Kamisama Kiss

 11

Story & Art by
Julietta Suzuki

CHARACTERS

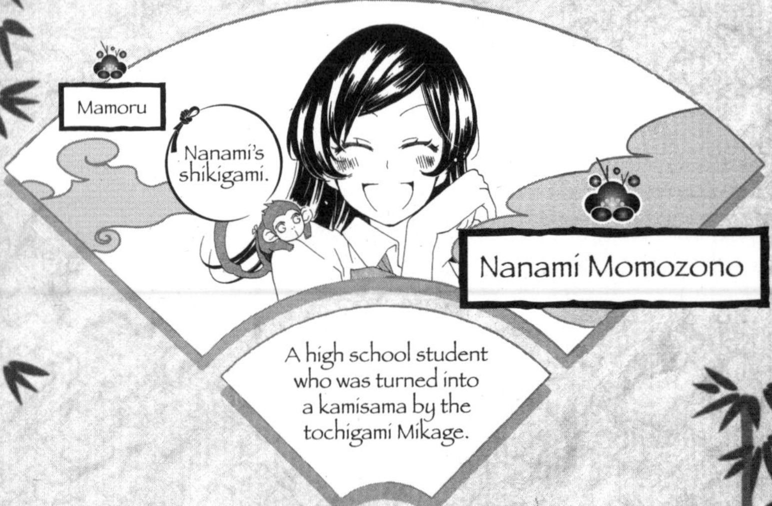
Mamoru
Nanami's shikigami.
Nanami Momozono
A high school student who was turned into a kamisama by the tochigami Mikage.

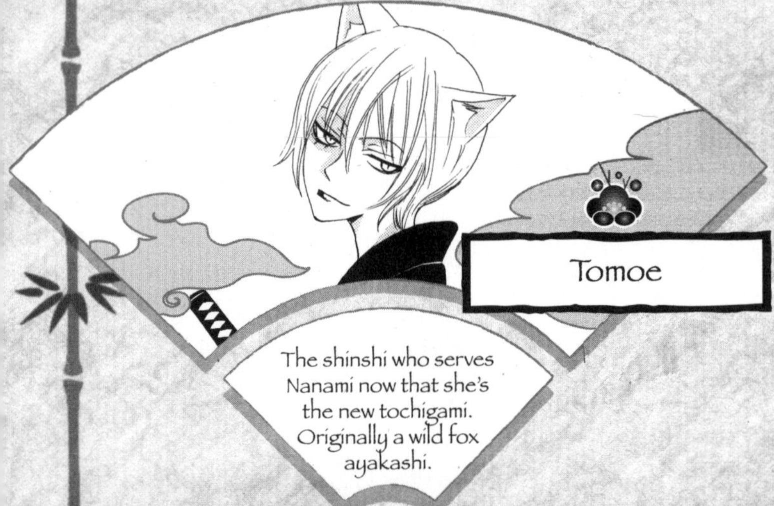
Tomoe
The shinshi who serves Nanami now that she's the new tochigami. Originally a wild fox ayakashi.

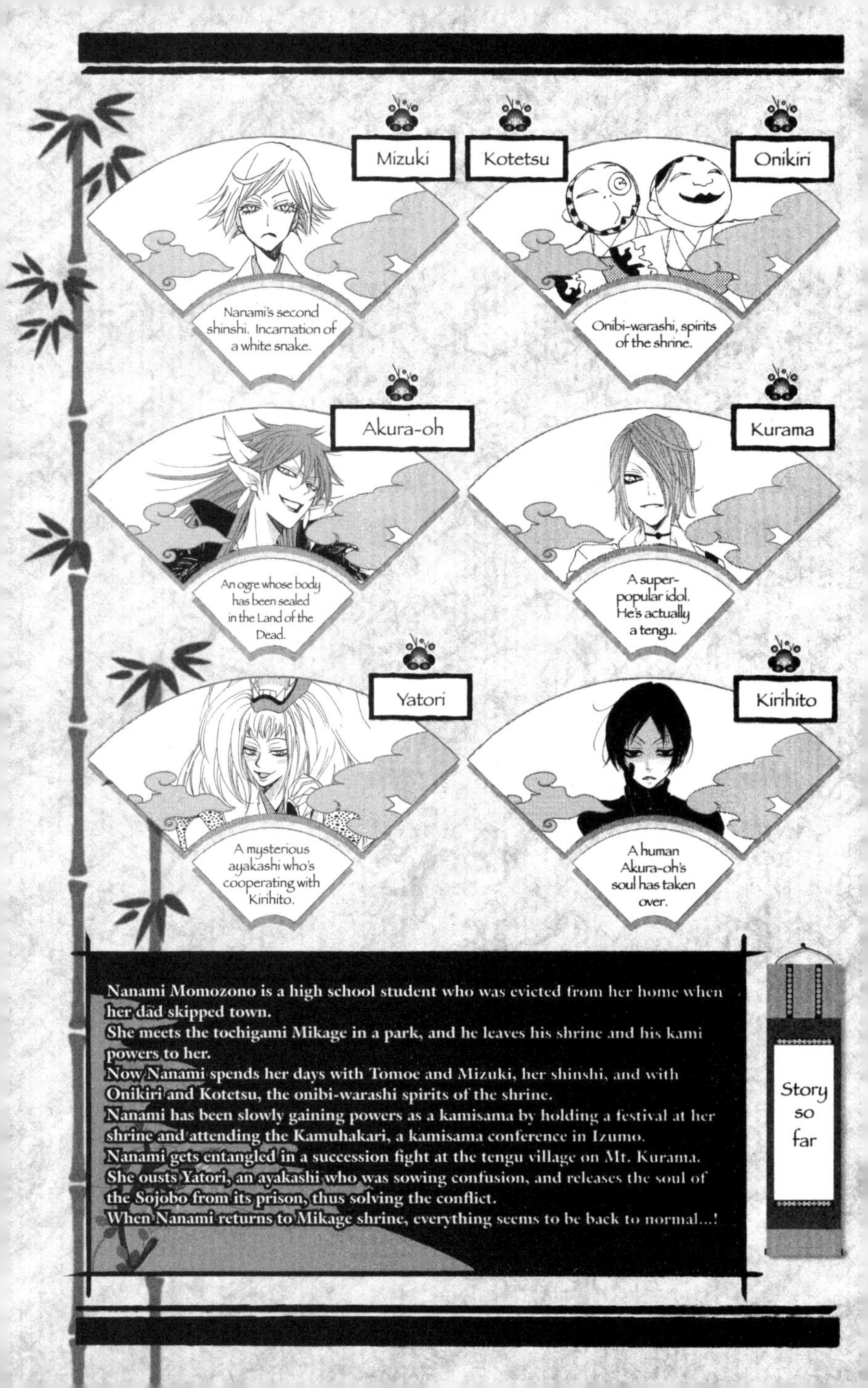
Onikiri
Kotetsu
Onibi-warashi, spirits of the shrine.
Mizuki
Nanami's second shinshi. Incarnation of a white snake.
Kurama
A super-popular idol. He's actually a tengu.
Akura-oh
An ogre whose body has been sealed in the Land of the Dead.
Kirihito
A human Akura-oh's soul has taken over.
Yatori
A mysterious ayakashi who's cooperating with Kirihito.

Story so far

Nanami Momozono is a high school student who was evicted from her home when her dad skipped town.
She meets the tochigami Mikage in a park, and he leaves his shrine and his kami powers to her.
Now Nanami spends her days with Tomoe and Mizuki, her shinshi, and with Onikiri and Kotetsu, the onibi-warashi spirits of the shrine.
Nanami has been slowly gaining powers as a kamisama by holding a festival at her shrine and attending the Kamuhakari, a kamisama conference in Izumo.
Nanami gets entangled in a succession fight at the tengu village on Mt. Kurama.
She ousts Yatori, an ayakashi who was sowing confusion, and releases the soul of the Sojobo from its prison, thus solving the conflict.
When Nanami returns to Mikage shrine, everything seems to be back to normal...!

Kamisama Kiss

Volume 11
CONTENTS

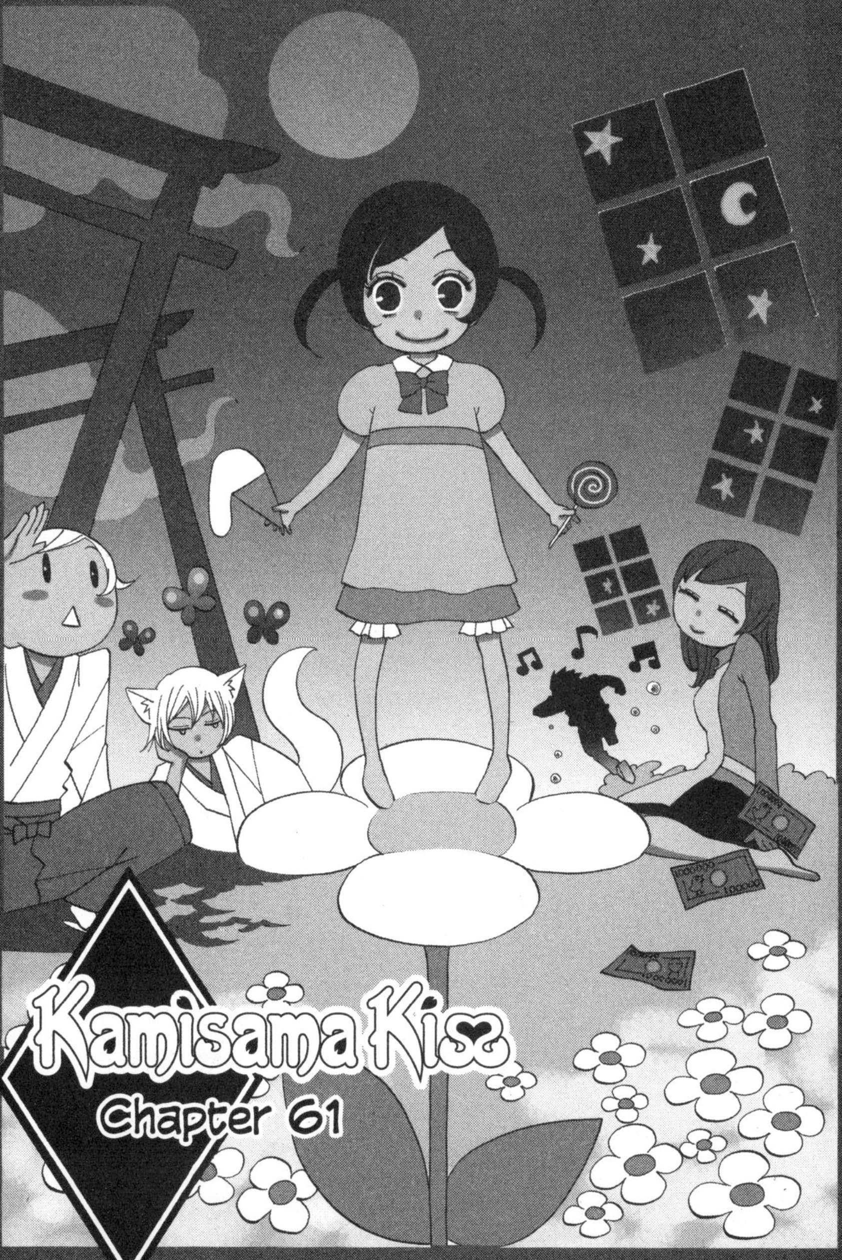
Kamisama Kiss
Chapter 61

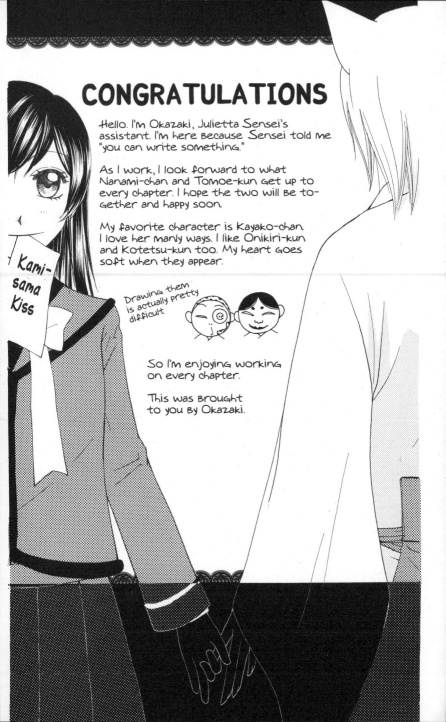

CONGRATULATIONS

Kami-sama Kiss

Hello. I'm Okazaki, Julietta Sensei's assistant. I'm here because Sensei told me "you can write something."

As I work, I look forward to what Nanami-chan and Tomoe-kun get up to every chapter. I hope the two will be together and happy soon.

My favorite character is Kayako-chan. I love her manly ways. I like Onikiri-kun and Kotetsu-kun too. My heart goes soft when they appear.

Drawing them is actually pretty difficult

So I'm enjoying working on every chapter.

This was brought to you by Okazaki.

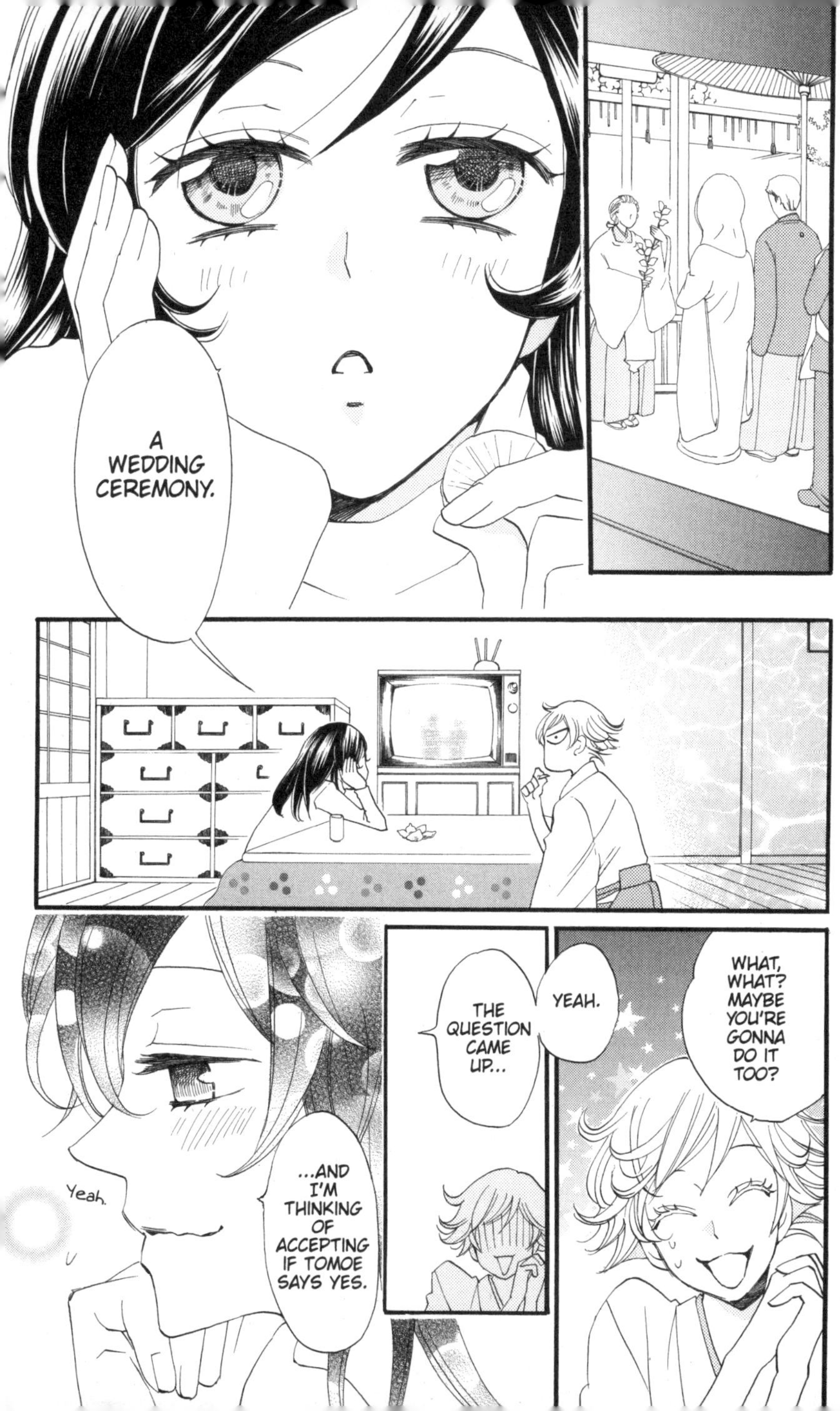
A WEDDING CEREMONY.
WHAT, WHAT? MAYBE YOU'RE GONNA DO IT TOO?
YEAH.
THE QUESTION CAME UP...
...AND I'M THINKING OF ACCEPTING IF TOMOE SAYS YES.
Yeah.

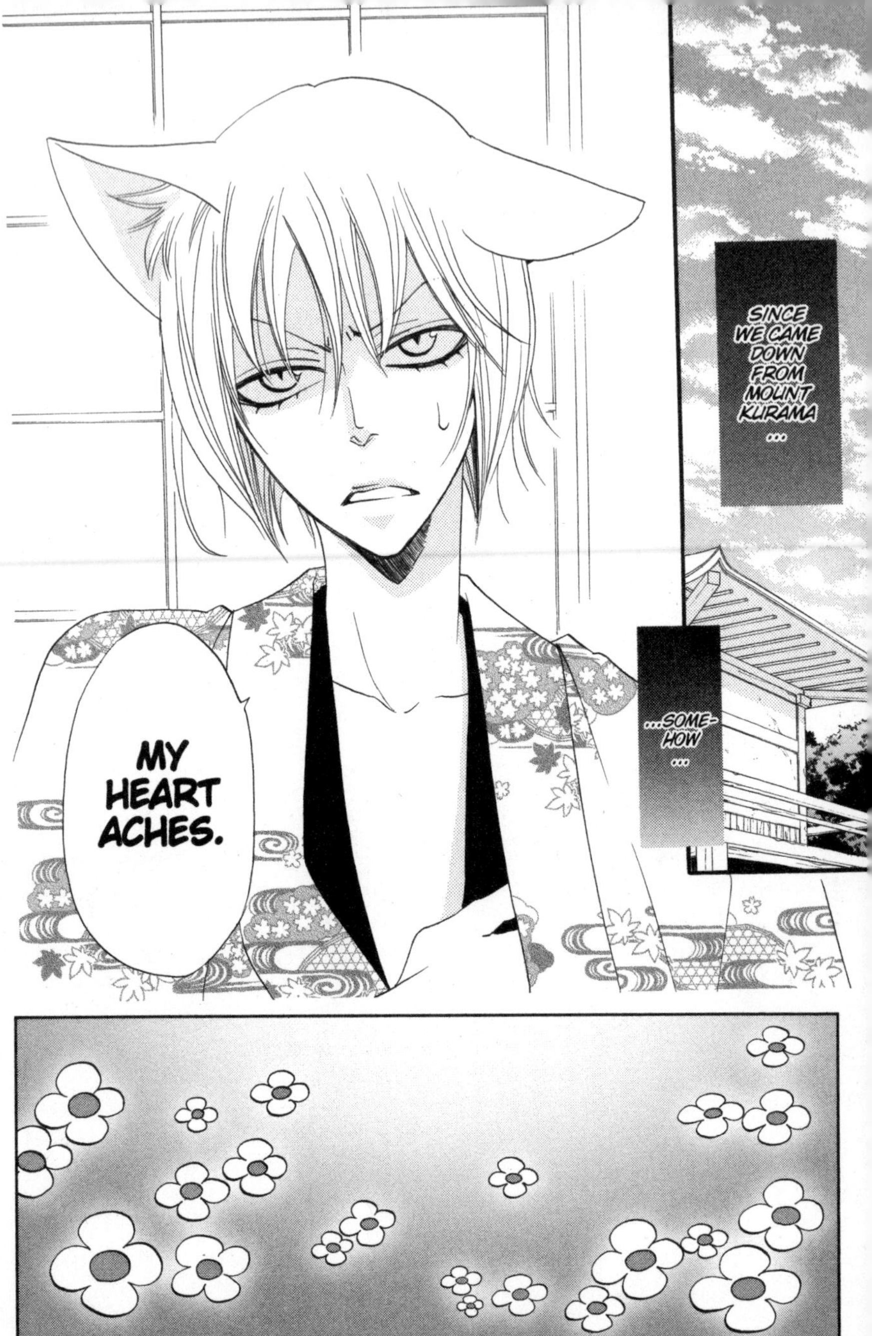
SINCE WE CAME DOWN FROM MOUNT KURAMA ...
...SOME-HOW ...
MY HEART ACHES.

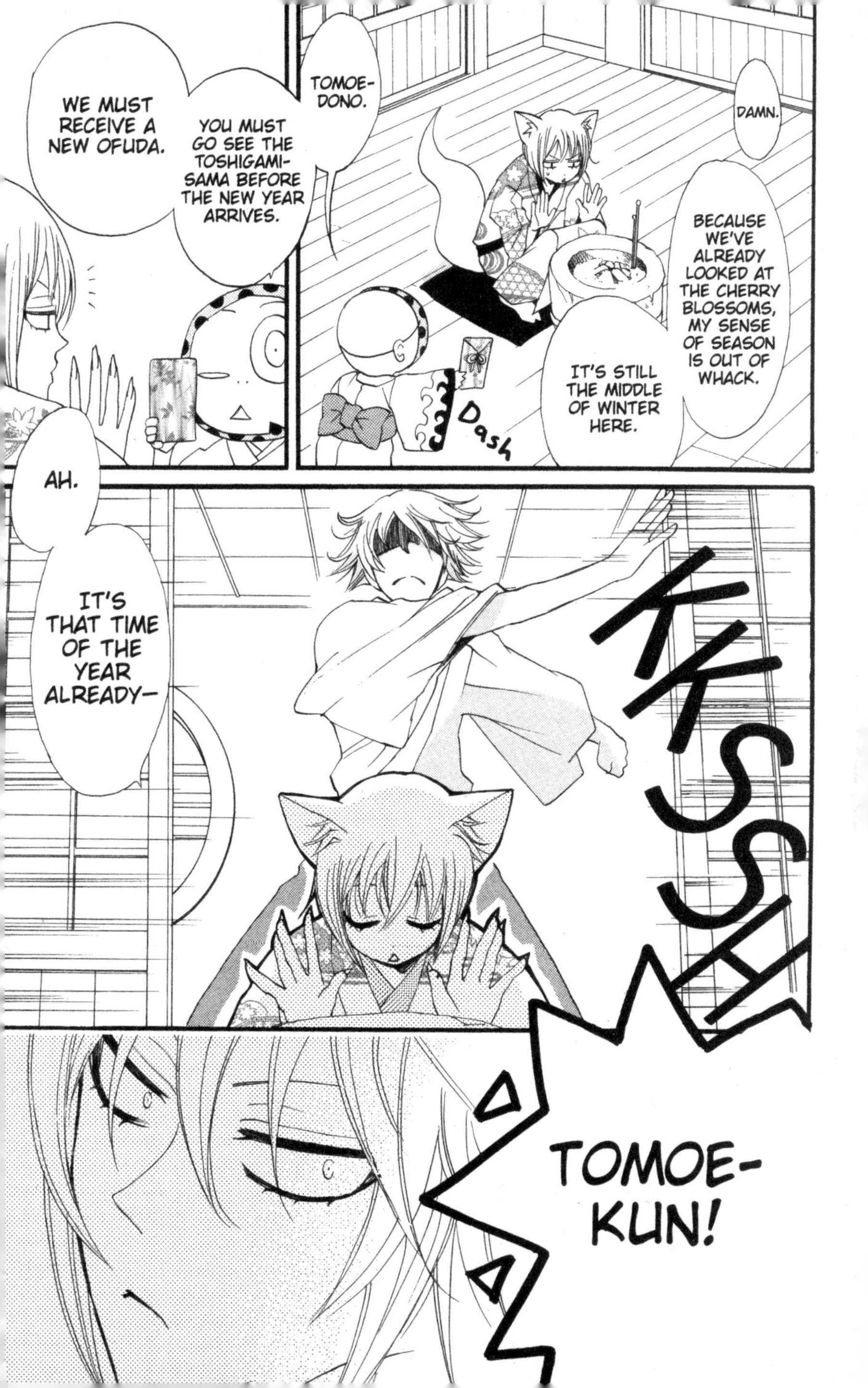
DAMN.
BECAUSE WE'VE ALREADY LOOKED AT THE CHERRY BLOSSOMS, MY SENSE OF SEASON IS OUT OF WHACK.
IT'S STILL THE MIDDLE OF WINTER HERE.
Dash
TOMOE-DONO.
YOU MUST GO SEE THE TOSHIGAMI-SAMA BEFORE THE NEW YEAR ARRIVES.
WE MUST RECEIVE A NEW OFUDA.
KKSSSH
AH.
IT'S THAT TIME OF THE YEAR ALREADY—
TOMOE-KUN!

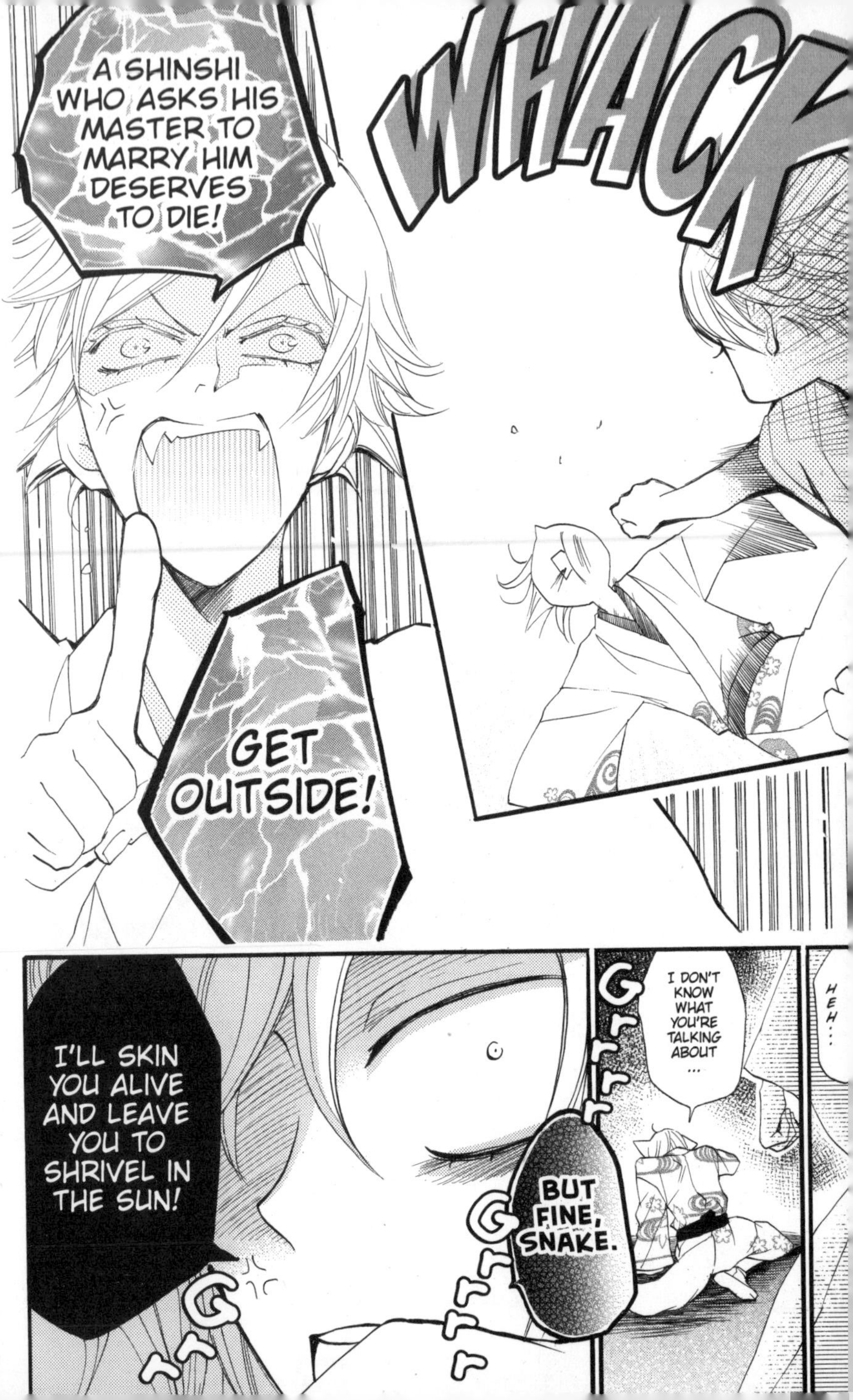
WHACK
A SHINSHI WHO ASKS HIS MASTER TO MARRY HIM DESERVES TO DIE!
GET OUTSIDE!
HEH...
I DON'T KNOW WHAT YOU'RE TALKING ABOUT...
BUT FINE, SNAKE.
Grrrr
Grrrr
Grrrr
I'LL SKIN YOU ALIVE AND LEAVE YOU TO SHRIVEL IN THE SUN!

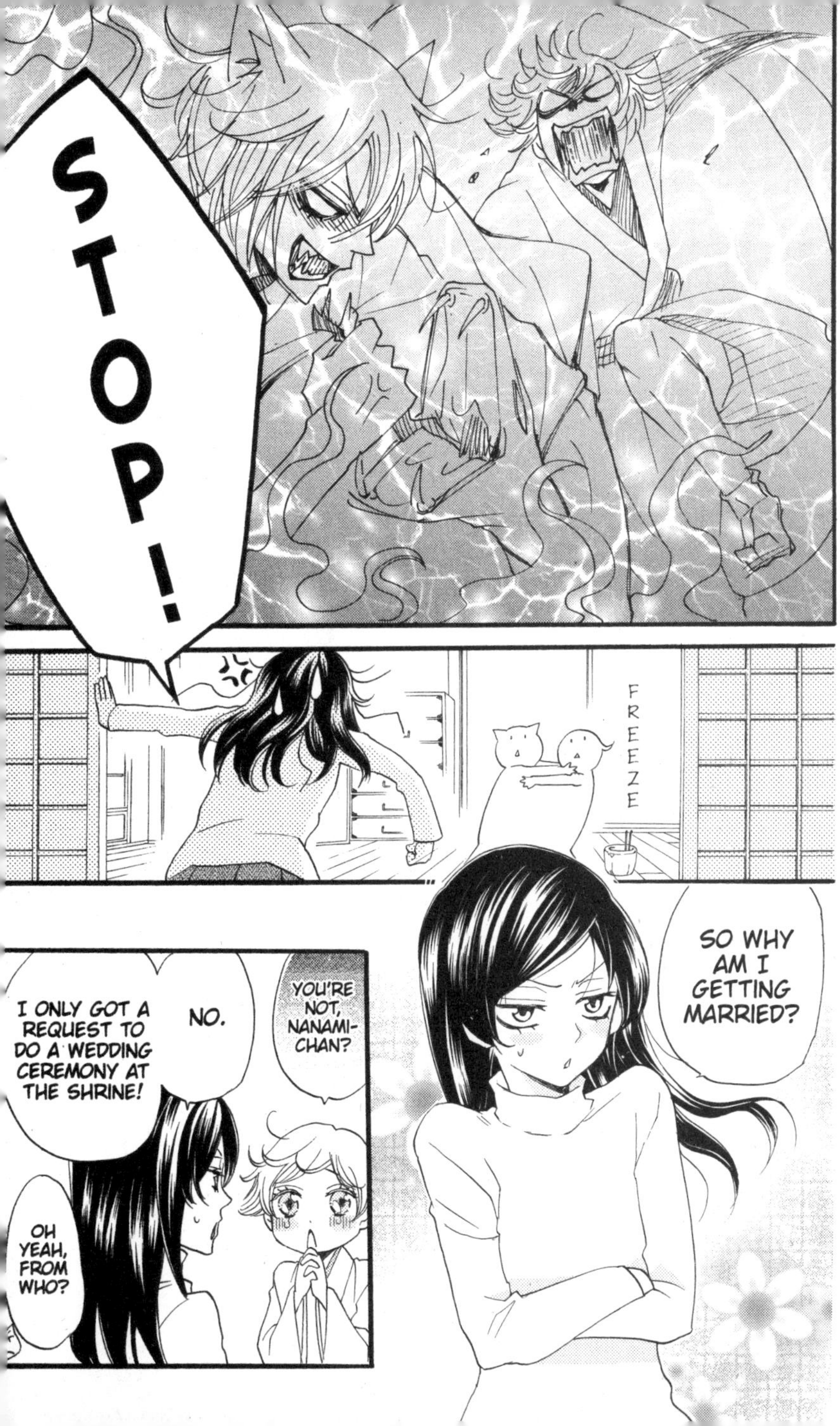
STOP!
FREEZE
SO WHY AM I GETTING MARRIED?
YOU'RE NOT, NANAMI-CHAN?
NO.
I ONLY GOT A REQUEST TO DO A WEDDING CEREMONY AT THE SHRINE!
OH YEAH, FROM WHO?

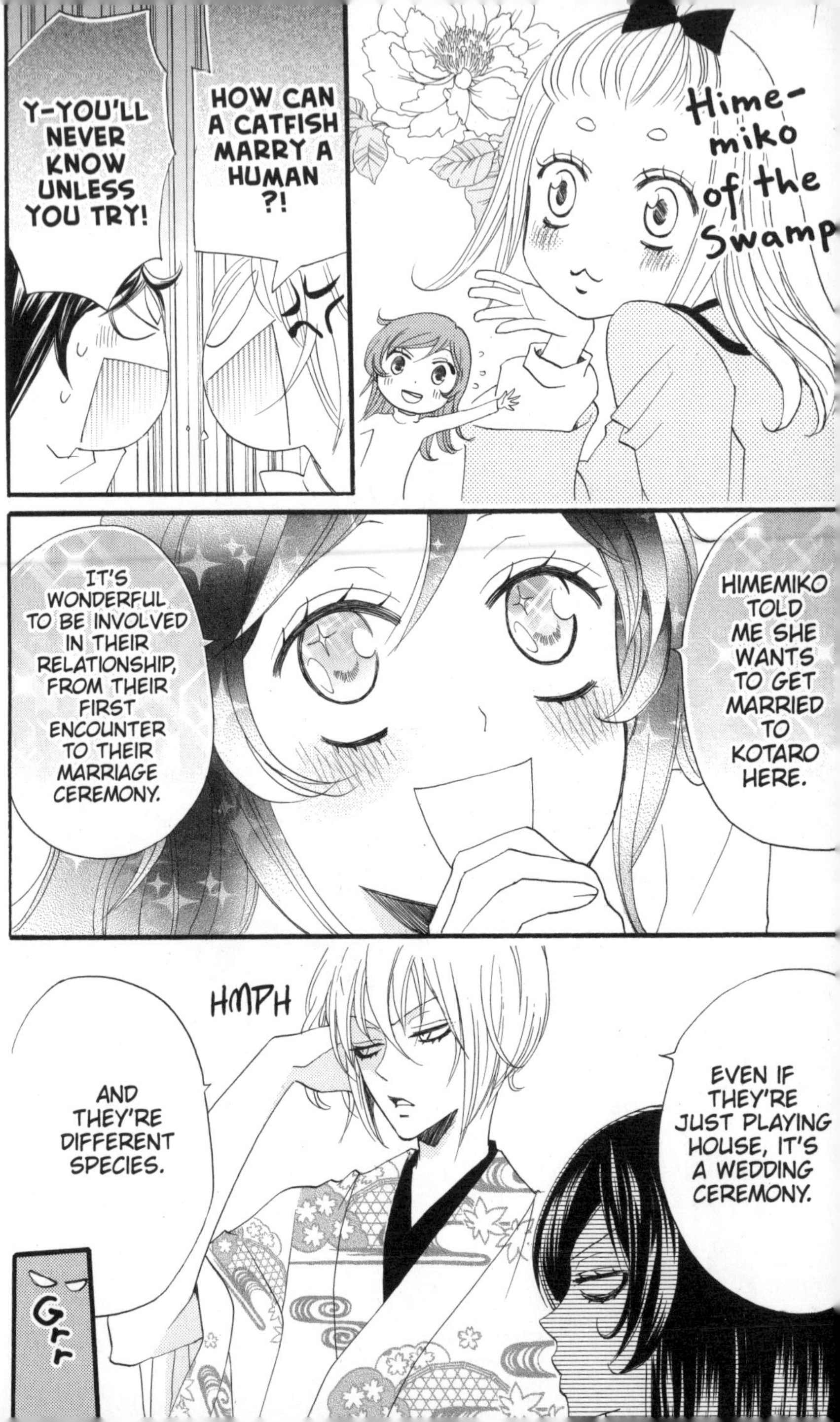
Hime-miko of the Swamp
HOW CAN A CATFISH MARRY A HUMAN?!
Y-YOU'LL NEVER KNOW UNLESS YOU TRY!
HIMEMIKO TOLD ME SHE WANTS TO GET MARRIED TO KOTARO HERE.
IT'S WONDERFUL TO BE INVOLVED IN THEIR RELATIONSHIP, FROM THEIR FIRST ENCOUNTER TO THEIR MARRIAGE CEREMONY.
EVEN IF THEY'RE JUST PLAYING HOUSE, IT'S A WEDDING CEREMONY.
HMPH
AND THEY'RE DIFFERENT SPECIES.
Grr

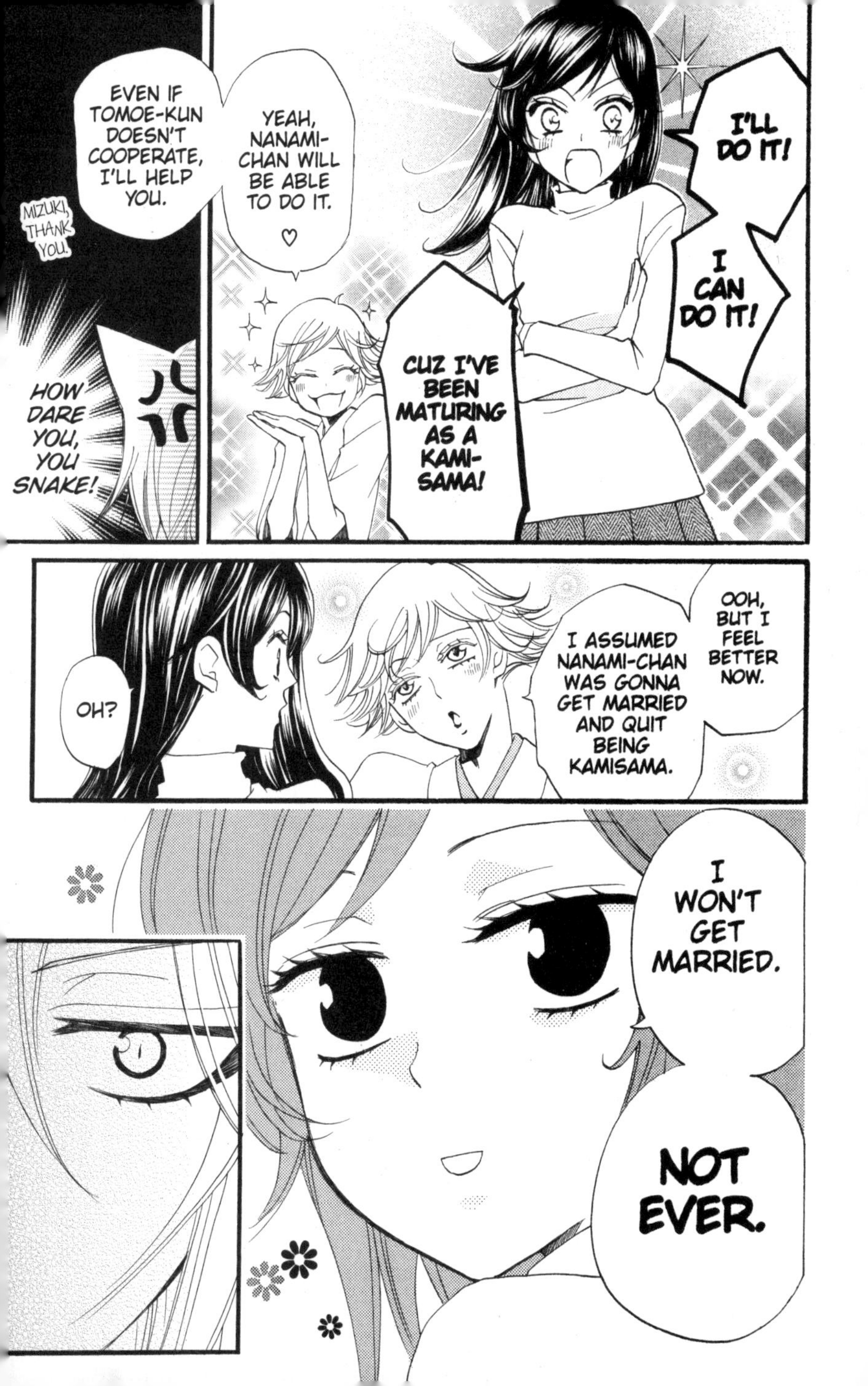
I'LL DO IT!
I CAN DO IT!
CUZ I'VE BEEN MATURING AS A KAMI-SAMA!
YEAH, NANAMI-CHAN WILL BE ABLE TO DO IT. ♡
EVEN IF TOMOE-KUN DOESN'T COOPERATE, I'LL HELP YOU.
MIZUKI, THANK YOU.
HOW DARE YOU, YOU SNAKE!
OOH, BUT I FEEL BETTER NOW.
I ASSUMED NANAMI-CHAN WAS GONNA GET MARRIED AND QUIT BEING KAMISAMA.
OH?
I WON'T GET MARRIED.
NOT EVER.

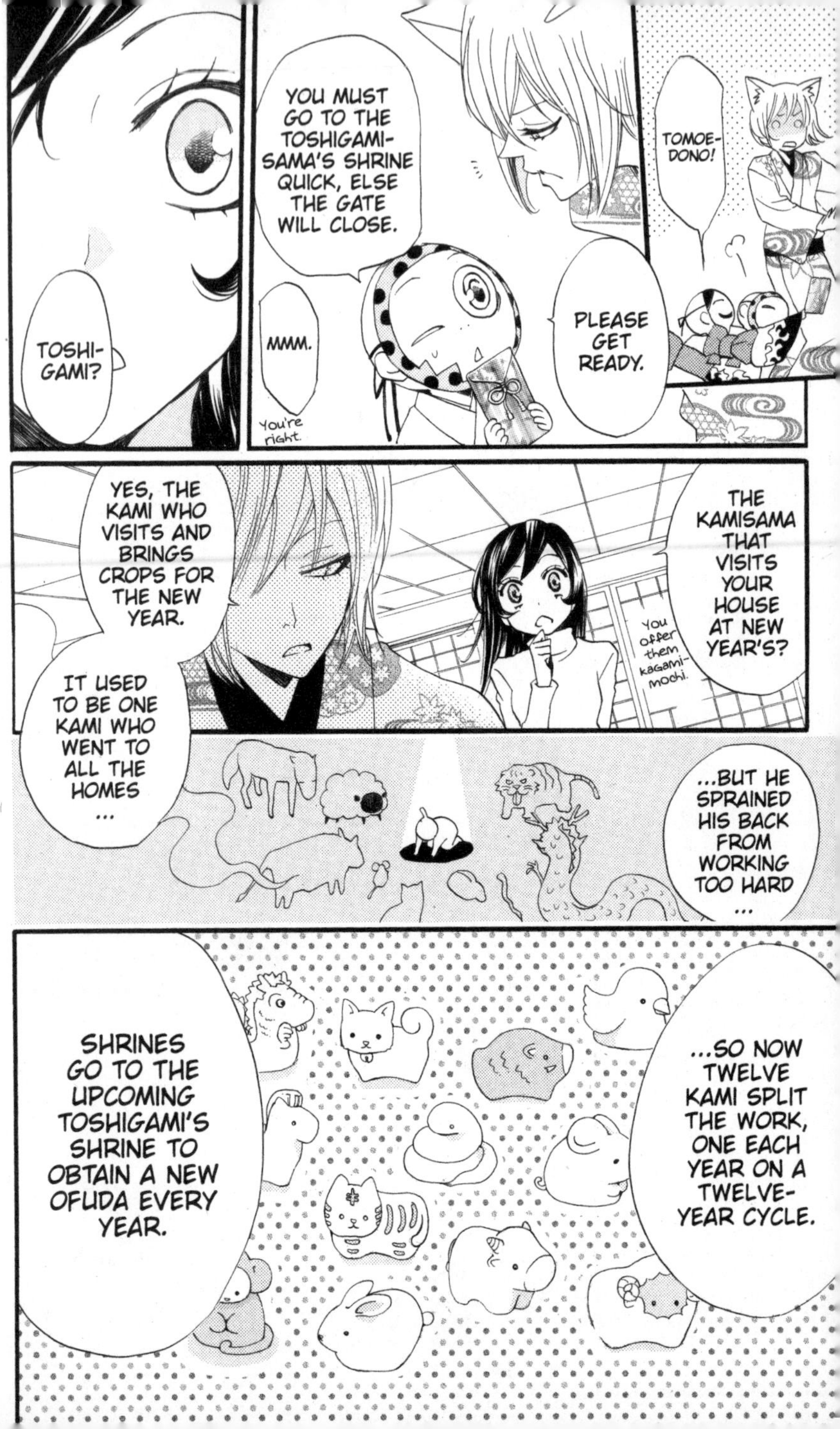
TOMOE-DONO!
PLEASE GET READY.
YOU MUST GO TO THE TOSHIGAMI-SAMA'S SHRINE QUICK, ELSE THE GATE WILL CLOSE.
MMM.
You're right.
TOSHIGAMI?
THE KAMISAMA THAT VISITS YOUR HOUSE AT NEW YEAR'S?
You offer them kagami-mochi.
YES, THE KAMI WHO VISITS AND BRINGS CROPS FOR THE NEW YEAR.
IT USED TO BE ONE KAMI WHO WENT TO ALL THE HOMES...
...BUT HE SPRAINED HIS BACK FROM WORKING TOO HARD...
...SO NOW TWELVE KAMI SPLIT THE WORK, ONE EACH YEAR ON A TWELVE-YEAR CYCLE.
SHRINES GO TO THE UPCOMING TOSHIGAMI'S SHRINE TO OBTAIN A NEW OFUDA EVERY YEAR.

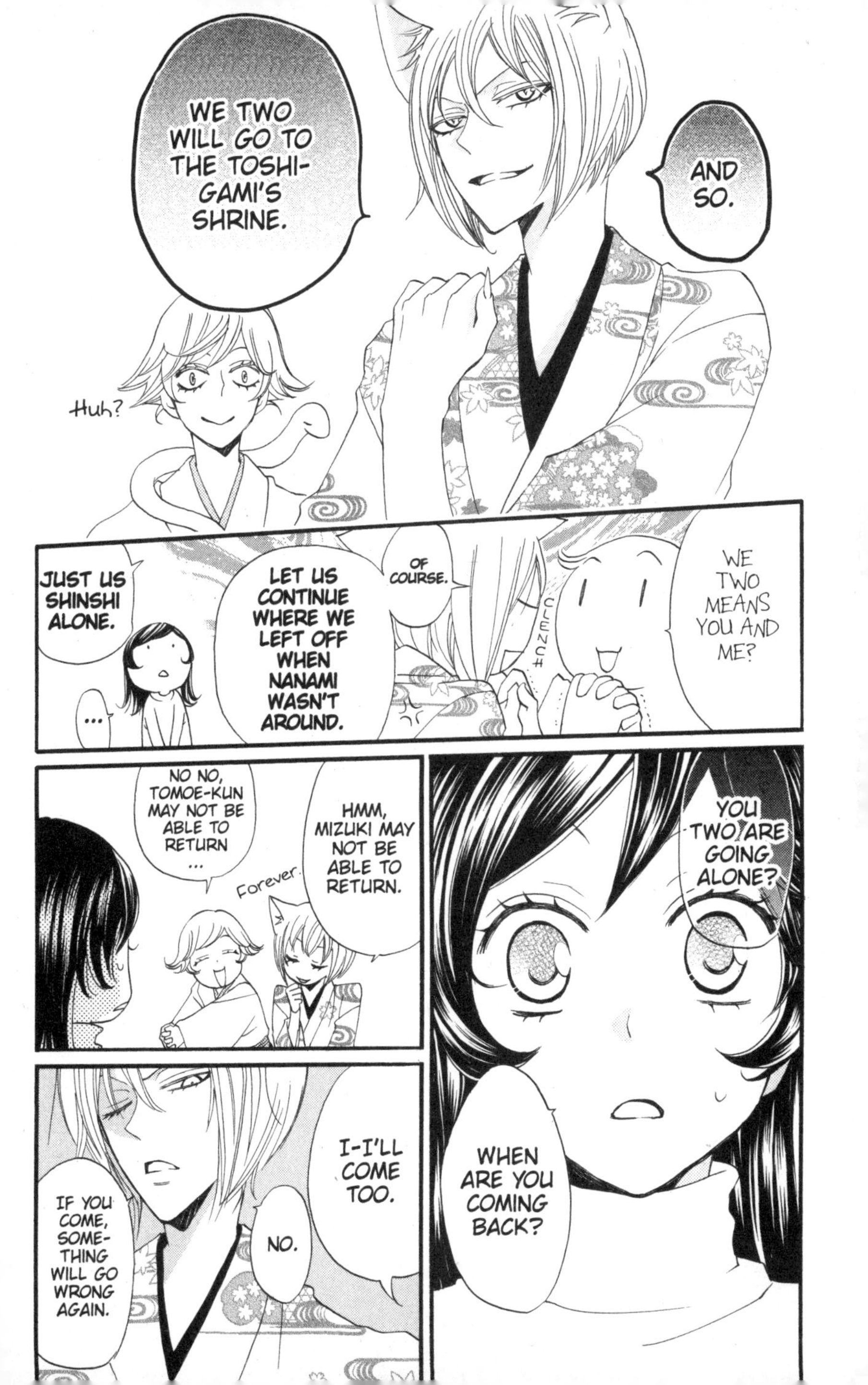
AND SO.
WE TWO WILL GO TO THE TOSHI-GAMI'S SHRINE.
Huh?
WE TWO MEANS YOU AND ME?
CLENCH
OF COURSE.
LET US CONTINUE WHERE WE LEFT OFF WHEN NANAMI WASN'T AROUND.
JUST US SHINSHI ALONE.
...
YOU TWO ARE GOING ALONE?
WHEN ARE YOU COMING BACK?
HMM, MIZUKI MAY NOT BE ABLE TO RETURN.
Forever.
NO NO, TOMOE-KUN MAY NOT BE ABLE TO RETURN ...
I-I'LL COME TOO.
NO.
IF YOU COME, SOME-THING WILL GO WRONG AGAIN.

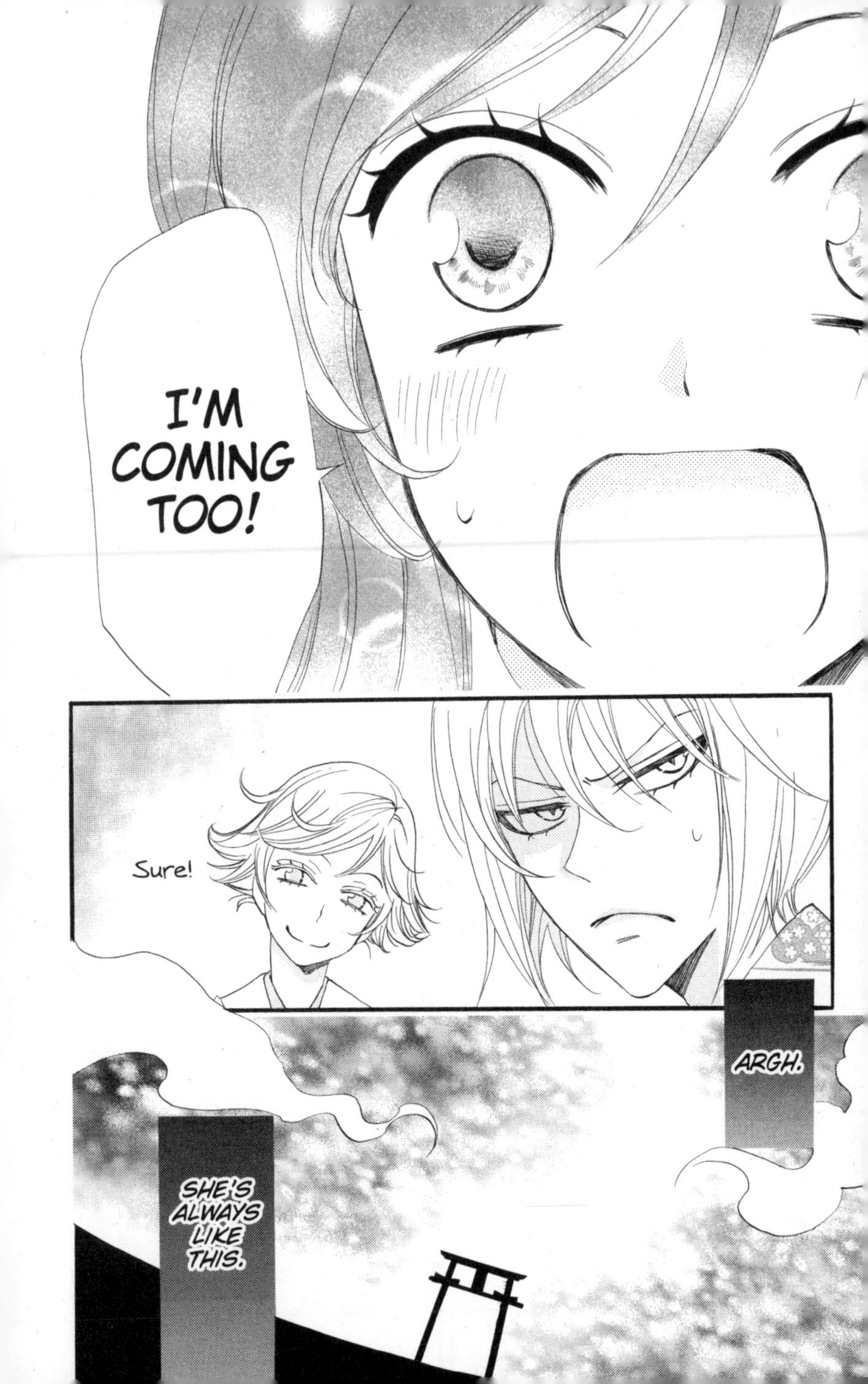
I'M COMING TOO!
Sure!
ARGH.
SHE'S ALWAYS LIKE THIS.

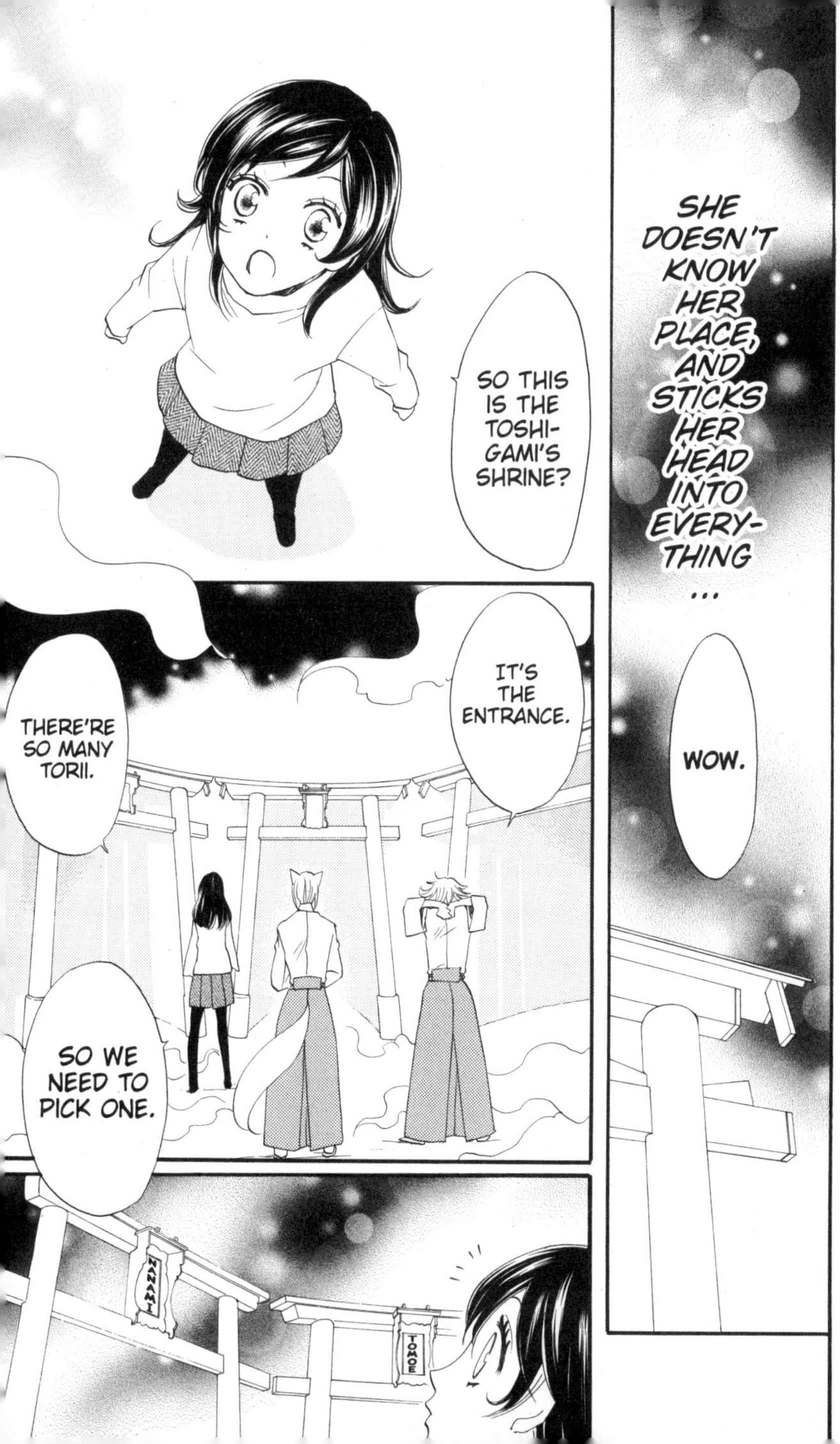
SHE DOESN'T KNOW HER PLACE, AND STICKS HER HEAD INTO EVERY-THING...
WOW.
SO THIS IS THE TOSHI-GAMI'S SHRINE?
IT'S THE ENTRANCE.
THERE'RE SO MANY TORII.
SO WE NEED TO PICK ONE.
NANAMI
TOMOE

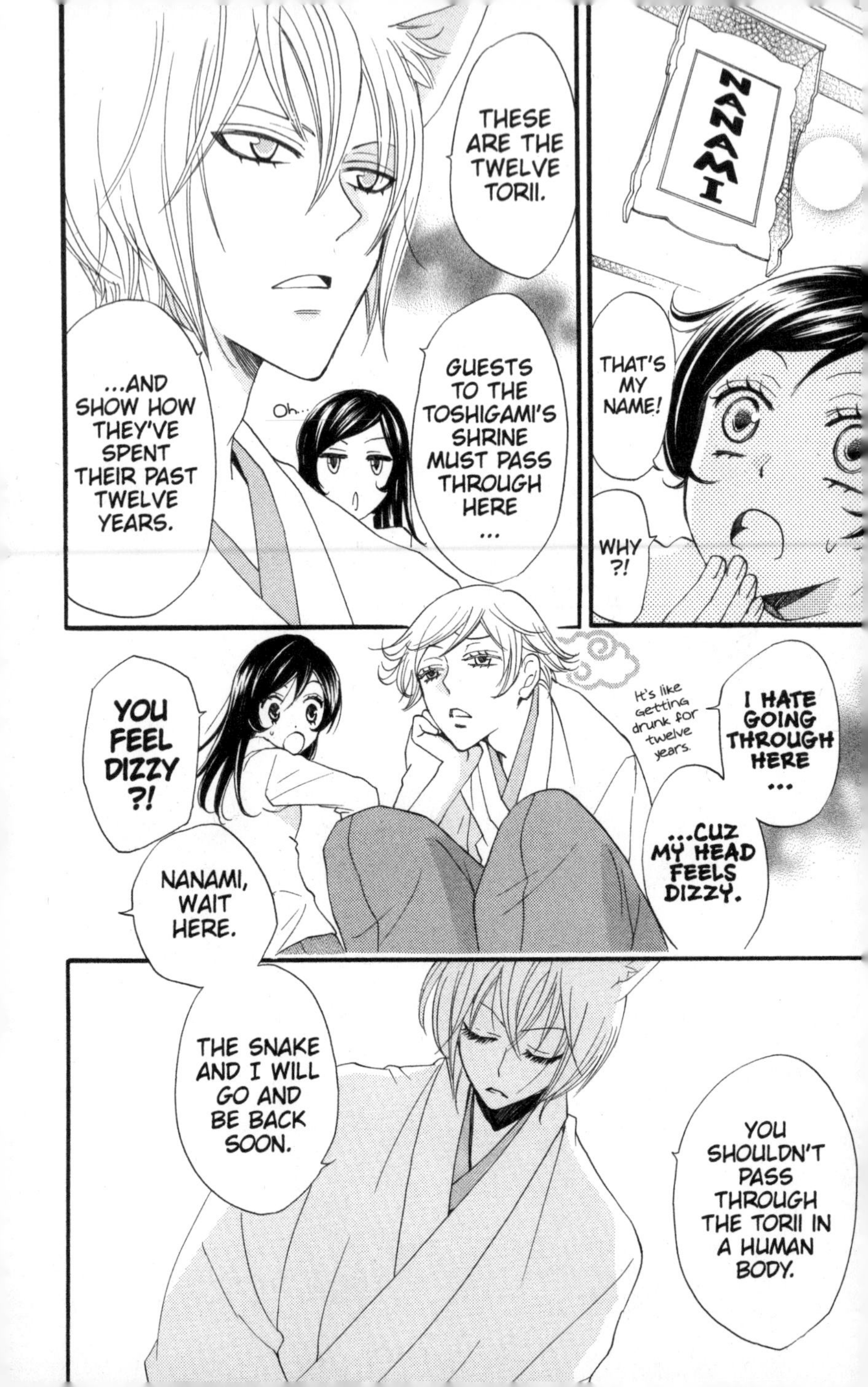
NANAMI
THAT'S MY NAME!
WHY?!
THESE ARE THE TWELVE TORII.
GUESTS TO THE TOSHIGAMI'S SHRINE MUST PASS THROUGH HERE...
Oh...
...AND SHOW HOW THEY'VE SPENT THEIR PAST TWELVE YEARS.
I HATE GOING THROUGH HERE...
It's like getting drunk for twelve years.
...CUZ MY HEAD FEELS DIZZY.
YOU FEEL DIZZY?!
NANAMI, WAIT HERE.
THE SNAKE AND I WILL GO AND BE BACK SOON.
YOU SHOULDN'T PASS THROUGH THE TORII IN A HUMAN BODY.

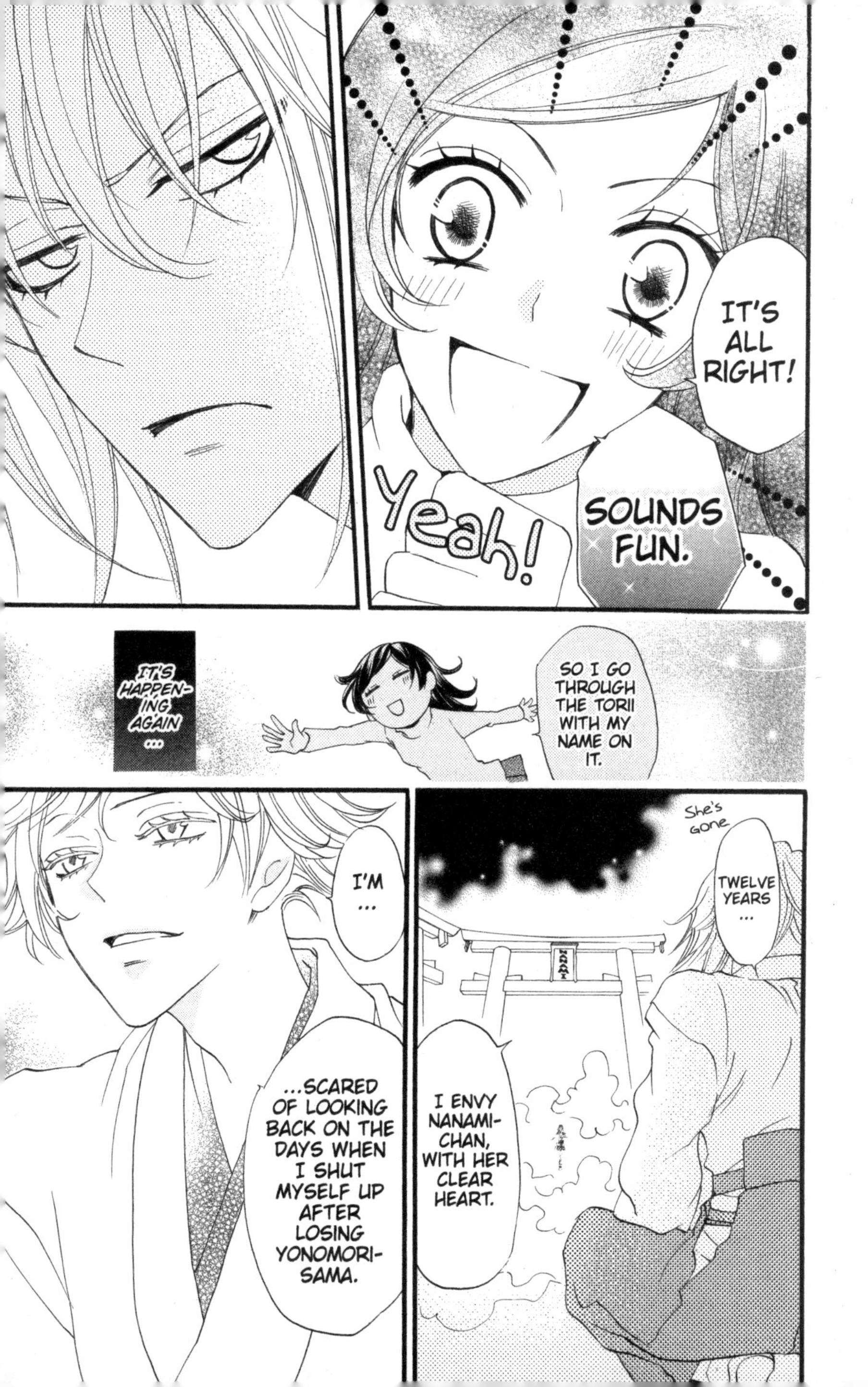

IT'S ALL RIGHT!
SOUNDS FUN.
Yeah!
SO I GO THROUGH THE TORII WITH MY NAME ON IT.
IT'S HAPPENING AGAIN ...
She's Gone
TWELVE YEARS ...
I ENVY NANAMI-CHAN, WITH HER CLEAR HEART.
I'M ...
...SCARED OF LOOKING BACK ON THE DAYS WHEN I SHUT MYSELF UP AFTER LOSING YONOMORI-SAMA.

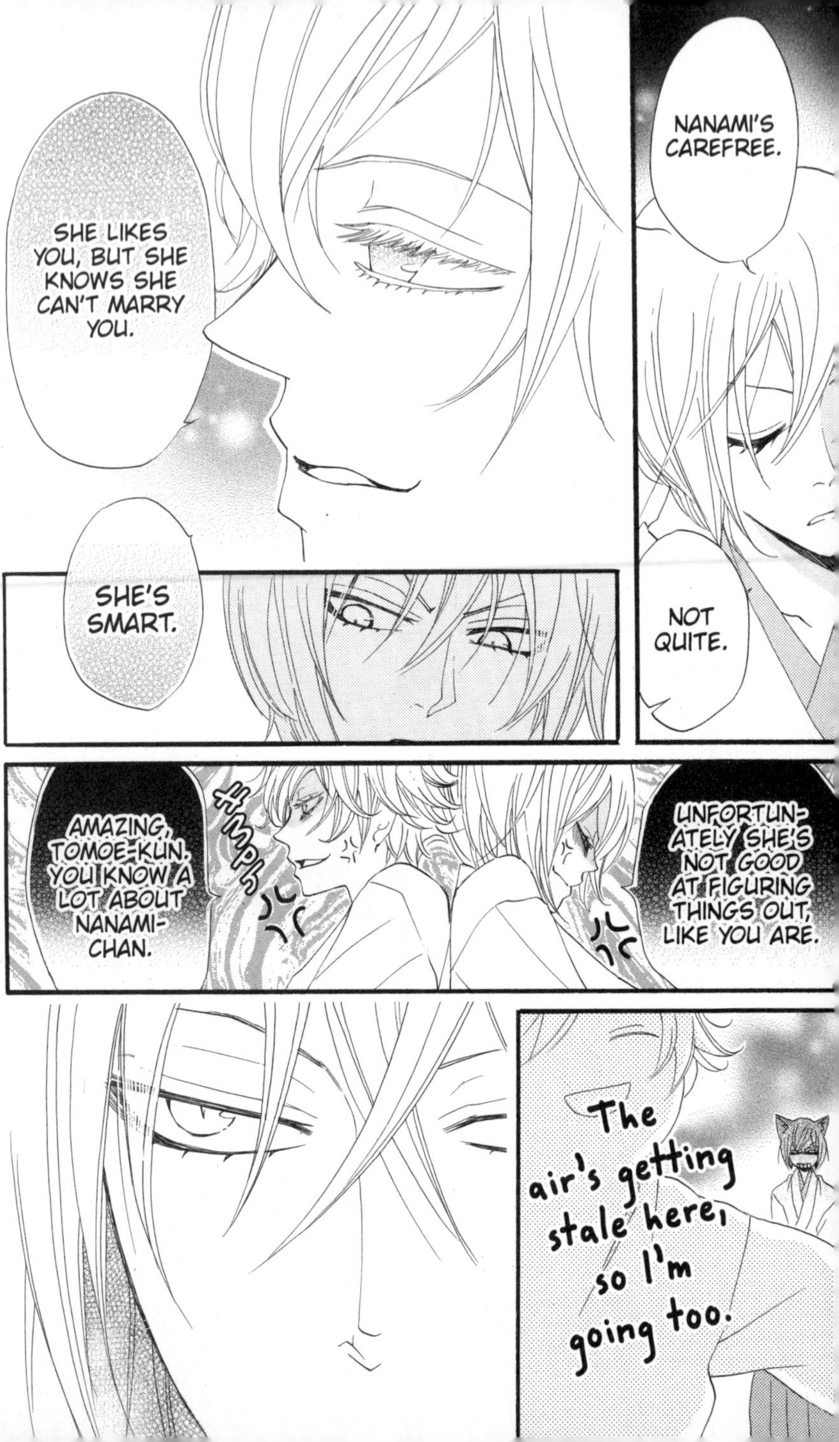
NANAMI'S CAREFREE.
NOT QUITE.
SHE LIKES YOU, BUT SHE KNOWS SHE CAN'T MARRY YOU.
SHE'S SMART.
UNFORTUNATELY SHE'S NOT GOOD AT FIGURING THINGS OUT, LIKE YOU ARE.
HMPH
AMAZING, TOMOE-KUN. YOU KNOW A LOT ABOUT NANAMI-CHAN.
The air's getting stale here, so I'm going too.

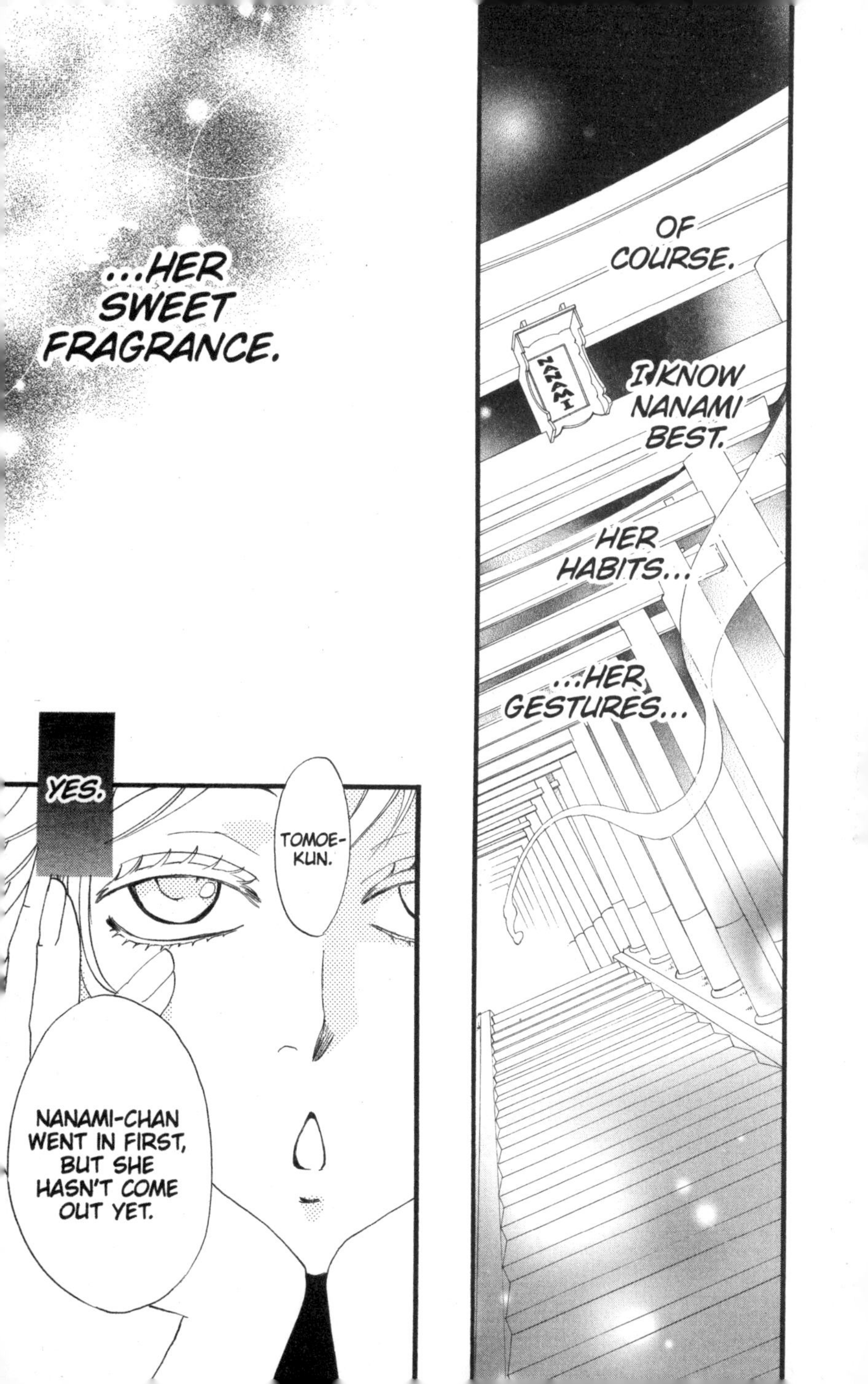
OF COURSE.
NANAMI
I KNOW NANAMI BEST.
HER HABITS...
...HER GESTURES...
...HER SWEET FRAGRANCE.
YES.
TOMOE-KUN.
NANAMI-CHAN WENT IN FIRST, BUT SHE HASN'T COME OUT YET.

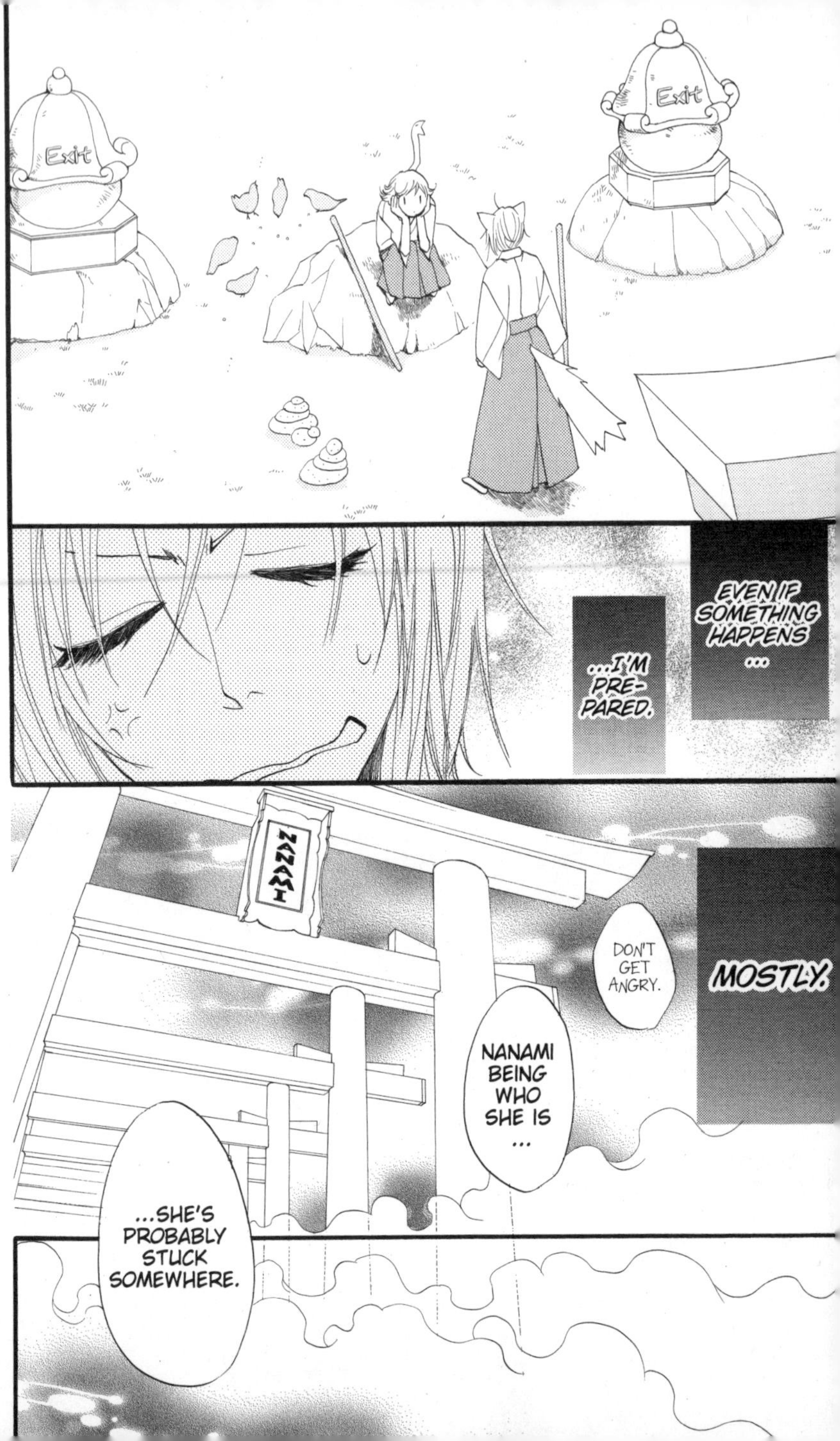
Exit
Exit
EVEN IF SOMETHING HAPPENS...
...I'M PREPARED.
NANAMI
MOSTLY.
DON'T GET ANGRY.
NANAMI BEING WHO SHE IS...
...SHE'S PROBABLY STUCK SOMEWHERE.

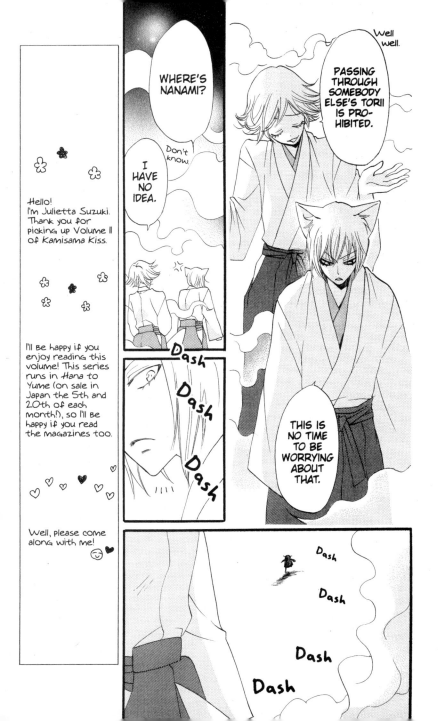

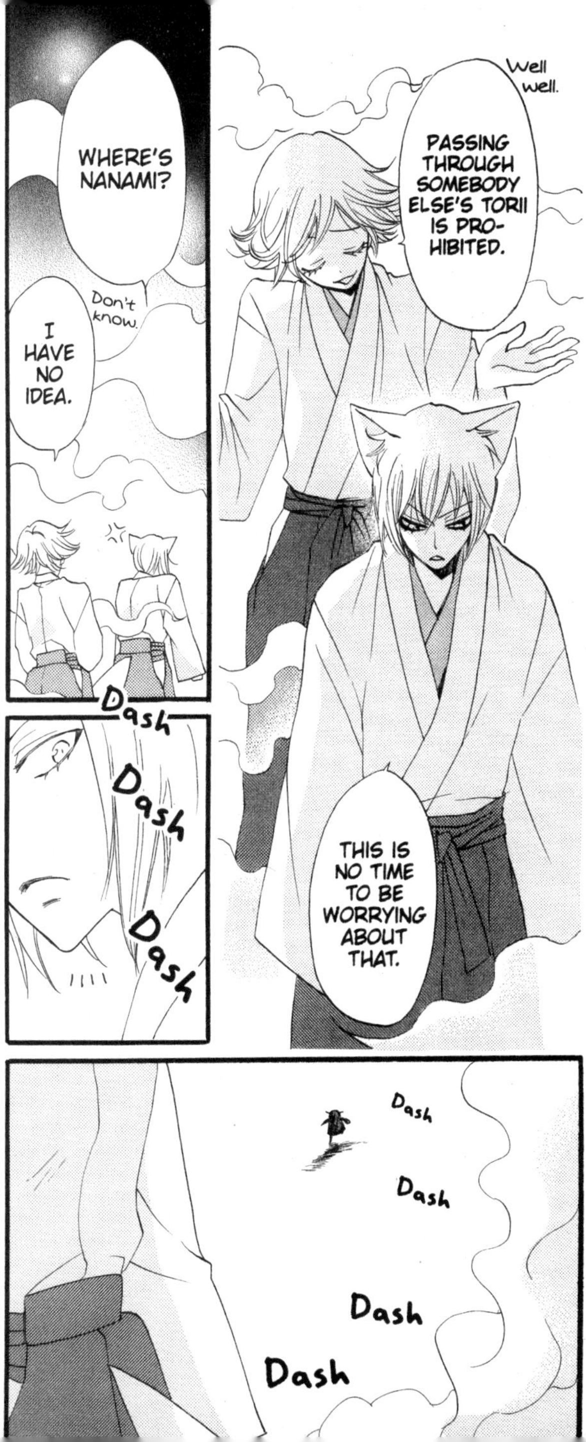
Well well.
PASSING THROUGH SOMEBODY ELSE'S TORII IS PROHIBITED.
THIS IS NO TIME TO BE WORRYING ABOUT THAT.
WHERE'S NANAMI?
Don't know.
I HAVE NO IDEA.
Dash
Dash
Dash
Dash
Dash
Dash
Dash

Hello!
I'm Julietta Suzuki.
Thank you for picking up Volume 11 of Kamisama Kiss.

I'll be happy if you enjoy reading this volume! This series runs in *Hana to Yume* (on sale in Japan the 5th and 20th of each month!), so I'll be happy if you read the magazines too.

Well, please come along with me!

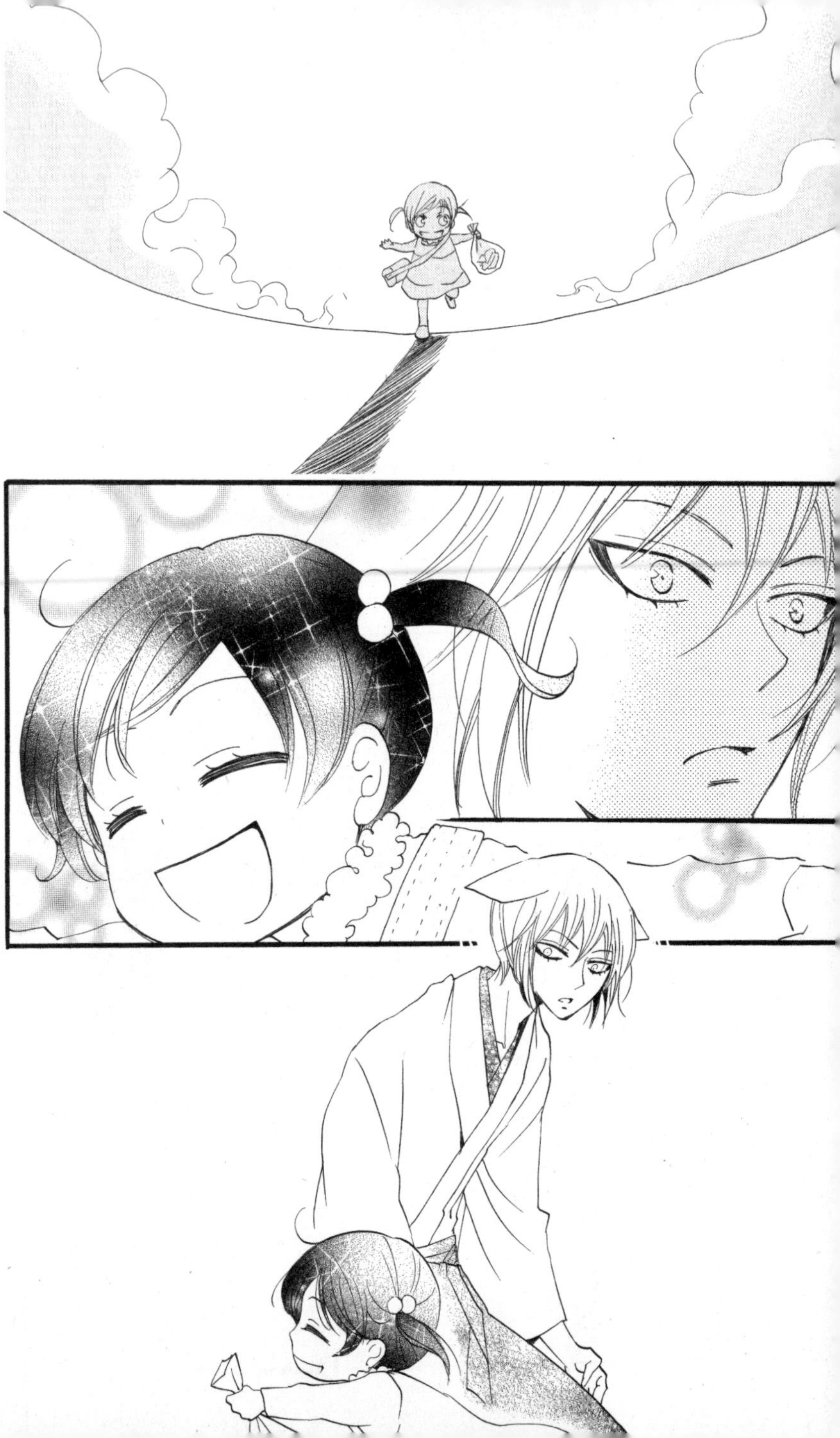

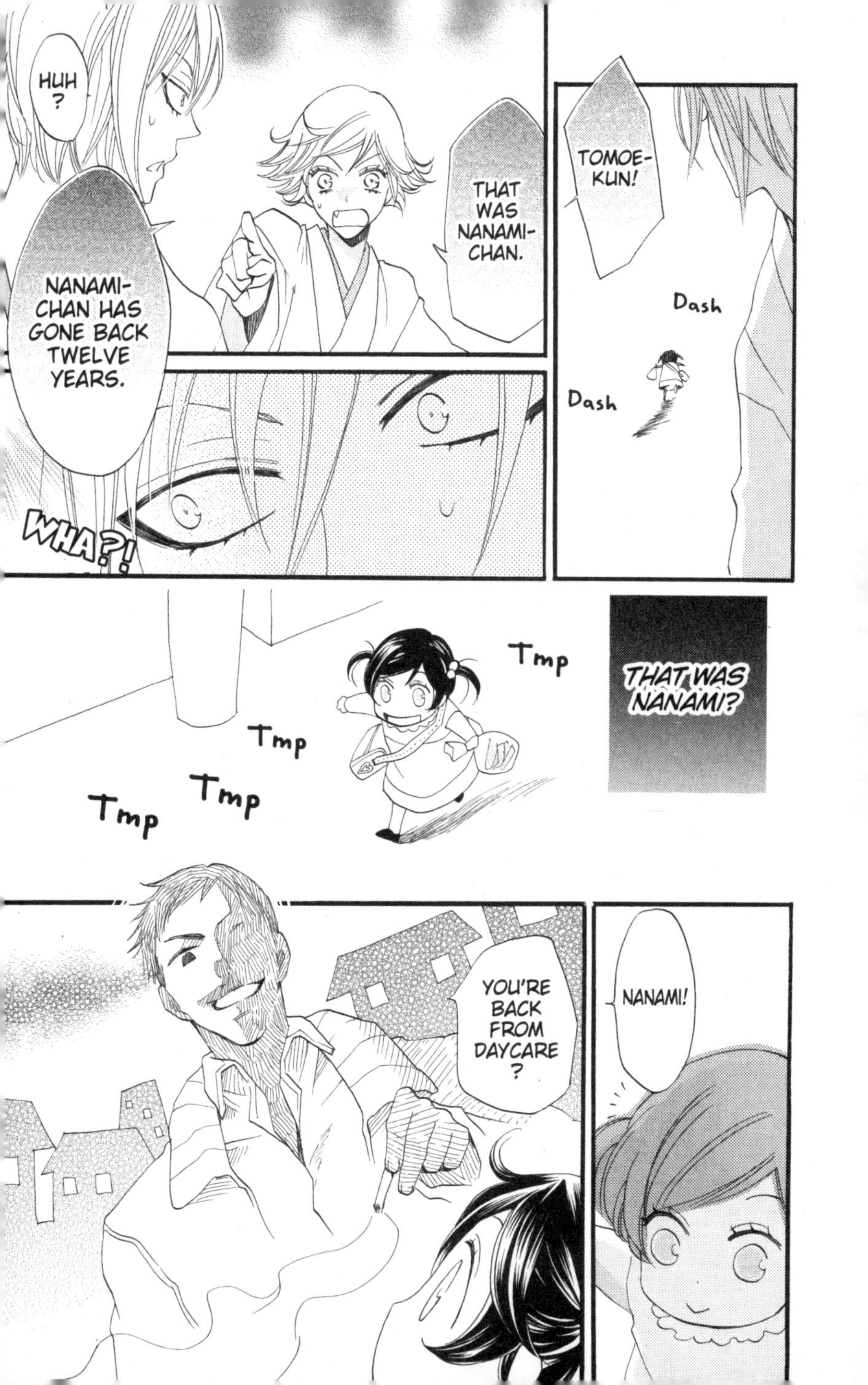
TOMOE-KUN!
Dash
Dash
THAT WAS NANAMI-CHAN.
HUH?
NANAMI-CHAN HAS GONE BACK TWELVE YEARS.
WHA?!
THAT WAS NANAMI?
Tmp
Tmp
Tmp
Tmp
NANAMI!
YOU'RE BACK FROM DAYCARE?

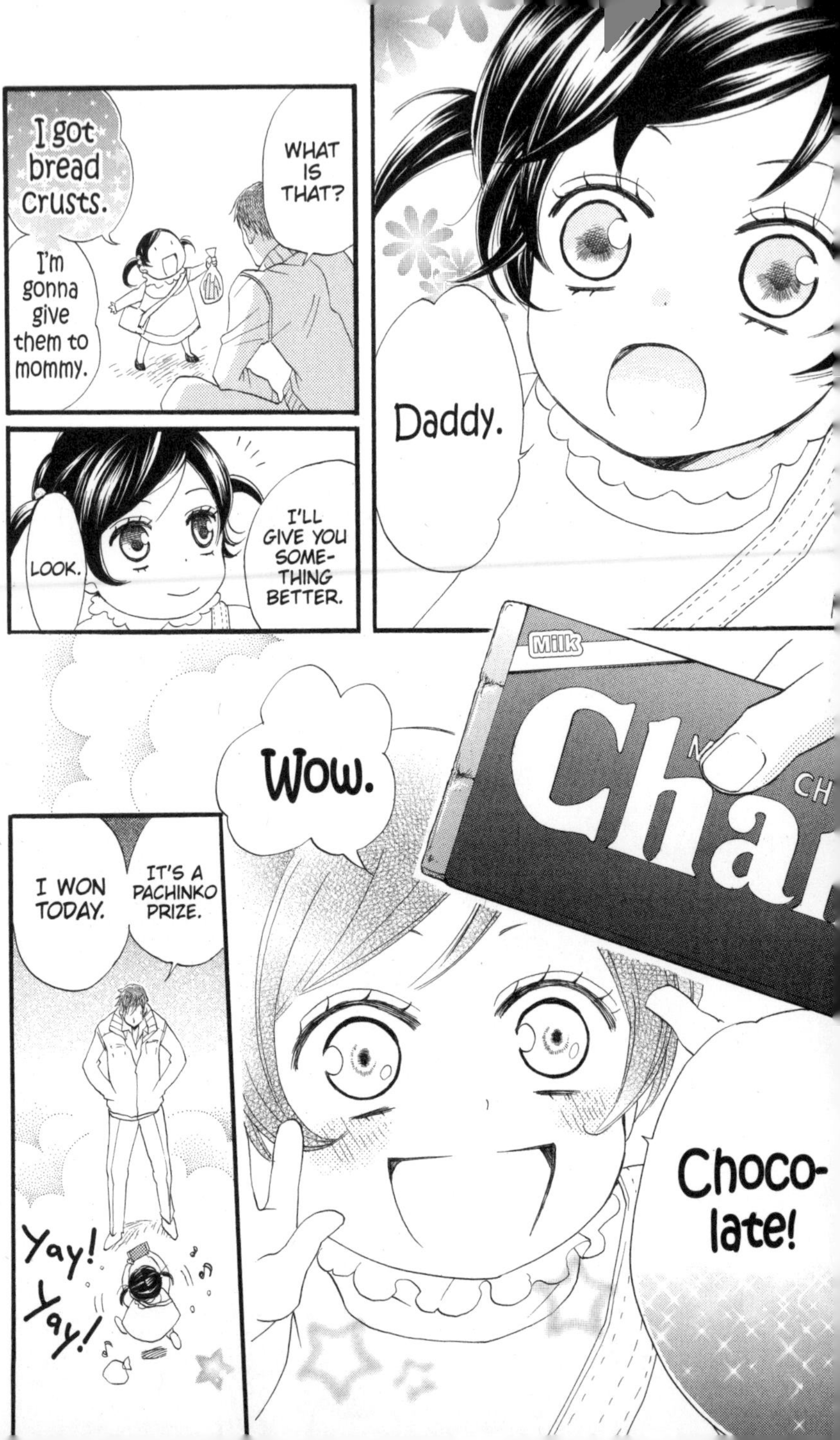
Daddy.
WHAT IS THAT?
I got bread crusts.
I'm gonna give them to mommy.
I'LL GIVE YOU SOME-THING BETTER.
LOOK.
Milk
Wow.
Choco-late!
IT'S A PACHINKO PRIZE.
I WON TODAY.
Yay! Yay!

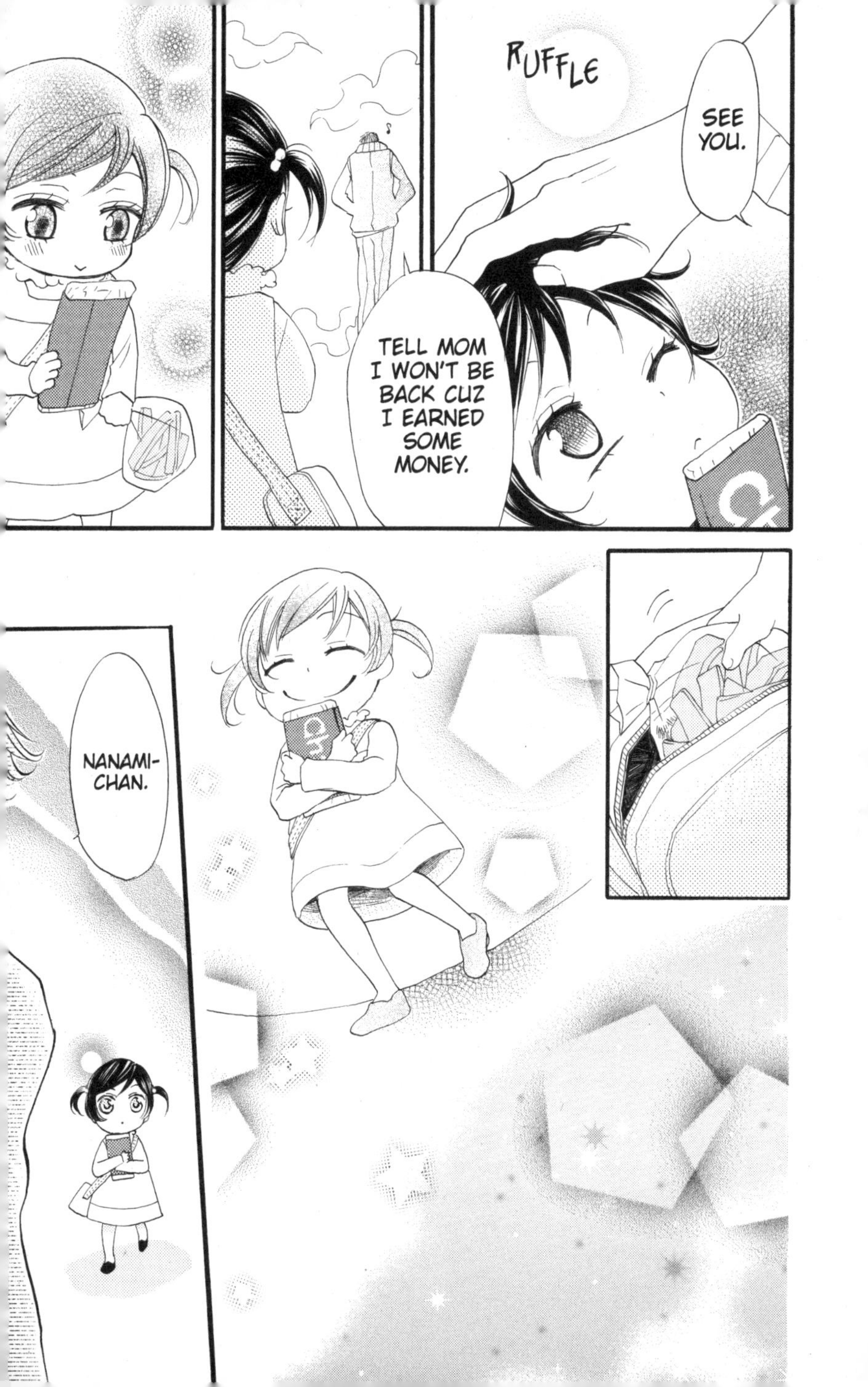
SEE YOU.
RUFFLE
TELL MOM I WON'T BE BACK CUZ I EARNED SOME MONEY.
NANAMI-CHAN.

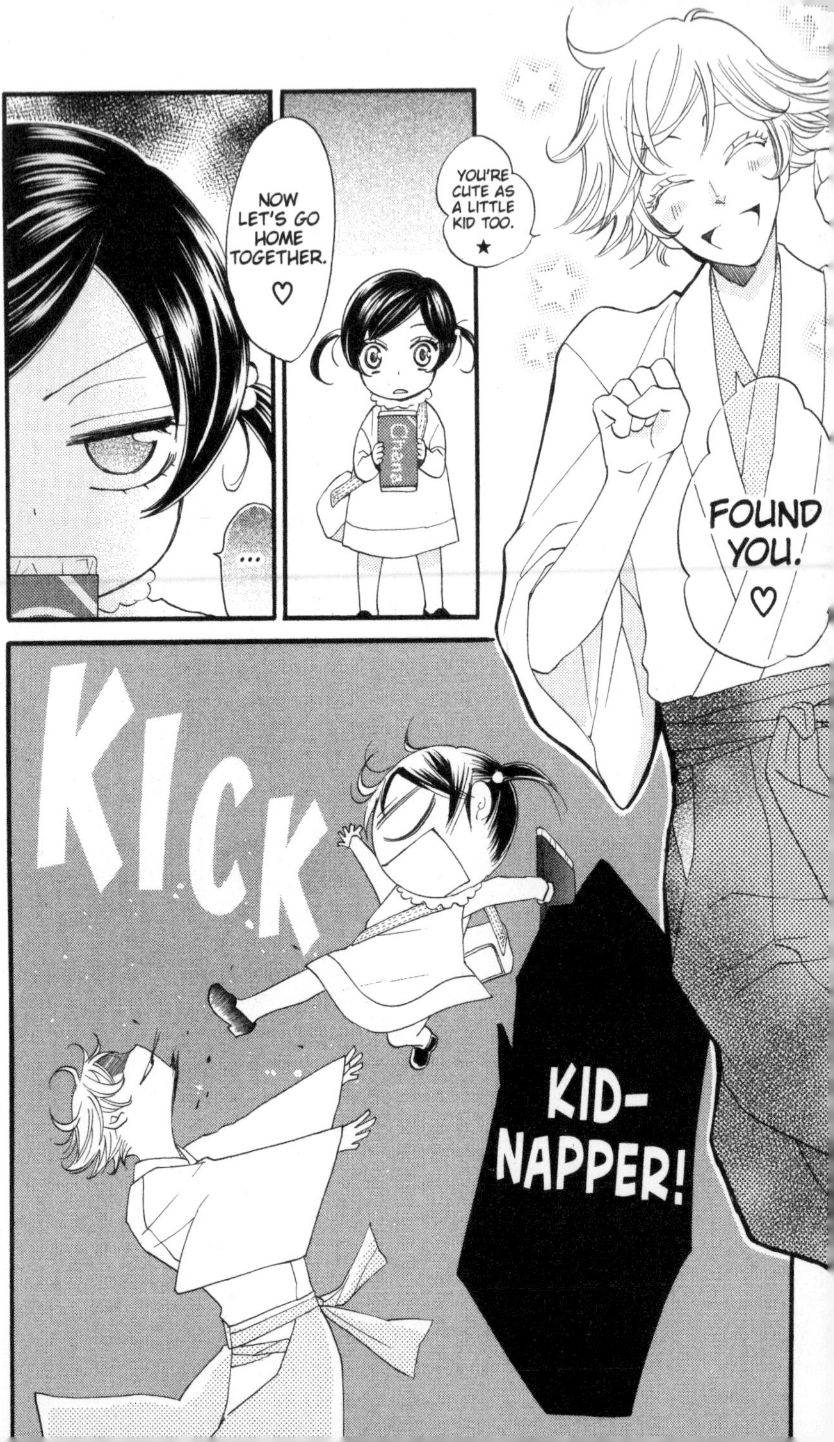
FOUND YOU. ♡
YOU'RE CUTE AS A LITTLE KID TOO. ★
NOW LET'S GO HOME TOGETHER. ♡
...
KICK
KID-NAPPER!

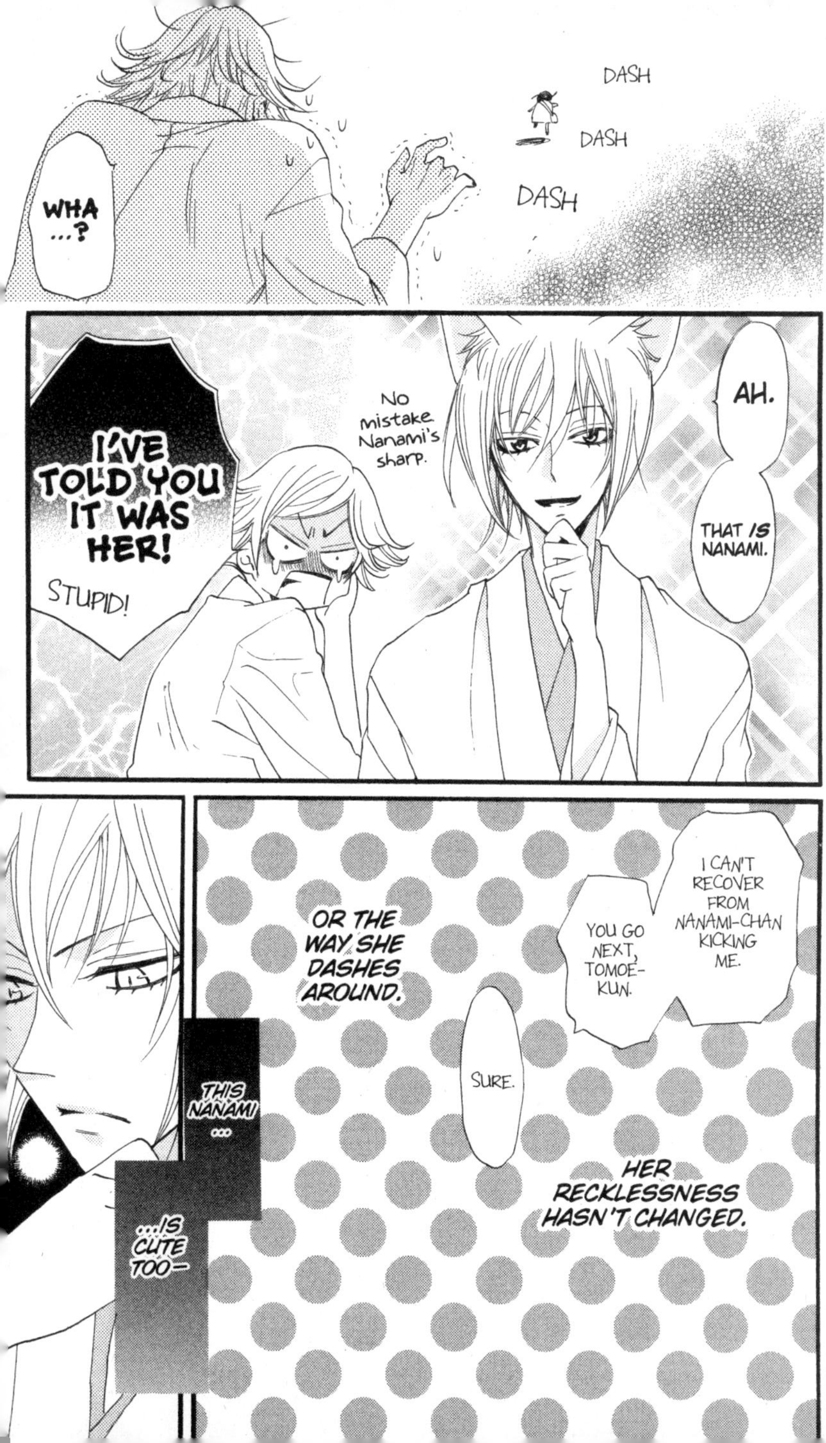
DASH
DASH
DASH
WHA ...?
AH.
THAT *IS* NANAMI.
No mistake. Nanami's sharp.
I'VE TOLD YOU IT WAS HER!
STUPID!
I CAN'T RECOVER FROM NANAMI-CHAN KICKING ME.
YOU GO NEXT, TOMOE-KUN.
SURE.
HER RECKLESSNESS HASN'T CHANGED.
OR THE WAY SHE DASHES AROUND.
THIS NANAMI ...
...IS CUTE TOO—

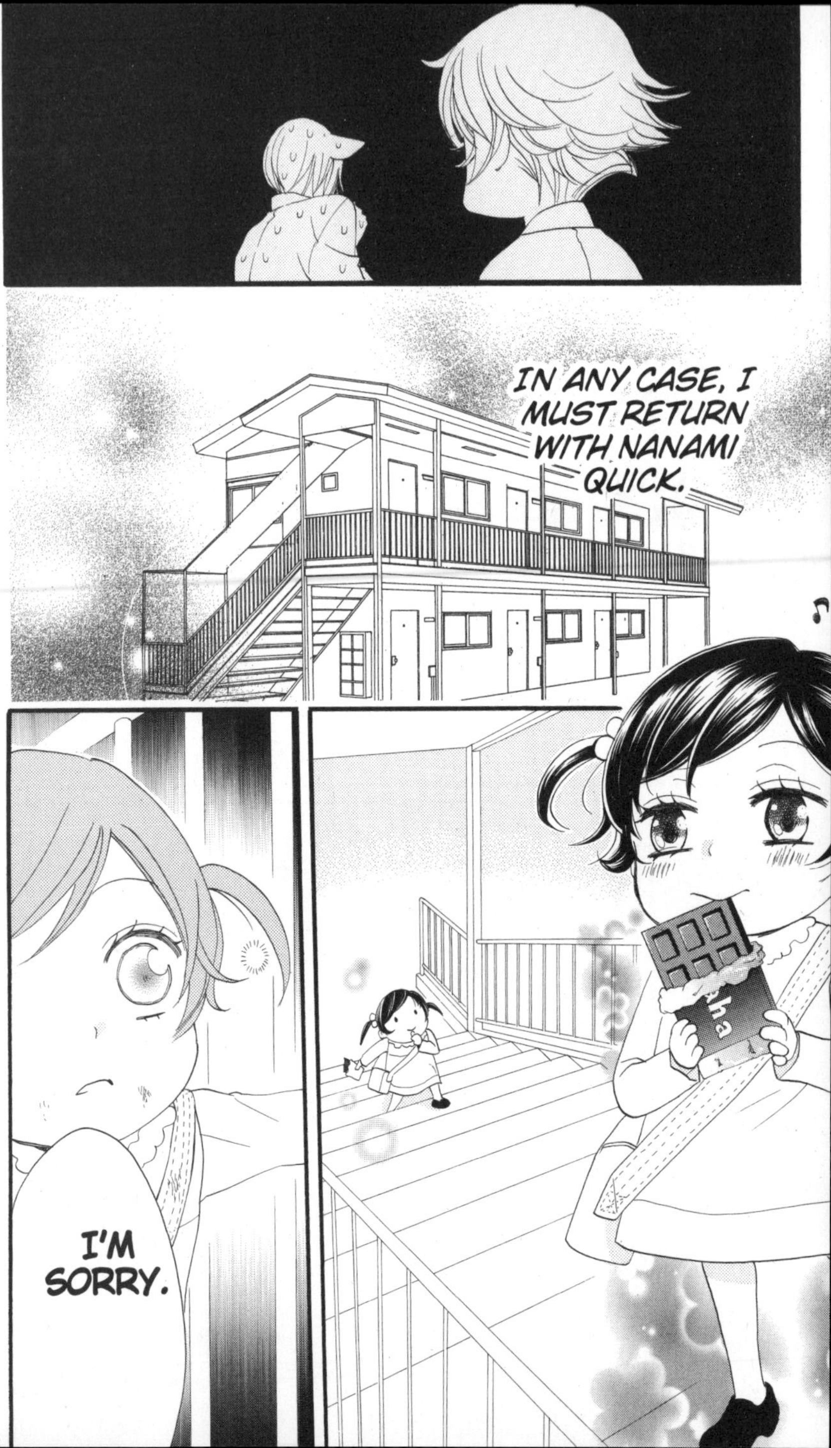
IN ANY CASE, I MUST RETURN WITH NANAMI QUICK.
I'M SORRY.

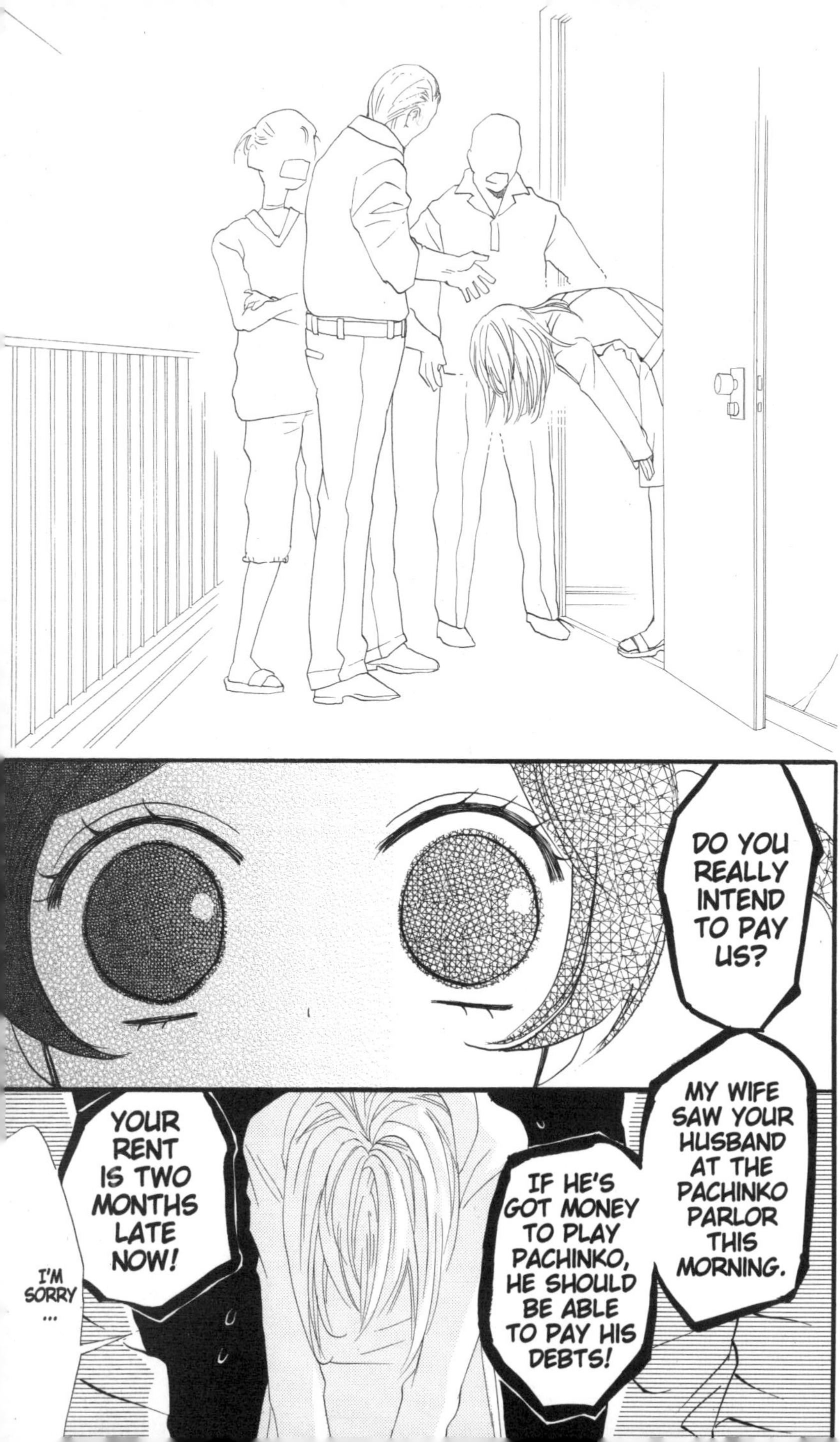
DO YOU REALLY INTEND TO PAY US?
MY WIFE SAW YOUR HUSBAND AT THE PACHINKO PARLOR THIS MORNING.
IF HE'S GOT MONEY TO PLAY PACHINKO, HE SHOULD BE ABLE TO PAY HIS DEBTS!
YOUR RENT IS TWO MONTHS LATE NOW!
I'M SORRY ...

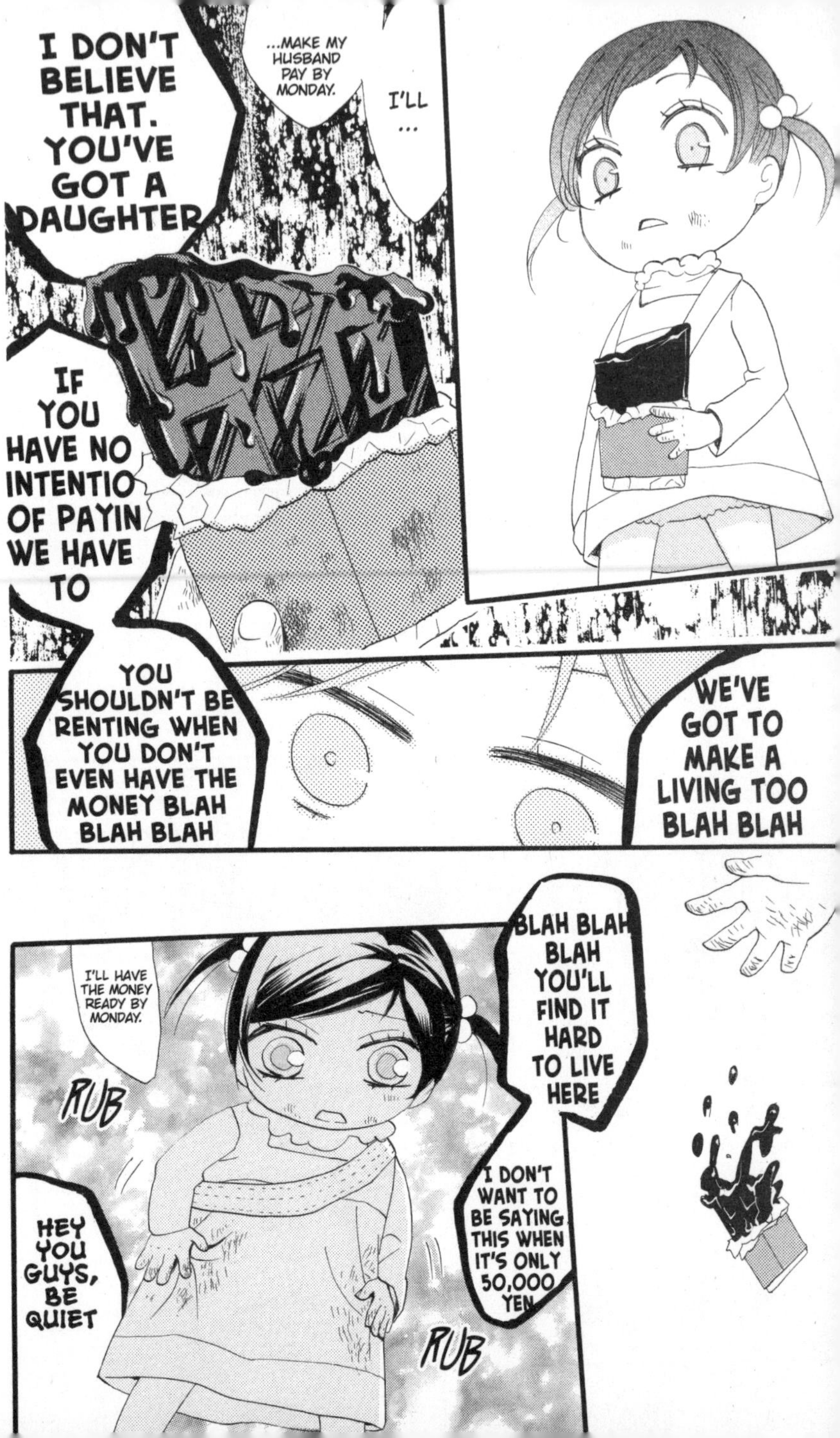
I'LL ...
...MAKE MY HUSBAND PAY BY MONDAY.
I DON'T BELIEVE THAT. YOU'VE GOT A DAUGHTER
IF YOU HAVE NO INTENTIO OF PAYIN WE HAVE TO
WE'VE GOT TO MAKE A LIVING TOO BLAH BLAH
YOU SHOULDN'T BE RENTING WHEN YOU DON'T EVEN HAVE THE MONEY BLAH BLAH BLAH
BLAH BLAH BLAH YOU'LL FIND IT HARD TO LIVE HERE
I DON'T WANT TO BE SAYING THIS WHEN IT'S ONLY 50,000 YEN
I'LL HAVE THE MONEY READY BY MONDAY.
RUB
HEY YOU GUYS, BE QUIET
RUB

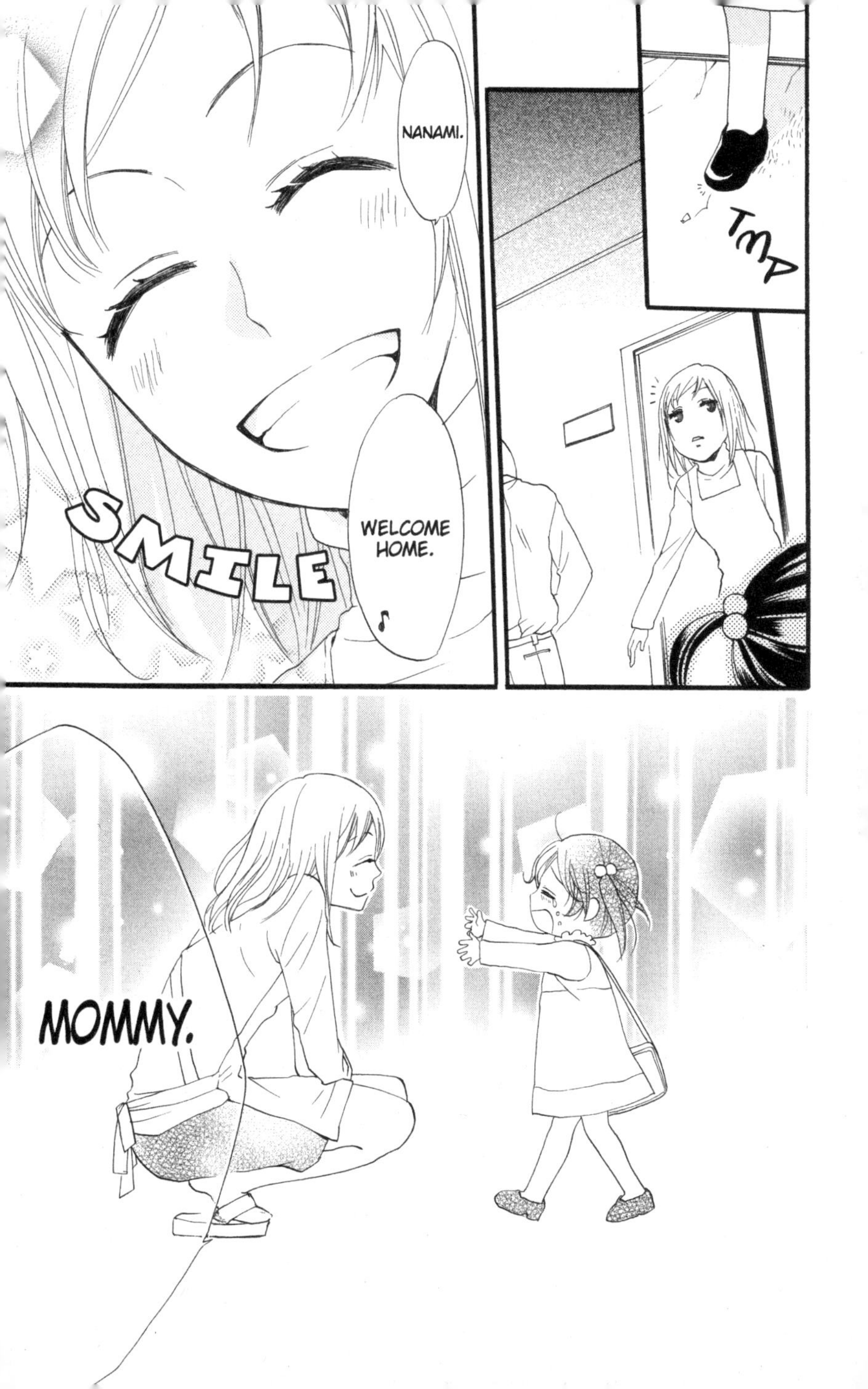
TMP
NANAMI.
WELCOME HOME. ♪
SMILE
MOMMY.

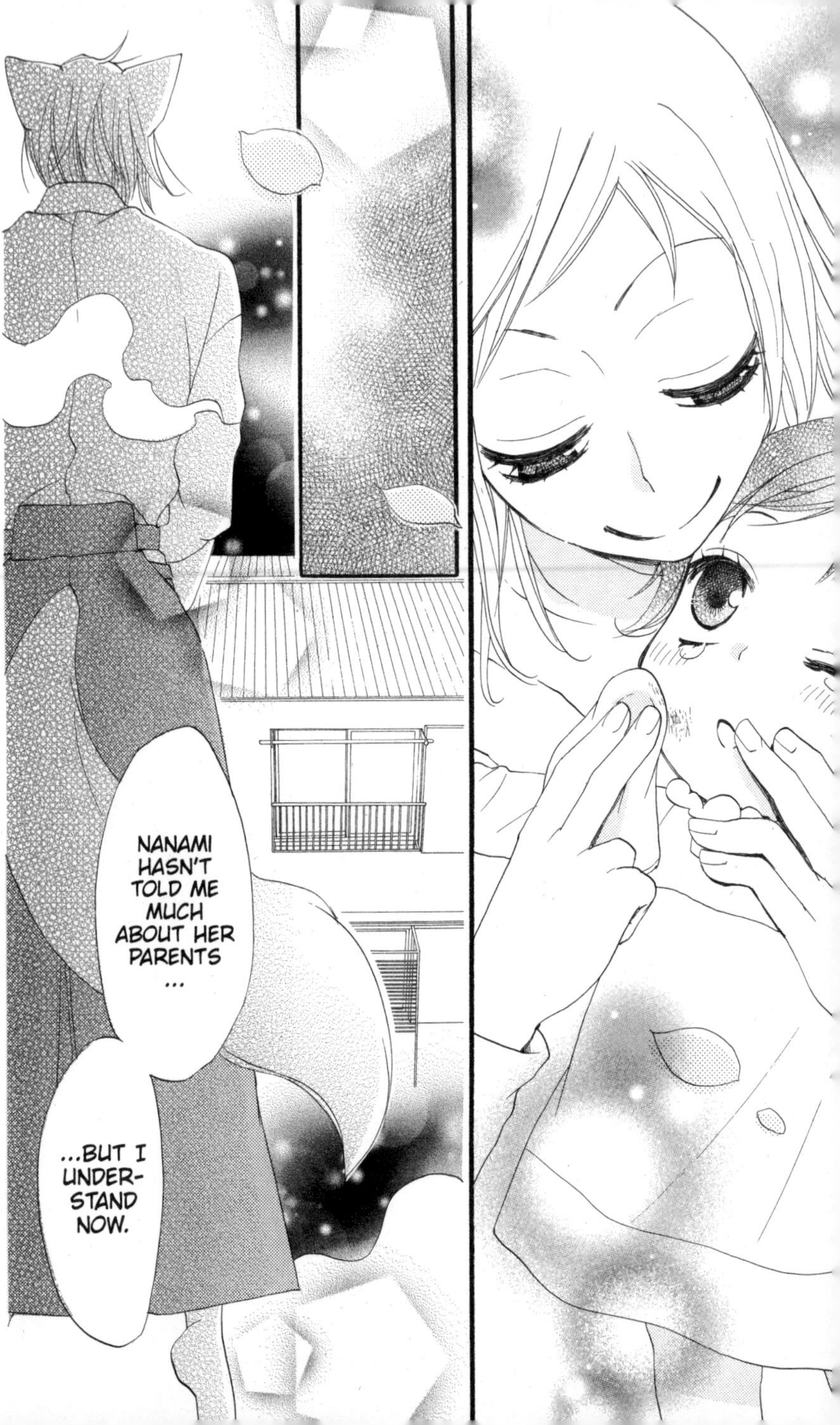
NANAMI HASN'T TOLD ME MUCH ABOUT HER PARENTS ...
...BUT I UNDER-STAND NOW.

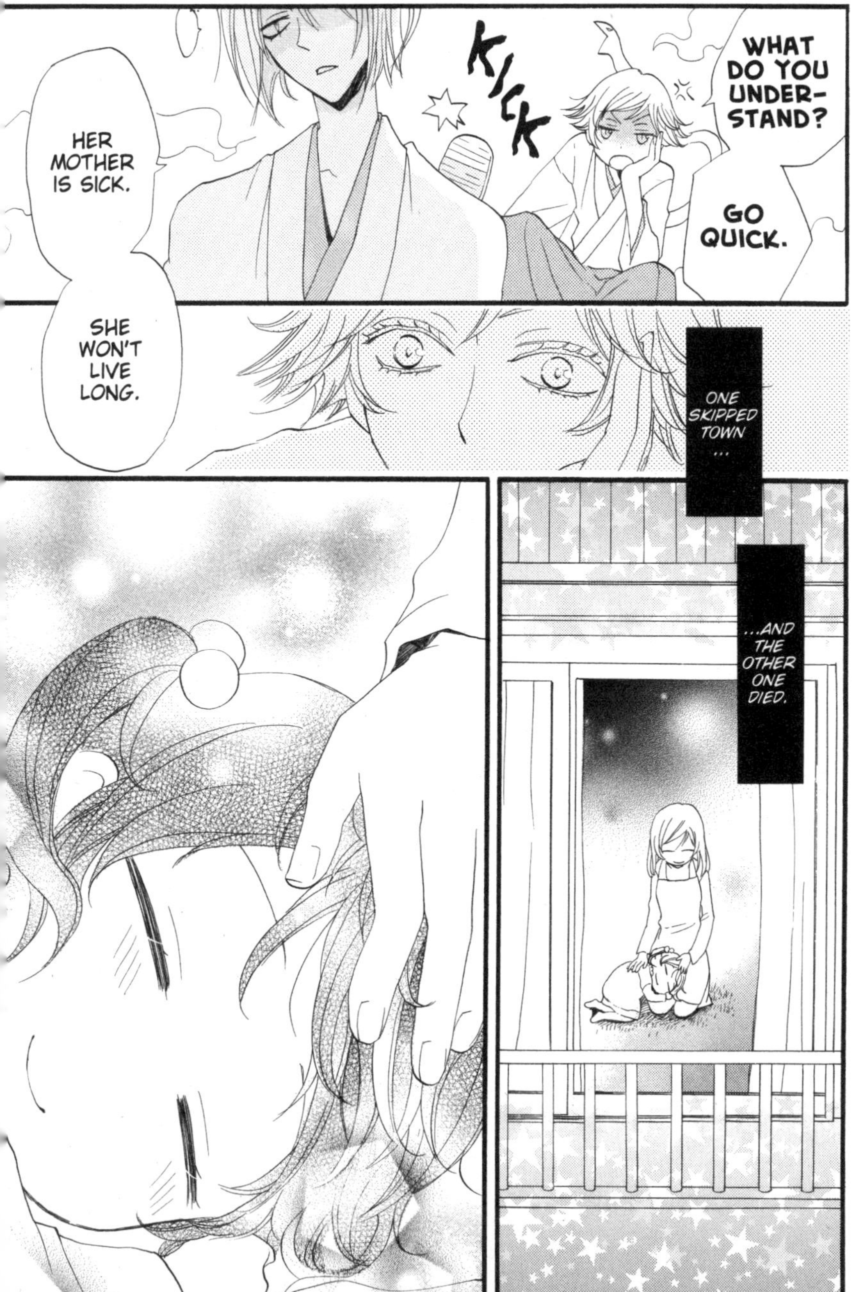
WHAT DO YOU UNDER-STAND?
GO QUICK.
KICK
HER MOTHER IS SICK.
SHE WON'T LIVE LONG.
ONE SKIPPED TOWN ...
...AND THE OTHER ONE DIED.

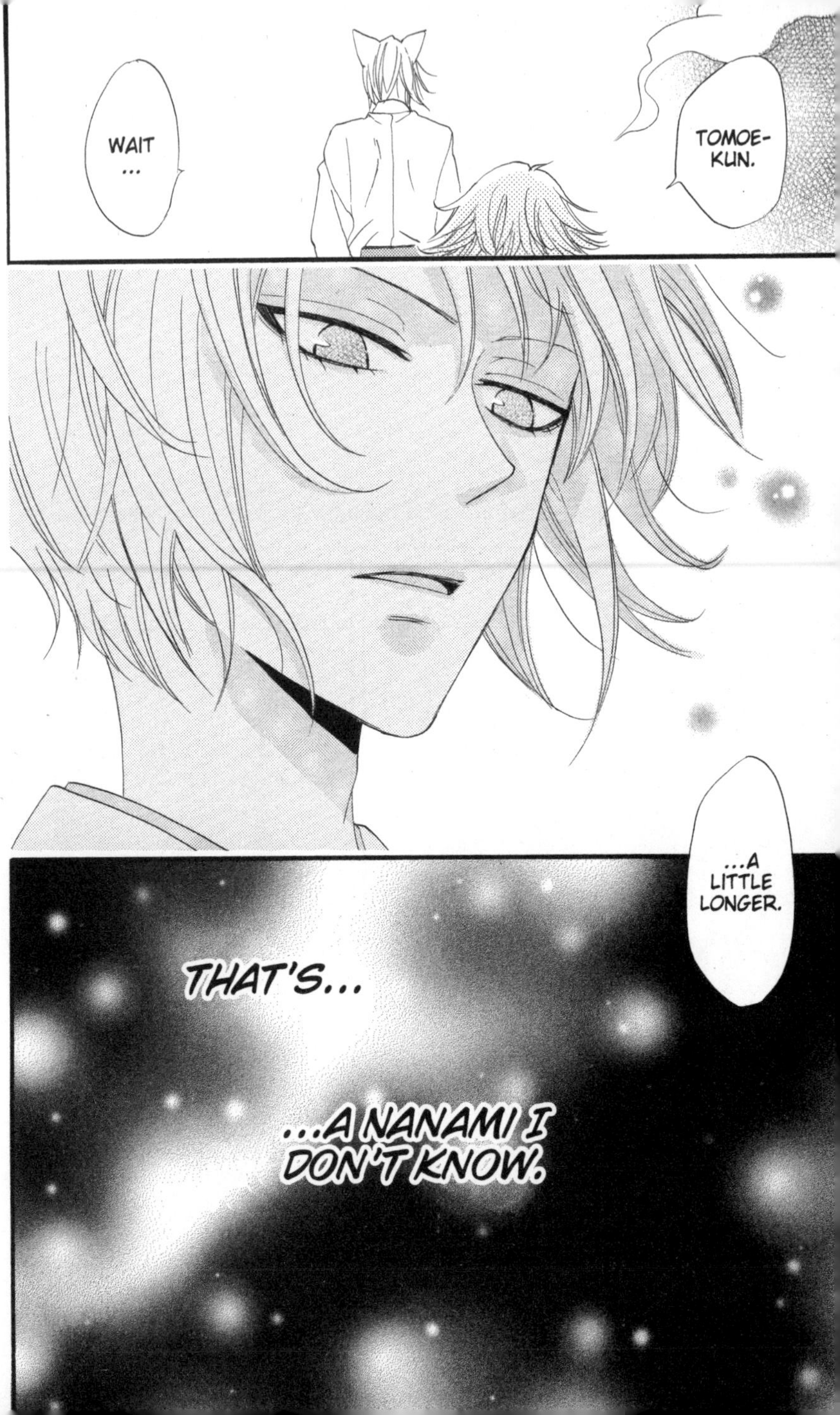
TOMOE-KUN.
WAIT ...
...A LITTLE LONGER.
THAT'S...
...A NANAMI I DON'T KNOW.

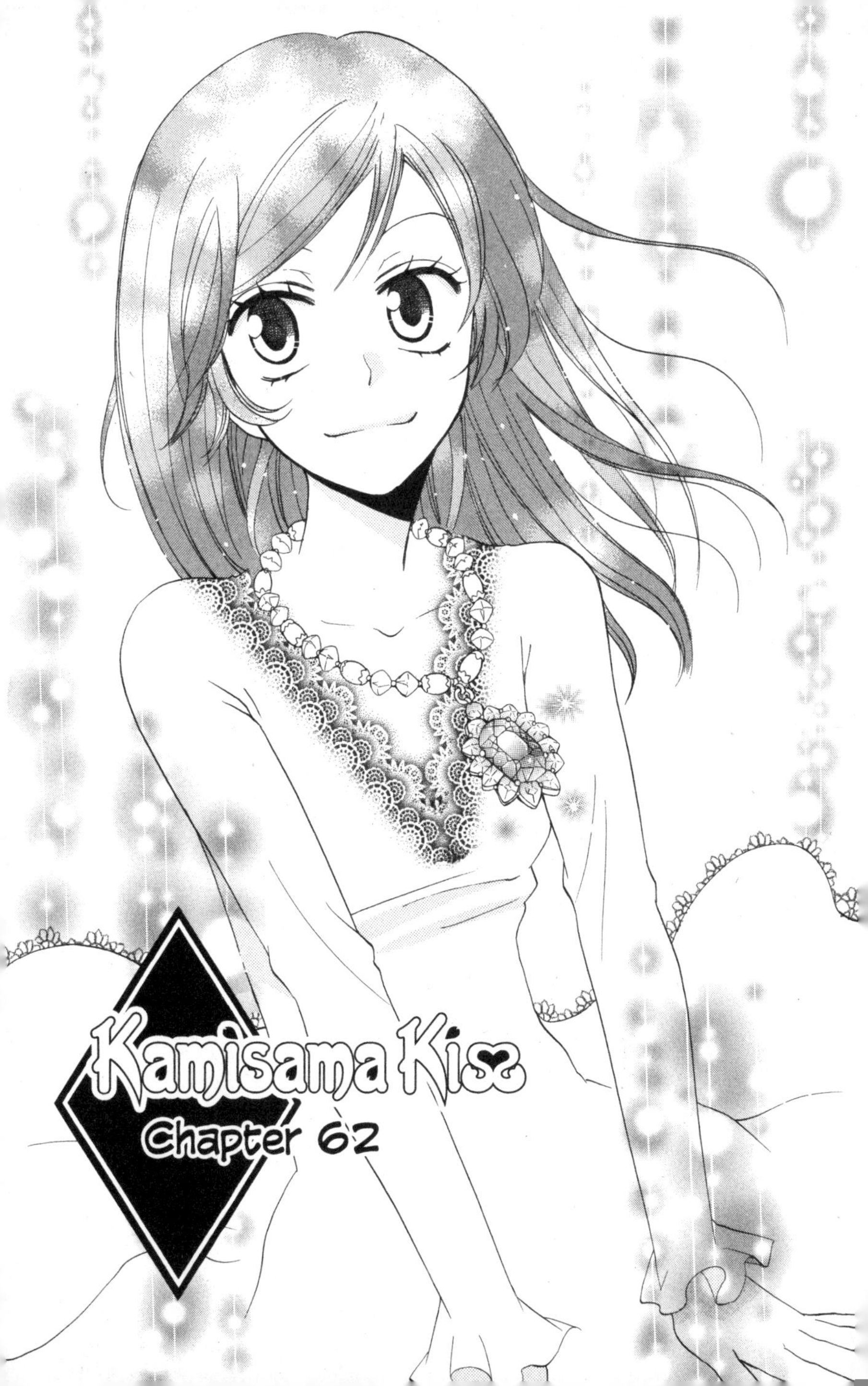
Kamisama Kiss
Chapter 62

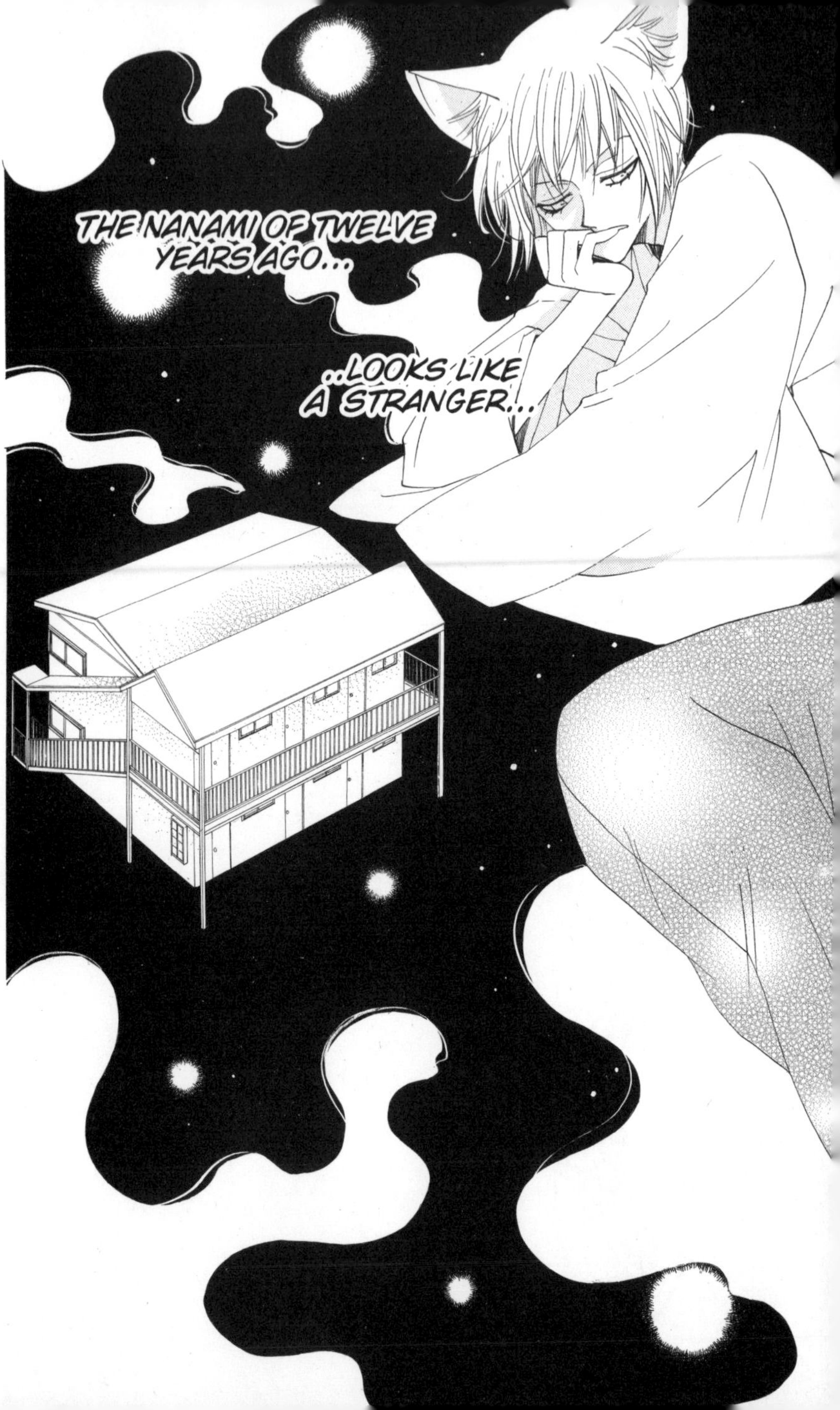
THE NANAMI OF TWELVE YEARS AGO...
...LOOKS LIKE A STRANGER...

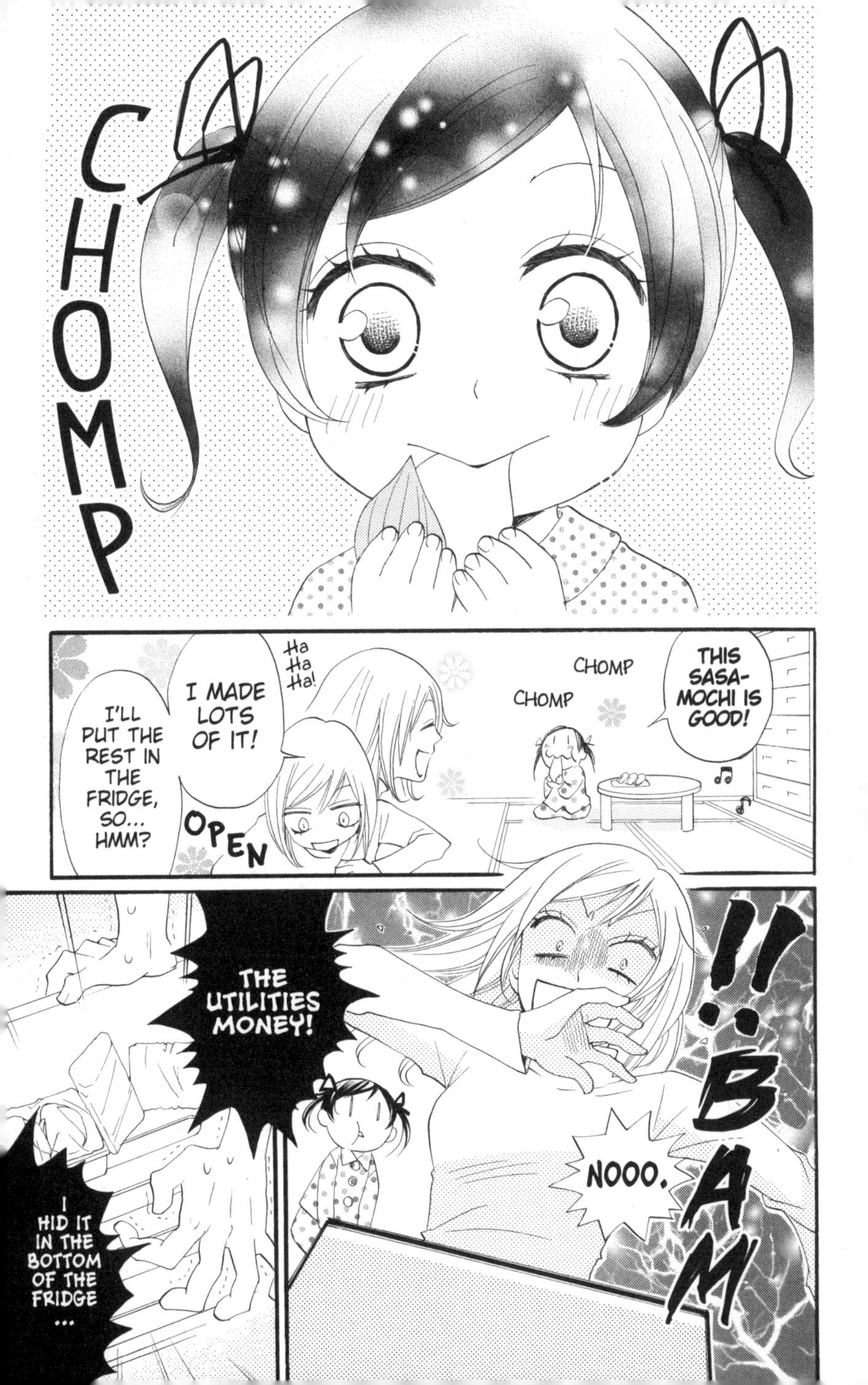
CHOMP
THIS SASA-MOCHI IS GOOD!
CHOMP
CHOMP
Ha Ha Ha!
I MADE LOTS OF IT!
I'LL PUT THE REST IN THE FRIDGE, SO... HMM?
OPEN
BAM!!
NOOO.
THE UTILITIES MONEY!
I HID IT IN THE BOTTOM OF THE FRIDGE...

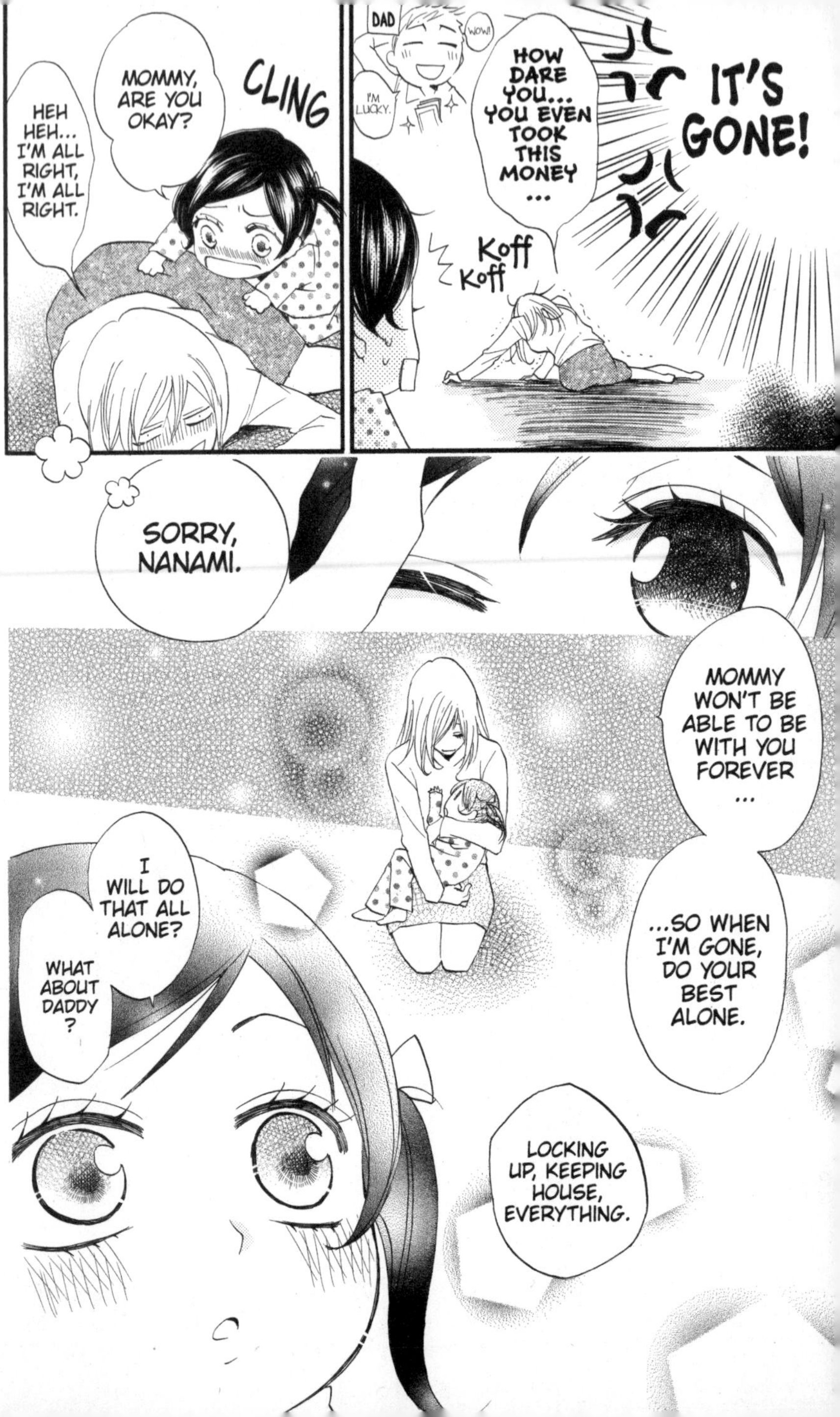
IT'S GONE!
HOW DARE YOU... YOU EVEN TOOK THIS MONEY...
WOW!
DAD
I'M LUCKY.
Koff Koff
CLING
MOMMY, ARE YOU OKAY?
HEH HEH... I'M ALL RIGHT, I'M ALL RIGHT.
SORRY, NANAMI.
MOMMY WON'T BE ABLE TO BE WITH YOU FOREVER...
...SO WHEN I'M GONE, DO YOUR BEST ALONE.
I WILL DO THAT ALL ALONE?
WHAT ABOUT DADDY?
LOCKING UP, KEEPING HOUSE, EVERYTHING.

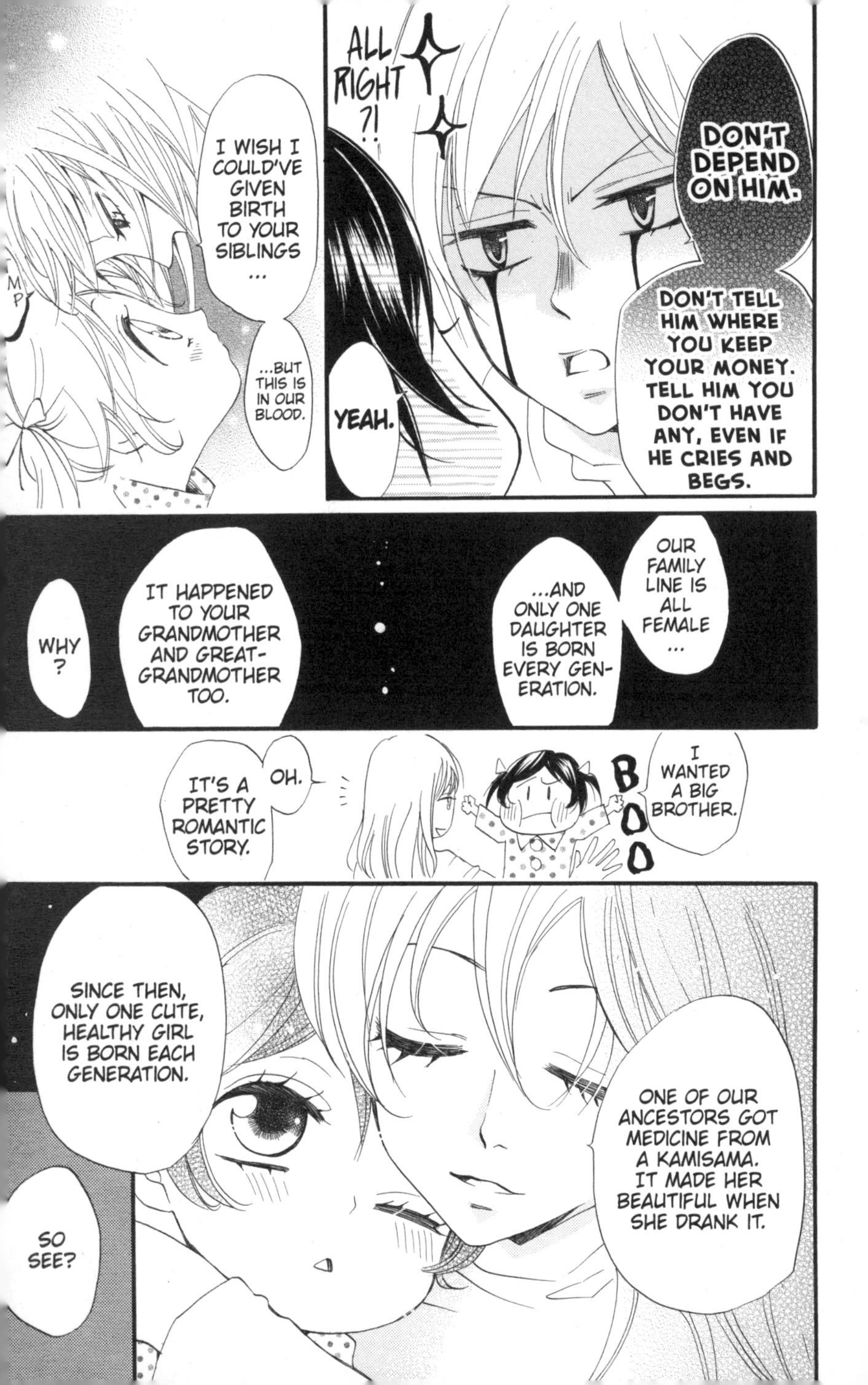
DON'T DEPEND ON HIM.
DON'T TELL HIM WHERE YOU KEEP YOUR MONEY. TELL HIM YOU DON'T HAVE ANY, EVEN IF HE CRIES AND BEGS.
ALL RIGHT ?!
YEAH.
I WISH I COULD'VE GIVEN BIRTH TO YOUR SIBLINGS...
...BUT THIS IS IN OUR BLOOD.
OUR FAMILY LINE IS ALL FEMALE...
...AND ONLY ONE DAUGHTER IS BORN EVERY GENERATION.
IT HAPPENED TO YOUR GRANDMOTHER AND GREAT-GRANDMOTHER TOO.
WHY?
I WANTED A BIG BROTHER.
BOO
OH.
IT'S A PRETTY ROMANTIC STORY.
ONE OF OUR ANCESTORS GOT MEDICINE FROM A KAMISAMA. IT MADE HER BEAUTIFUL WHEN SHE DRANK IT.
SINCE THEN, ONLY ONE CUTE, HEALTHY GIRL IS BORN EACH GENERATION.
SO SEE?

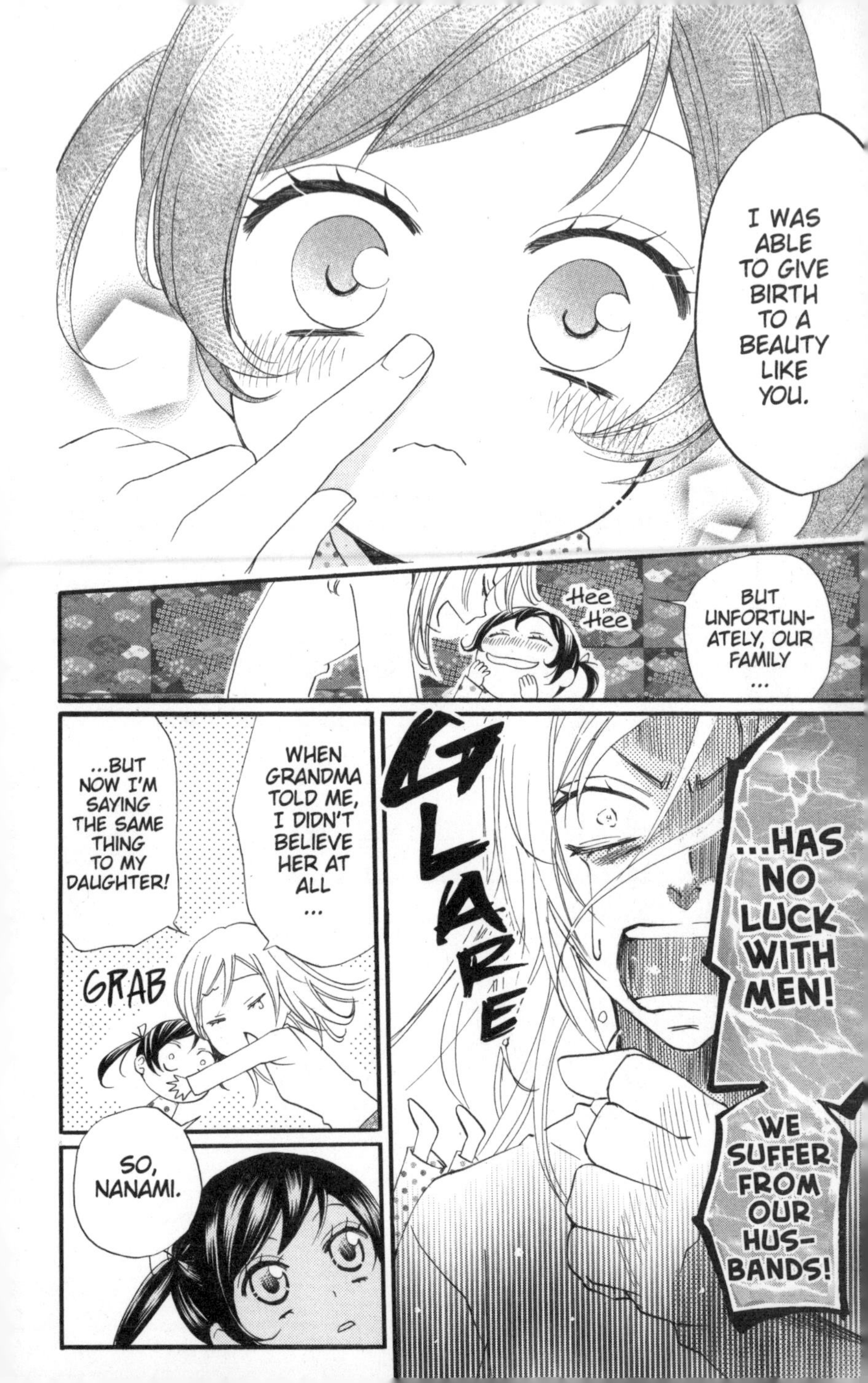
I WAS ABLE TO GIVE BIRTH TO A BEAUTY LIKE YOU.
BUT UNFORTUNATELY, OUR FAMILY ...
Hee Hee
...HAS NO LUCK WITH MEN!
WE SUFFER FROM OUR HUSBANDS!
GLARE
WHEN GRANDMA TOLD ME, I DIDN'T BELIEVE HER AT ALL ...
...BUT NOW I'M SAYING THE SAME THING TO MY DAUGHTER!
GRAB
SO, NANAMI.

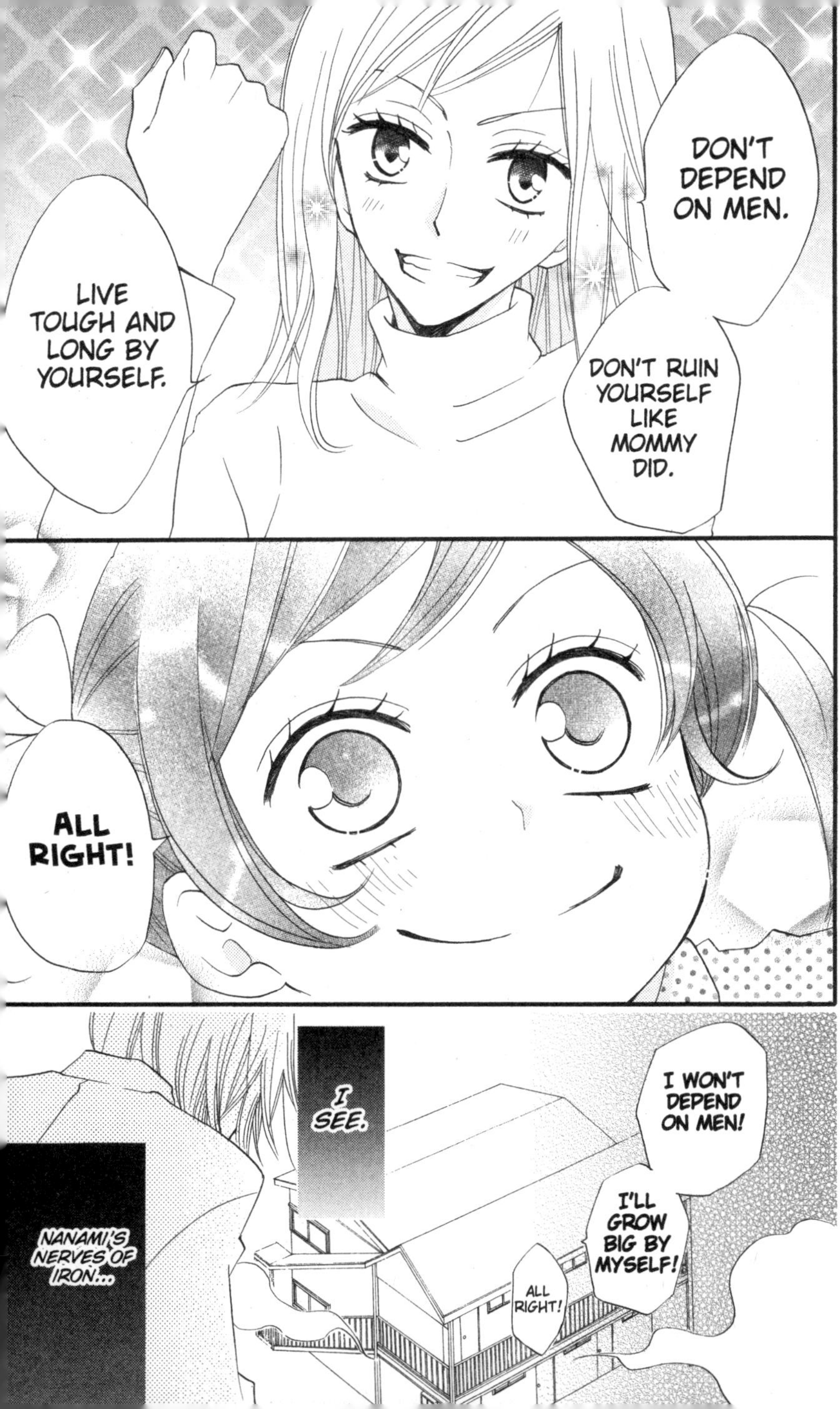
DON'T DEPEND ON MEN.
DON'T RUIN YOURSELF LIKE MOMMY DID.
LIVE TOUGH AND LONG BY YOURSELF.
ALL RIGHT!
I WON'T DEPEND ON MEN!
I'LL GROW BIG BY MYSELF!
ALL RIGHT!
I SEE.
NANAMI'S NERVES OF IRON...

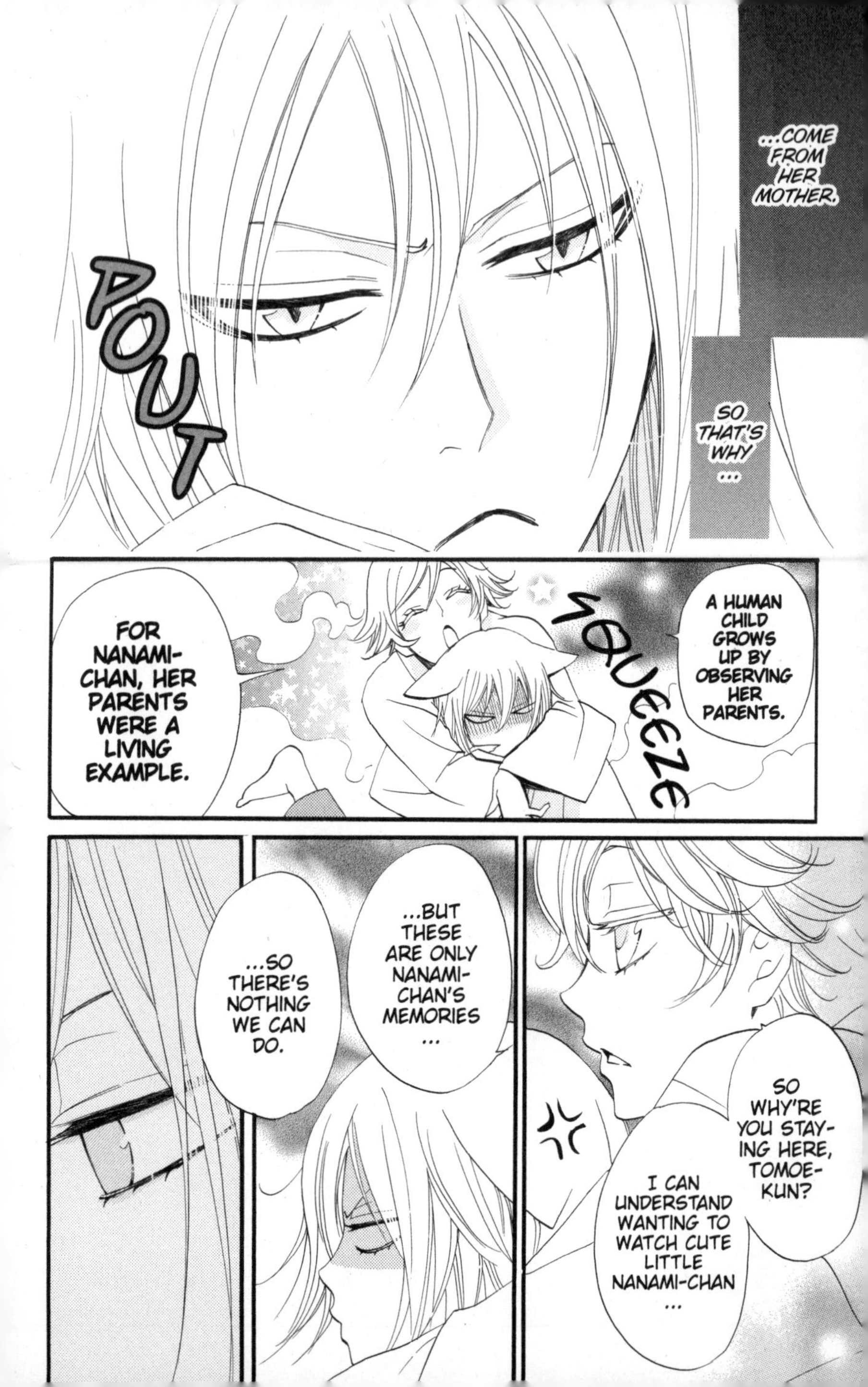
...COME FROM HER MOTHER.
SO THAT'S WHY ...
POUT
A HUMAN CHILD GROWS UP BY OBSERVING HER PARENTS.
SQUEEZE
FOR NANAMI-CHAN, HER PARENTS WERE A LIVING EXAMPLE.
SO WHY'RE YOU STAYING HERE, TOMOE-KUN?
I CAN UNDERSTAND WANTING TO WATCH CUTE LITTLE NANAMI-CHAN ...
...BUT THESE ARE ONLY NANAMI-CHAN'S MEMORIES ...
...SO THERE'S NOTHING WE CAN DO.

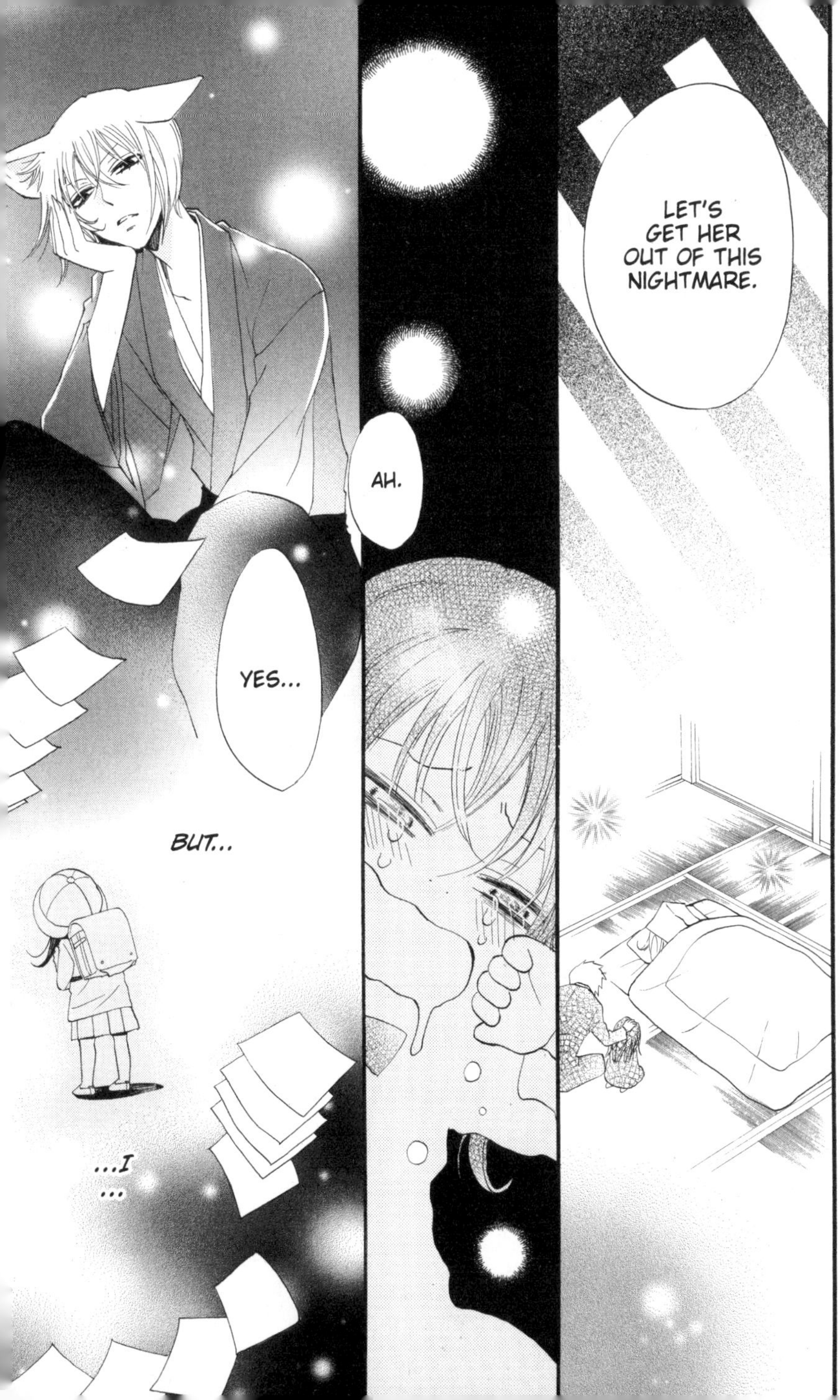
LET'S GET HER OUT OF THIS NIGHTMARE.
AH.
YES...
BUT...
...I ...

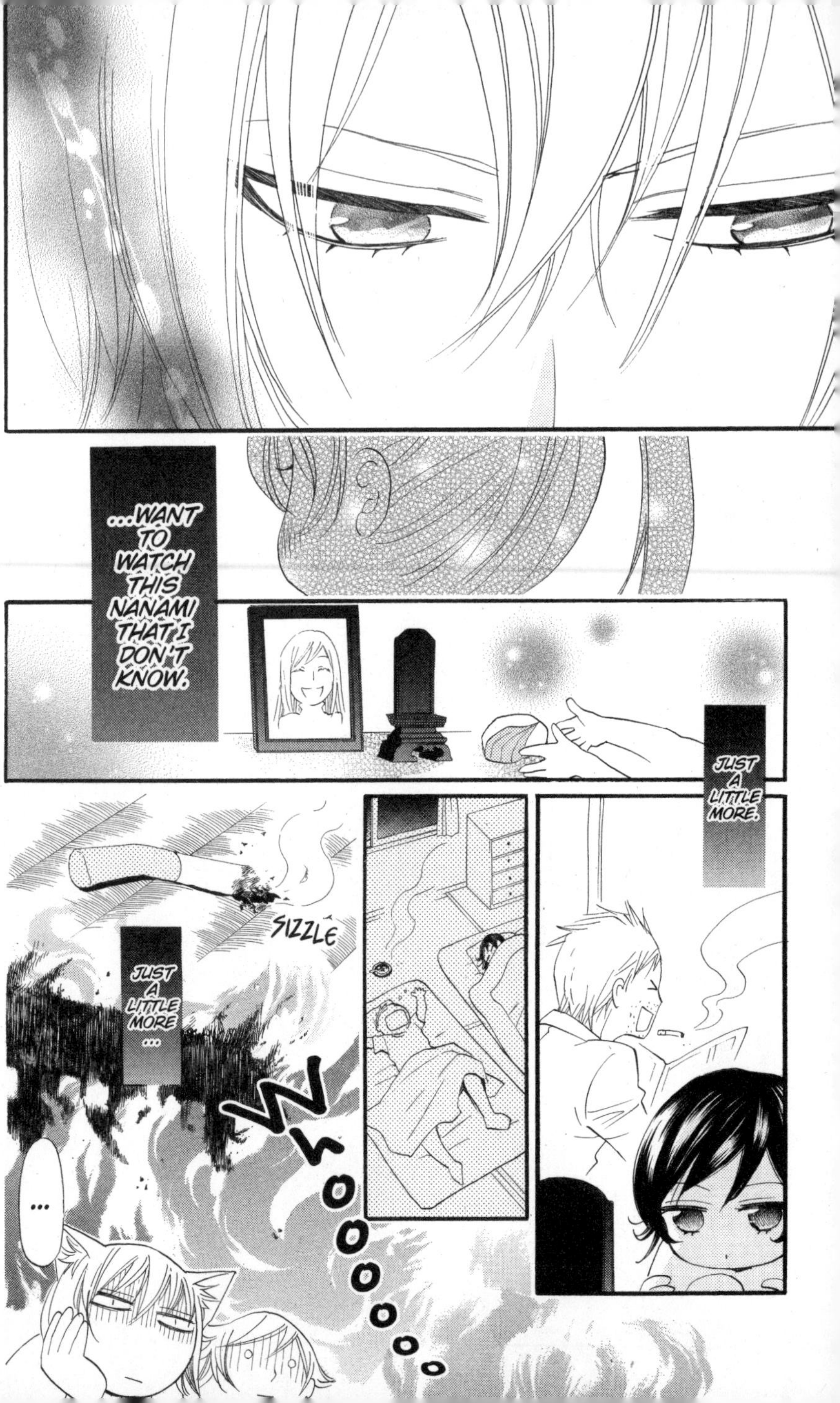
...WANT TO WATCH THIS NANAMI THAT I DON'T KNOW.
JUST A LITTLE MORE.
SIZZLE
JUST A LITTLE MORE...
WHOOOOOOO
...

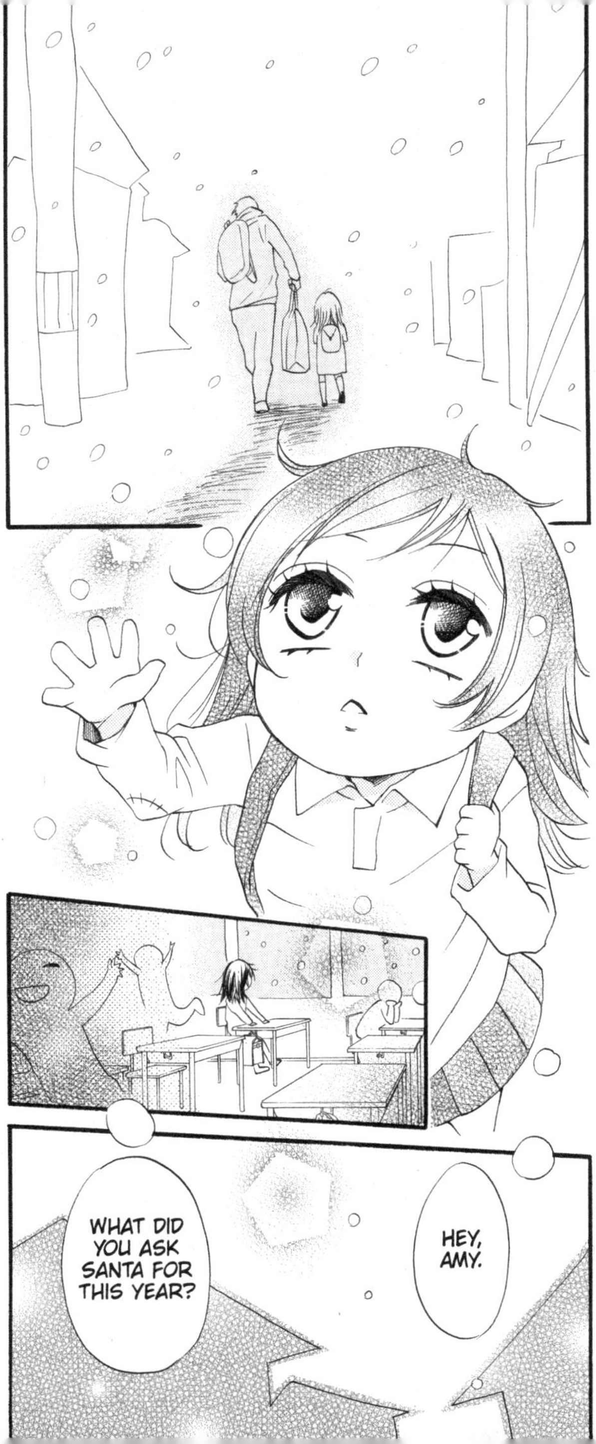
HEY, AMY.
WHAT DID YOU ASK SANTA FOR THIS YEAR?

The day Kamisama 11 comes out in Japan, a book of my one-shots is coming out as well.

It's manga I sent in before I made my debut, and my debut manga is in it. Actually, the one-shots were all drawn around the time I made my debut, so you can tell I still had a lot to learn about drawing manga. I hope you'll take a look...

There're re-runs of the Moomin anime on TV nowadays, and I enjoy watching it every morning. I got the DVD boxset too! It hasn't arrived yet, but I'm looking forward to it. Moomin! Moomin! My favorite character is Moomin Mama. She soothes me.

When I said I'd like to go to Finland someday, I was told that 2013 is the year for watching the aurora borealis! So my heart is swaying. 2013! What will I be doing then?

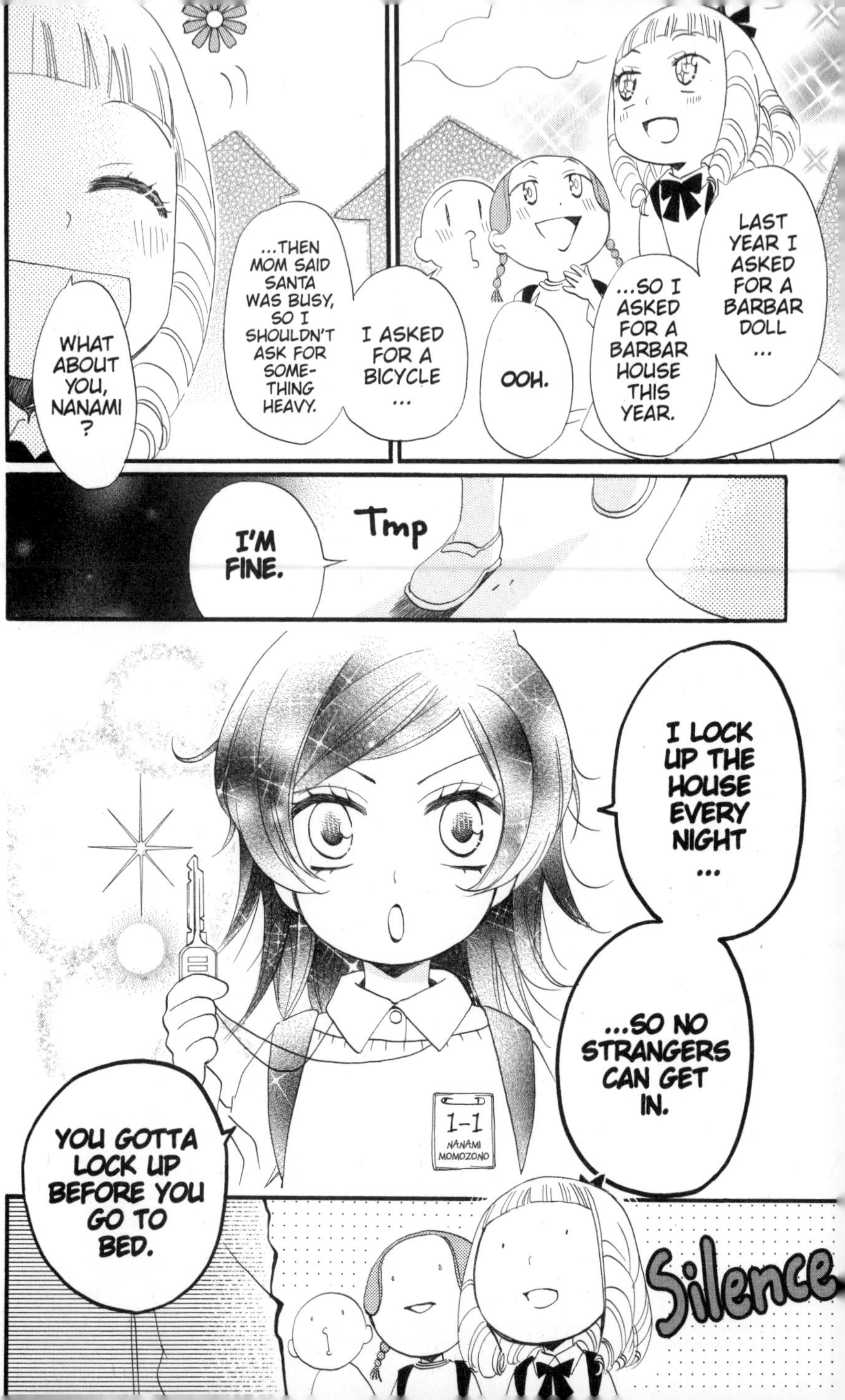
LAST YEAR I ASKED FOR A BARBAR DOLL ...
...SO I ASKED FOR A BARBAR HOUSE THIS YEAR.
OOH.
I ASKED FOR A BICYCLE ...
...THEN MOM SAID SANTA WAS BUSY, SO I SHOULDN'T ASK FOR SOME-THING HEAVY.
WHAT ABOUT YOU, NANAMI?
Tmp
I'M FINE.
I LOCK UP THE HOUSE EVERY NIGHT ...
...SO NO STRANGERS CAN GET IN.
1-1
NANAMI MOMOZONO
YOU GOTTA LOCK UP BEFORE YOU GO TO BED.
Silence

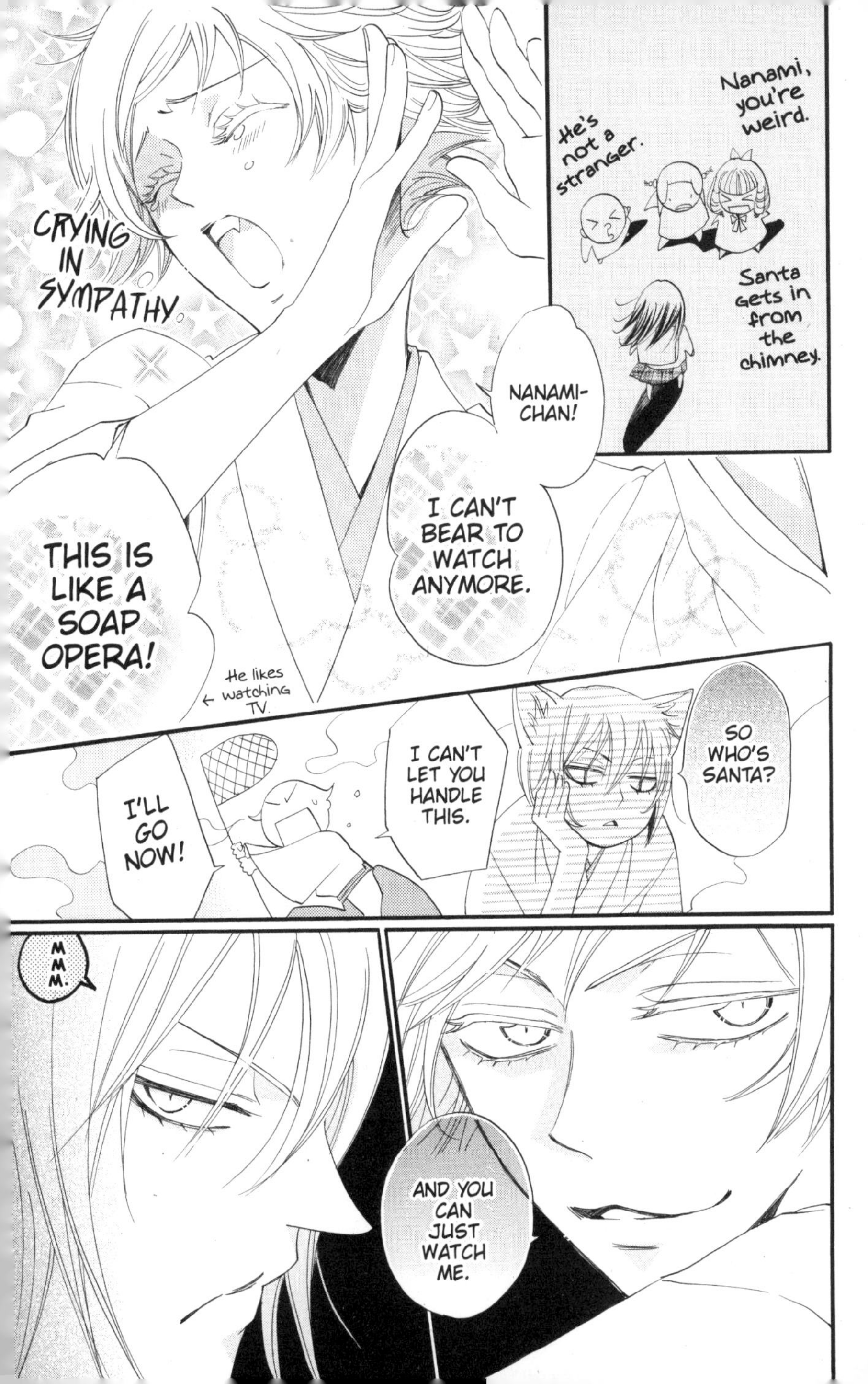
Nanami, you're weird.
He's not a stranger.
Santa gets in from the chimney.
NANAMI-CHAN!
I CAN'T BEAR TO WATCH ANYMORE.
CRYING IN SYMPATHY
THIS IS LIKE A SOAP OPERA!
He likes watching TV.
SO WHO'S SANTA?
I CAN'T LET YOU HANDLE THIS.
I'LL GO NOW!
AND YOU CAN JUST WATCH ME.
MMM.

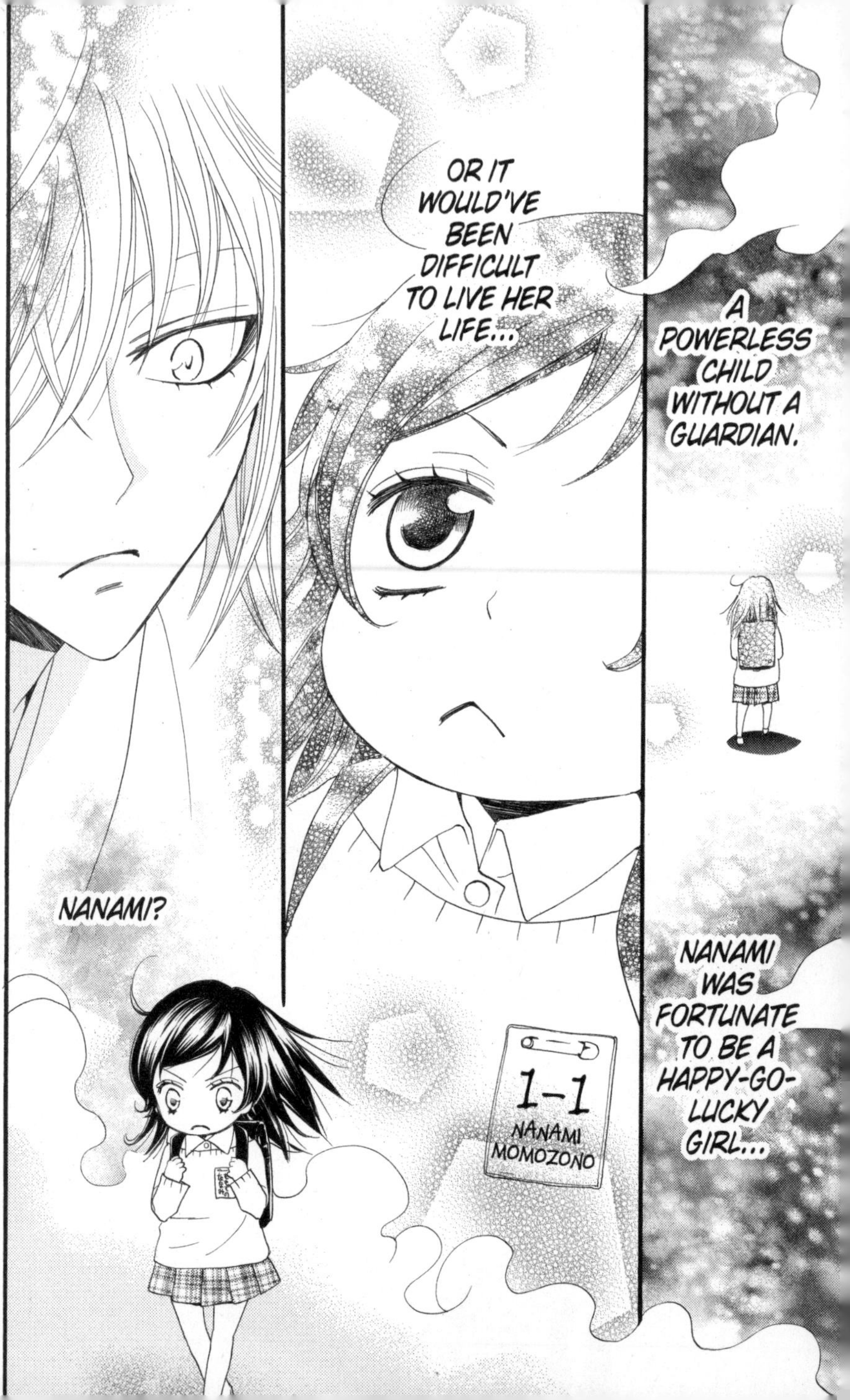
A POWERLESS CHILD WITHOUT A GUARDIAN.
NANAMI WAS FORTUNATE TO BE A HAPPY-GO-LUCKY GIRL...
OR IT WOULD'VE BEEN DIFFICULT TO LIVE HER LIFE...
NANAMI?
1-1
NANAMI MOMOZONO

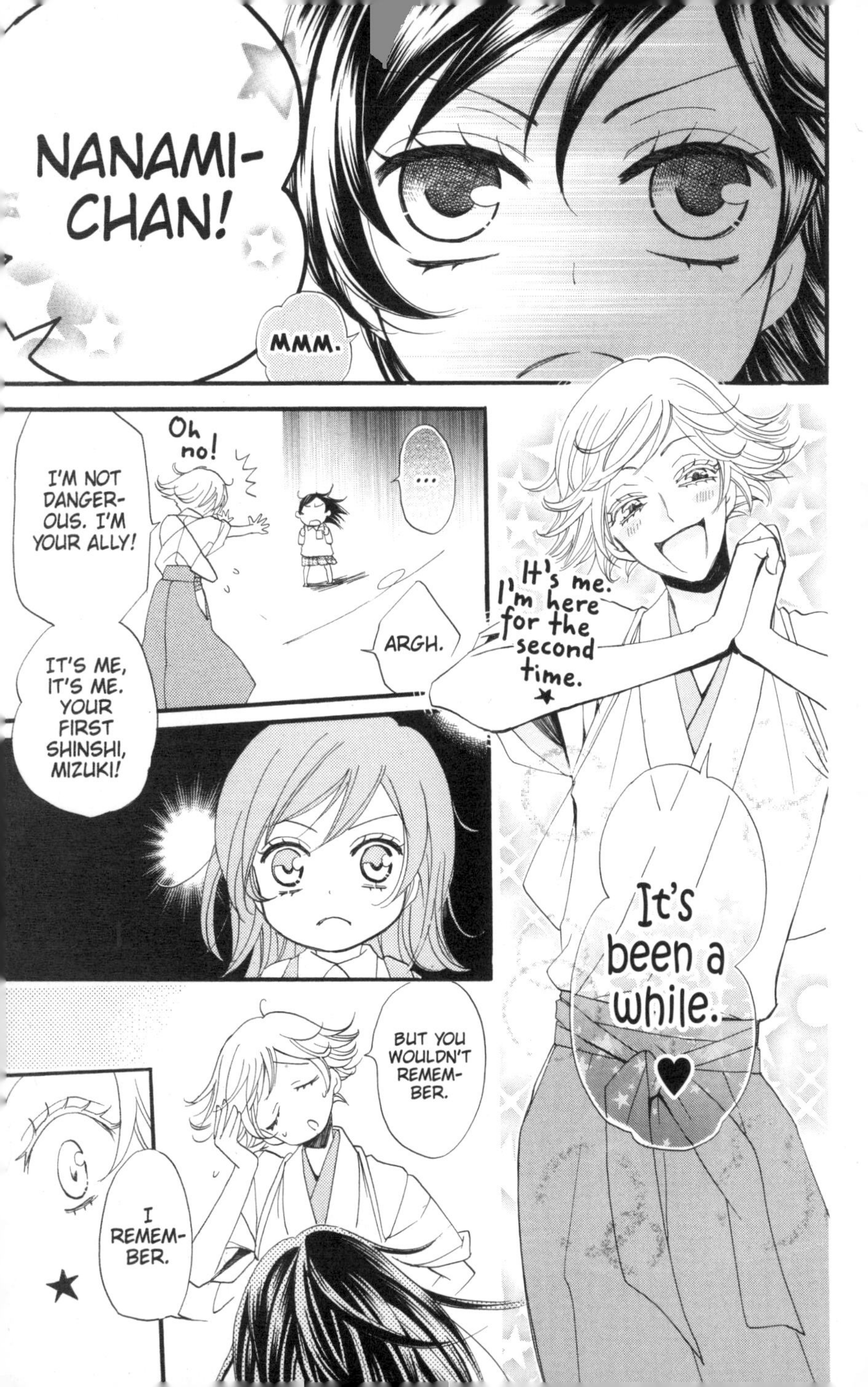
NANAMI-CHAN!
MMM.
It's me. I'm here for the second time. ★
It's been a while. ♥
...
Oh no!
I'M NOT DANGEROUS. I'M YOUR ALLY!
ARGH.
IT'S ME, IT'S ME. YOUR FIRST SHINSHI, MIZUKI!
BUT YOU WOULDN'T REMEMBER.
I REMEMBER.

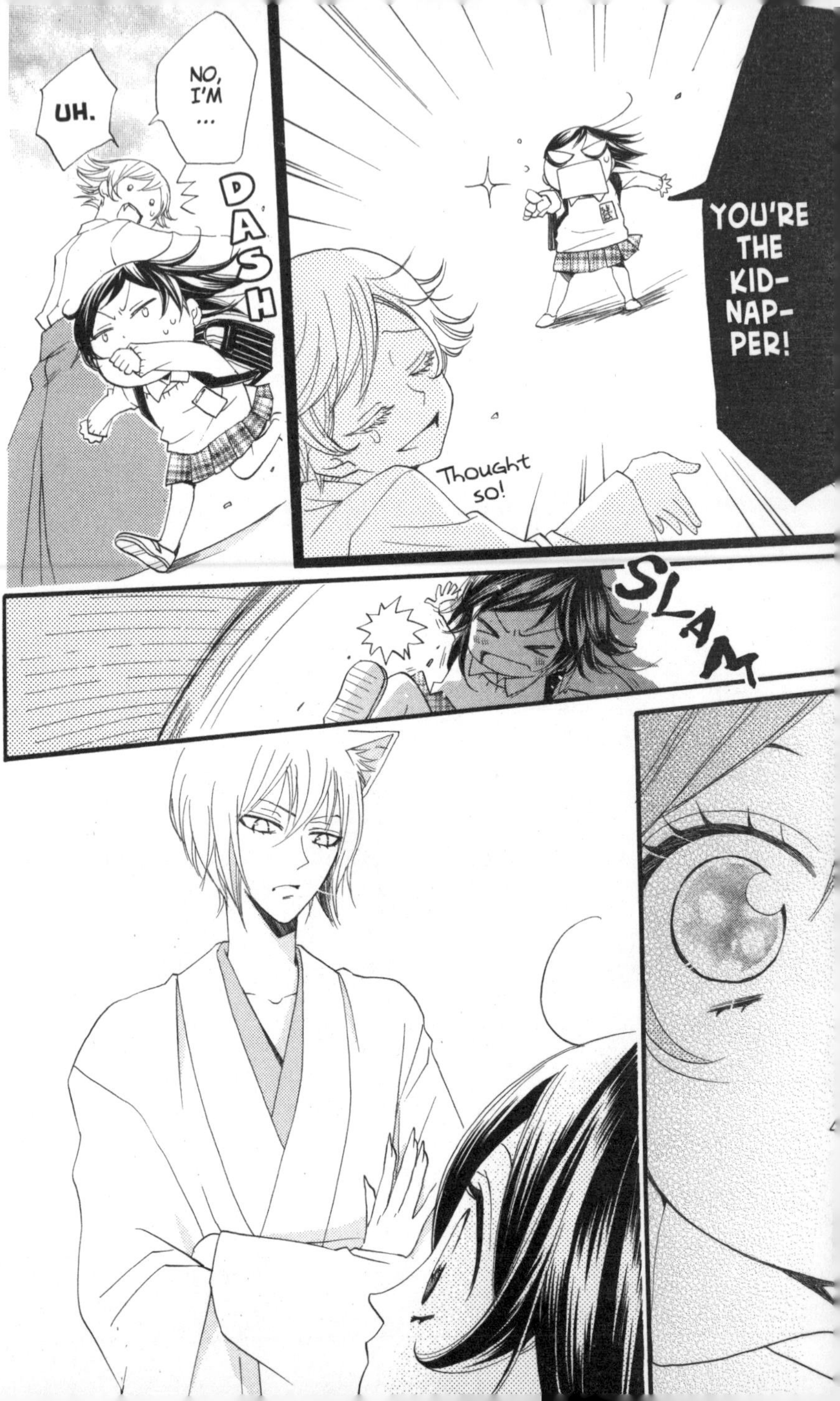
YOU'RE THE KID-NAP-PER!
Thought so!
NO, I'M ...
UH.
DASH
SLAM

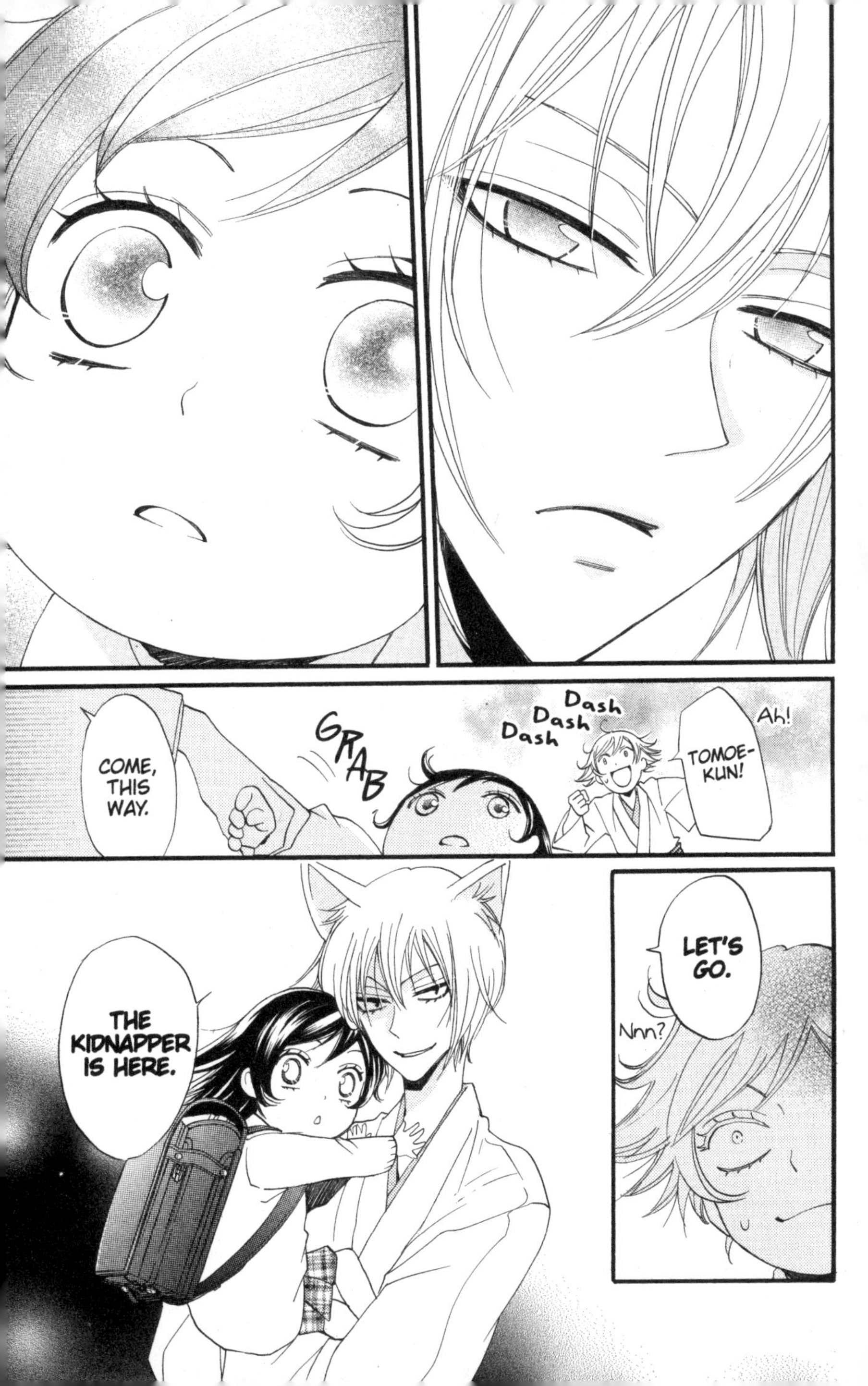
Ah!
TOMOE-KUN!
Dash Dash Dash
GRAB
COME, THIS WAY.
LET'S GO.
Nnn?
THE KIDNAPPER IS HERE.

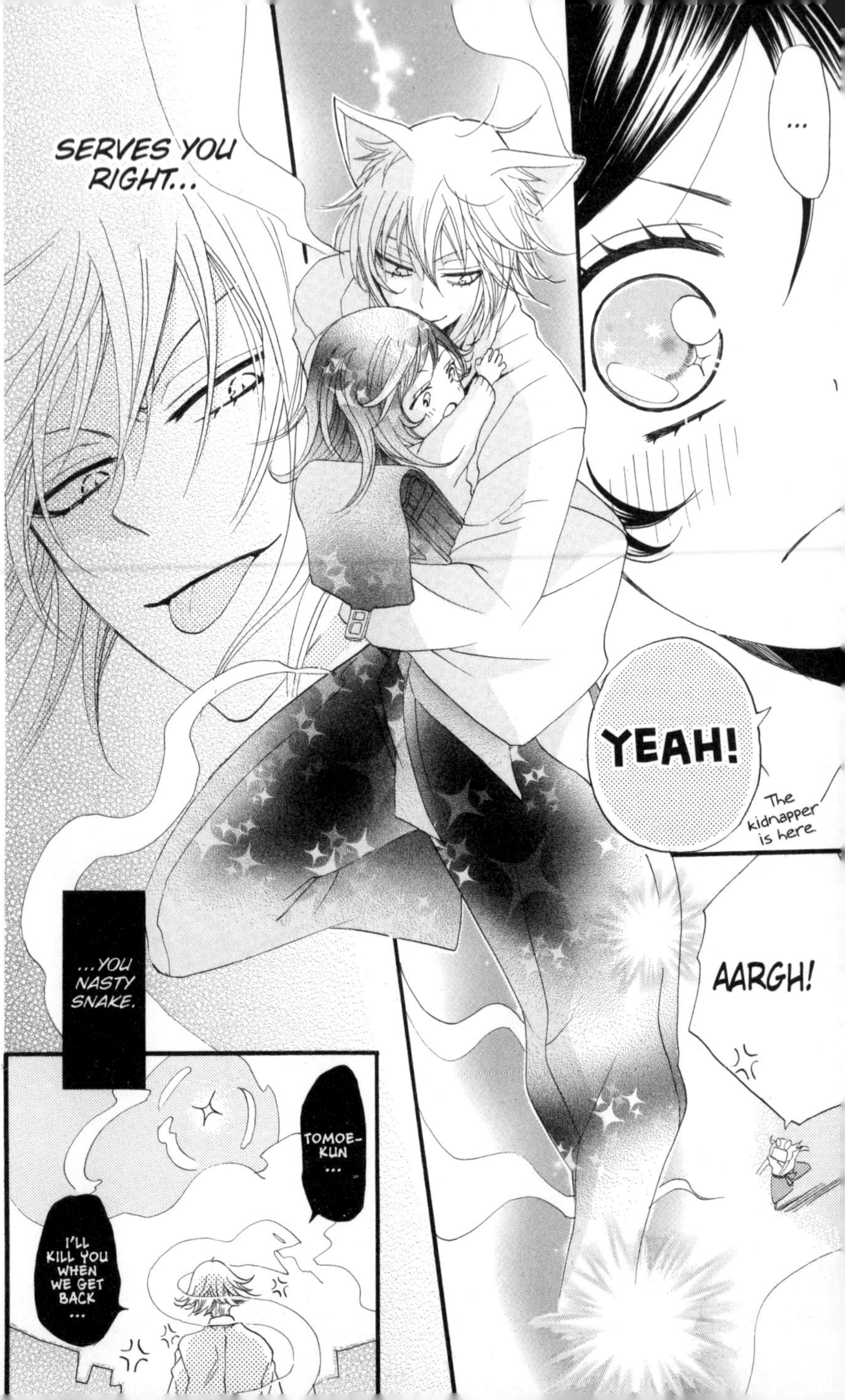
...
YEAH!
The kidnapper is here.
SERVES YOU RIGHT...
...YOU NASTY SNAKE.
AARGH!
TOMOE-KUN...
I'LL KILL YOU WHEN WE GET BACK...

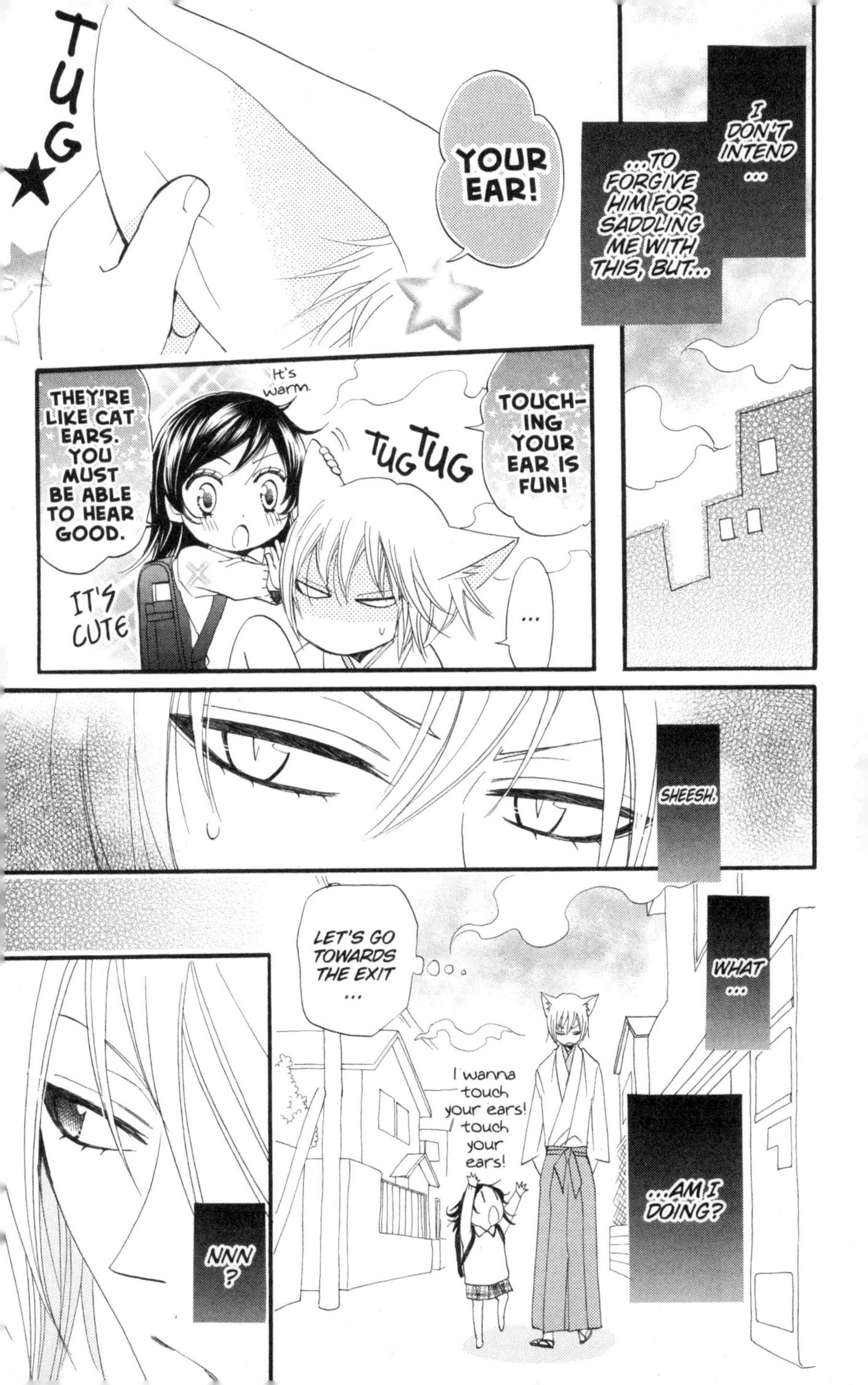
I DON'T INTEND...
...TO FORGIVE HIM FOR SADDLING ME WITH THIS, BUT...
YOUR EAR!
TUG★
TOUCHING YOUR EAR IS FUN!
TUG TUG
It's warm.
THEY'RE LIKE CAT EARS. YOU MUST BE ABLE TO HEAR GOOD.
IT'S CUTE
...
SHEESH.
WHAT...
...AM I DOING?
LET'S GO TOWARDS THE EXIT...
I wanna touch your ears! touch your ears!
NNN?

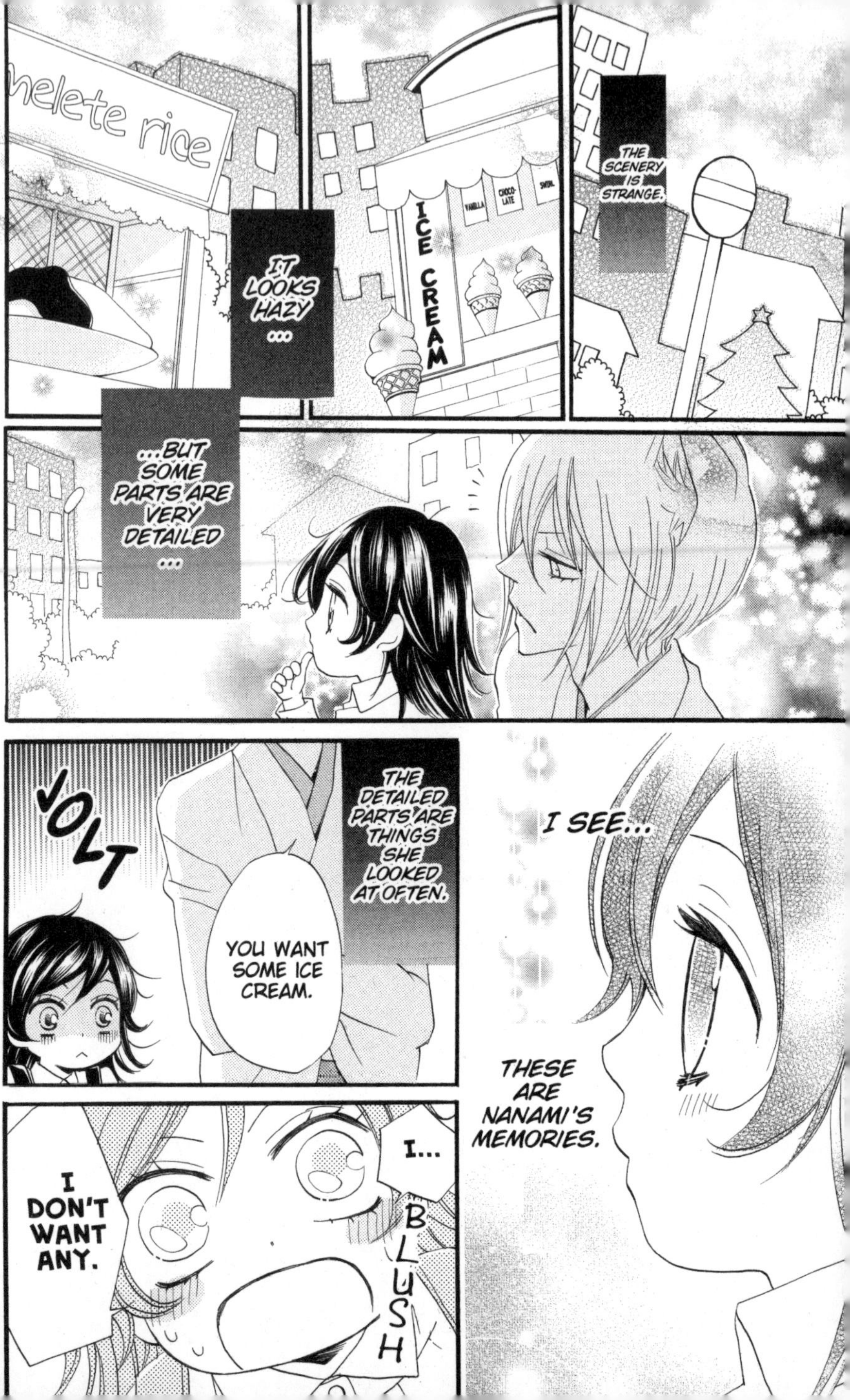
THE SCENERY IS STRANGE.
ICE CREAM
VANILLA
CHOCOLATE
SWIRL
IT LOOKS HAZY ...
melete rice
...BUT SOME PARTS ARE VERY DETAILED ...
I SEE...
THESE ARE NANAMI'S MEMORIES.
THE DETAILED PARTS ARE THINGS SHE LOOKED AT OFTEN.
VOLT
YOU WANT SOME ICE CREAM.
I...
BLUSH
I DON'T WANT ANY.

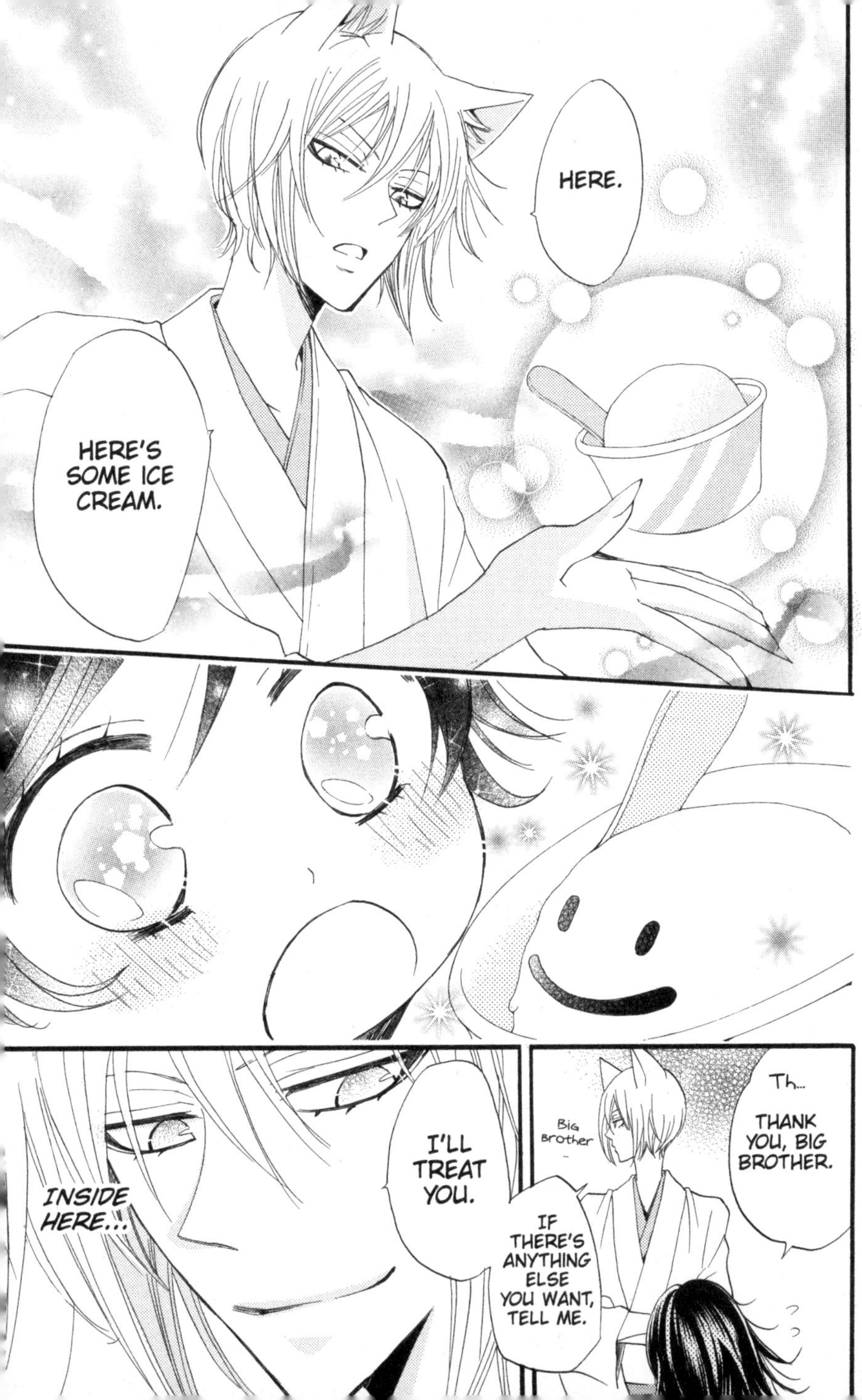
HERE.
HERE'S SOME ICE CREAM.
Th...
THANK YOU, BIG BROTHER.
Big Brother...
IF THERE'S ANYTHING ELSE YOU WANT, TELL ME.
I'LL TREAT YOU.
INSIDE HERE...

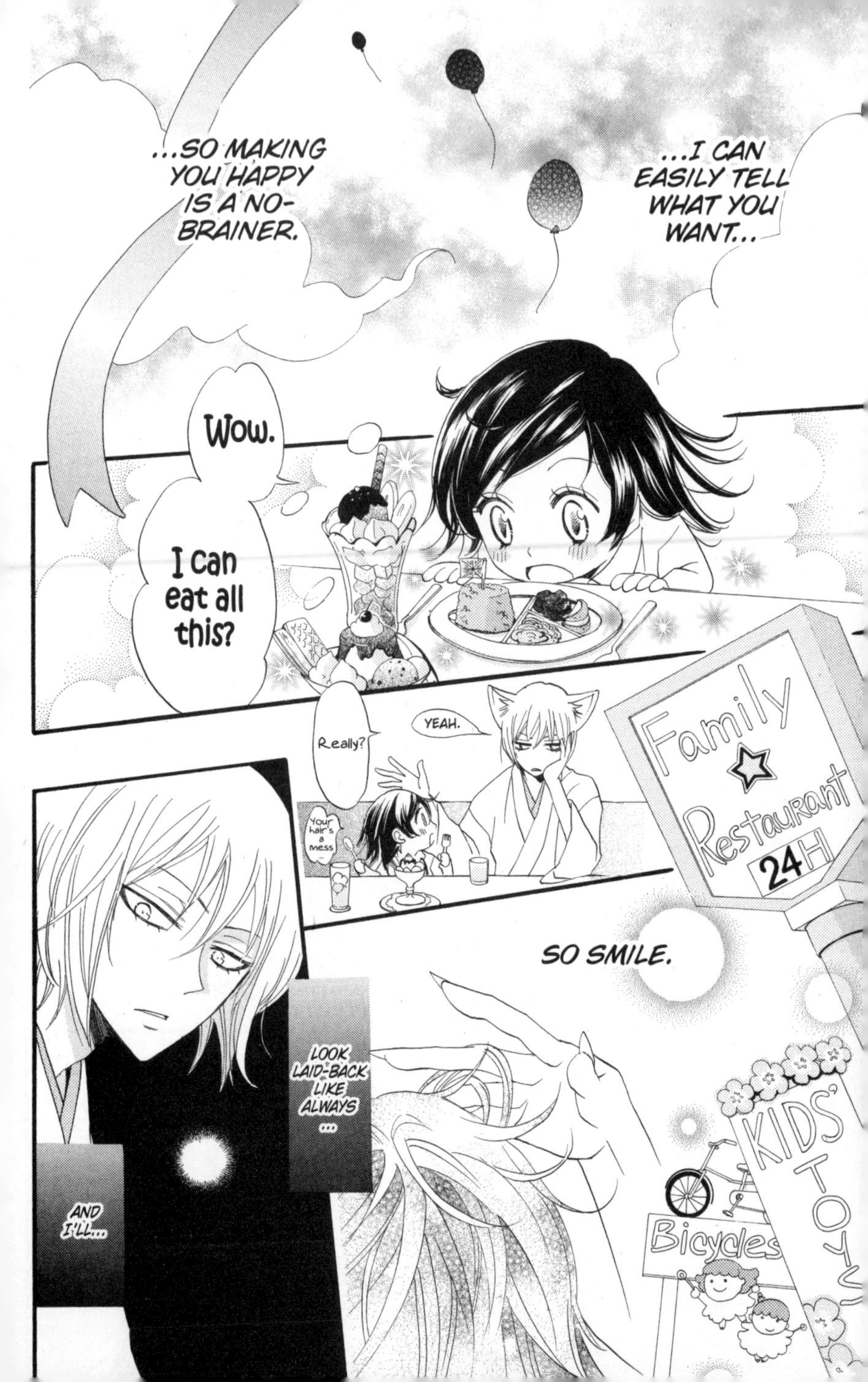
...I CAN EASILY TELL WHAT YOU WANT...
...SO MAKING YOU HAPPY IS A NO-BRAINER.
Wow.
I can eat all this?
Family Restaurant 24H
Really?
YEAH.
Your hair's a mess...
SO SMILE.
KIDS' TOY
Bicycles
LOOK LAID-BACK LIKE ALWAYS...
AND I'LL...

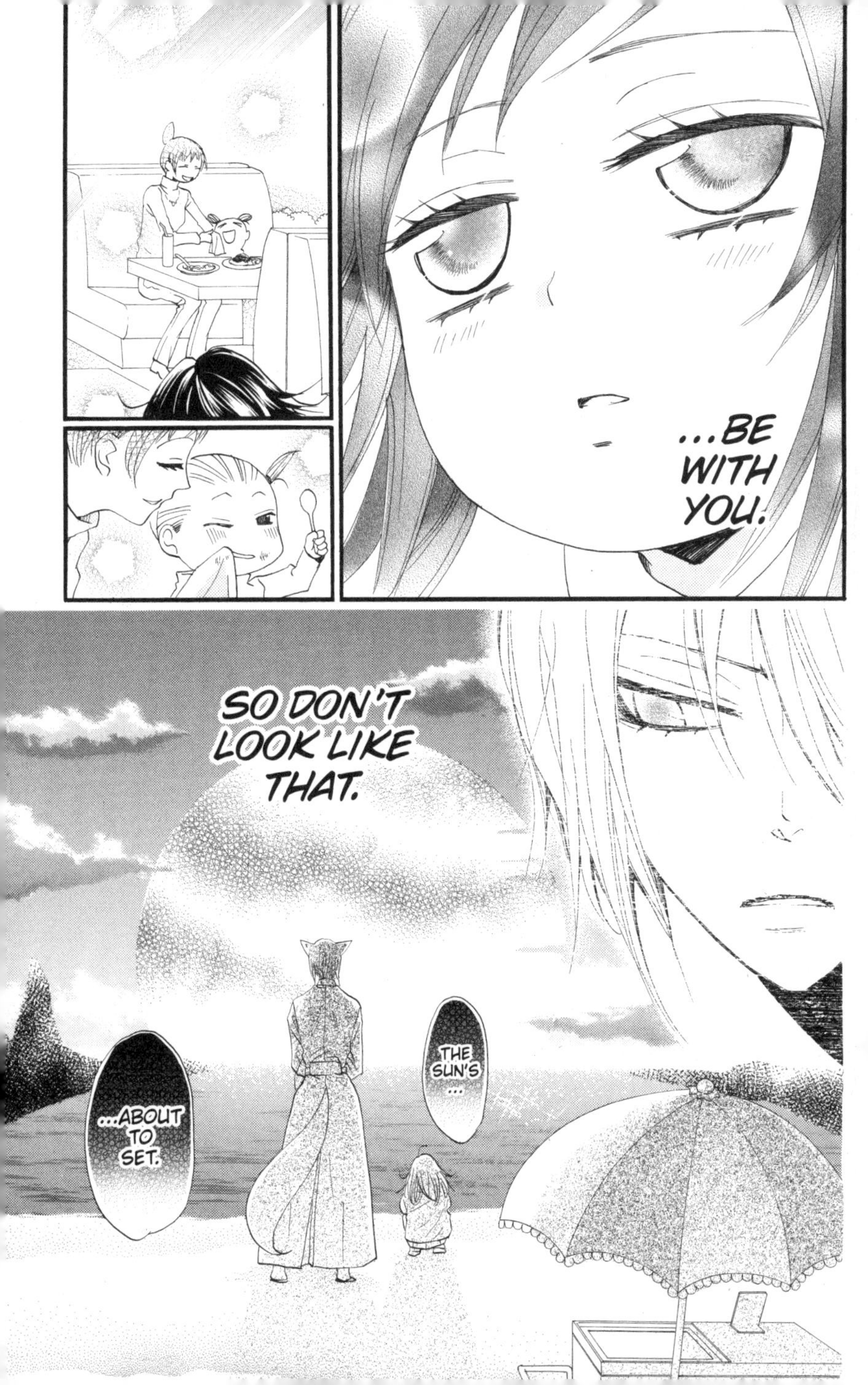
...BE WITH YOU.
SO DON'T LOOK LIKE THAT.
THE SUN'S...
...ABOUT TO SET.

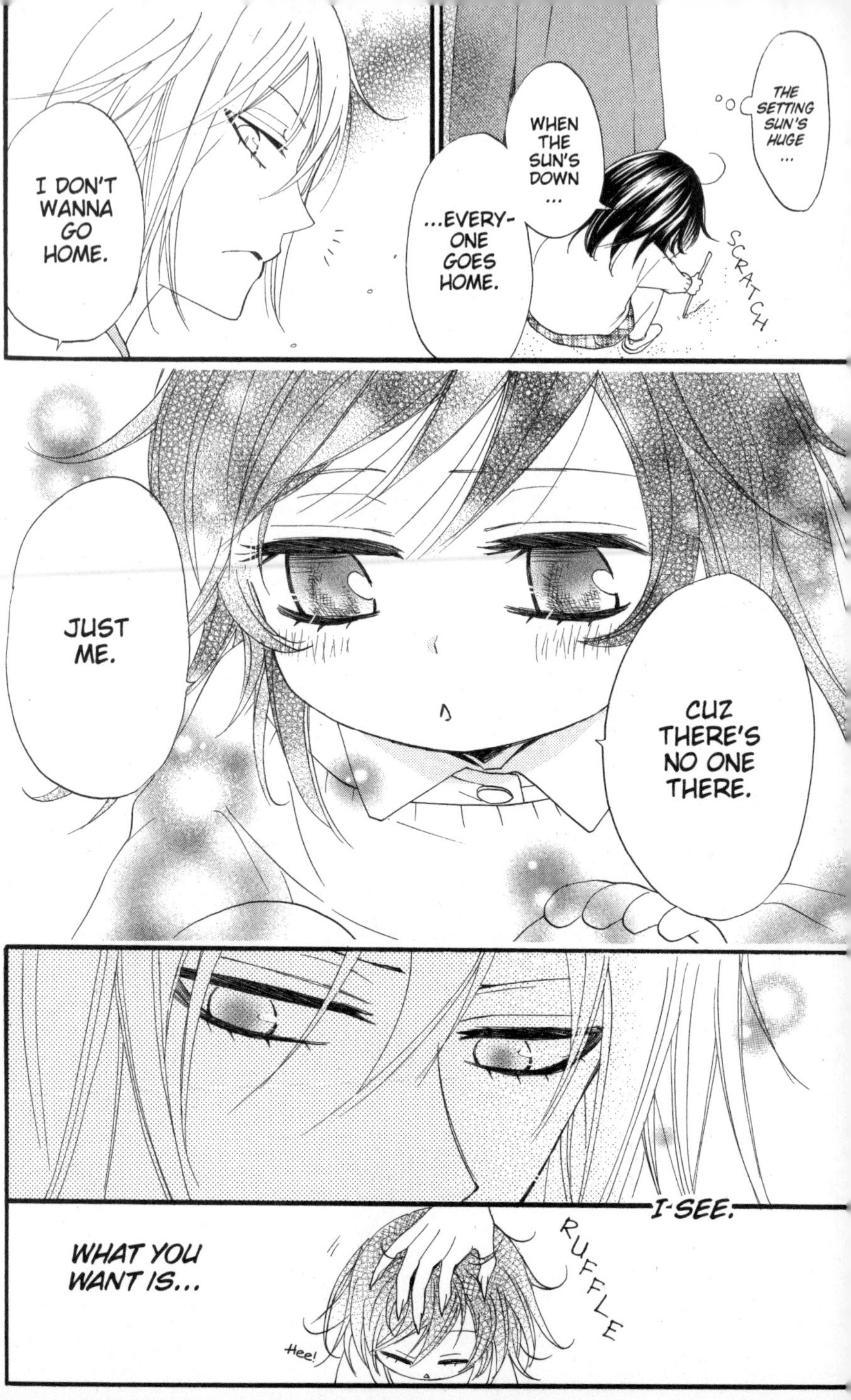
THE SETTING SUN'S HUGE ...
SCRATCH
WHEN THE SUN'S DOWN ...
...EVERY-ONE GOES HOME.
I DON'T WANNA GO HOME.
CUZ THERE'S NO ONE THERE.
JUST ME.
I SEE.
RUFFLE
WHAT YOU WANT IS...
Hee!

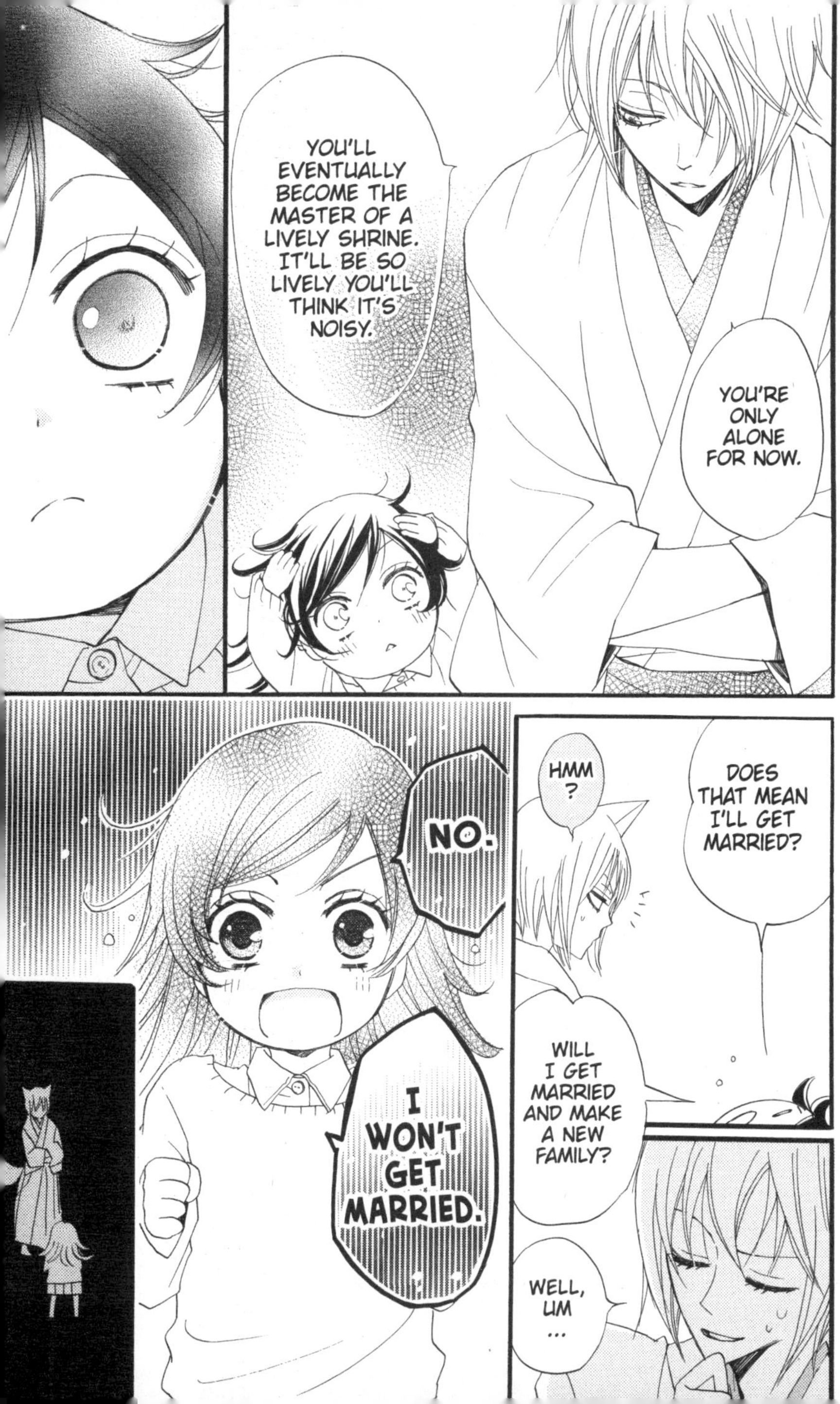
YOU'RE ONLY ALONE FOR NOW.
YOU'LL EVENTUALLY BECOME THE MASTER OF A LIVELY SHRINE. IT'LL BE SO LIVELY YOU'LL THINK IT'S NOISY.
DOES THAT MEAN I'LL GET MARRIED?
HMM?
WILL I GET MARRIED AND MAKE A NEW FAMILY?
WELL, UM...
NO.
I WON'T GET MARRIED.

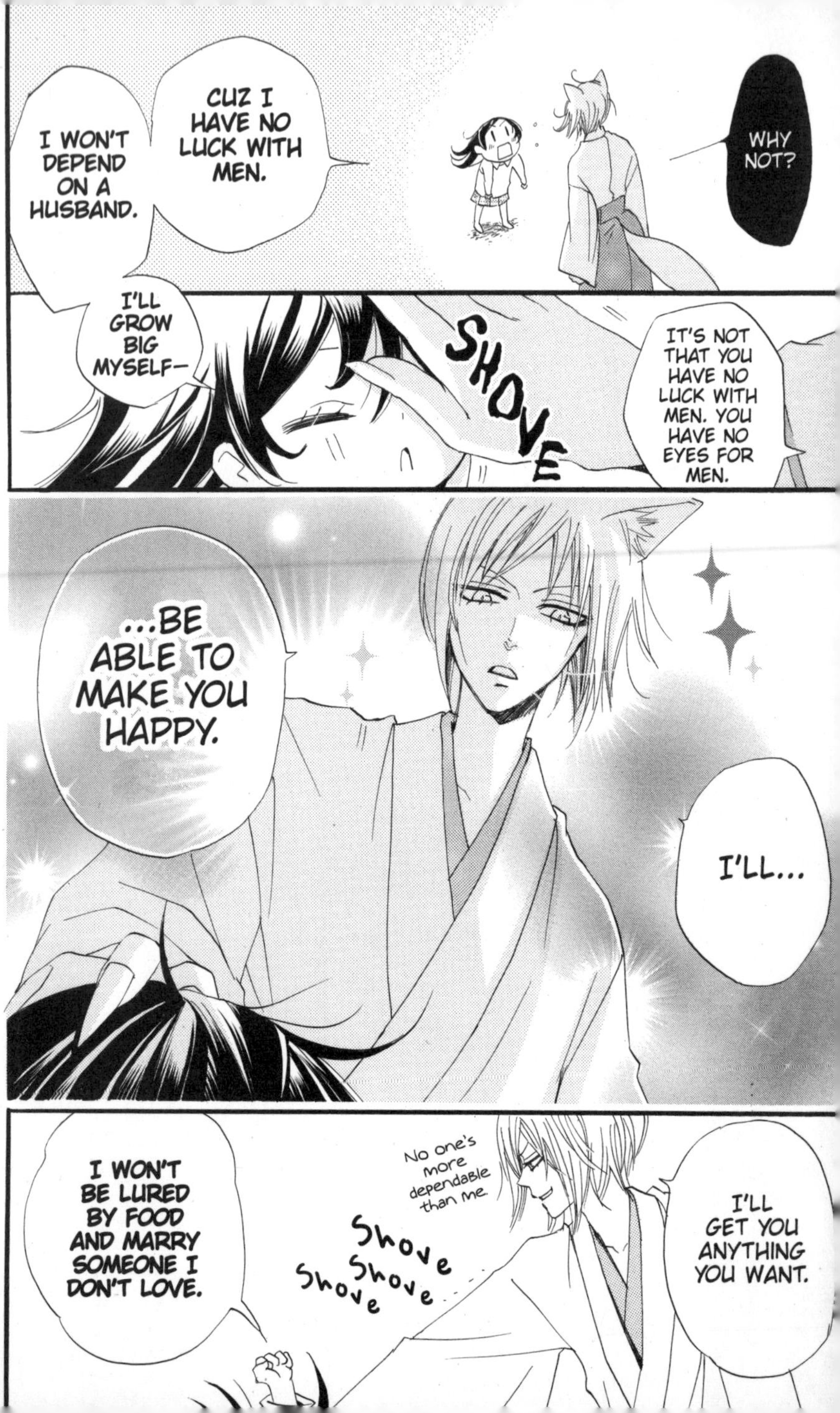
WHY NOT?
CUZ I HAVE NO LUCK WITH MEN.
I WON'T DEPEND ON A HUSBAND.
I'LL GROW BIG MYSELF—
SHOVE
IT'S NOT THAT YOU HAVE NO LUCK WITH MEN. YOU HAVE NO EYES FOR MEN.
I'LL...
...BE ABLE TO MAKE YOU HAPPY.
I'LL GET YOU ANYTHING YOU WANT.
No one's more dependable than me.
Shove Shove Shove
I WON'T BE LURED BY FOOD AND MARRY SOMEONE I DON'T LOVE.

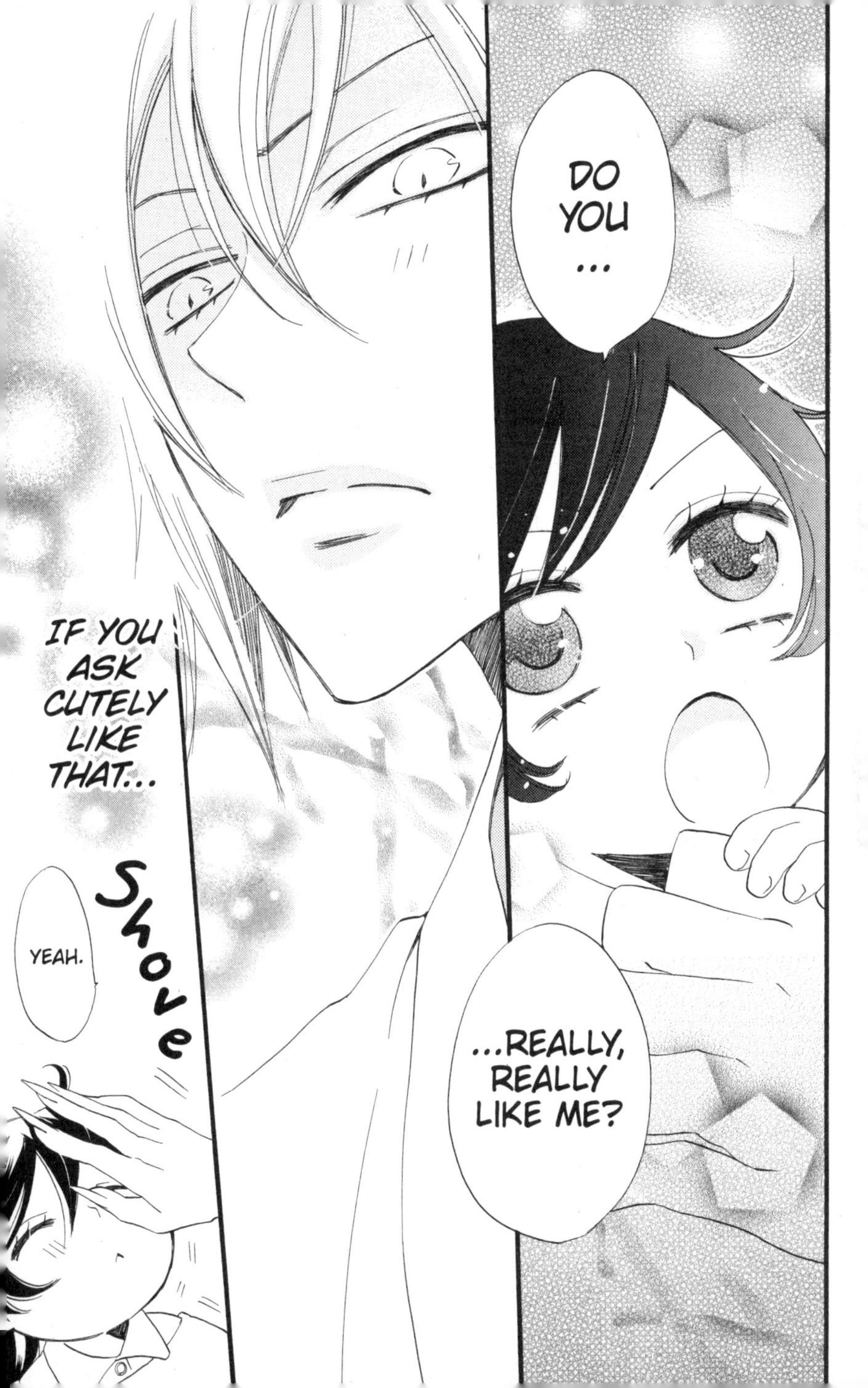
DO YOU ...
...REALLY, REALLY LIKE ME?
IF YOU ASK CUTELY LIKE THAT...
Shove
YEAH.

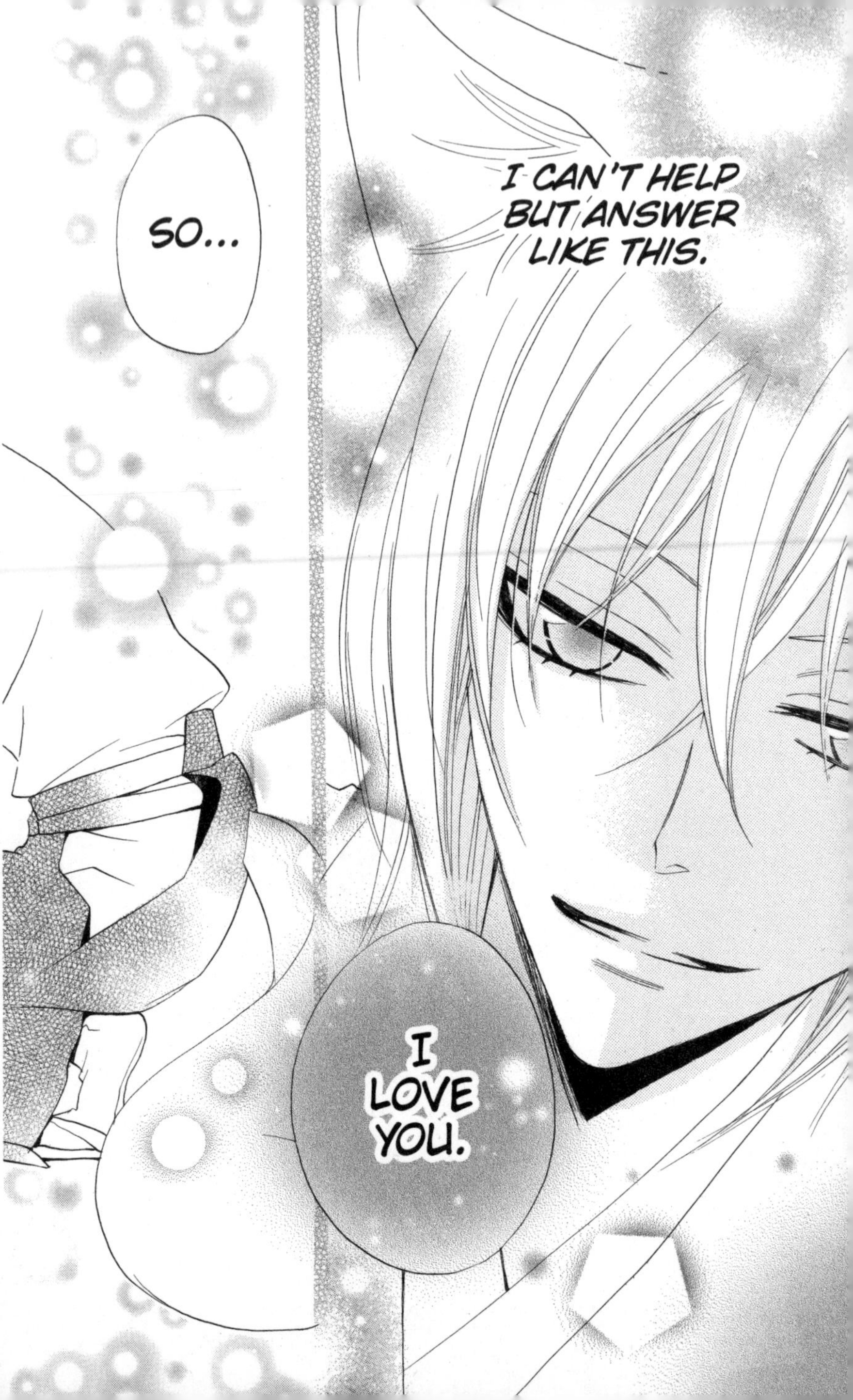
I CAN'T HELP BUT ANSWER LIKE THIS.
I LOVE YOU.
SO...

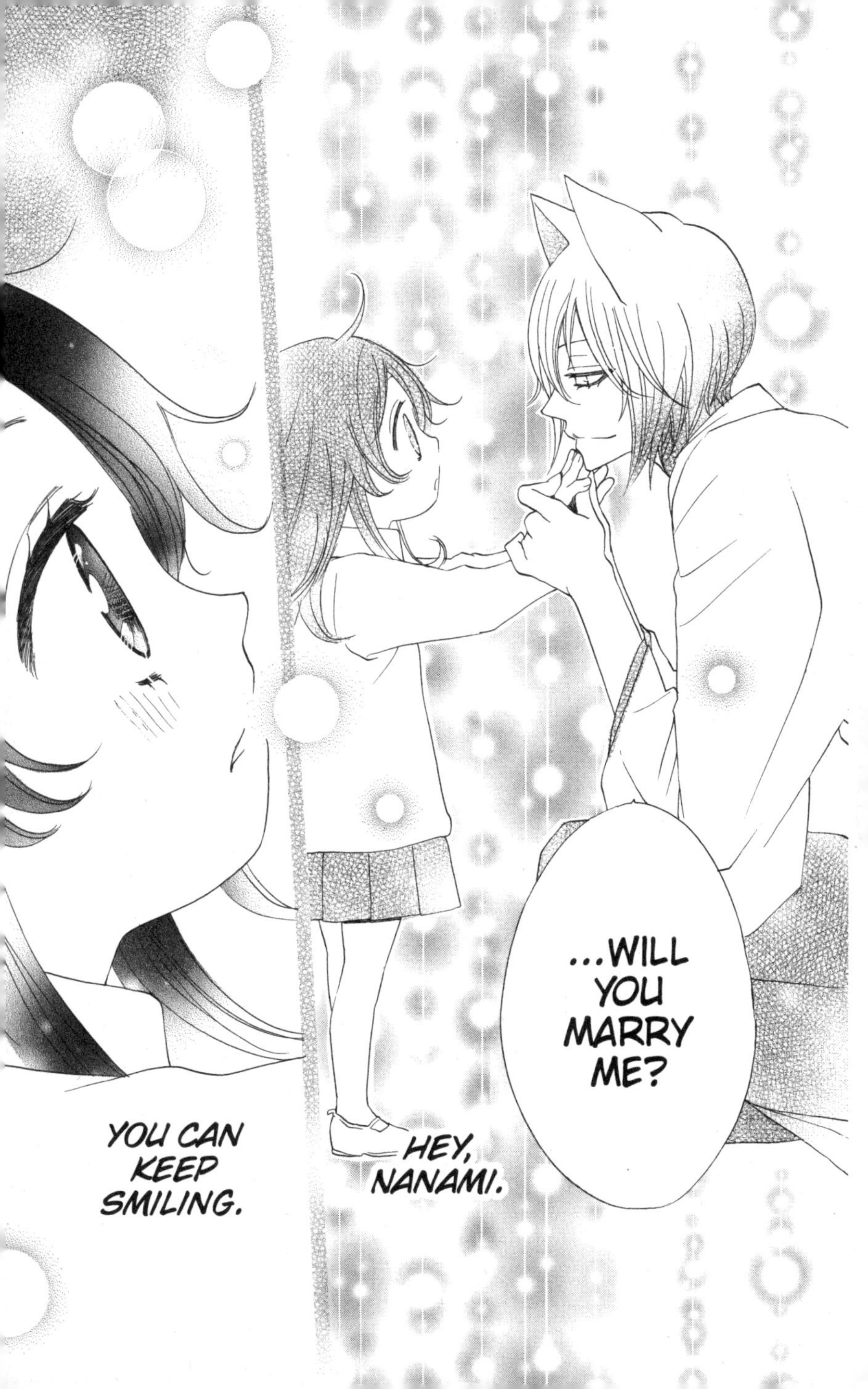
...WILL YOU MARRY ME?
HEY, NANAMI.
YOU CAN KEEP SMILING.

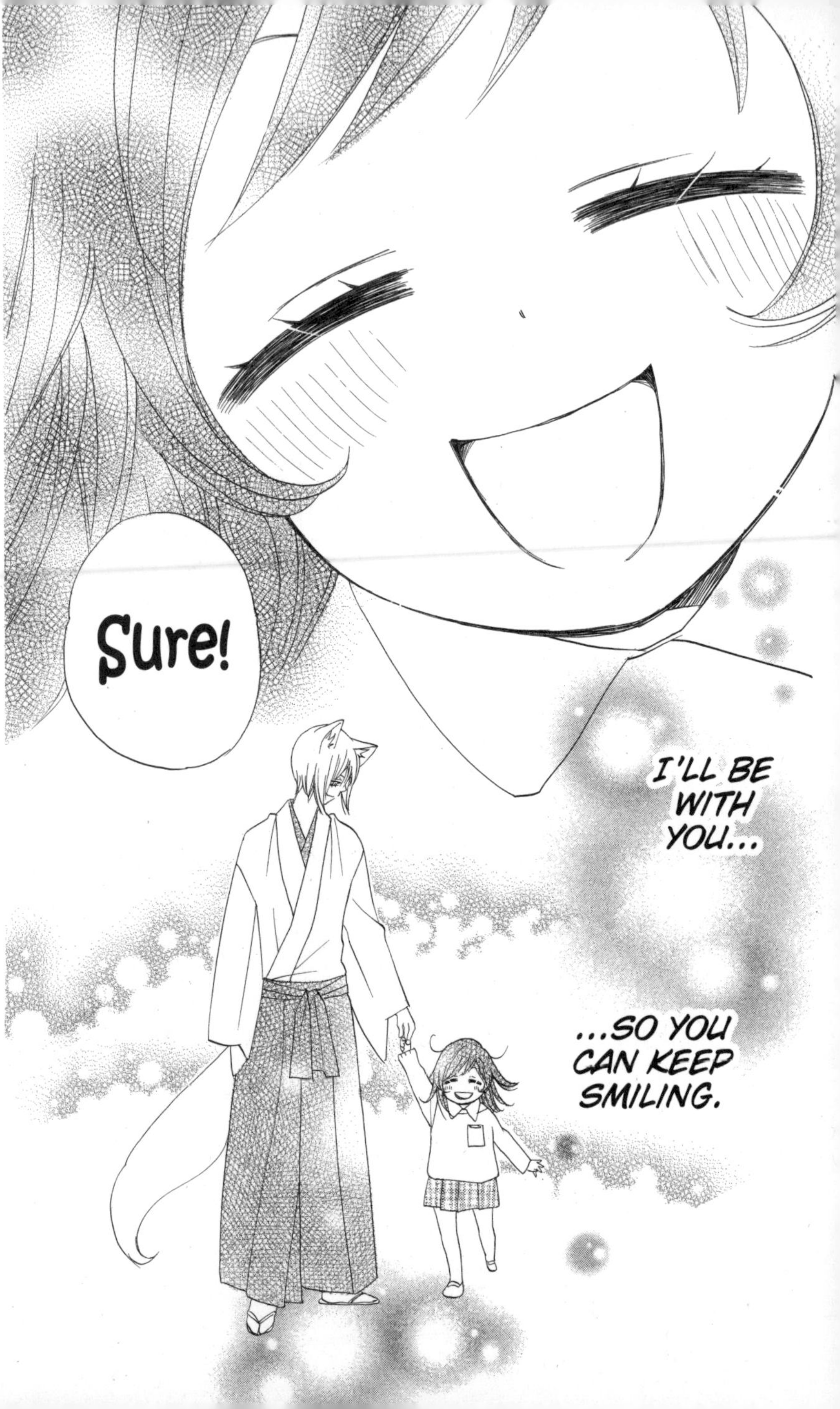
Sure!
I'LL BE WITH YOU...
...SO YOU CAN KEEP SMILING.

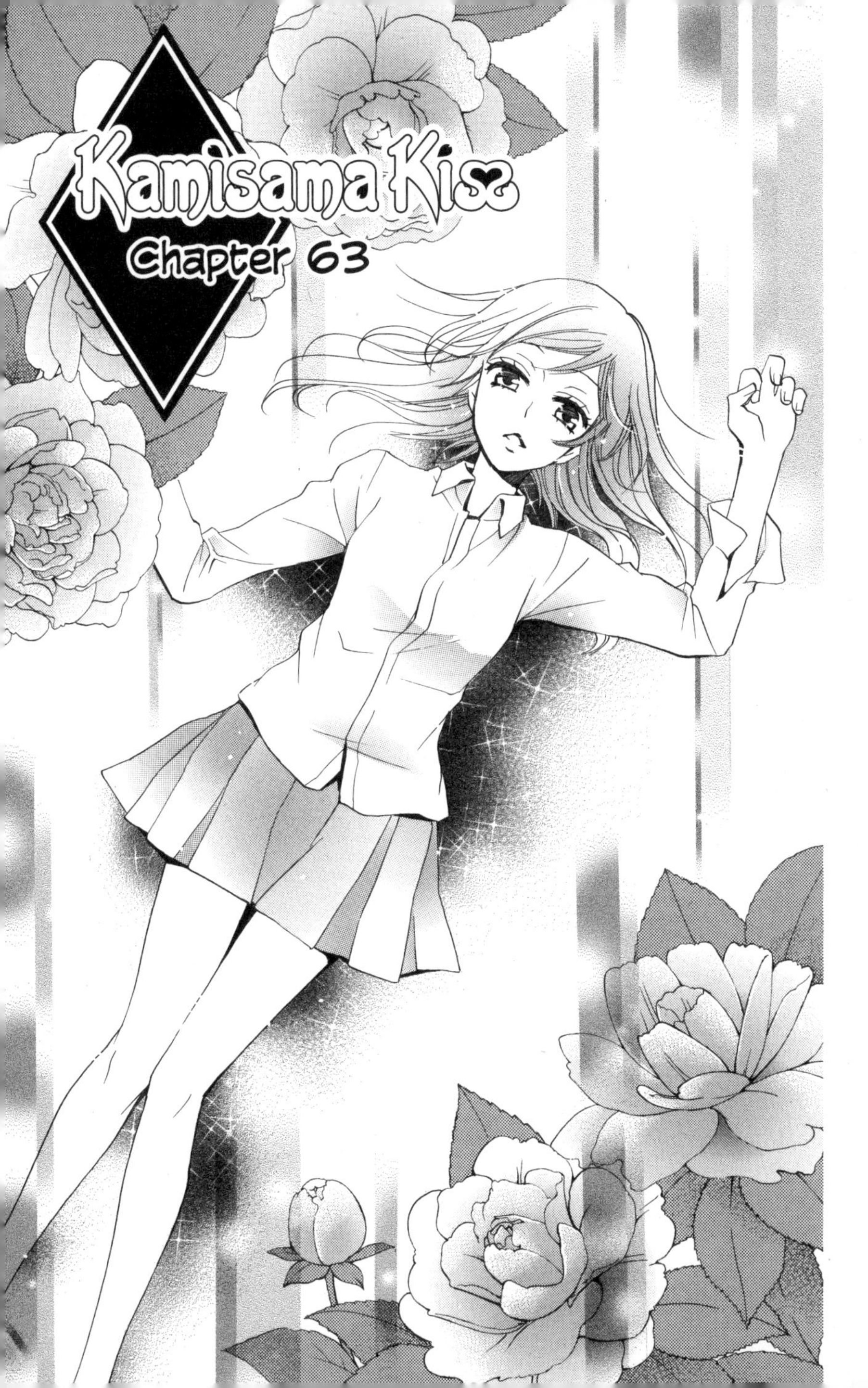
Kamisama Kiss
Chapter 63

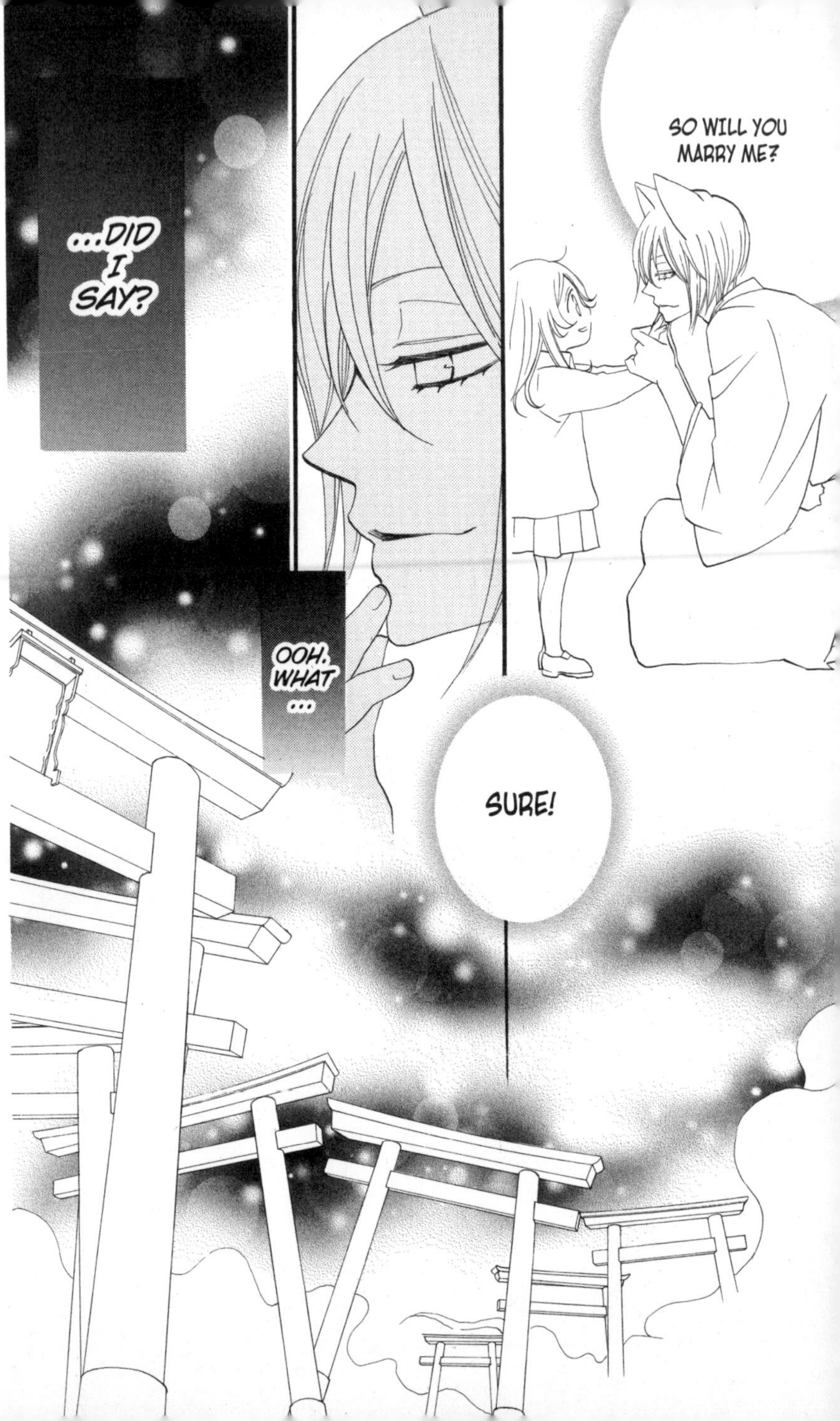
SO WILL YOU MARRY ME?
SURE!
OOH. WHAT ...
...DID I SAY?

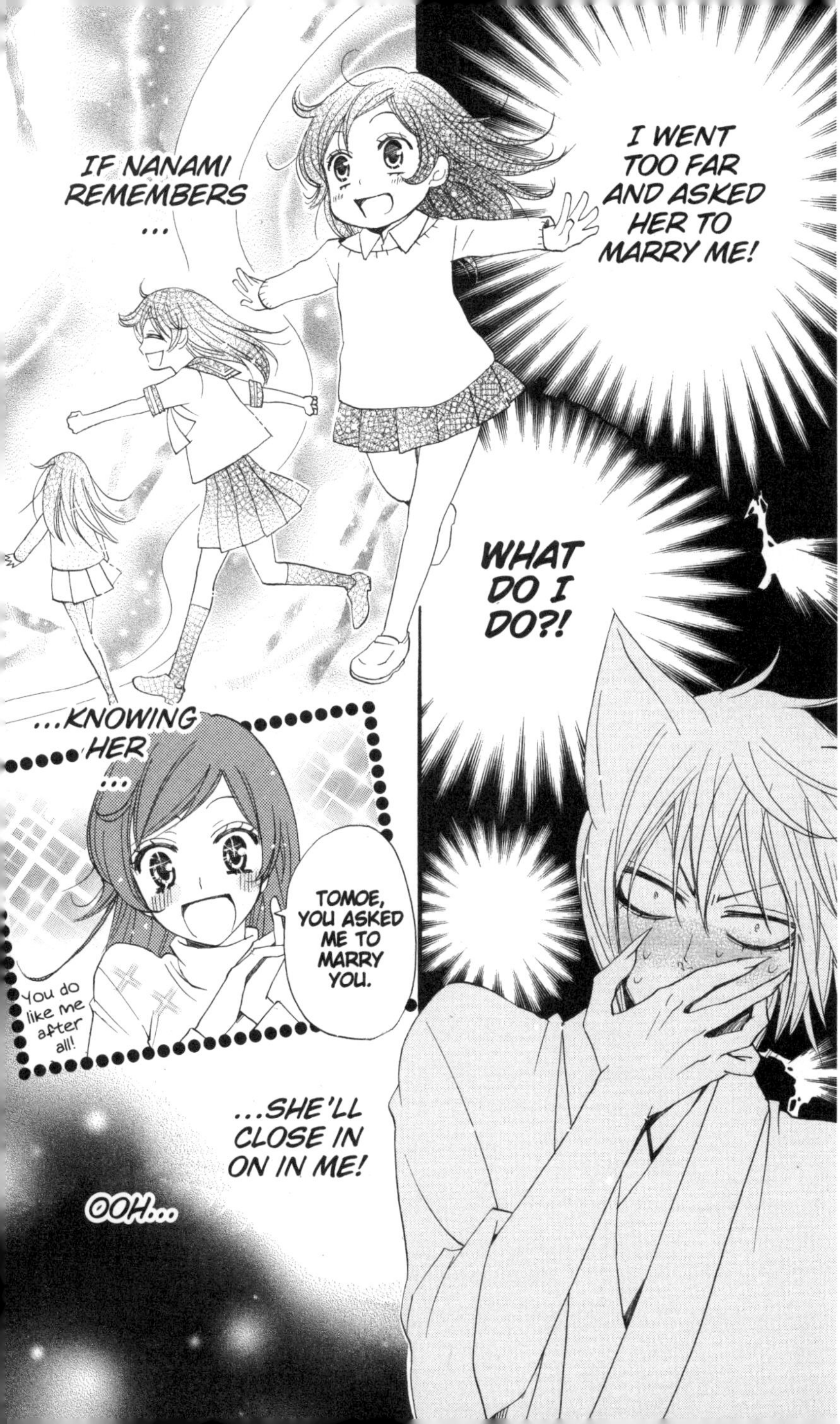

I WENT TOO FAR AND ASKED HER TO MARRY ME!
WHAT DO I DO?!
IF NANAMI REMEMBERS ...
...KNOWING HER ...
TOMOE, YOU ASKED ME TO MARRY YOU.
You do like me after all!
...SHE'LL CLOSE IN ON IN ME!
OOH...

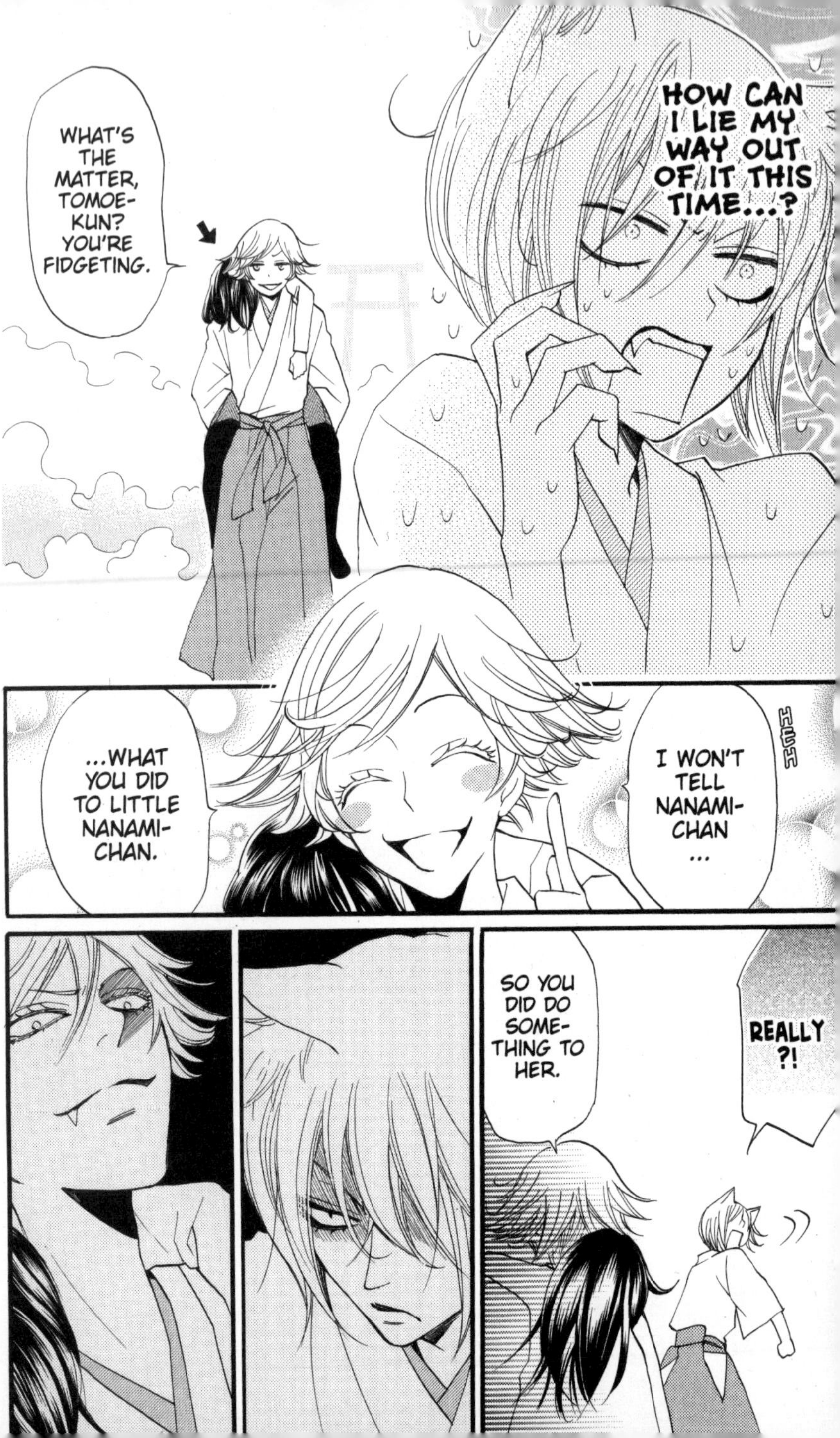
HOW CAN I LIE MY WAY OUT OF IT THIS TIME...?
WHAT'S THE MATTER, TOMOE-KUN? YOU'RE FIDGETING.
HEH HEH
I WON'T TELL NANAMI-CHAN ...
...WHAT YOU DID TO LITTLE NANAMI-CHAN.
REALLY?!
SO YOU DID DO SOME-THING TO HER.

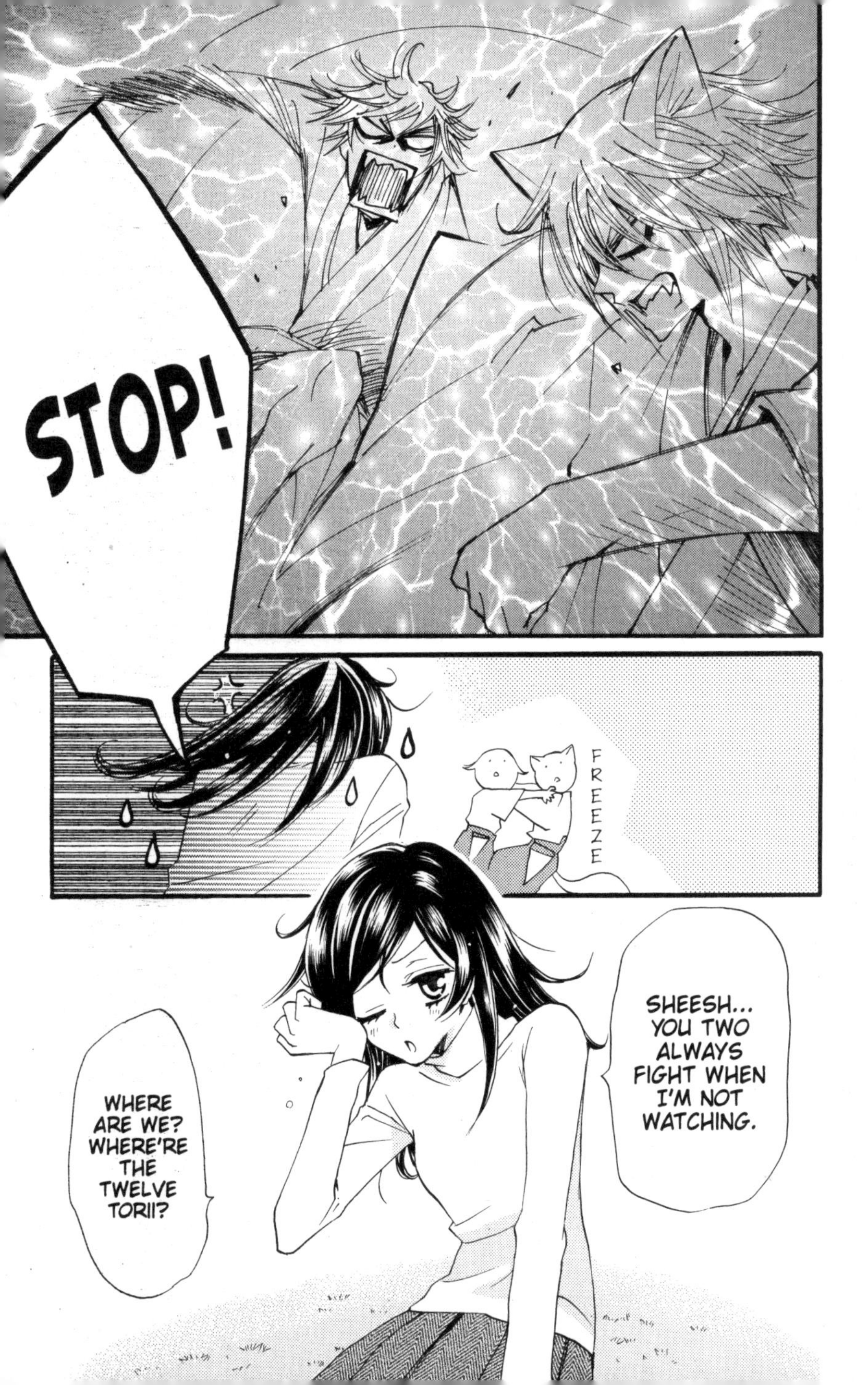
STOP!
FREEZE
SHEESH... YOU TWO ALWAYS FIGHT WHEN I'M NOT WATCHING.
WHERE ARE WE? WHERE'RE THE TWELVE TORII?

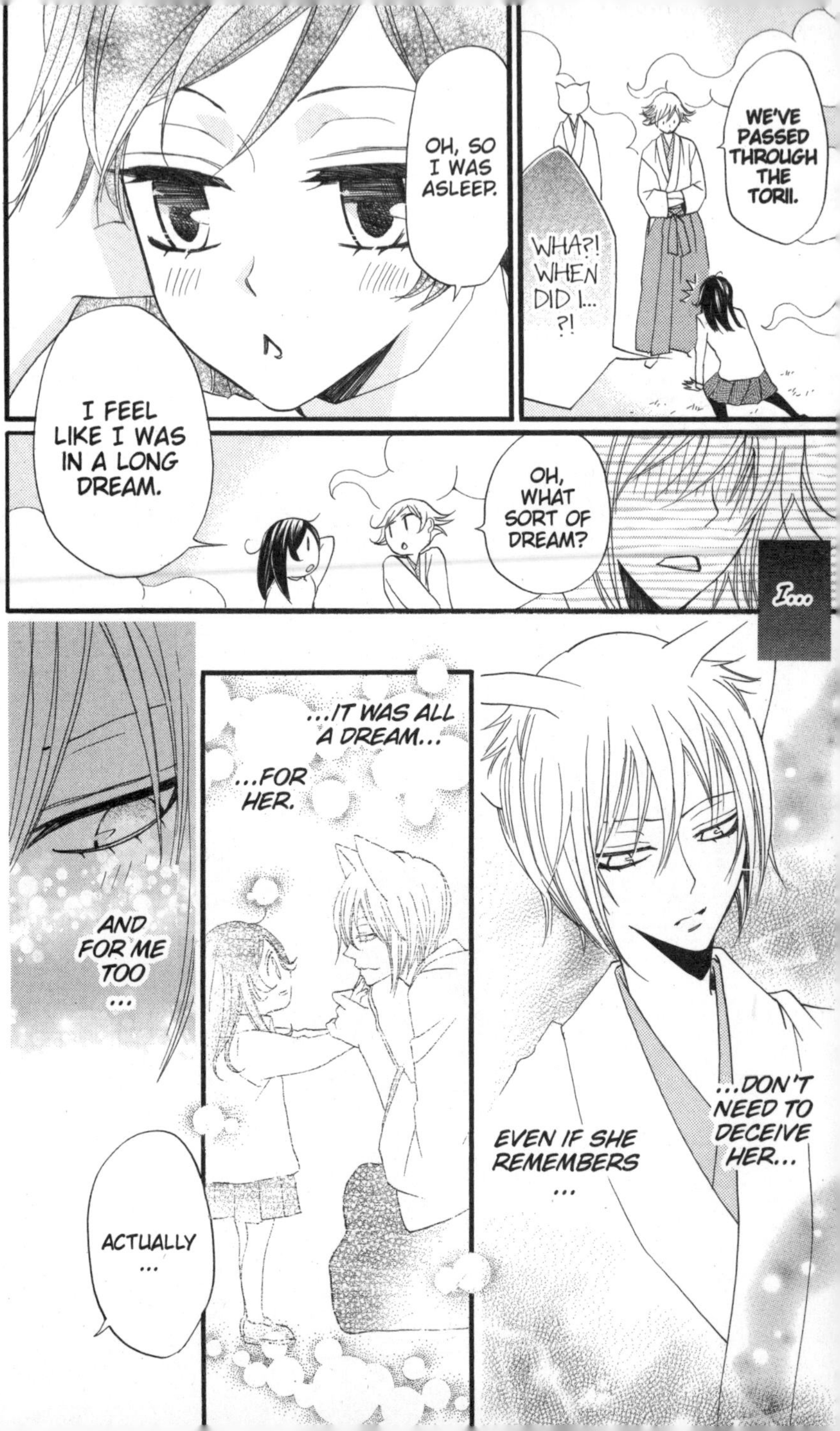
WE'VE PASSED THROUGH THE TORII.
WHA?! WHEN DID I... ?!
OH, SO I WAS ASLEEP.
I FEEL LIKE I WAS IN A LONG DREAM.
OH, WHAT SORT OF DREAM?
I...
...DON'T NEED TO DECEIVE HER...
EVEN IF SHE REMEMBERS ...
...IT WAS ALL A DREAM...
...FOR HER.
AND FOR ME TOO ...
ACTUALLY ...

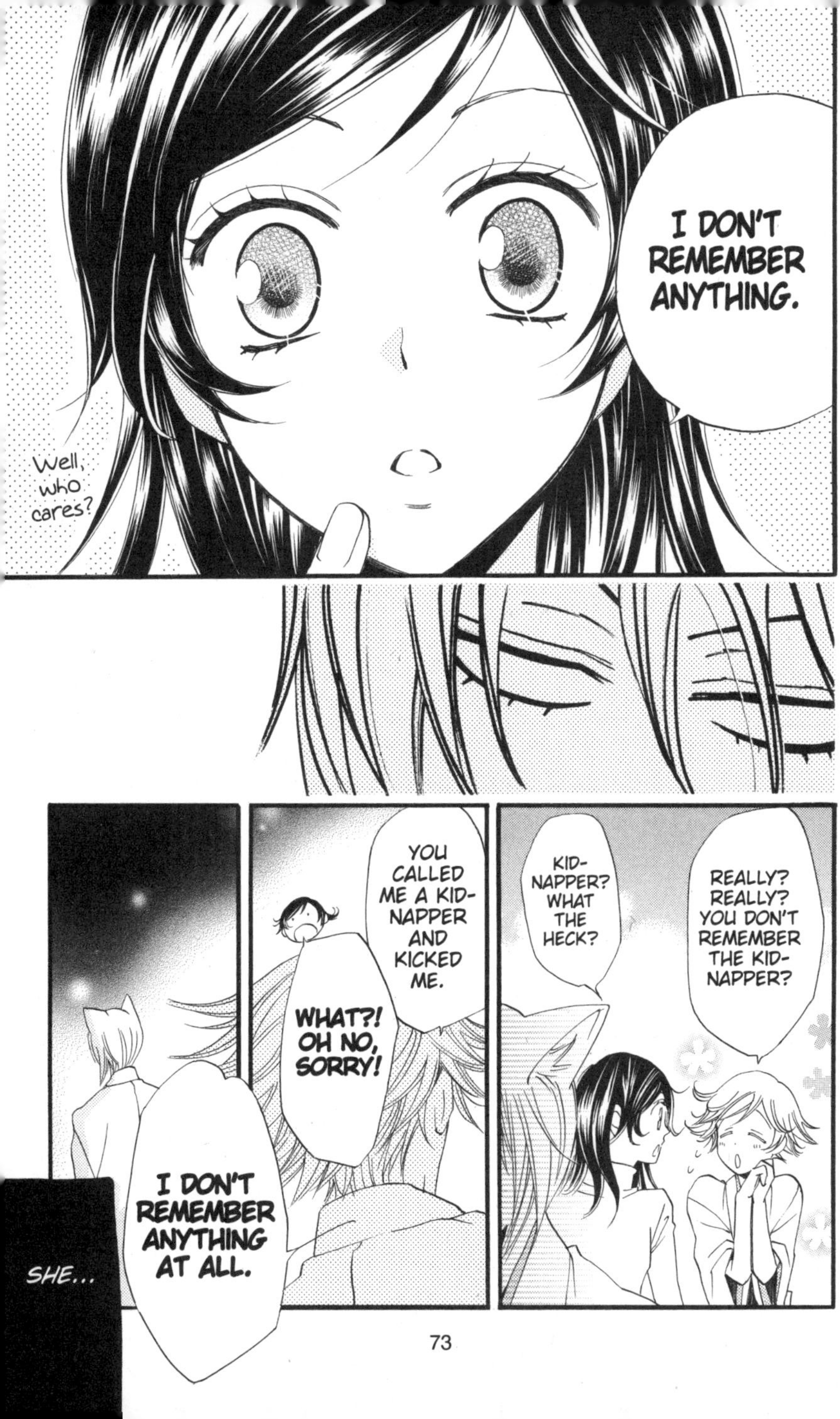
I DON'T REMEMBER ANYTHING.
Well, who cares?
REALLY? REALLY? YOU DON'T REMEMBER THE KID-NAPPER?
KID-NAPPER? WHAT THE HECK?
YOU CALLED ME A KID-NAPPER AND KICKED ME.
WHAT?! OH NO, SORRY!
I DON'T REMEMBER ANYTHING AT ALL.
SHE...

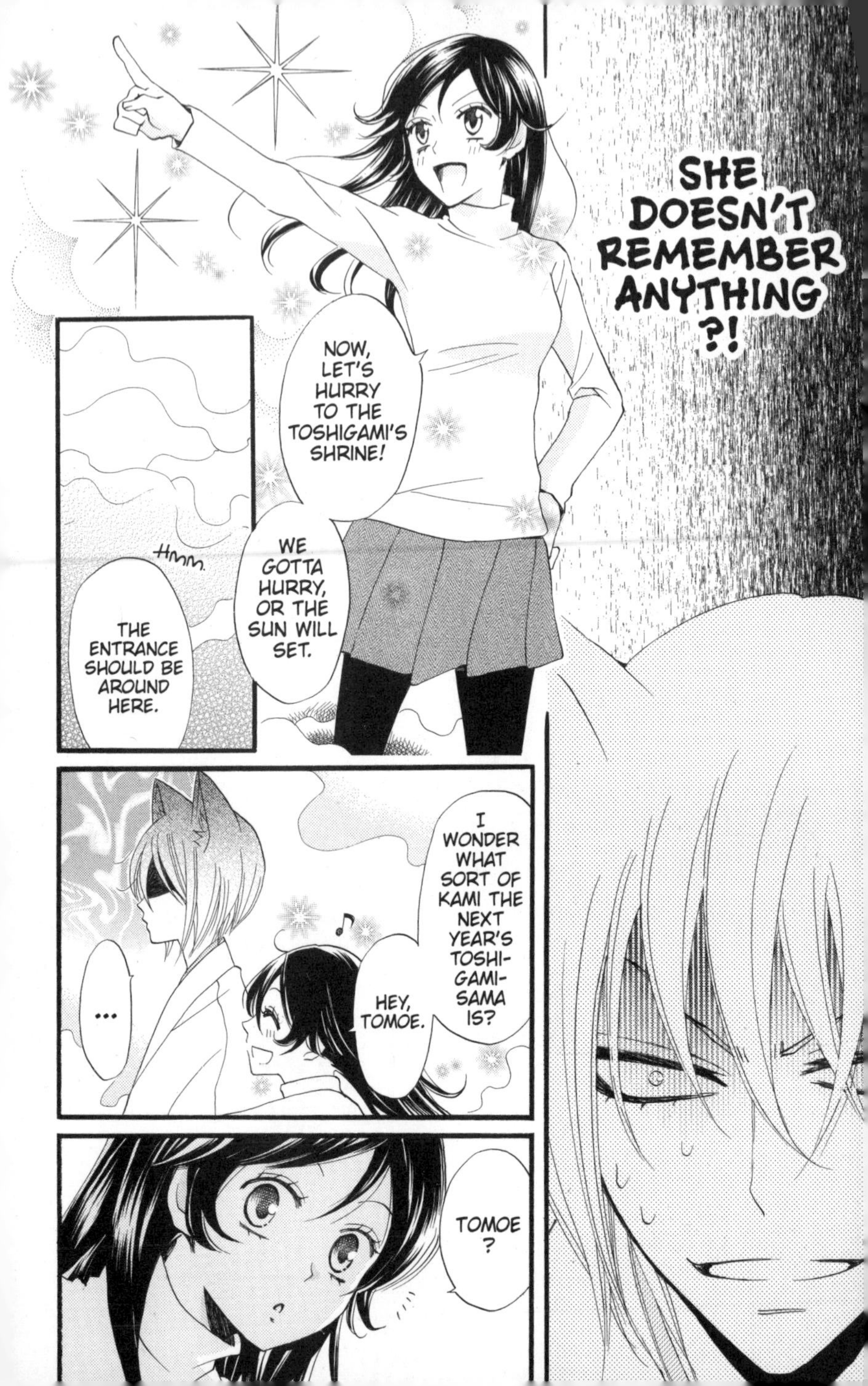

NOW, LET'S HURRY TO THE TOSHIGAMI'S SHRINE!
WE GOTTA HURRY, OR THE SUN WILL SET.
Hmm.
THE ENTRANCE SHOULD BE AROUND HERE.
I WONDER WHAT SORT OF KAMI THE NEXT YEAR'S TOSHI-GAMI-SAMA IS?
HEY, TOMOE.
...
TOMOE?
SHE DOESN'T REMEMBER ANYTHING ?!

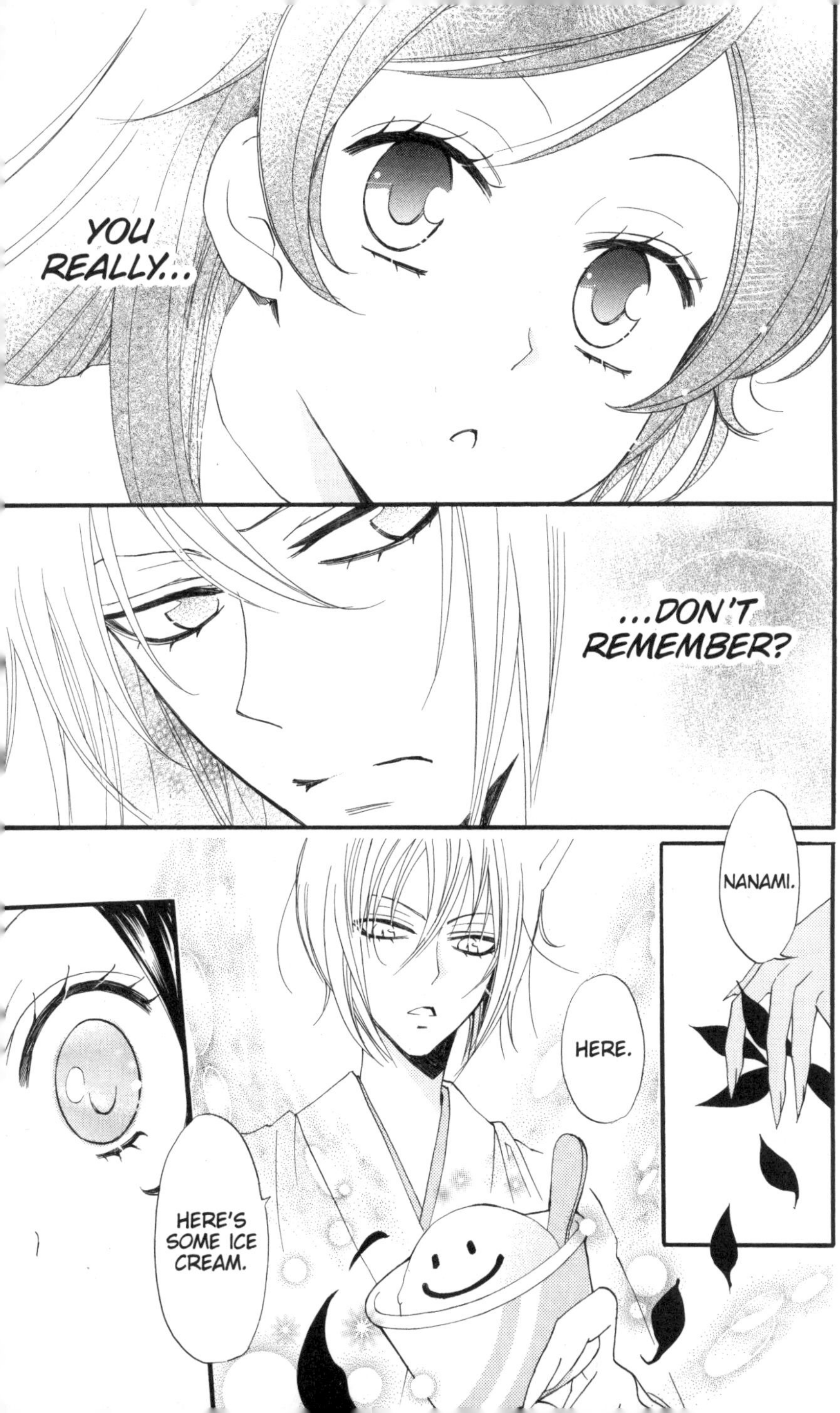
YOU REALLY...
...DON'T REMEMBER?
NANAMI.
HERE.
HERE'S SOME ICE CREAM.

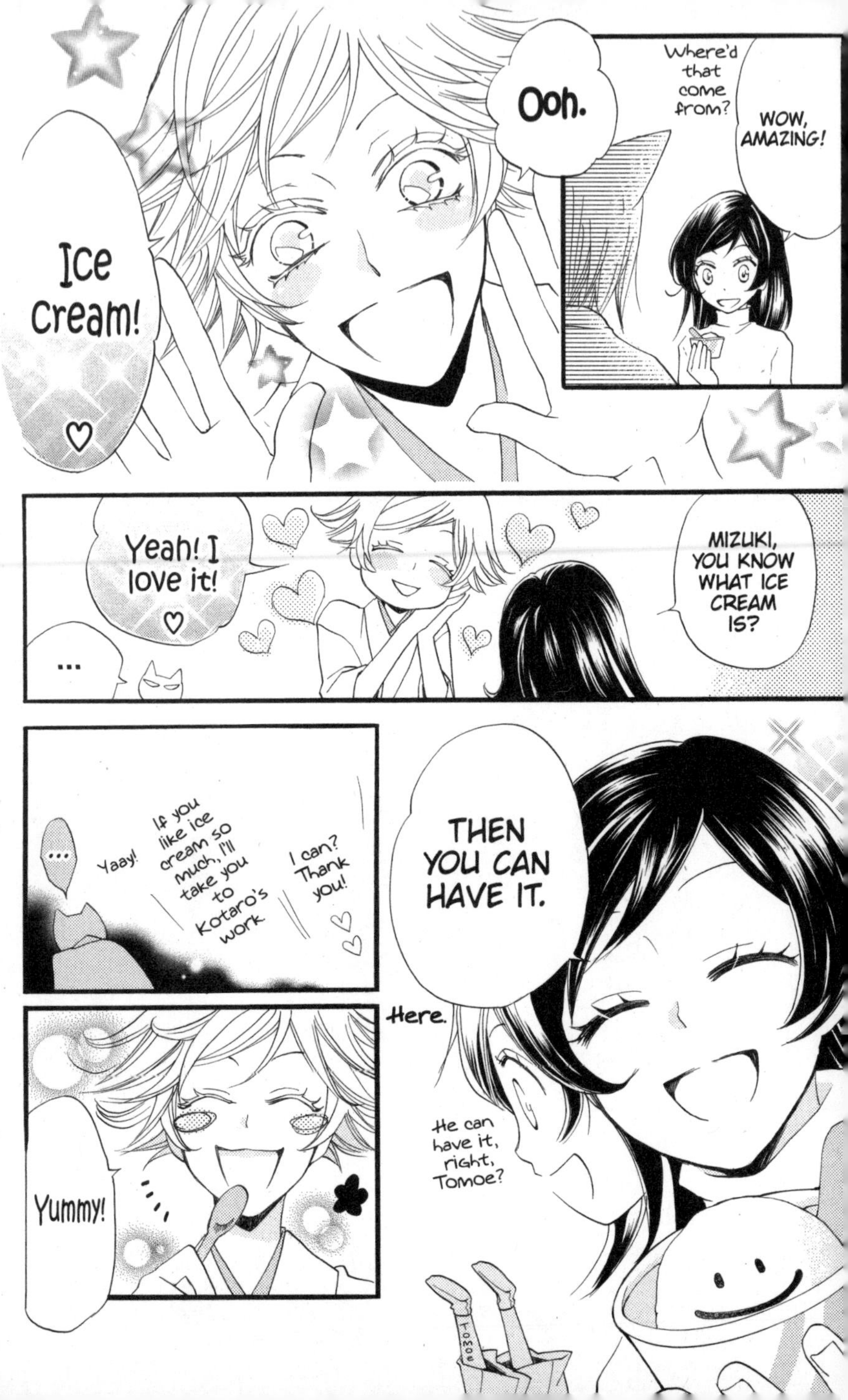
WOW, AMAZING!
Where'd that come from?
Ooh.
Ice Cream! ♡
MIZUKI, YOU KNOW WHAT ICE CREAM IS?
Yeah! I love it! ♡
...
THEN YOU CAN HAVE IT.
Here.
He can have it, right, Tomoe?
TOMOE
I can? Thank you!
If you like ice cream so much, I'll take you to Kotaro's work
Yaay!
...
Yummy!

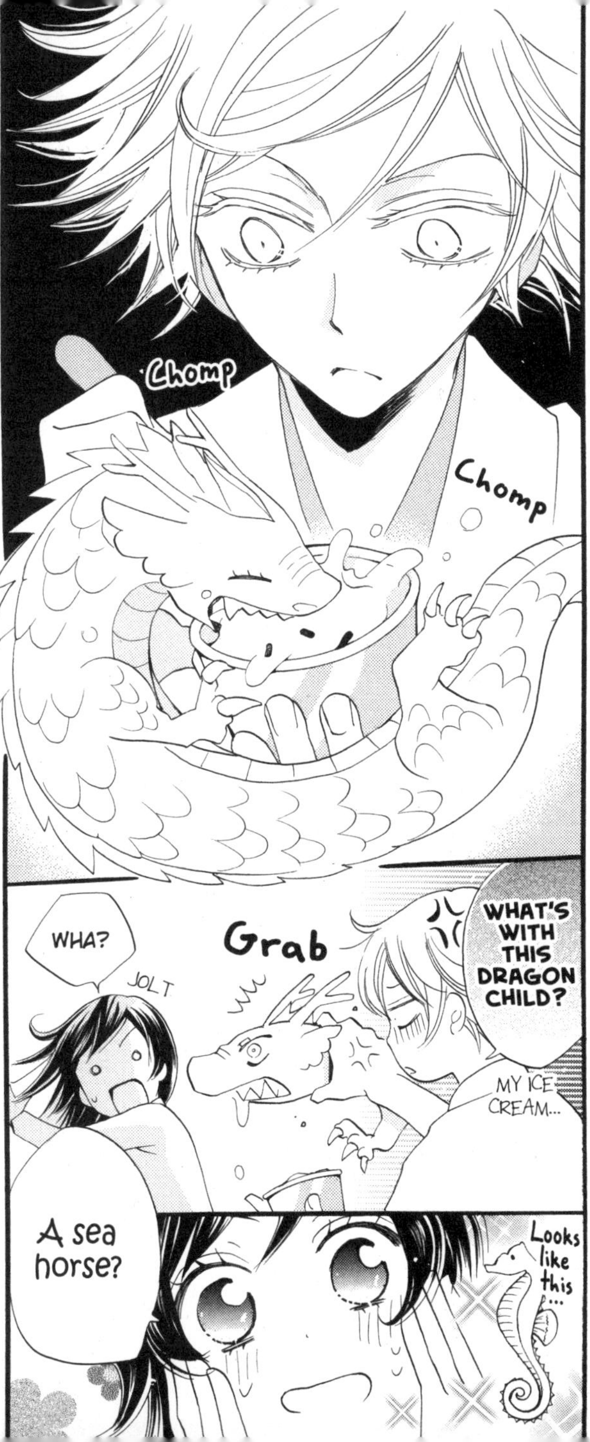
Chomp
Chomp
WHAT'S WITH THIS DRAGON CHILD?
MY ICE CREAM...
Grab
WHA?
JOLT
Looks like this...
A sea horse?

The "Zakkuri Cookie Choco" (from Kabaya Shokuhin) my assistant got for me are really good, and they're my favorite nowadays.

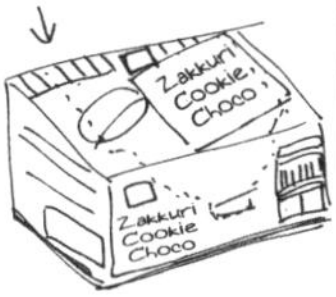
Zakkuri Cookie Choco
Zakkuri Cookie Choco

If you find it in a supermarket, grab a box!

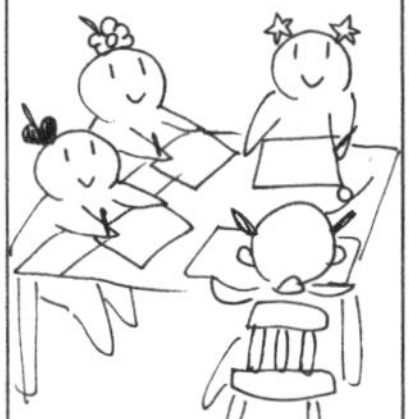

Nowadays, I've got three assistants working with me, so I'm able to work very efficiently. Thanks for coming.

For this volume...

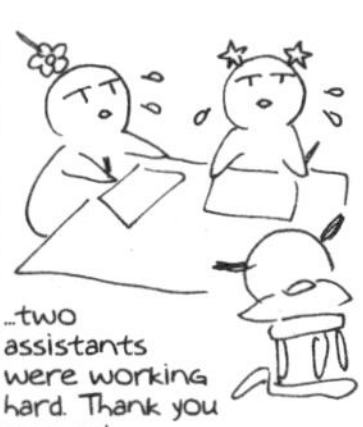

...two assistants were working hard. Thank you so much.

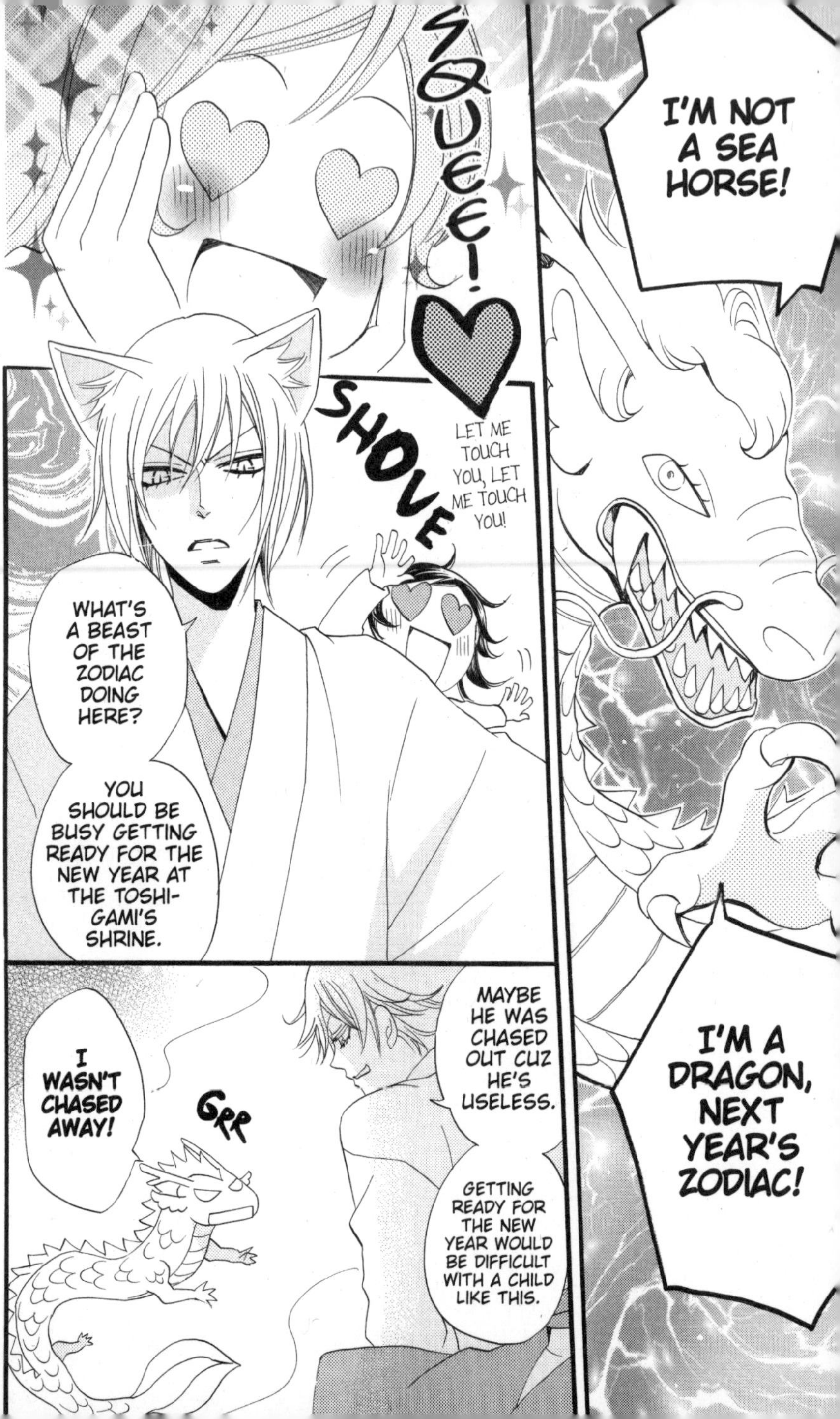
I'M NOT A SEA HORSE!
I'M A DRAGON, NEXT YEAR'S ZODIAC!
SQUEEE!
SHOVE
LET ME TOUCH YOU, LET ME TOUCH YOU!
WHAT'S A BEAST OF THE ZODIAC DOING HERE?
YOU SHOULD BE BUSY GETTING READY FOR THE NEW YEAR AT THE TOSHI-GAMI'S SHRINE.
MAYBE HE WAS CHASED OUT CUZ HE'S USELESS.
GETTING READY FOR THE NEW YEAR WOULD BE DIFFICULT WITH A CHILD LIKE THIS.
GRR
I WASN'T CHASED AWAY!

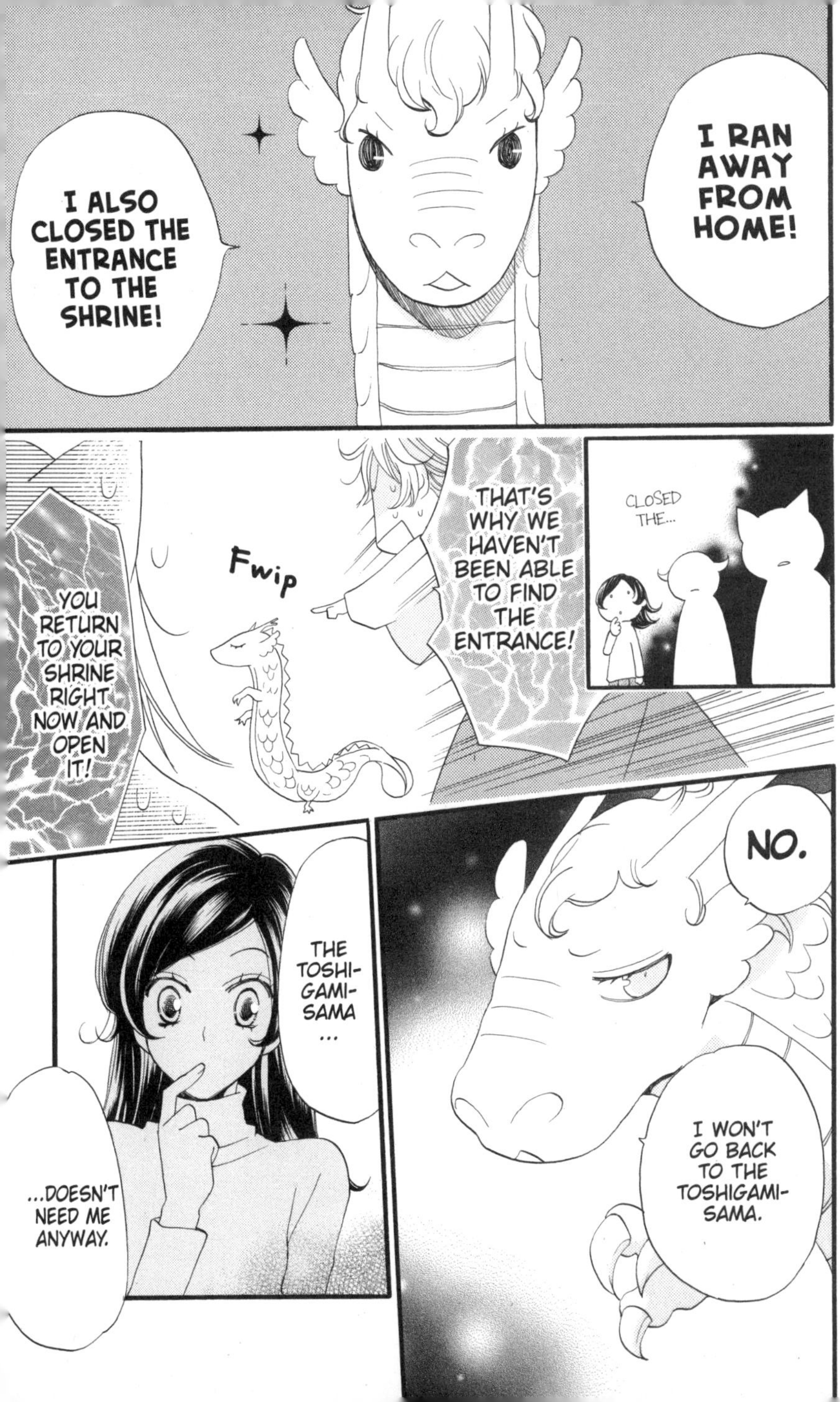
I RAN AWAY FROM HOME!
I ALSO CLOSED THE ENTRANCE TO THE SHRINE!
CLOSED THE...
THAT'S WHY WE HAVEN'T BEEN ABLE TO FIND THE ENTRANCE!
Fwip
YOU RETURN TO YOUR SHRINE RIGHT NOW AND OPEN IT!
NO.
I WON'T GO BACK TO THE TOSHIGAMI-SAMA.
THE TOSHIGAMI-SAMA...
...DOESN'T NEED ME ANYWAY.

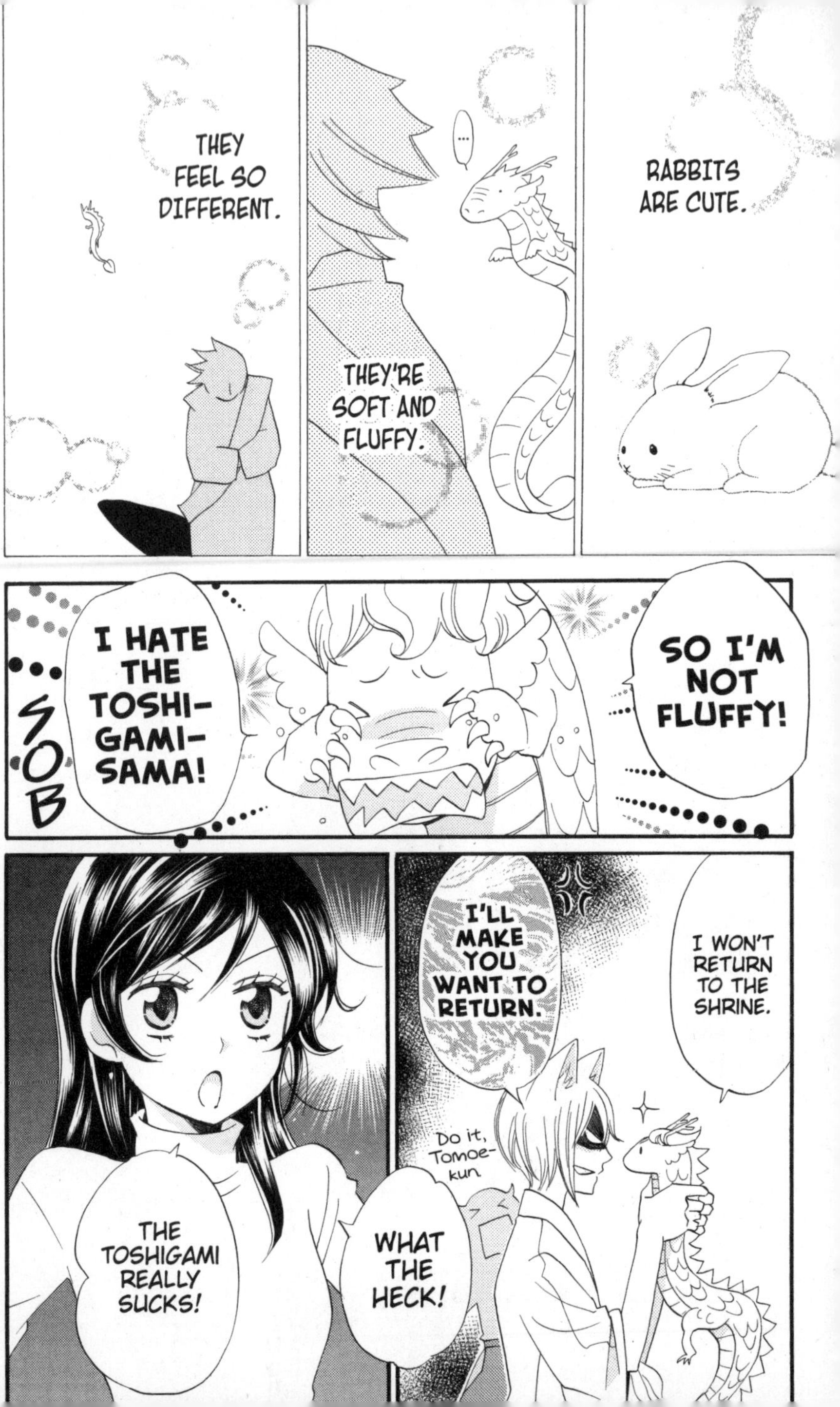
RABBITS ARE CUTE.
...
THEY'RE SOFT AND FLUFFY.
THEY FEEL SO DIFFERENT.
SO I'M NOT FLUFFY!
I HATE THE TOSHI-GAMI-SAMA!
SOB
I WON'T RETURN TO THE SHRINE.
I'LL MAKE YOU WANT TO RETURN.
Do it, Tomoe-kun.
WHAT THE HECK!
THE TOSHIGAMI REALLY SUCKS!

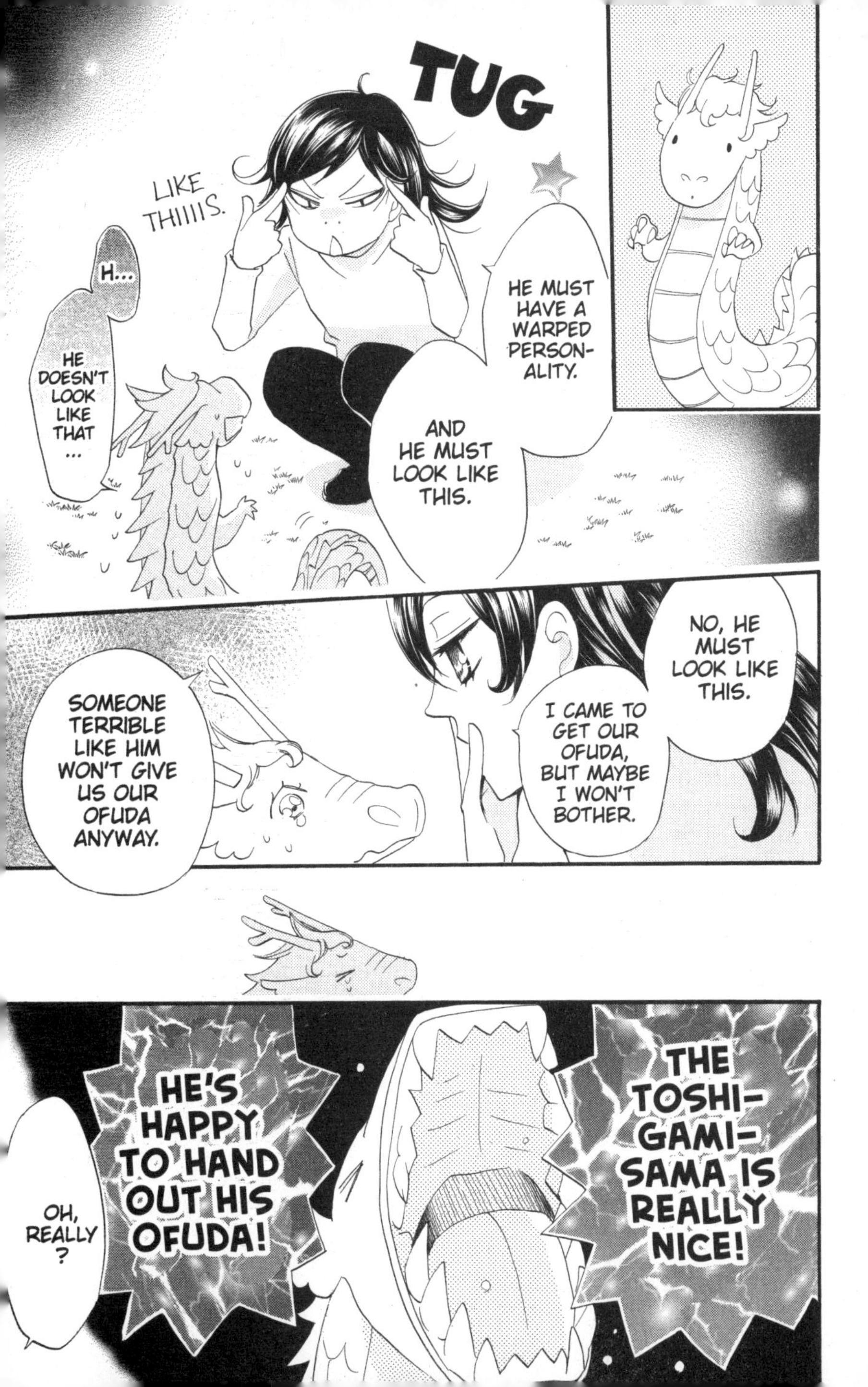
TUG
HE MUST HAVE A WARPED PERSONALITY.
AND HE MUST LOOK LIKE THIS.
LIKE THIIIIS.
H...
HE DOESN'T LOOK LIKE THAT...
NO, HE MUST LOOK LIKE THIS.
I CAME TO GET OUR OFUDA, BUT MAYBE I WON'T BOTHER.
SOMEONE TERRIBLE LIKE HIM WON'T GIVE US OUR OFUDA ANYWAY.
THE TOSHIGAMI-SAMA IS REALLY NICE!
HE'S HAPPY TO HAND OUT HIS OFUDA!
OH, REALLY?

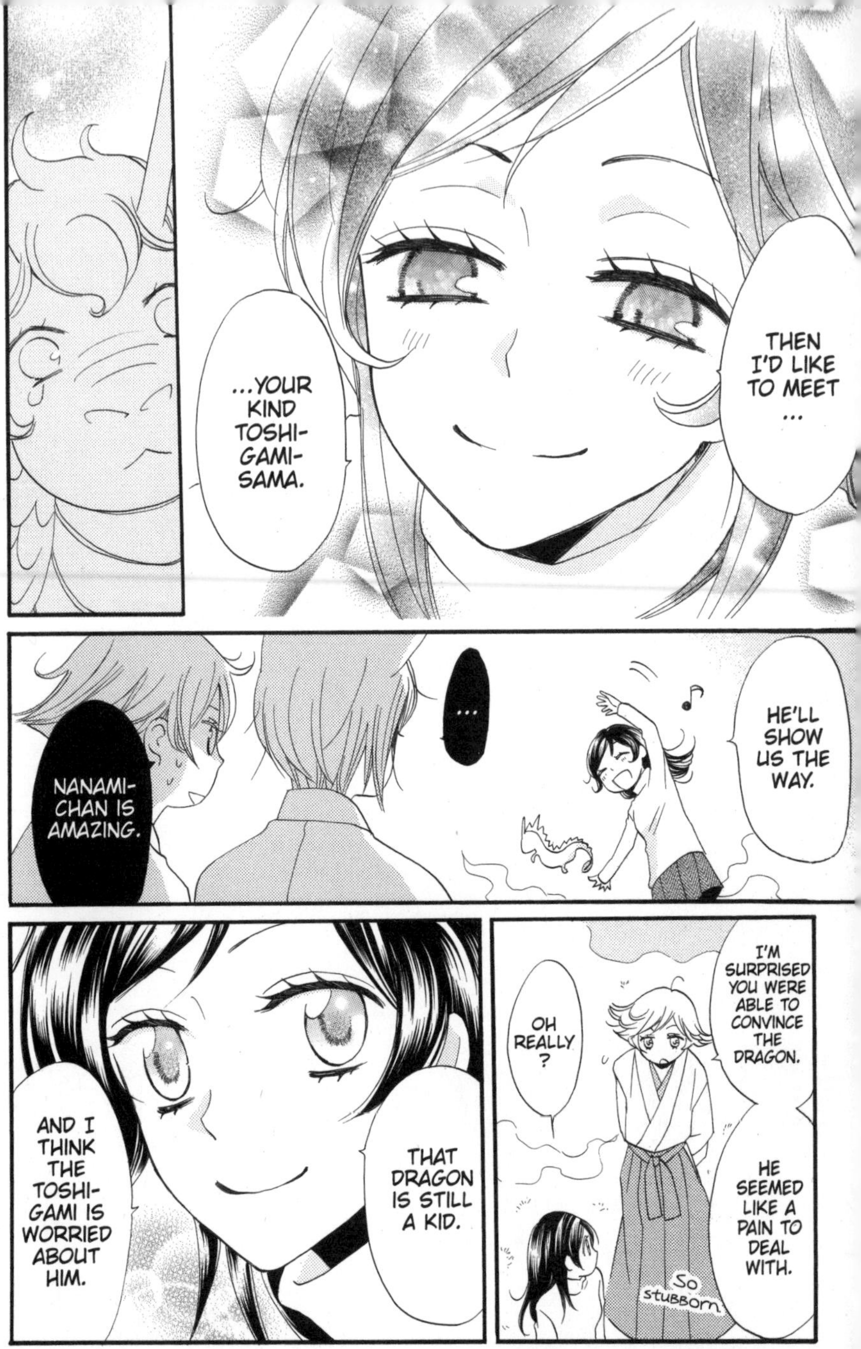
THEN I'D LIKE TO MEET ...
...YOUR KIND TOSHI-GAMI-SAMA.
HE'LL SHOW US THE WAY.
...
NANAMI-CHAN IS AMAZING.
I'M SURPRISED YOU WERE ABLE TO CONVINCE THE DRAGON.
OH REALLY?
HE SEEMED LIKE A PAIN TO DEAL WITH.
So stubborn.
THAT DRAGON IS STILL A KID.
AND I THINK THE TOSHI-GAMI IS WORRIED ABOUT HIM.

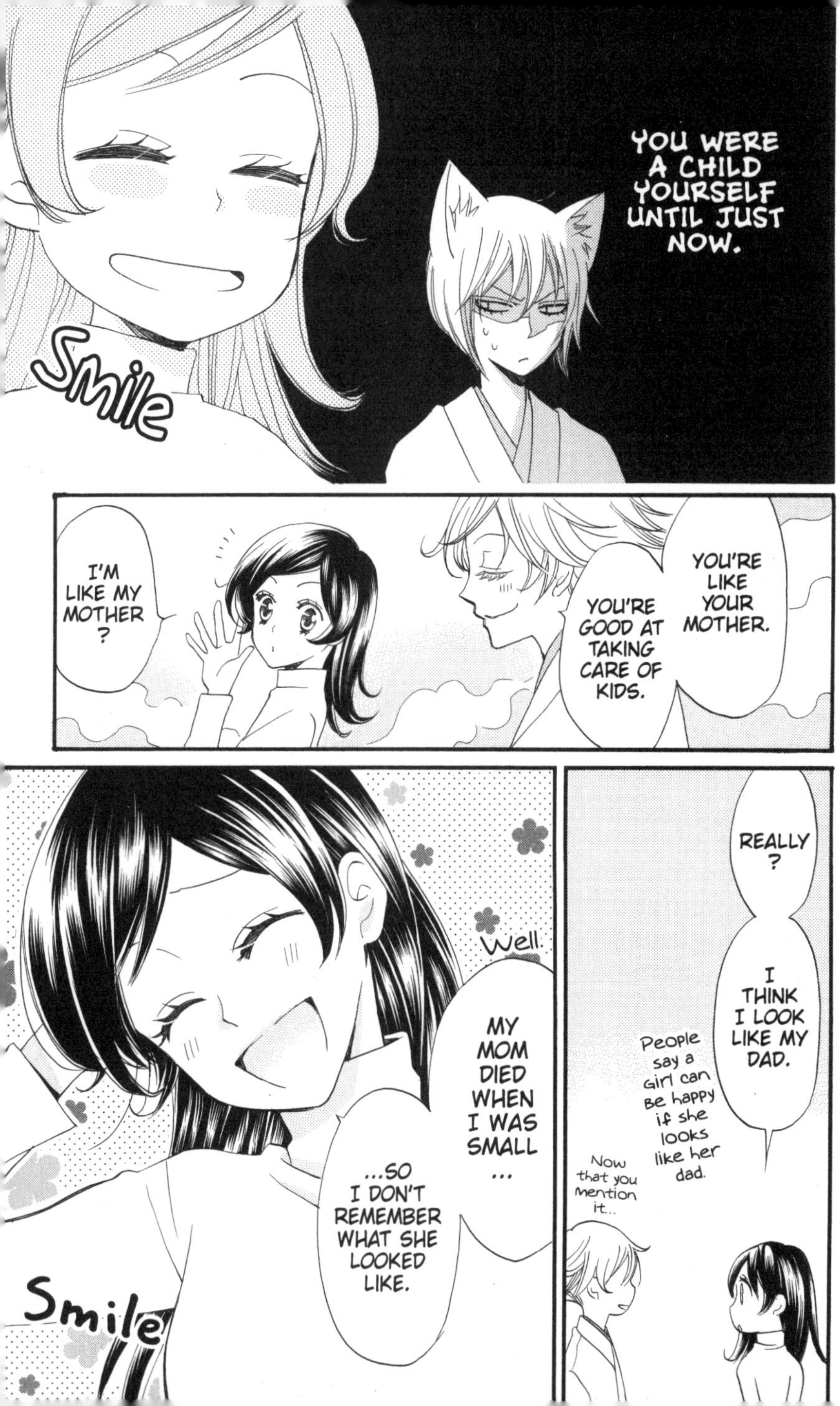
YOU WERE A CHILD YOURSELF UNTIL JUST NOW.
Smile
YOU'RE LIKE YOUR MOTHER.
YOU'RE GOOD AT TAKING CARE OF KIDS.
I'M LIKE MY MOTHER?
REALLY?
I THINK I LOOK LIKE MY DAD.
People say a girl can be happy if she looks like her dad.
Now that you mention it...
Well.
MY MOM DIED WHEN I WAS SMALL...
...SO I DON'T REMEMBER WHAT SHE LOOKED LIKE.
Smile

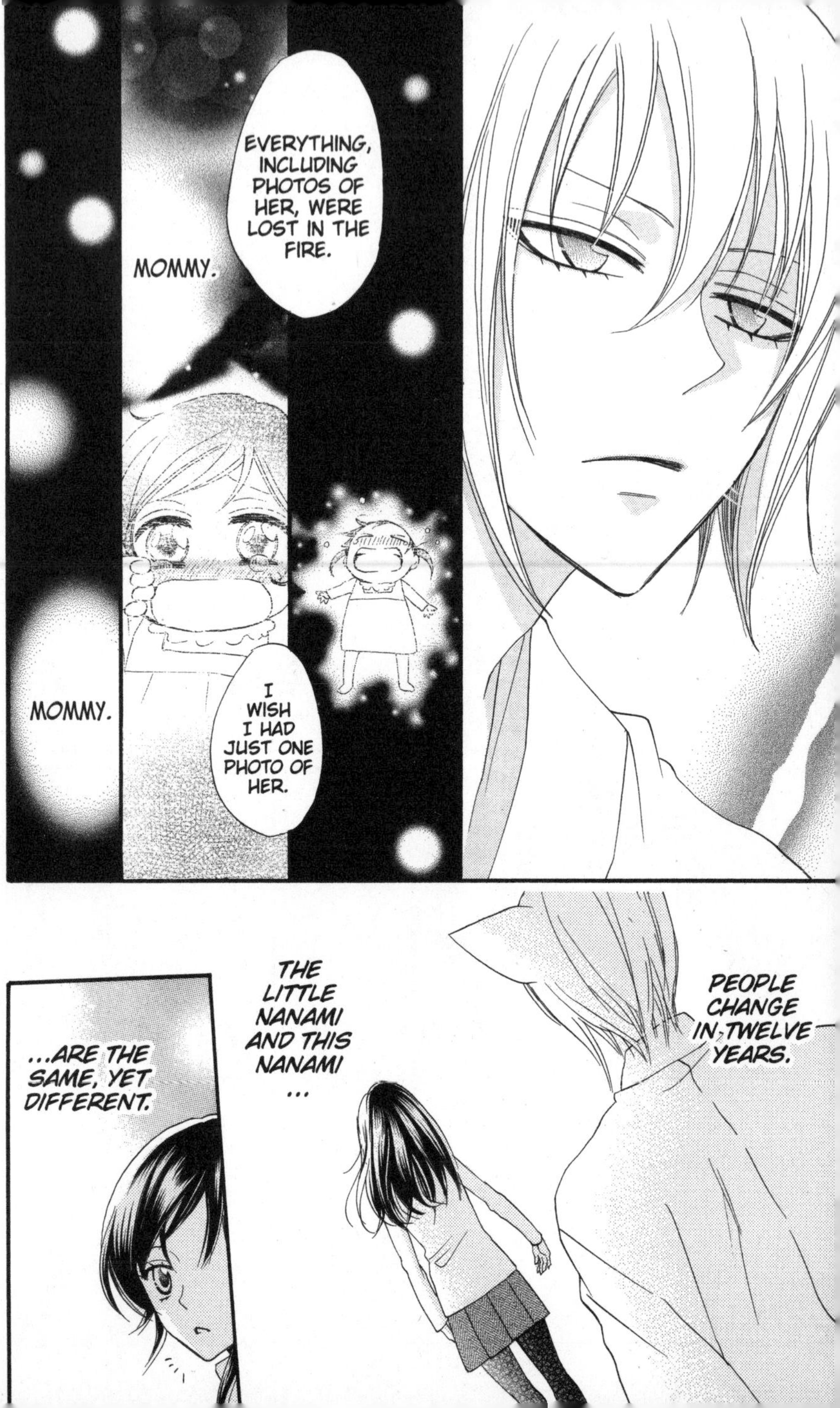
EVERYTHING, INCLUDING PHOTOS OF HER, WERE LOST IN THE FIRE.
MOMMY.
I WISH I HAD JUST ONE PHOTO OF HER.
MOMMY.
PEOPLE CHANGE IN TWELVE YEARS.
THE LITTLE NANAMI AND THIS NANAMI ...
...ARE THE SAME, YET DIFFERENT.

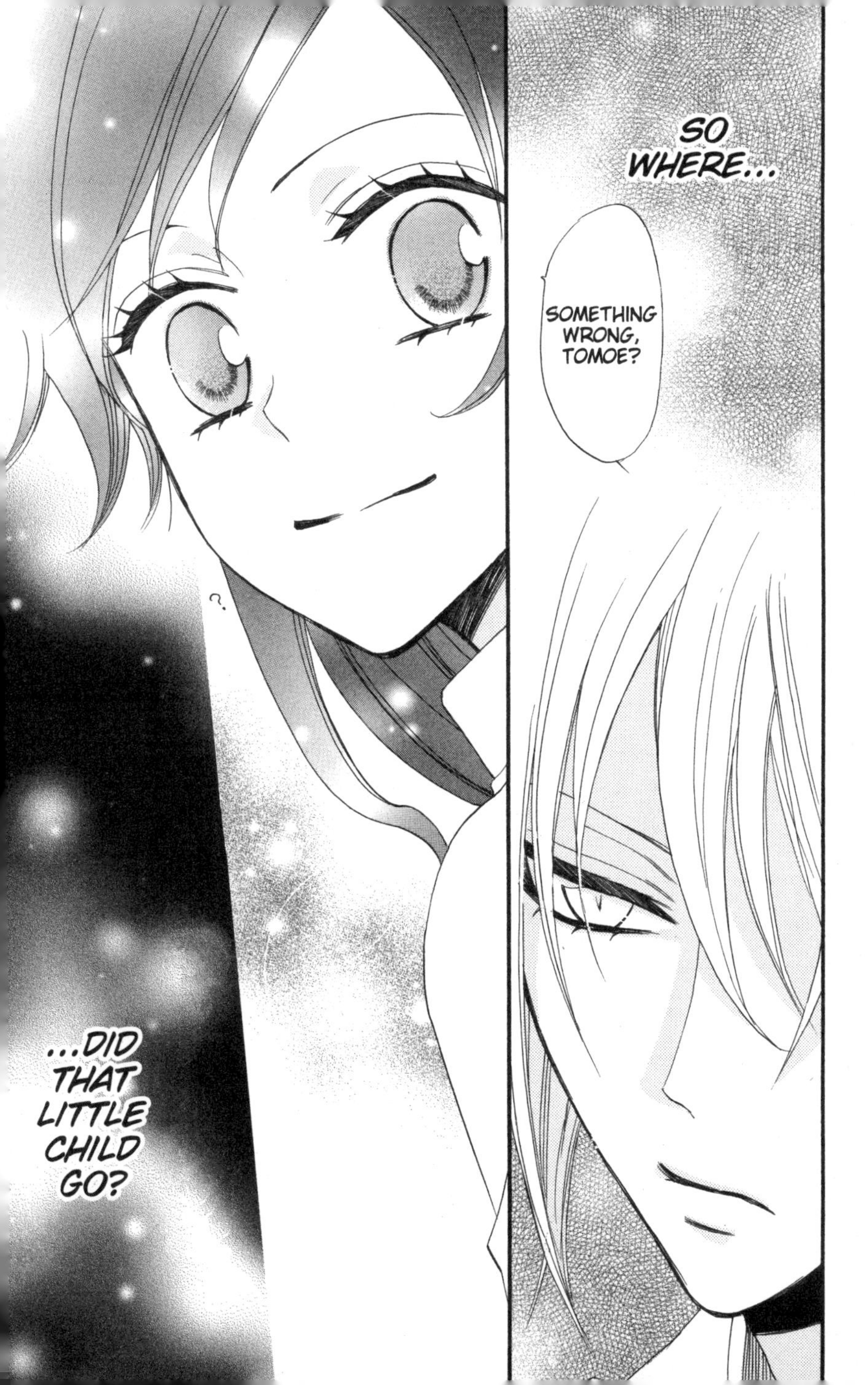
SO WHERE...
SOMETHING WRONG, TOMOE?
?
...DID THAT LITTLE CHILD GO?

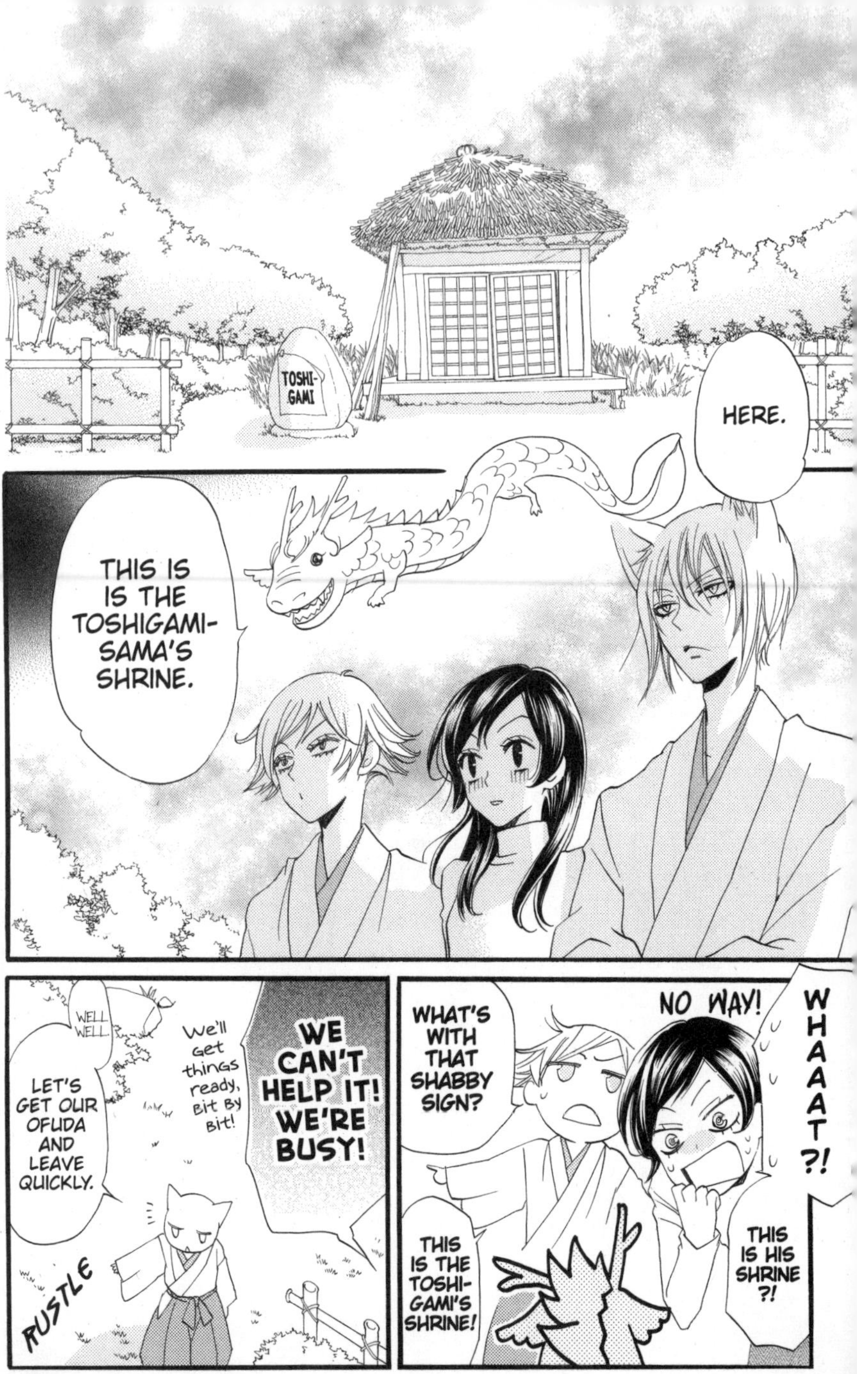
TOSHI-GAMI
HERE.
THIS IS IS THE TOSHIGAMI-SAMA'S SHRINE.
WHAAAT?!
NO WAY!
WHAT'S WITH THAT SHABBY SIGN?
THIS IS HIS SHRINE?!
THIS IS THE TOSHI-GAMI'S SHRINE!
WE CAN'T HELP IT! WE'RE BUSY!
We'll get things ready, bit by bit!
WELL WELL.
LET'S GET OUR OFUDA AND LEAVE QUICKLY.
RUSTLE

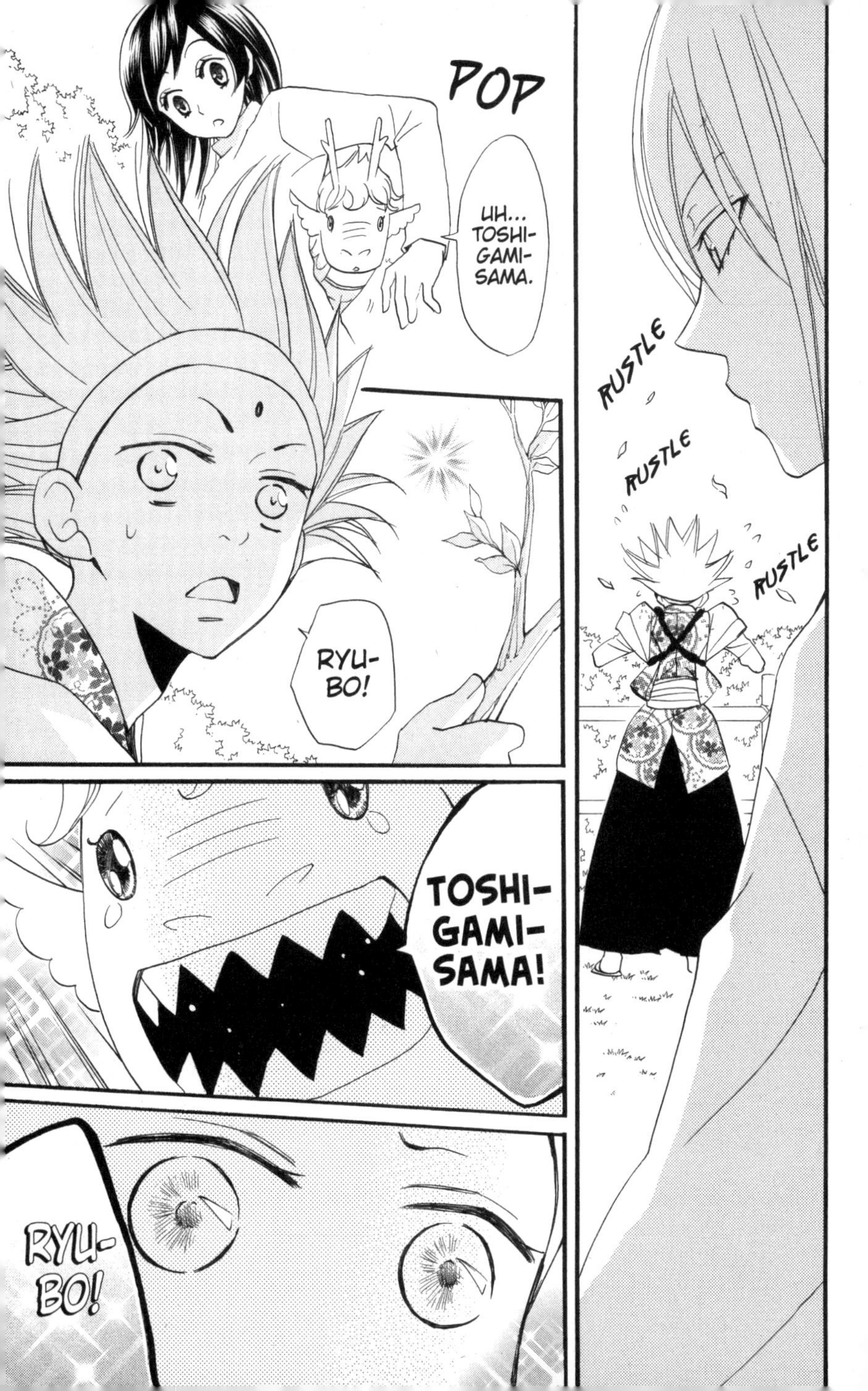
RUSTLE
RUSTLE
RUSTLE
POP
UH... TOSHI-GAMI-SAMA.
RYU-BO!
TOSHI-GAMI-SAMA!
RYU-BO!

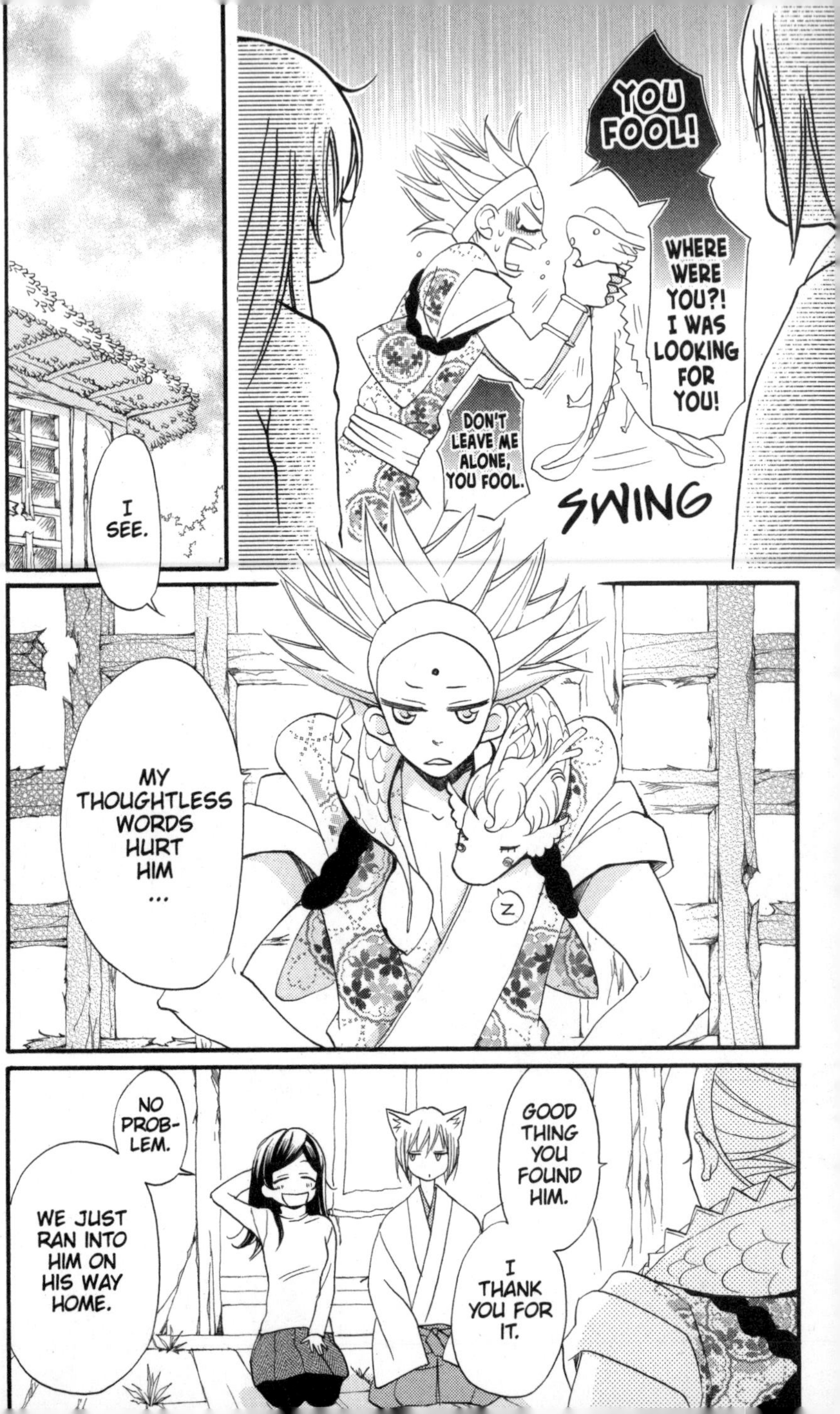
YOU FOOL!
WHERE WERE YOU?! I WAS LOOKING FOR YOU!
DON'T LEAVE ME ALONE, YOU FOOL.
SWING
I SEE.
MY THOUGHTLESS WORDS HURT HIM ...
Z
GOOD THING YOU FOUND HIM.
I THANK YOU FOR IT.
NO PROB-LEM.
WE JUST RAN INTO HIM ON HIS WAY HOME.

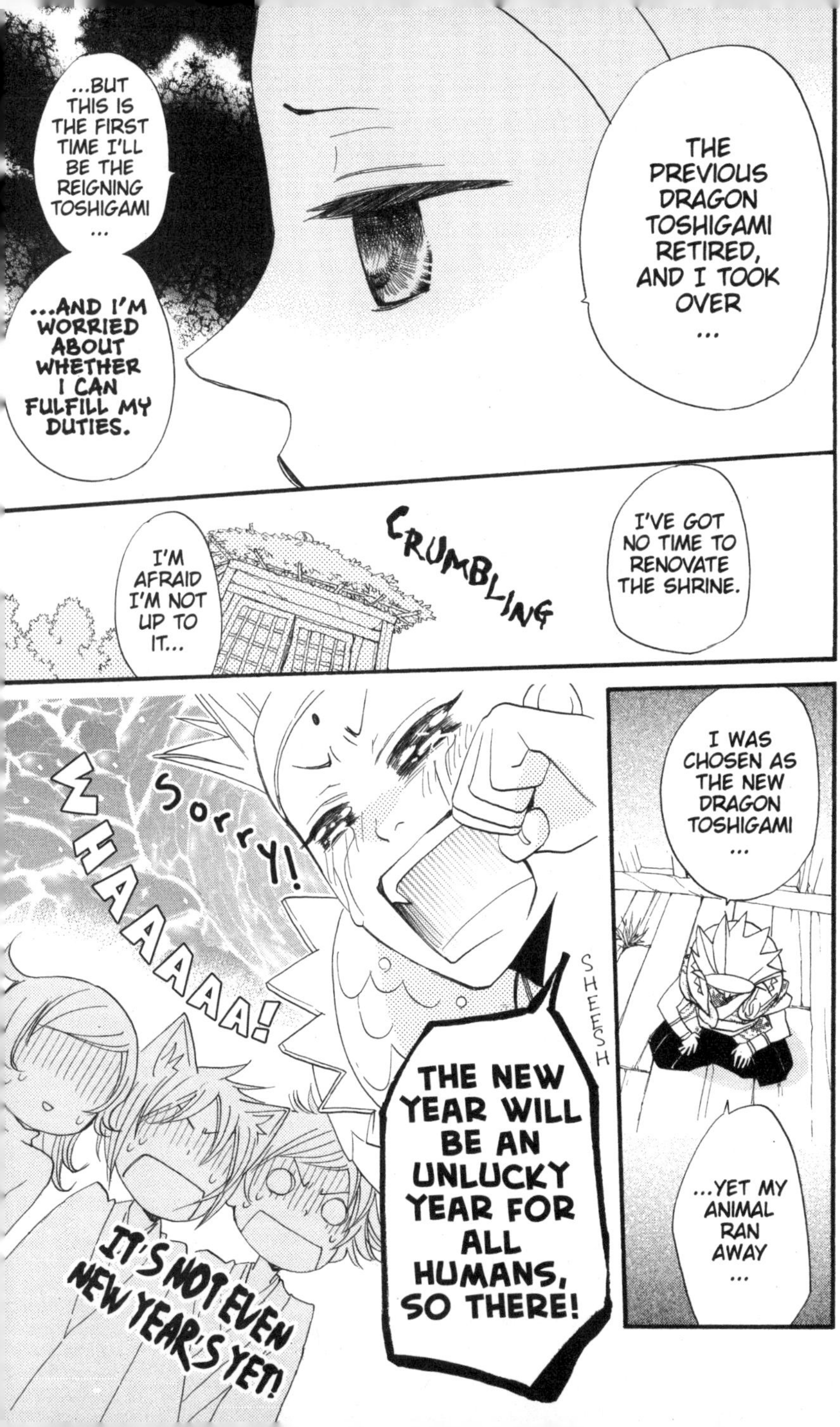
THE PREVIOUS DRAGON TOSHIGAMI RETIRED, AND I TOOK OVER...
...BUT THIS IS THE FIRST TIME I'LL BE THE REIGNING TOSHIGAMI...
...AND I'M WORRIED ABOUT WHETHER I CAN FULFILL MY DUTIES.
I'VE GOT NO TIME TO RENOVATE THE SHRINE.
CRUMBLING
I'M AFRAID I'M NOT UP TO IT...
I WAS CHOSEN AS THE NEW DRAGON TOSHIGAMI...
...YET MY ANIMAL RAN AWAY...
Sorry!
WHAAAAAA!
SHEESH
THE NEW YEAR WILL BE AN UNLUCKY YEAR FOR ALL HUMANS, SO THERE!
IT'S NOT EVEN NEW YEAR'S YET!

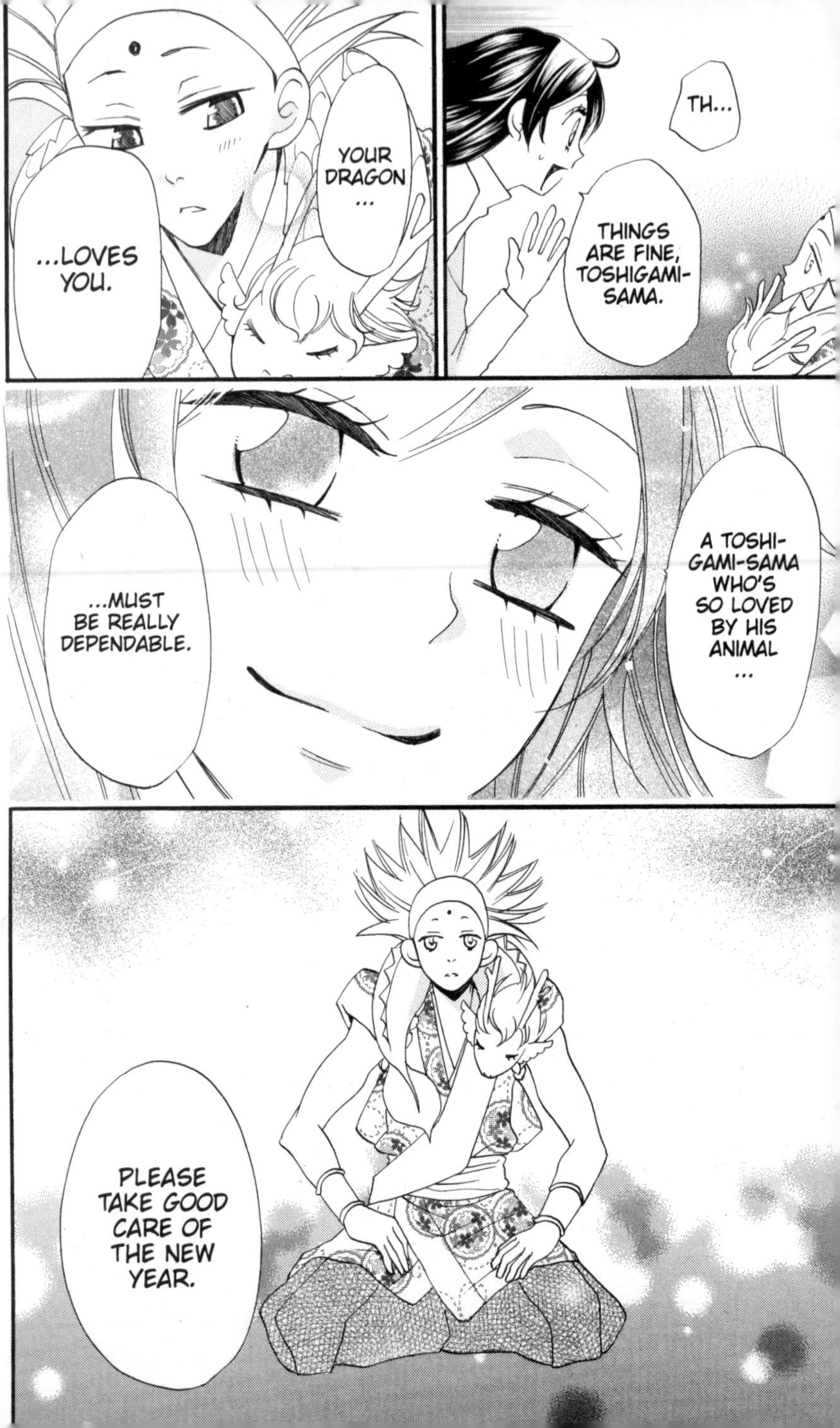
TH...
THINGS ARE FINE, TOSHIGAMI-SAMA.
YOUR DRAGON...
...LOVES YOU.
A TOSHIGAMI-SAMA WHO'S SO LOVED BY HIS ANIMAL...
...MUST BE REALLY DEPENDABLE.
PLEASE TAKE GOOD CARE OF THE NEW YEAR.

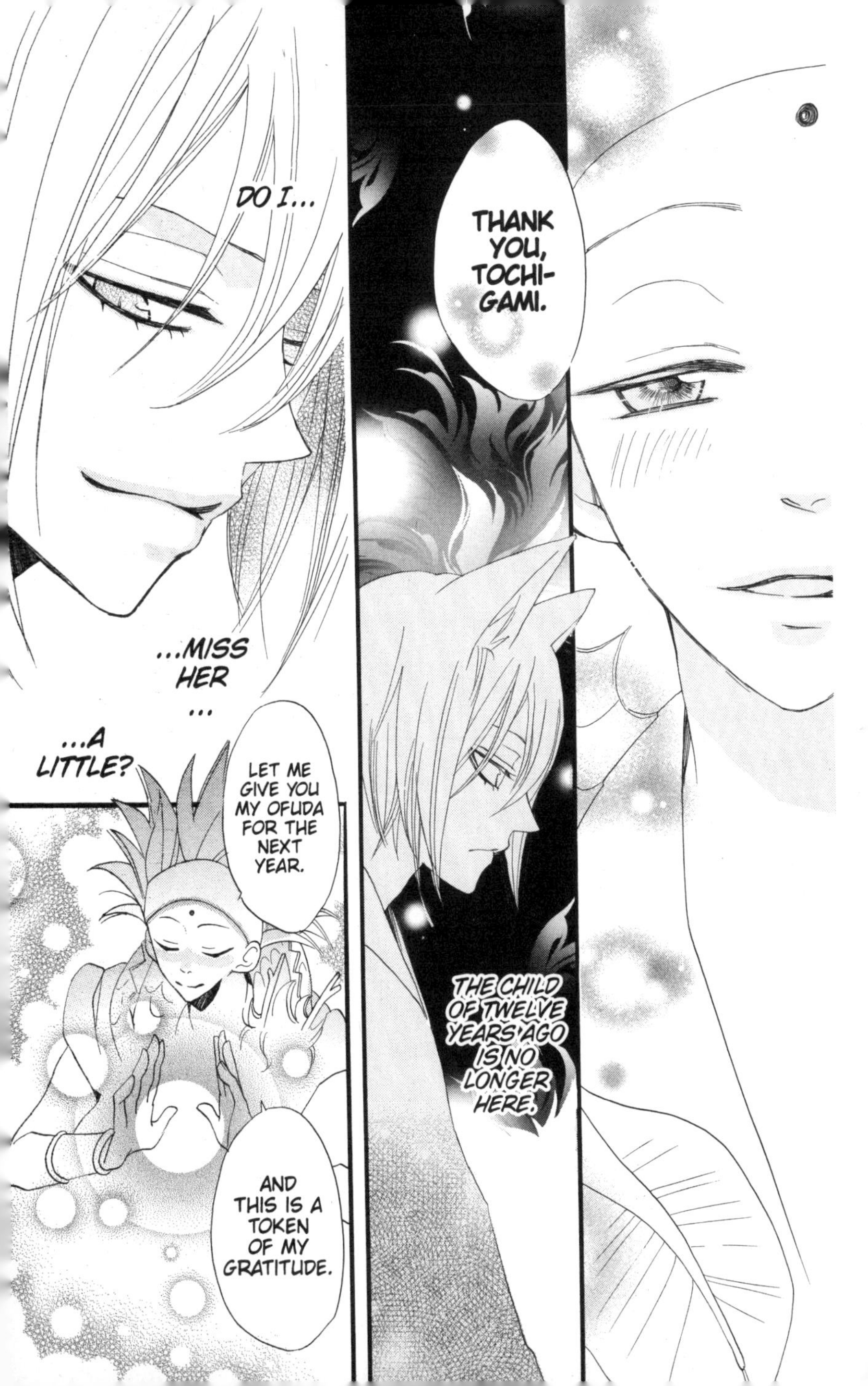
THANK YOU, TOCHI-GAMI.
THE CHILD OF TWELVE YEARS AGO IS NO LONGER HERE.
DO I...
...MISS HER...
...A LITTLE?
LET ME GIVE YOU MY OFUDA FOR THE NEXT YEAR.
AND THIS IS A TOKEN OF MY GRATITUDE.

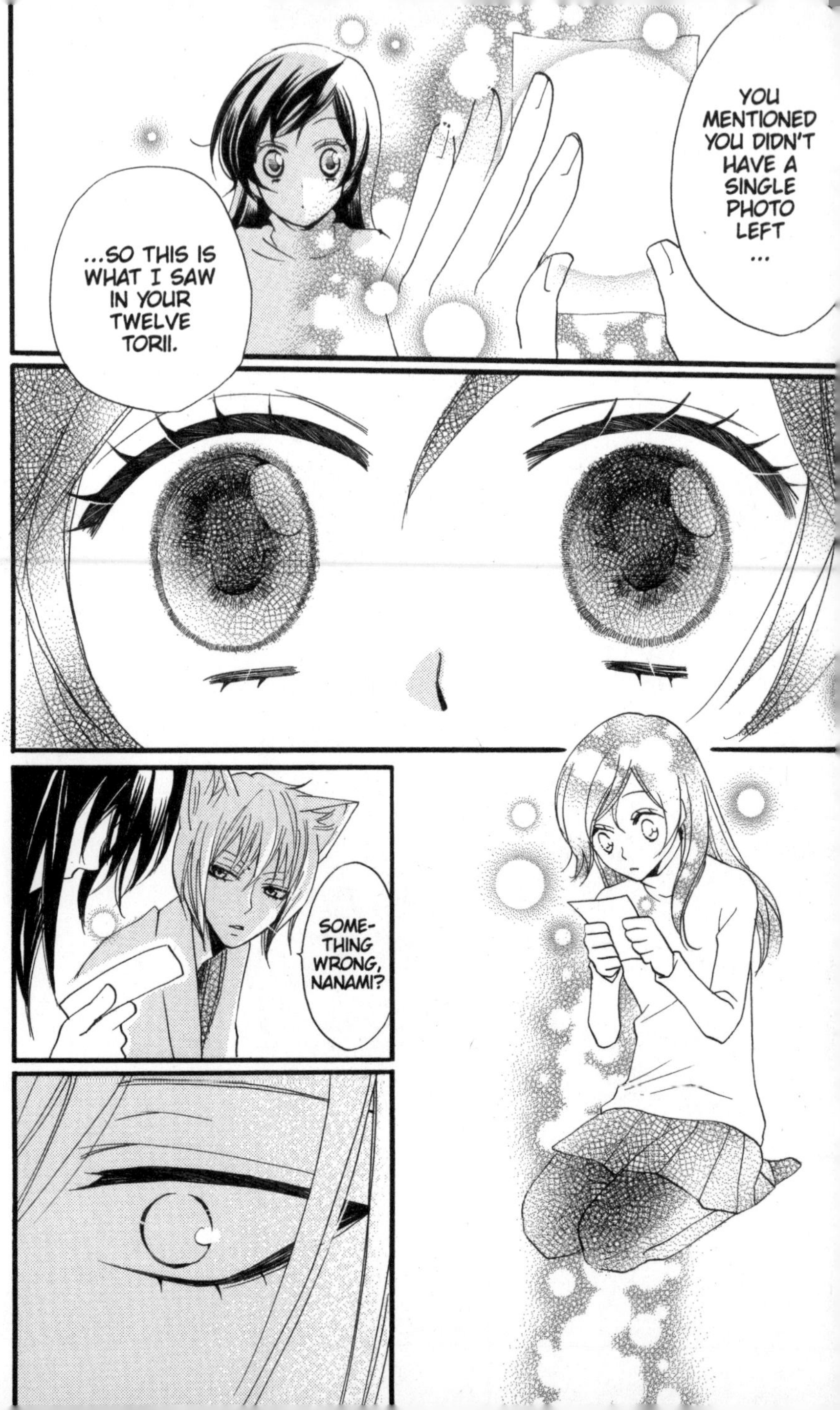
YOU MENTIONED YOU DIDN'T HAVE A SINGLE PHOTO LEFT ...
...SO THIS IS WHAT I SAW IN YOUR TWELVE TORII.
SOME-THING WRONG, NANAMI?

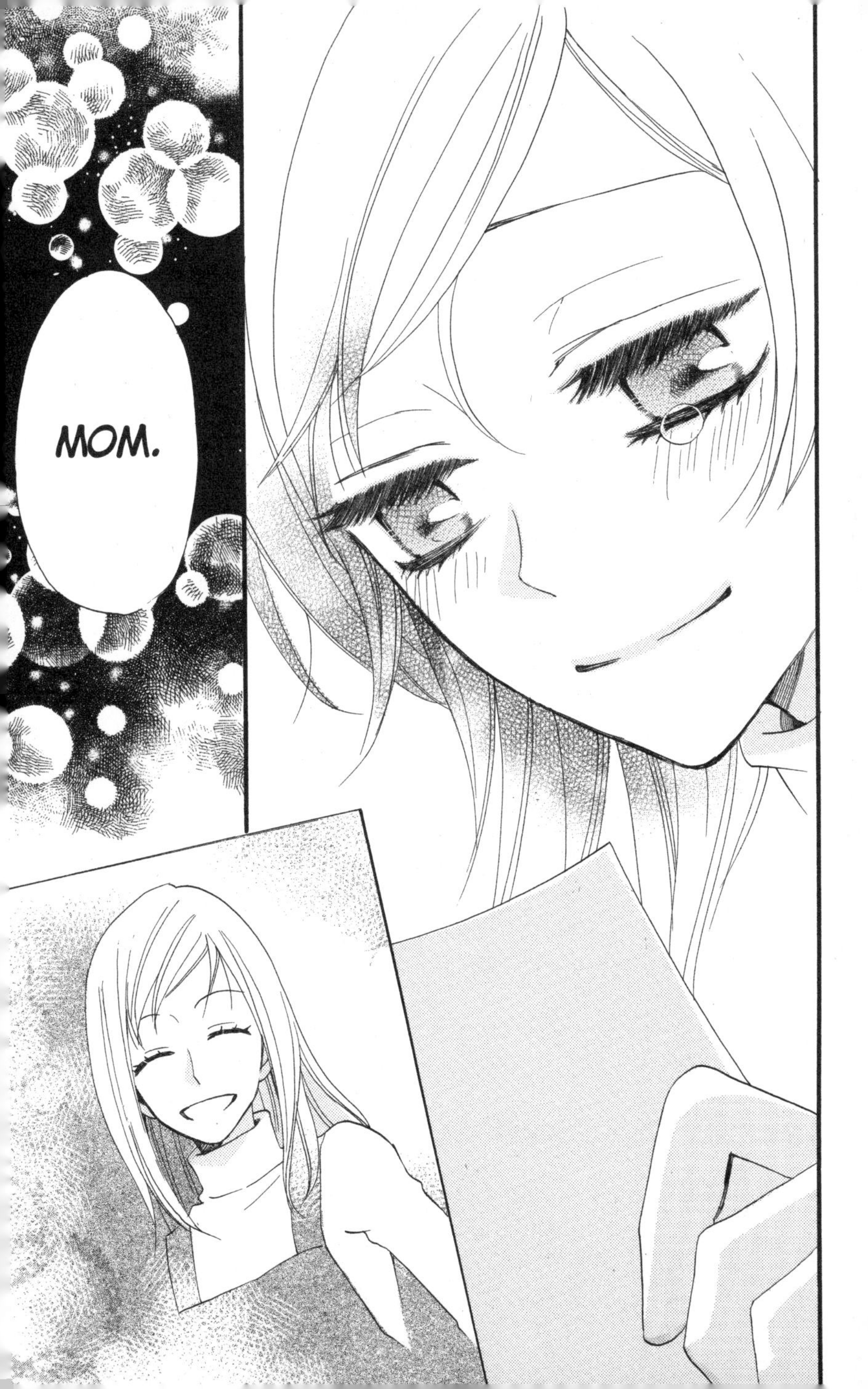
MOM.

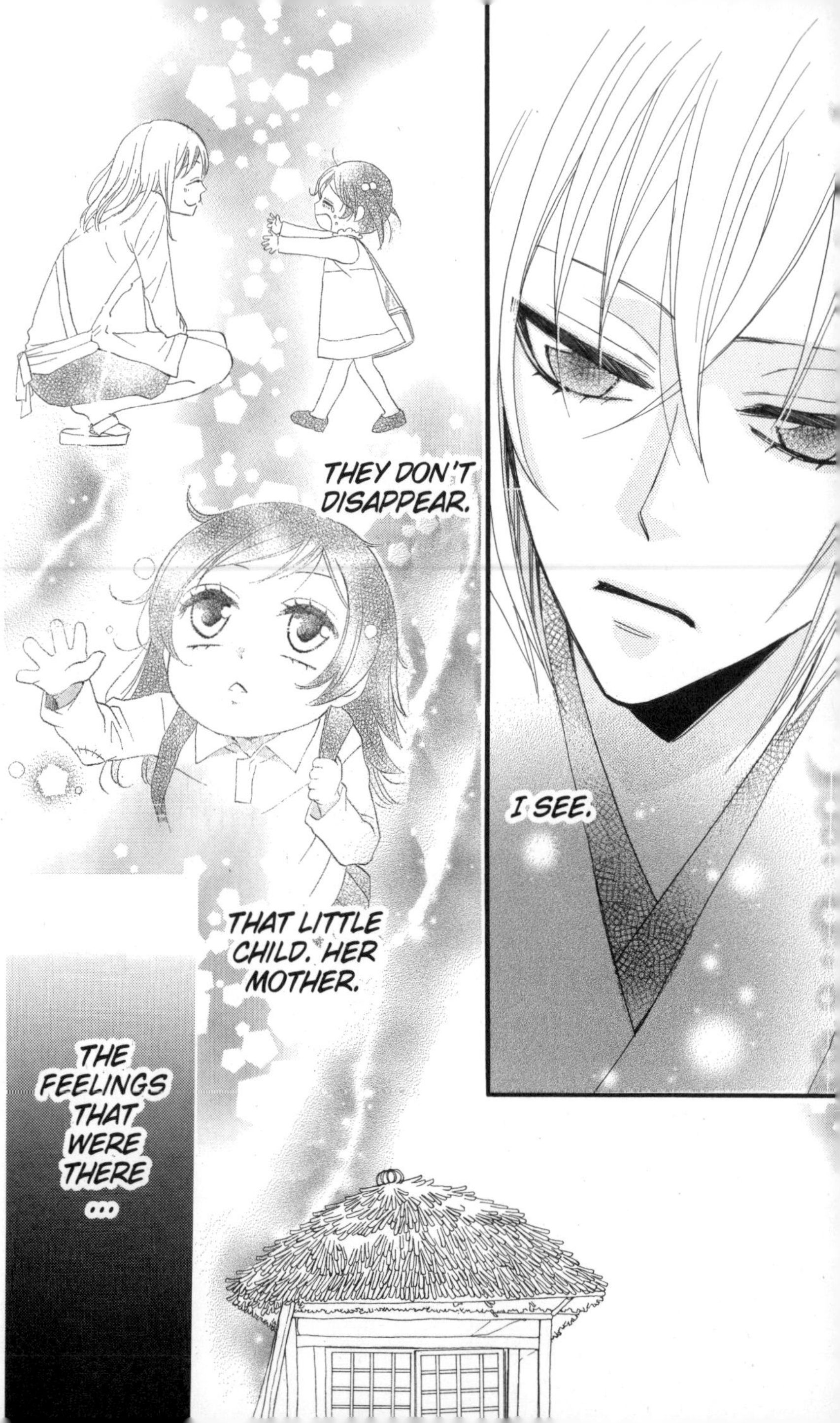
I SEE.
THEY DON'T DISAPPEAR.
THAT LITTLE CHILD. HER MOTHER.
THE FEELINGS THAT WERE THERE...

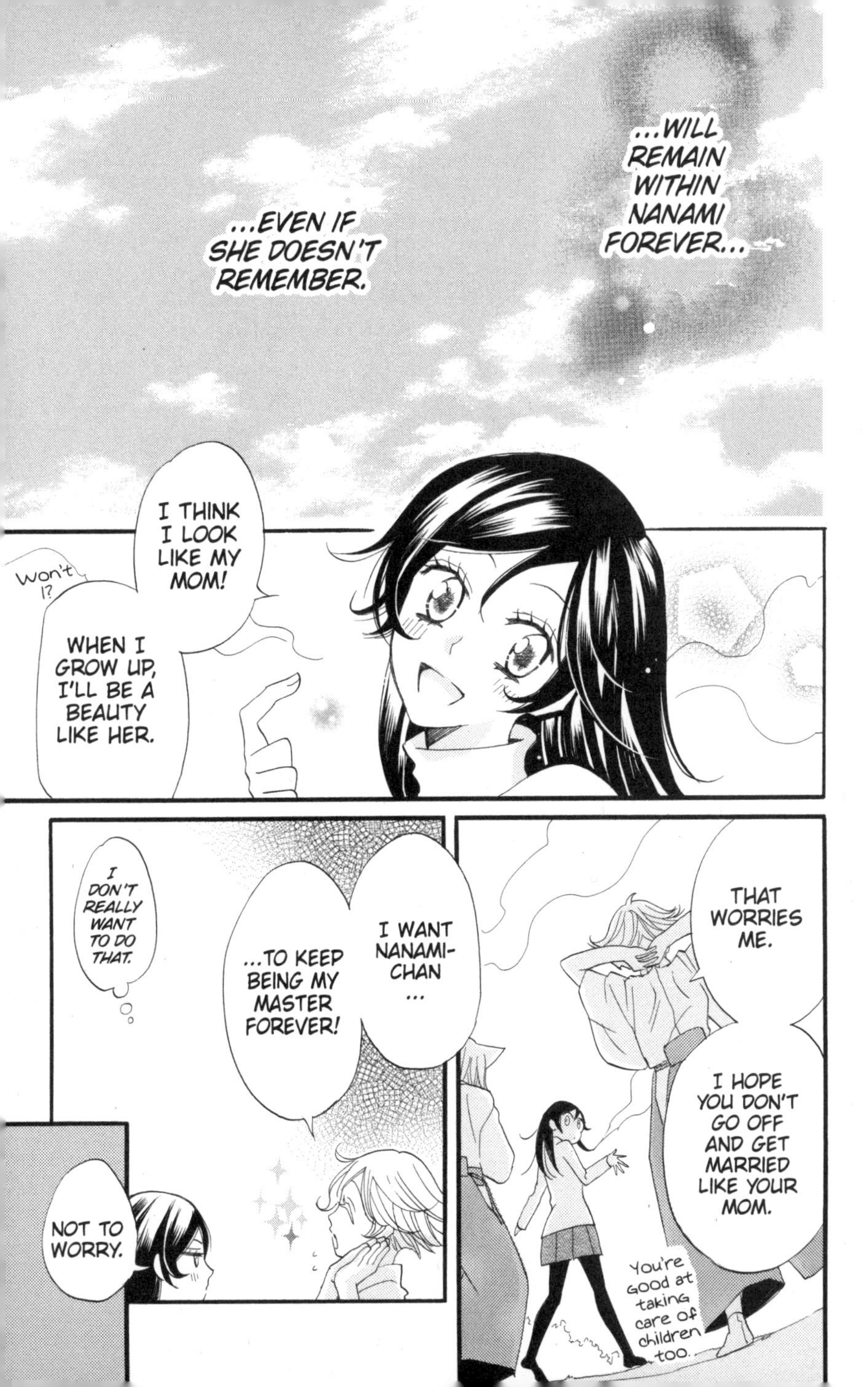
...WILL REMAIN WITHIN NANAMI FOREVER...
...EVEN IF SHE DOESN'T REMEMBER.
I THINK I LOOK LIKE MY MOM!
WHEN I GROW UP, I'LL BE A BEAUTY LIKE HER.
Won't I?
THAT WORRIES ME.
I HOPE YOU DON'T GO OFF AND GET MARRIED LIKE YOUR MOM.
You're good at taking care of children too.
I WANT NANAMI-CHAN...
...TO KEEP BEING MY MASTER FOREVER!
I DON'T REALLY WANT TO DO THAT.
NOT TO WORRY.

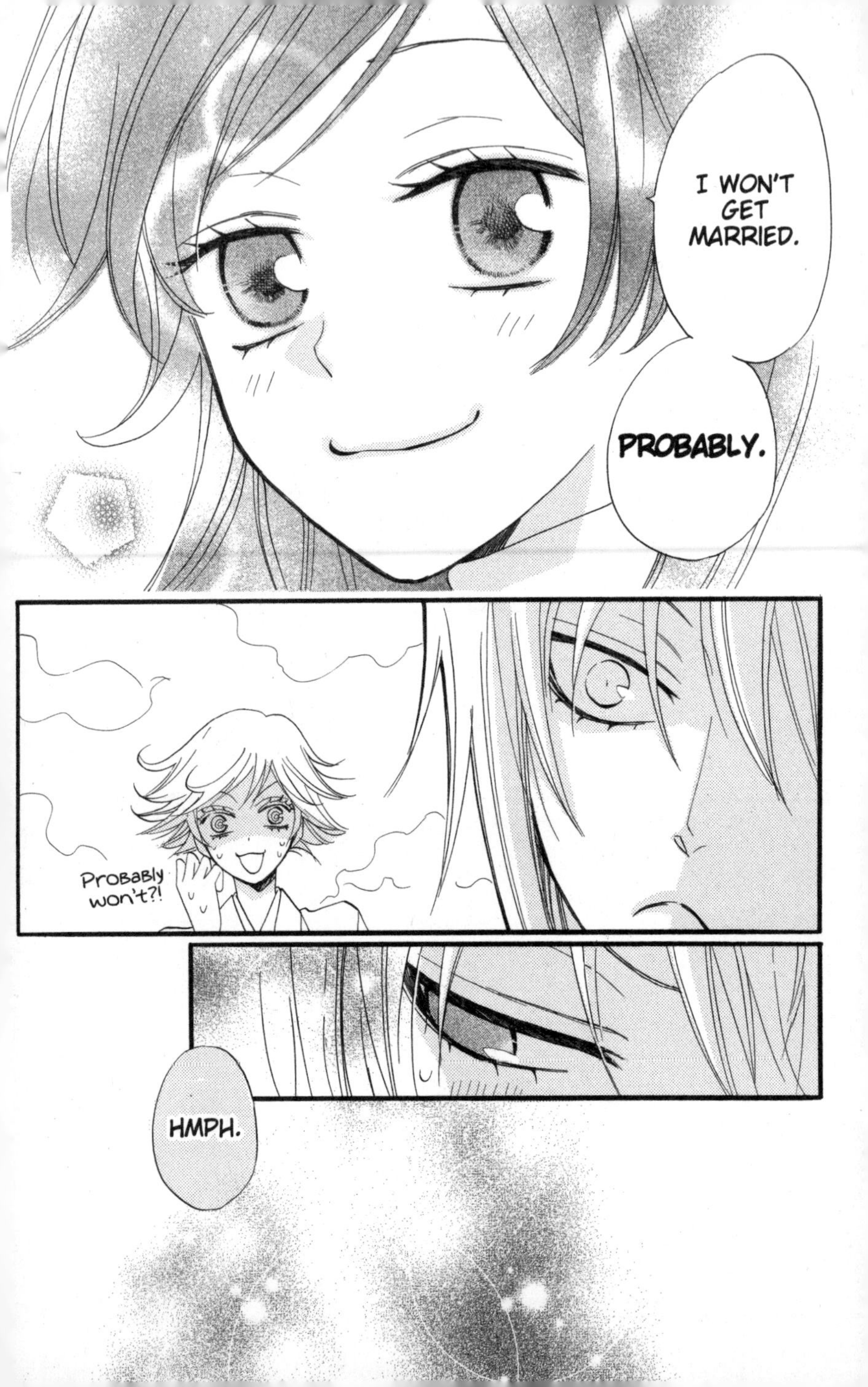
I WON'T GET MARRIED.
PROBABLY.
Probably won't?!
HMPH.

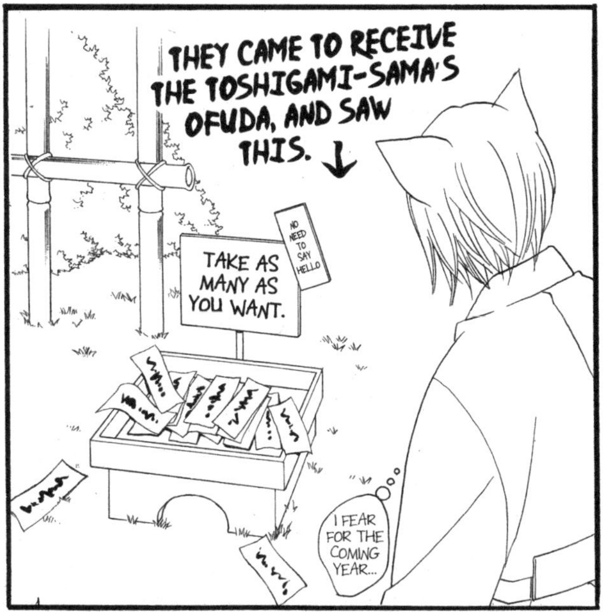
THEY CAME TO RECEIVE THE TOSHIGAMI-SAMA'S OFUDA, AND SAW THIS.
NO NEED TO SAY HELLO
TAKE AS MANY AS YOU WANT.
I FEAR FOR THE COMING YEAR...

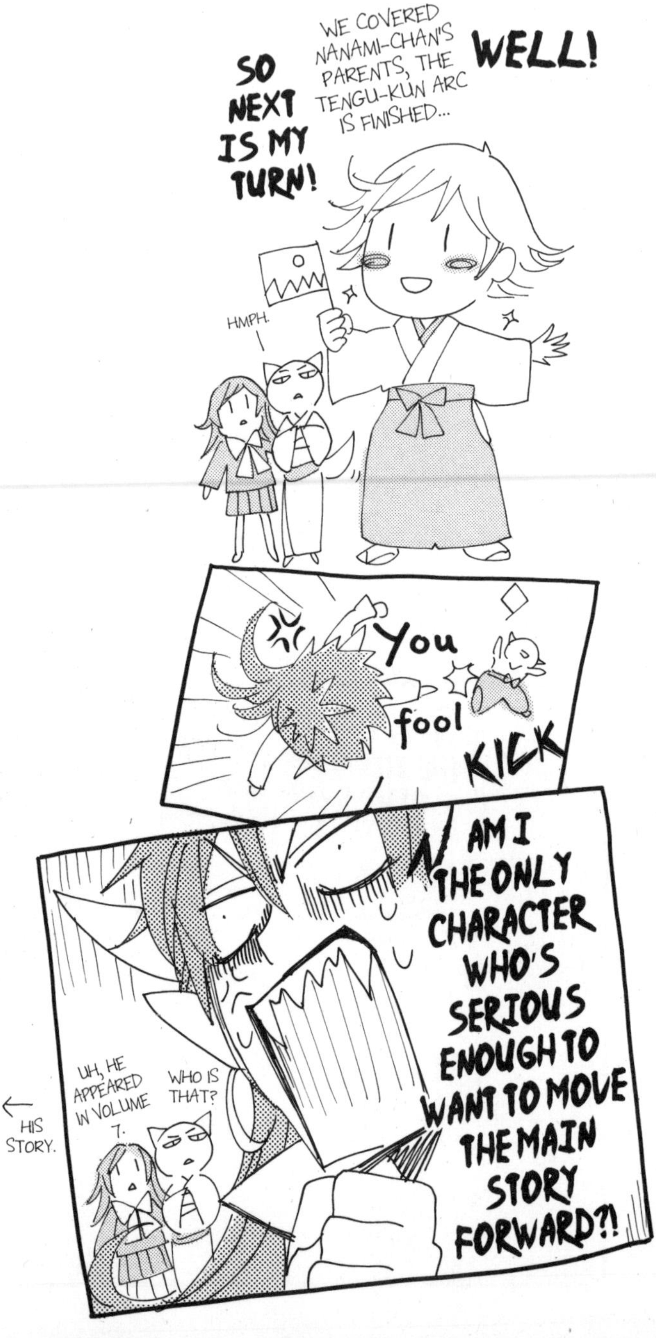
WELL!
WE COVERED NANAMI-CHAN'S PARENTS, THE TENGU-KUN ARC IS FINISHED...
SO NEXT IS MY TURN!
HMPH.
You fool
KICK
AM I THE ONLY CHARACTER WHO'S SERIOUS ENOUGH TO WANT TO MOVE THE MAIN STORY FORWARD?!
WHO IS THAT?
UH, HE APPEARED IN VOLUME 7.
← HIS STORY.

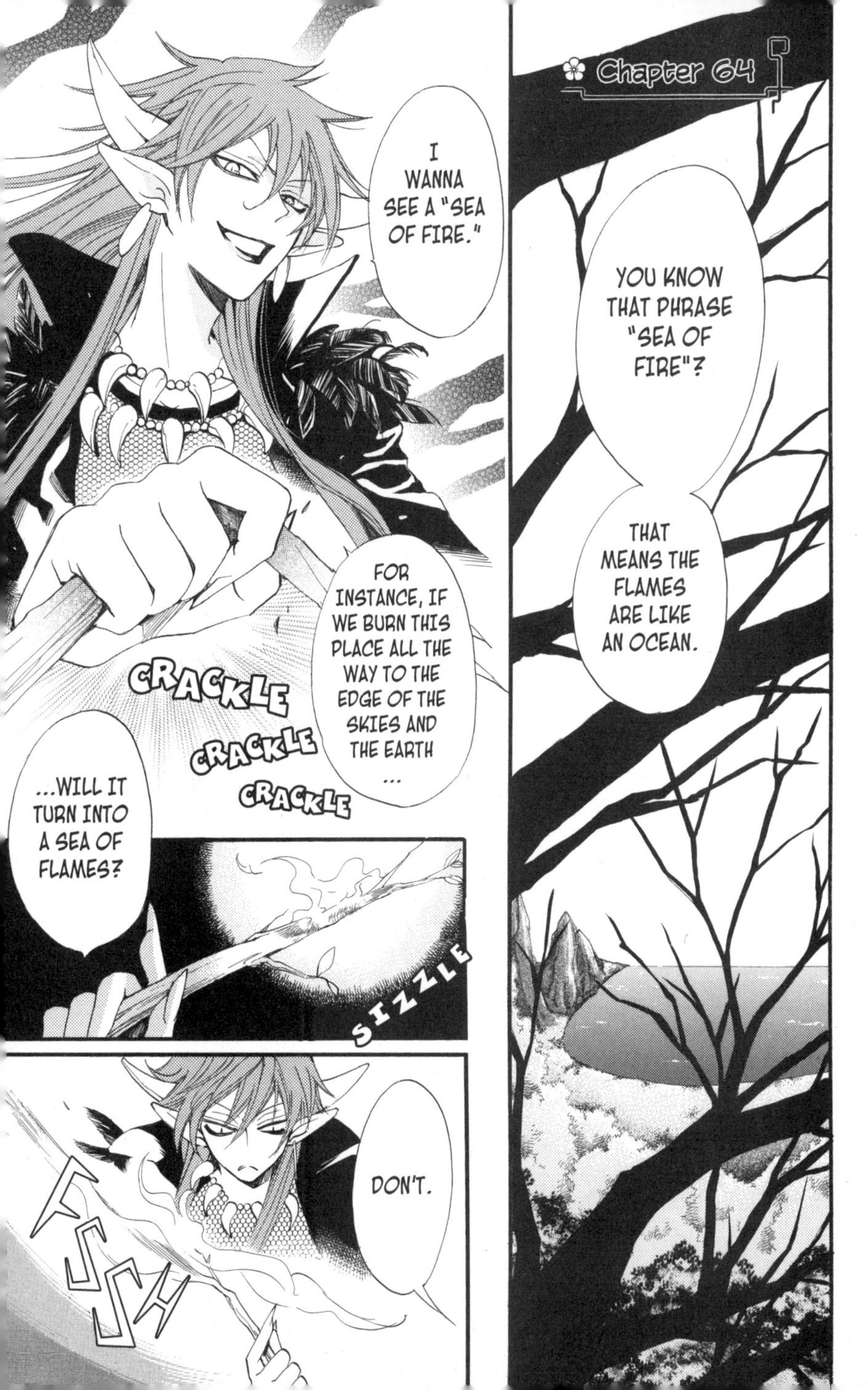
Chapter 64
YOU KNOW THAT PHRASE "SEA OF FIRE"?
THAT MEANS THE FLAMES ARE LIKE AN OCEAN.
I WANNA SEE A "SEA OF FIRE."
FOR INSTANCE, IF WE BURN THIS PLACE ALL THE WAY TO THE EDGE OF THE SKIES AND THE EARTH ...
CRACKLE
CRACKLE
CRACKLE
...WILL IT TURN INTO A SEA OF FLAMES?
SIZZLE
DON'T.
FSSH

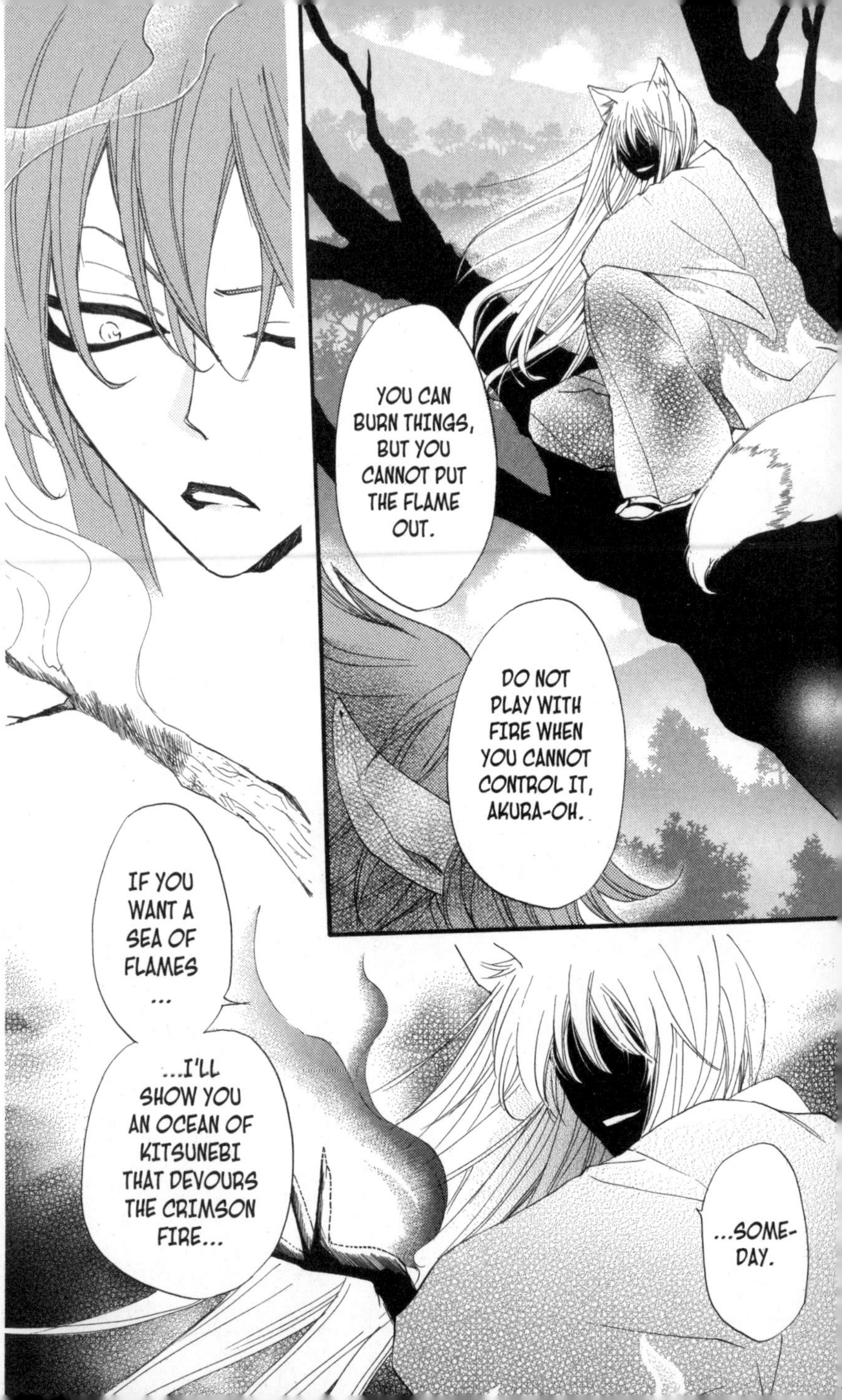
YOU CAN BURN THINGS, BUT YOU CANNOT PUT THE FLAME OUT.
DO NOT PLAY WITH FIRE WHEN YOU CANNOT CONTROL IT, AKURA-OH.
IF YOU WANT A SEA OF FLAMES ...
...I'LL SHOW YOU AN OCEAN OF KITSUNEBI THAT DEVOURS THE CRIMSON FIRE...
...SOME-DAY.

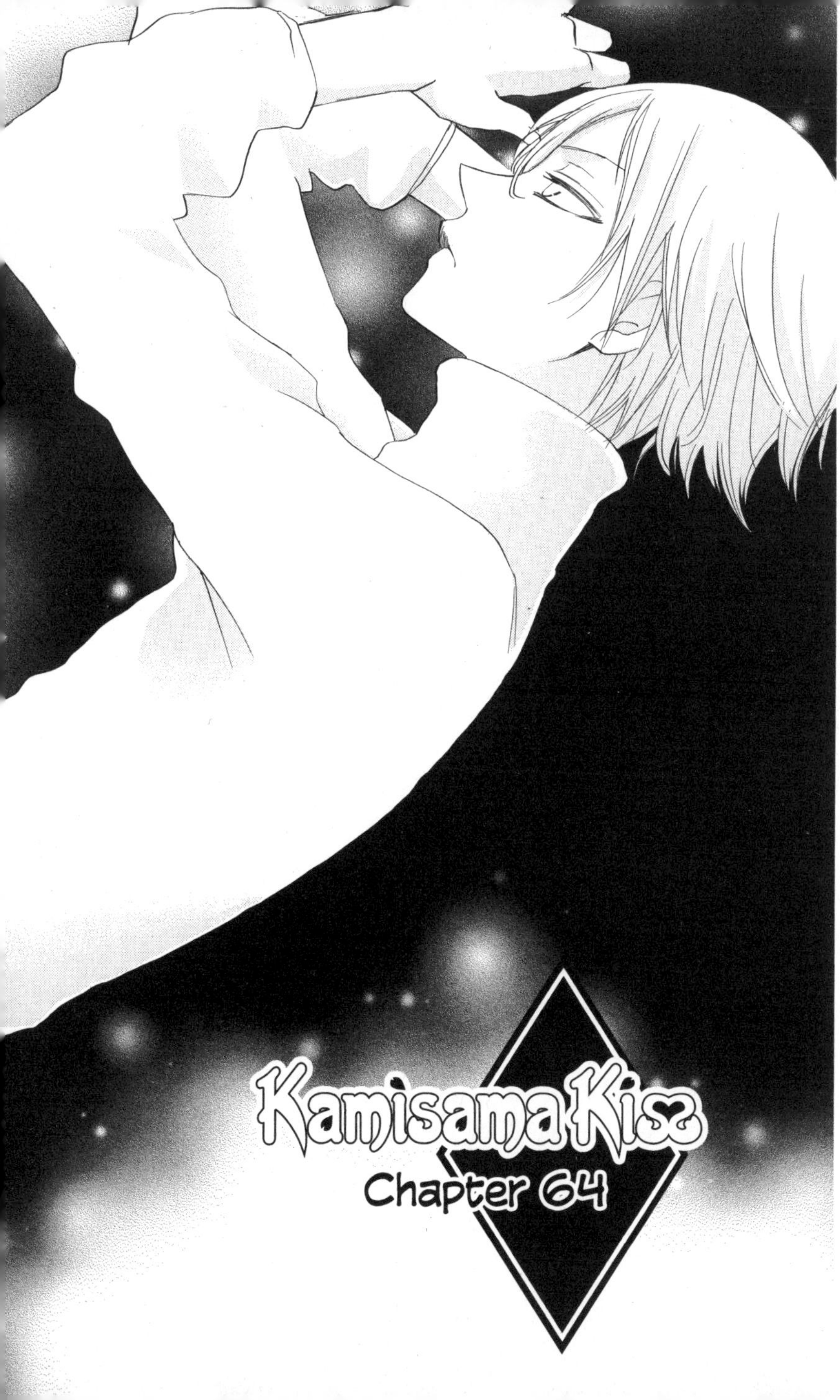
Kamisama Kiss
Chapter 64

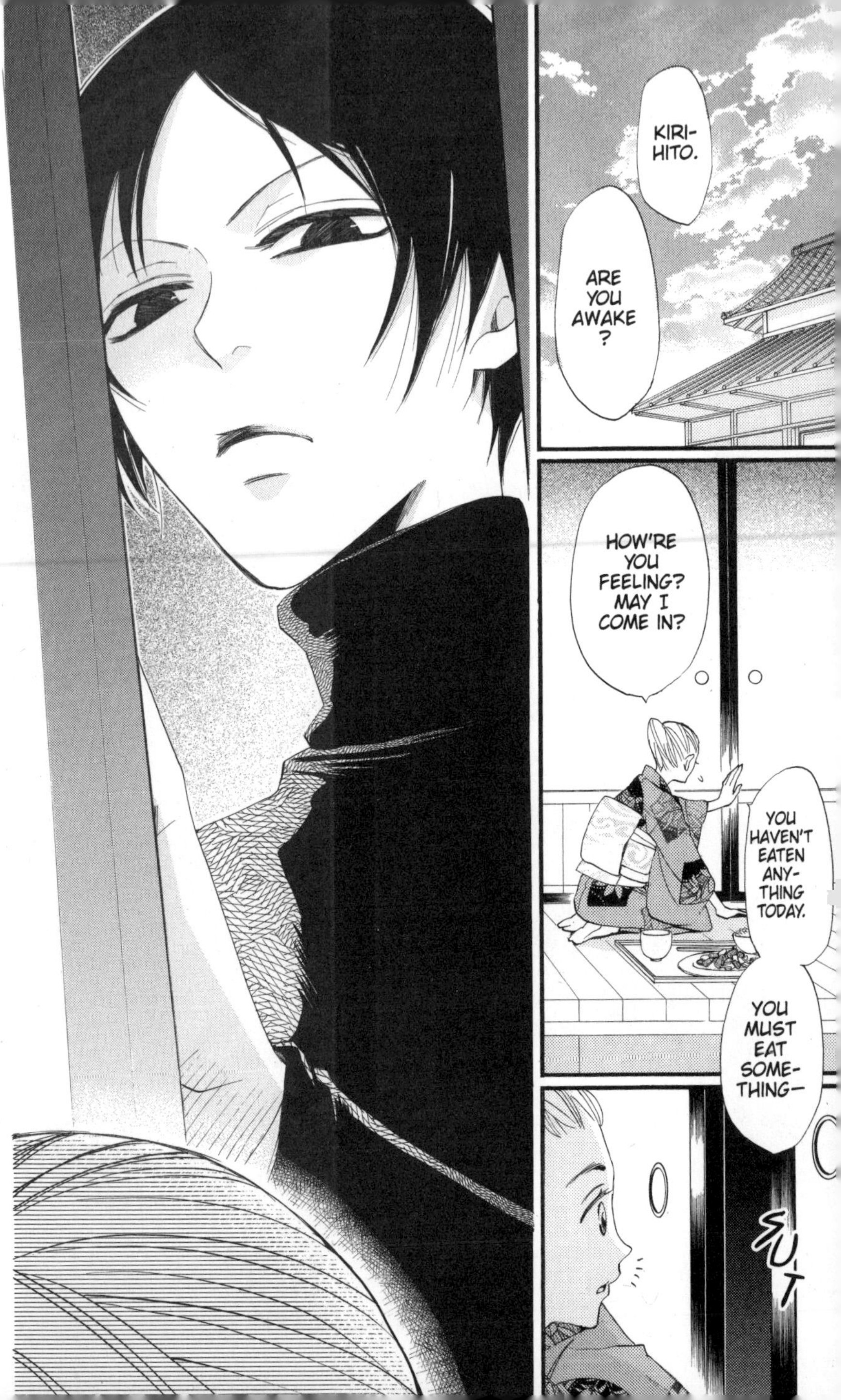
KIRI-HITO.
ARE YOU AWAKE?
HOW'RE YOU FEELING? MAY I COME IN?
YOU HAVEN'T EATEN ANY-THING TODAY.
YOU MUST EAT SOME-THING—
SHUT

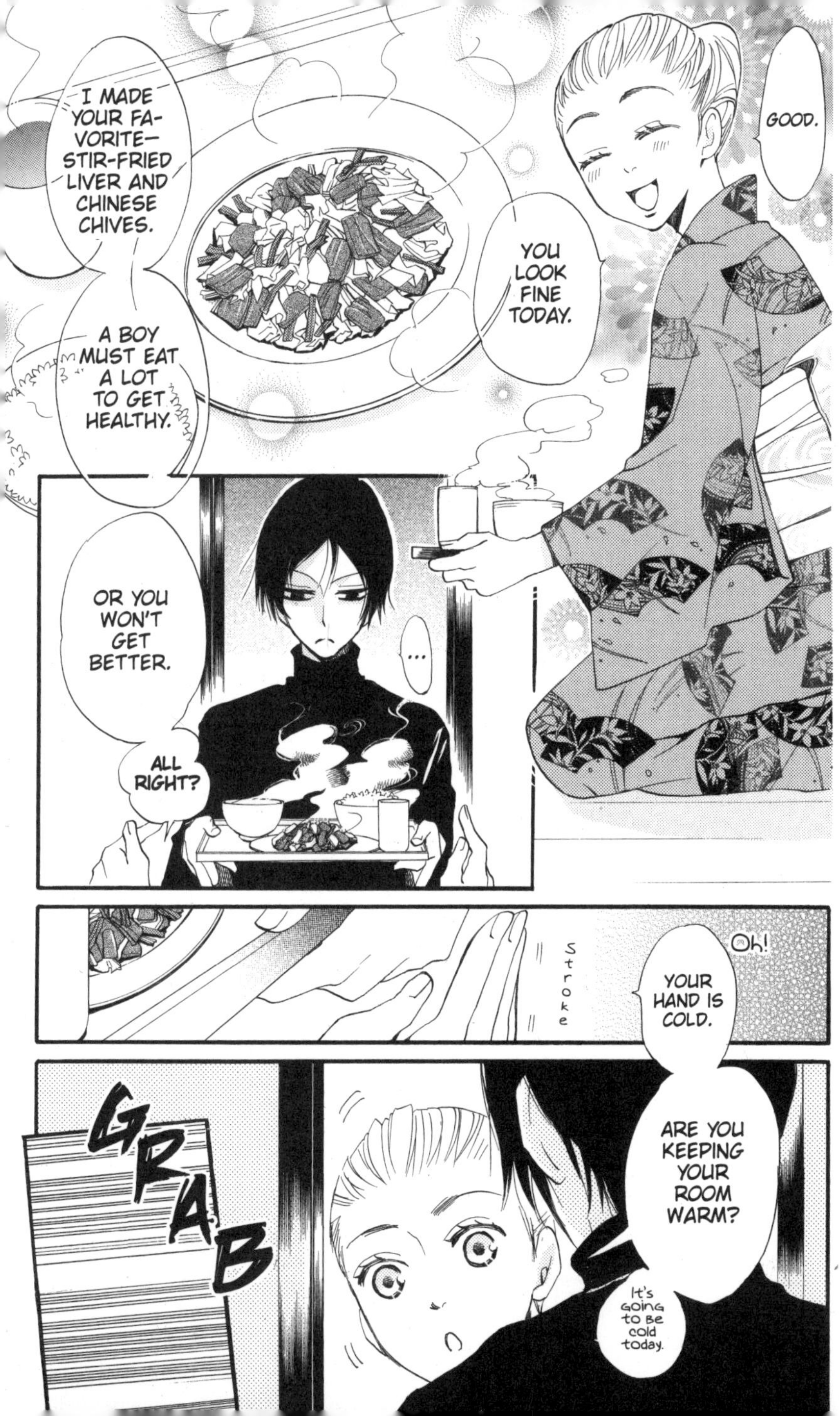
...
GOOD.
YOU LOOK FINE TODAY.
I MADE YOUR FAVORITE—STIR-FRIED LIVER AND CHINESE CHIVES.
A BOY MUST EAT A LOT TO GET HEALTHY.
OR YOU WON'T GET BETTER.
ALL RIGHT?
...
Oh!
YOUR HAND IS COLD.
Stroke
ARE YOU KEEPING YOUR ROOM WARM?
It's going to be cold today.
GRAB

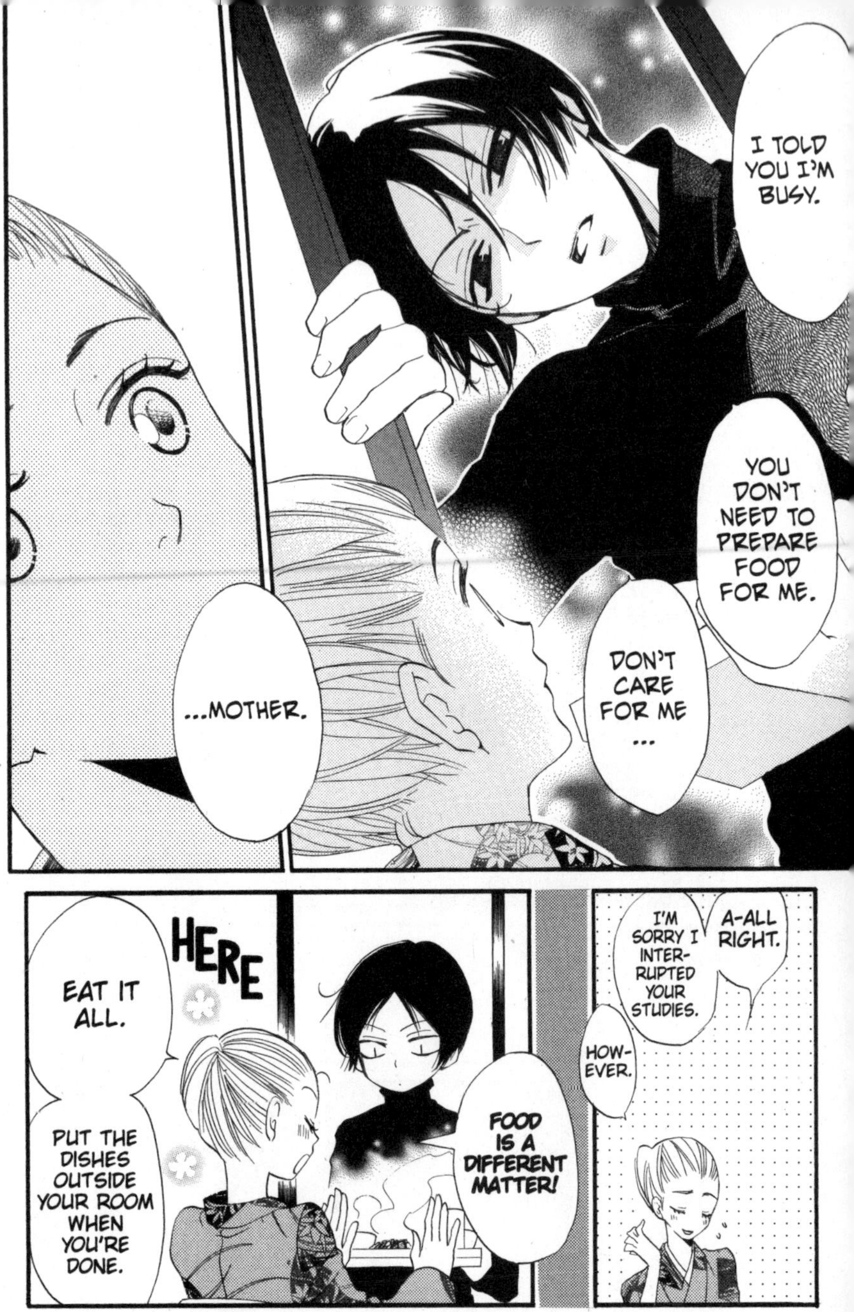
I TOLD YOU I'M BUSY.
YOU DON'T NEED TO PREPARE FOOD FOR ME.
DON'T CARE FOR ME ...
...MOTHER.
A-ALL RIGHT.
I'M SORRY I INTER-RUPTED YOUR STUDIES.
HOW-EVER.
FOOD IS A DIFFERENT MATTER!
HERE
EAT IT ALL.
PUT THE DISHES OUTSIDE YOUR ROOM WHEN YOU'RE DONE.

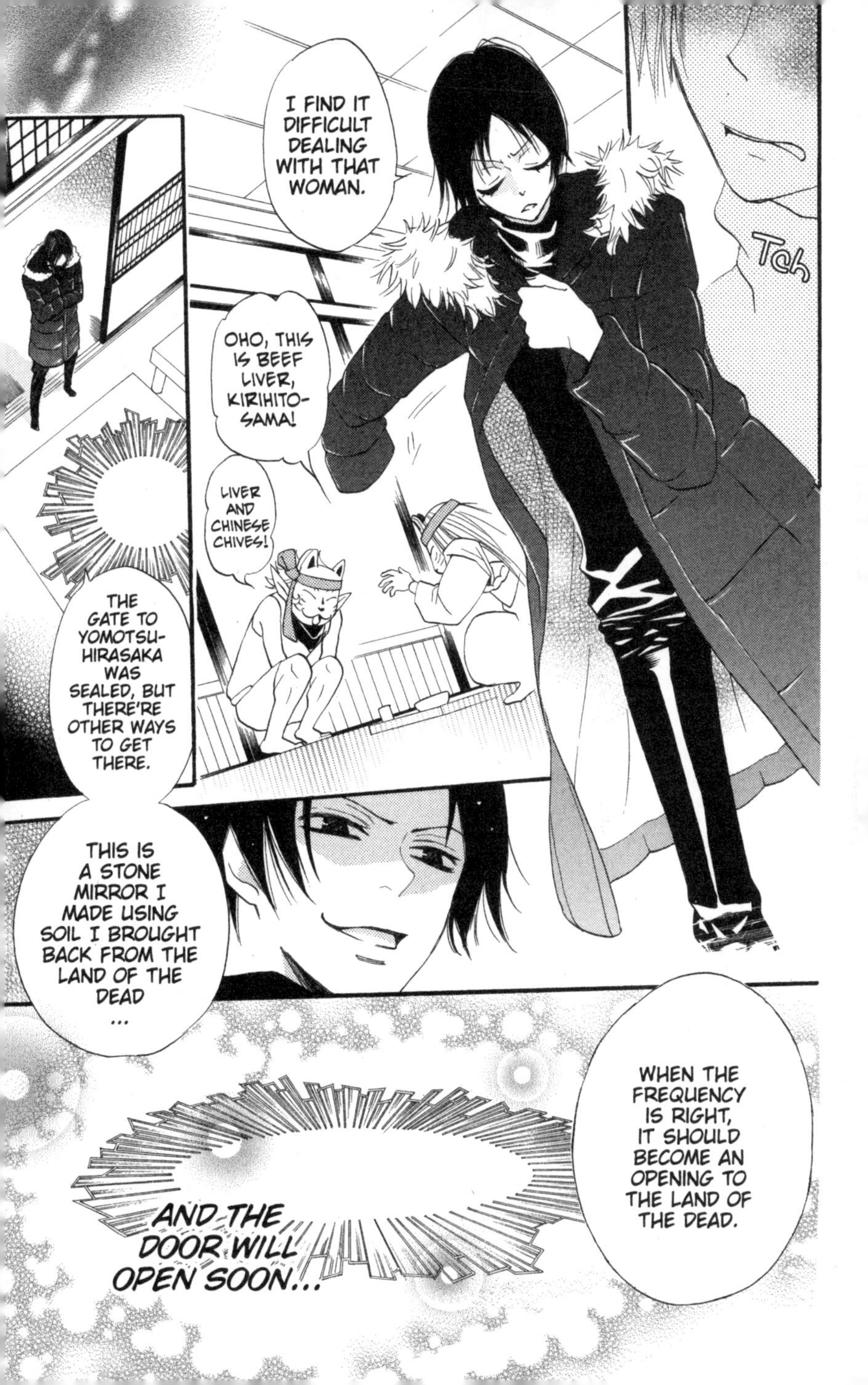
Tch
I FIND IT DIFFICULT DEALING WITH THAT WOMAN.
OHO, THIS IS BEEF LIVER, KIRIHITO-SAMA!
LIVER AND CHINESE CHIVES!
THE GATE TO YOMOTSU-HIRASAKA WAS SEALED, BUT THERE'RE OTHER WAYS TO GET THERE.
THIS IS A STONE MIRROR I MADE USING SOIL I BROUGHT BACK FROM THE LAND OF THE DEAD ...
WHEN THE FREQUENCY IS RIGHT, IT SHOULD BECOME AN OPENING TO THE LAND OF THE DEAD.
AND THE DOOR WILL OPEN SOON...

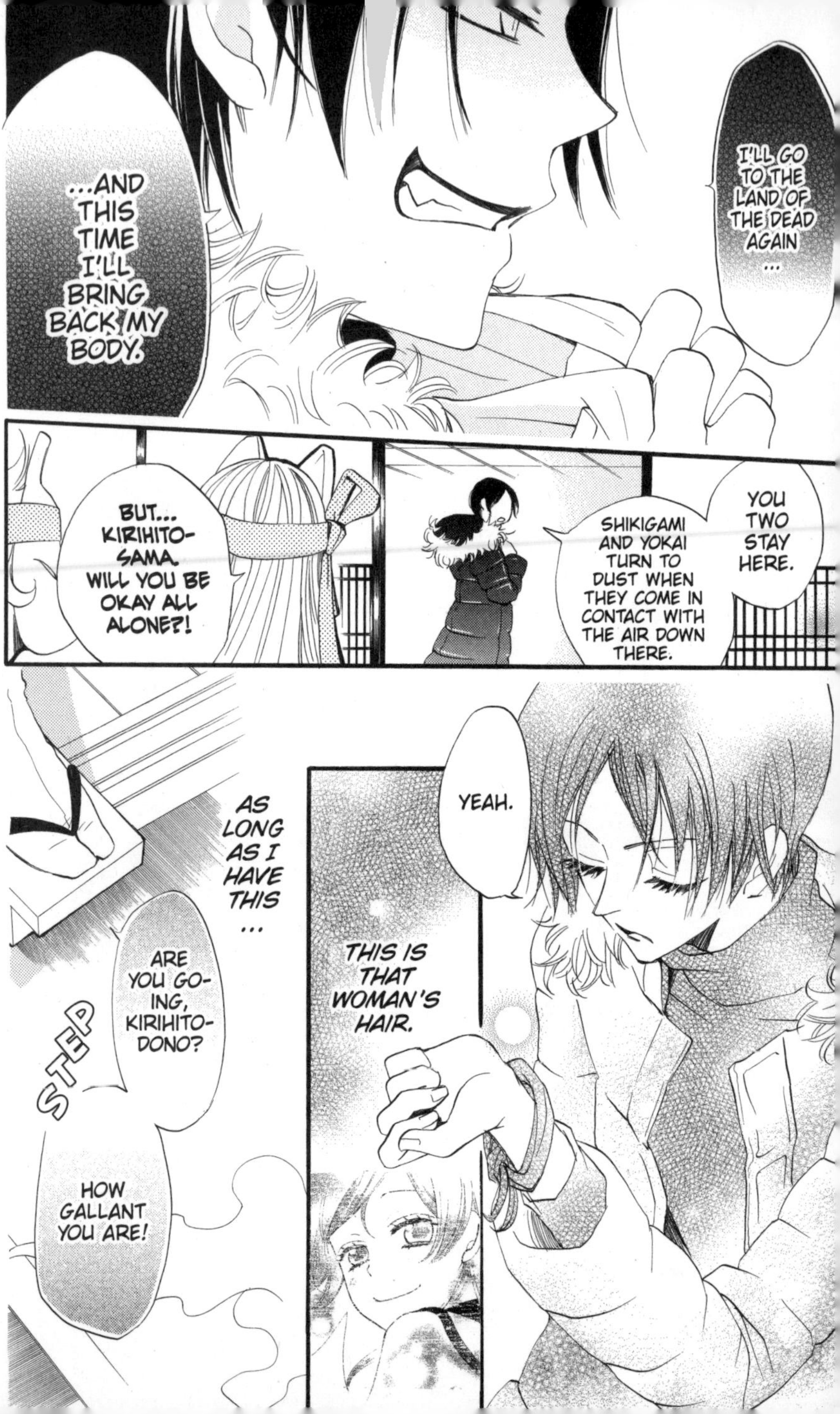
I'LL GO TO THE LAND OF THE DEAD AGAIN...
...AND THIS TIME I'LL BRING BACK MY BODY.
YOU TWO STAY HERE.
SHIKIGAMI AND YOKAI TURN TO DUST WHEN THEY COME IN CONTACT WITH THE AIR DOWN THERE.
BUT... KIRIHITO-SAMA. WILL YOU BE OKAY ALL ALONE?!
YEAH.
THIS IS THAT WOMAN'S HAIR.
AS LONG AS I HAVE THIS...
STEP
ARE YOU GOING, KIRIHITO-DONO?
HOW GALLANT YOU ARE!

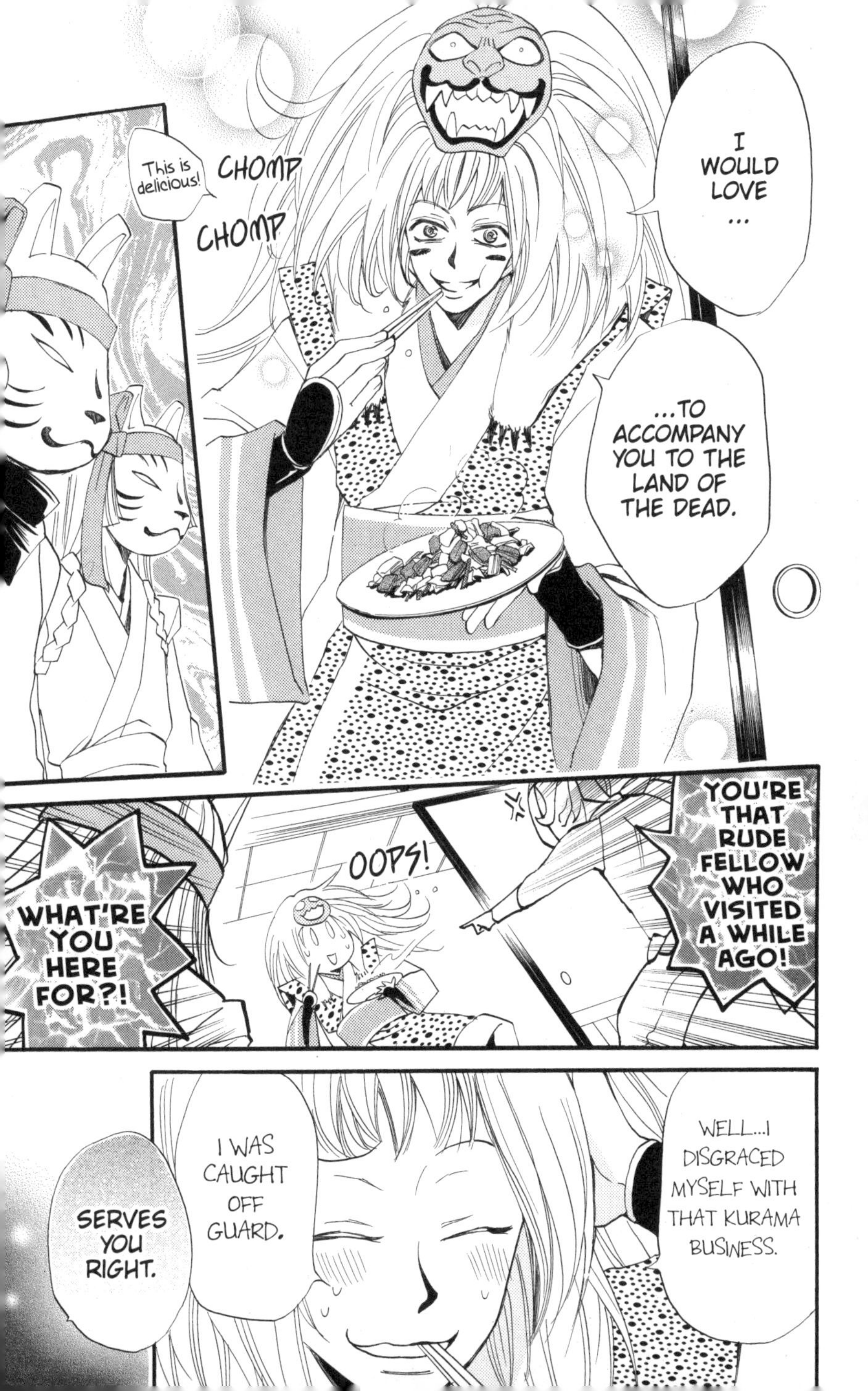
I WOULD LOVE ...
...TO ACCOMPANY YOU TO THE LAND OF THE DEAD.
This is delicious!
CHOMP
CHOMP
YOU'RE THAT RUDE FELLOW WHO VISITED A WHILE AGO!
OOPS!
WHAT'RE YOU HERE FOR?!
WELL...I DISGRACED MYSELF WITH THAT KURAMA BUSINESS.
I WAS CAUGHT OFF GUARD.
SERVES YOU RIGHT.

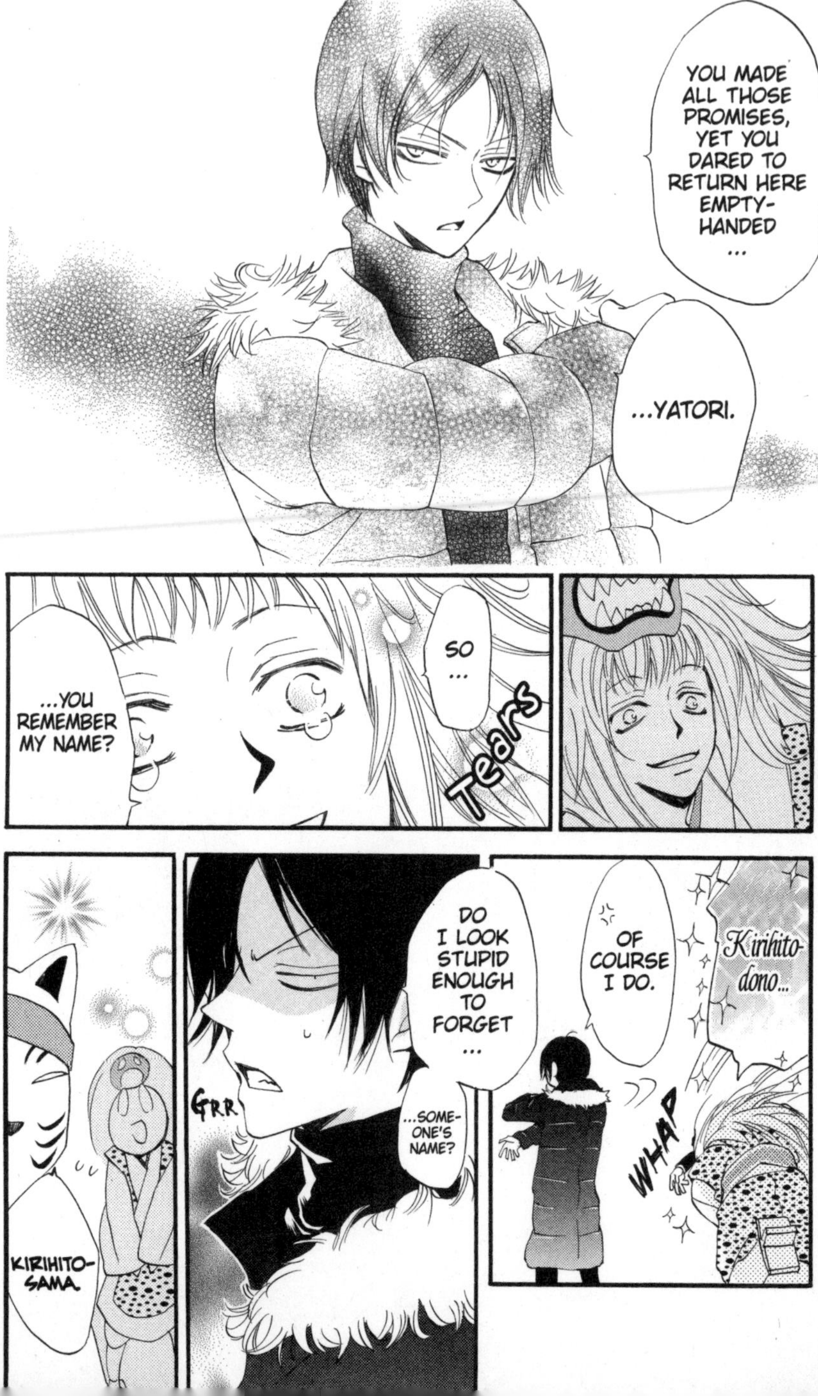
YOU MADE ALL THOSE PROMISES, YET YOU DARED TO RETURN HERE EMPTY-HANDED ...
...YATORI.
SO ...
Tears
...YOU REMEMBER MY NAME?
Kirihito-dono...
OF COURSE I DO.
WHAP
DO I LOOK STUPID ENOUGH TO FORGET ...
GRR
...SOME-ONE'S NAME?
KIRIHITO-SAMA.

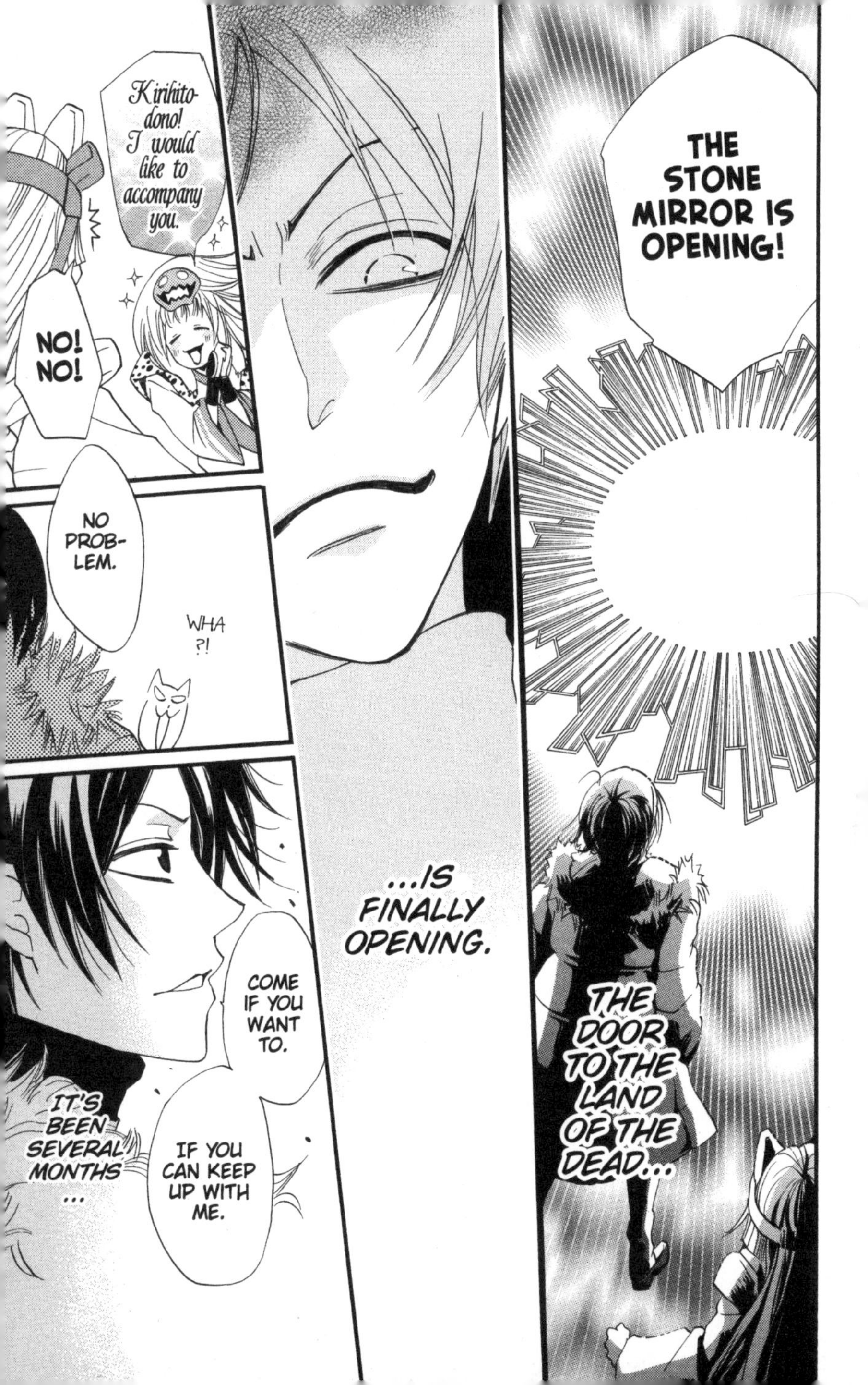
THE STONE MIRROR IS OPENING!
THE DOOR TO THE LAND OF THE DEAD...
...IS FINALLY OPENING.
Kirihito-dono! I would like to accompany you.
NO! NO!
NO PROBLEM.
WHA?!
COME IF YOU WANT TO.
IF YOU CAN KEEP UP WITH ME.
IT'S BEEN SEVERAL MONTHS...

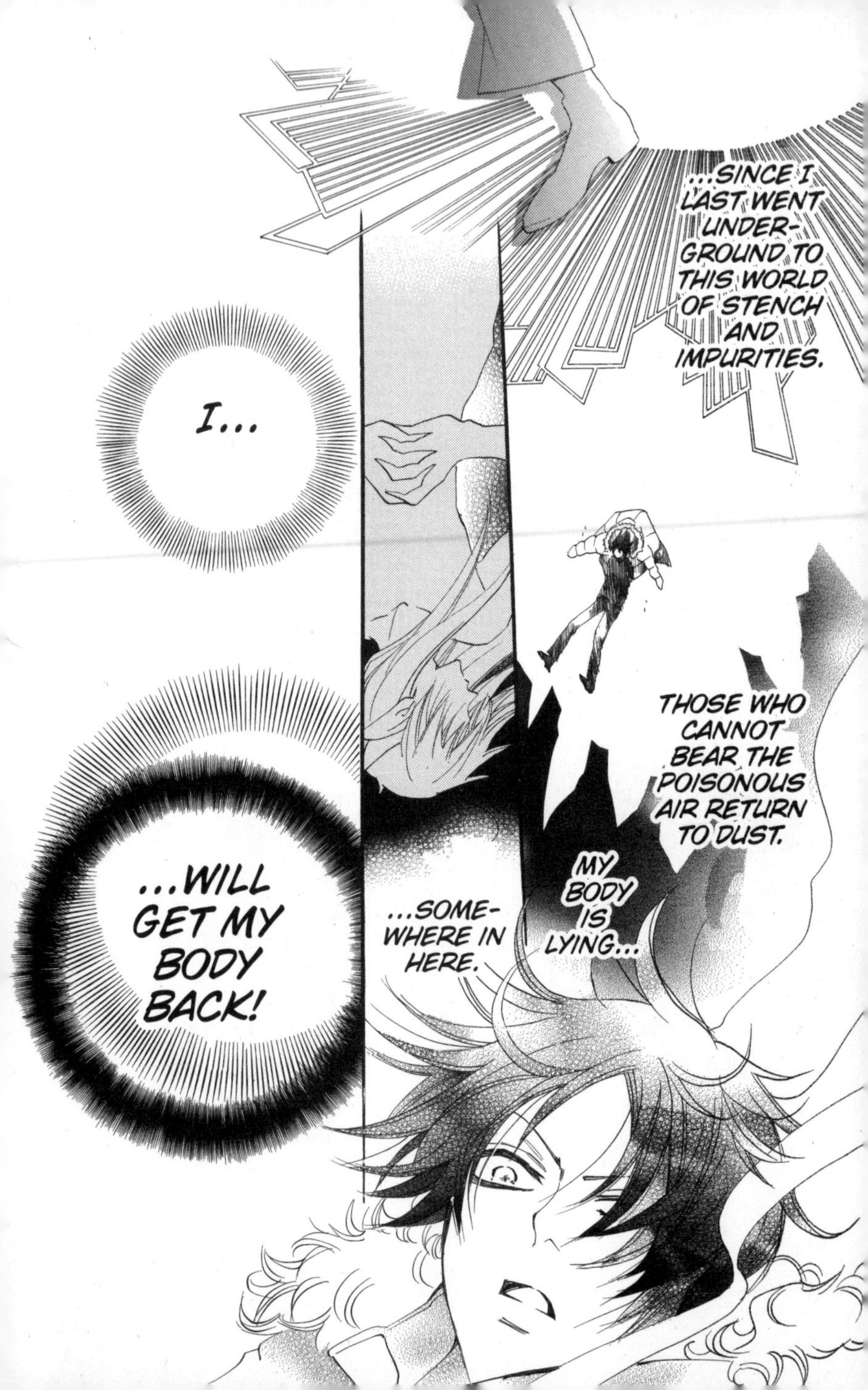
...SINCE I LAST WENT UNDER-GROUND TO THIS WORLD OF STENCH AND IMPURITIES.
THOSE WHO CANNOT BEAR THE POISONOUS AIR RETURN TO DUST.
MY BODY IS LYING...
...SOME-WHERE IN HERE.
I...
...WILL GET MY BODY BACK!

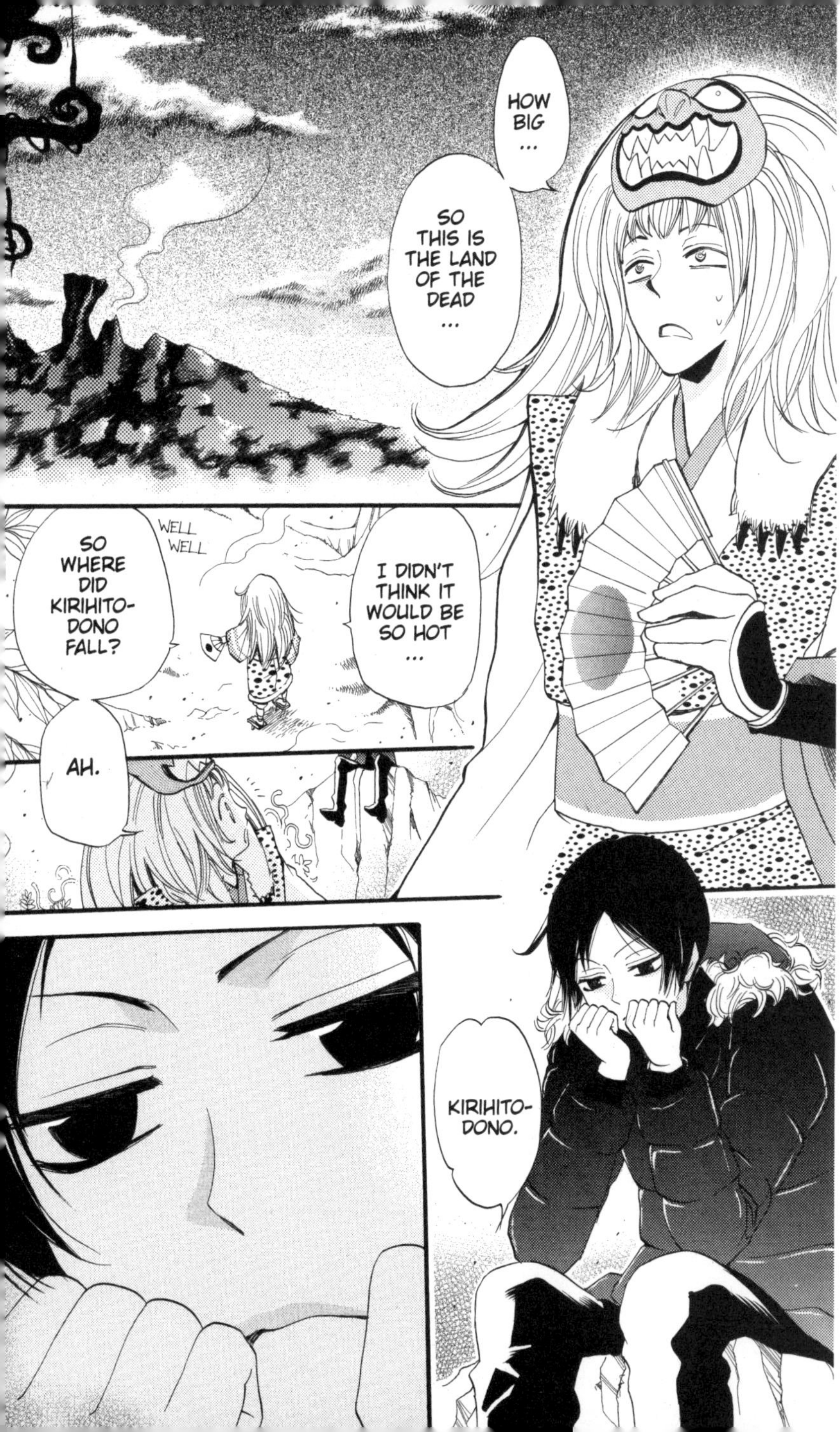
HOW BIG ...
SO THIS IS THE LAND OF THE DEAD ...
I DIDN'T THINK IT WOULD BE SO HOT ...
WELL WELL
SO WHERE DID KIRIHITO-DONO FALL?
AH.
KIRIHITO-DONO.

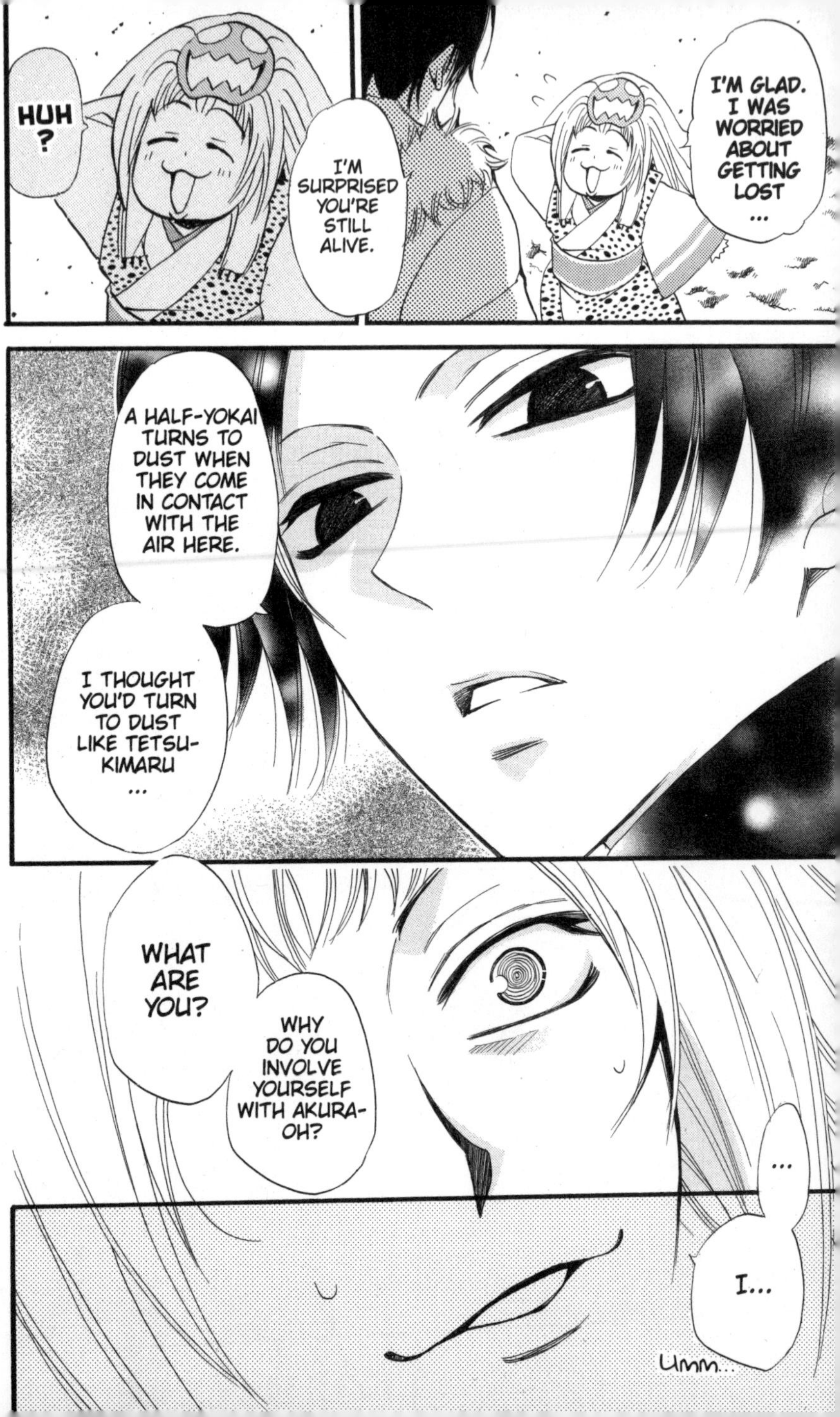
I'M GLAD. I WAS WORRIED ABOUT GETTING LOST ...
I'M SURPRISED YOU'RE STILL ALIVE.
HUH?
A HALF-YOKAI TURNS TO DUST WHEN THEY COME IN CONTACT WITH THE AIR HERE.
I THOUGHT YOU'D TURN TO DUST LIKE TETSU-KIMARU ...
WHAT ARE YOU?
WHY DO YOU INVOLVE YOURSELF WITH AKURA-OH?
...
I...
Umm...

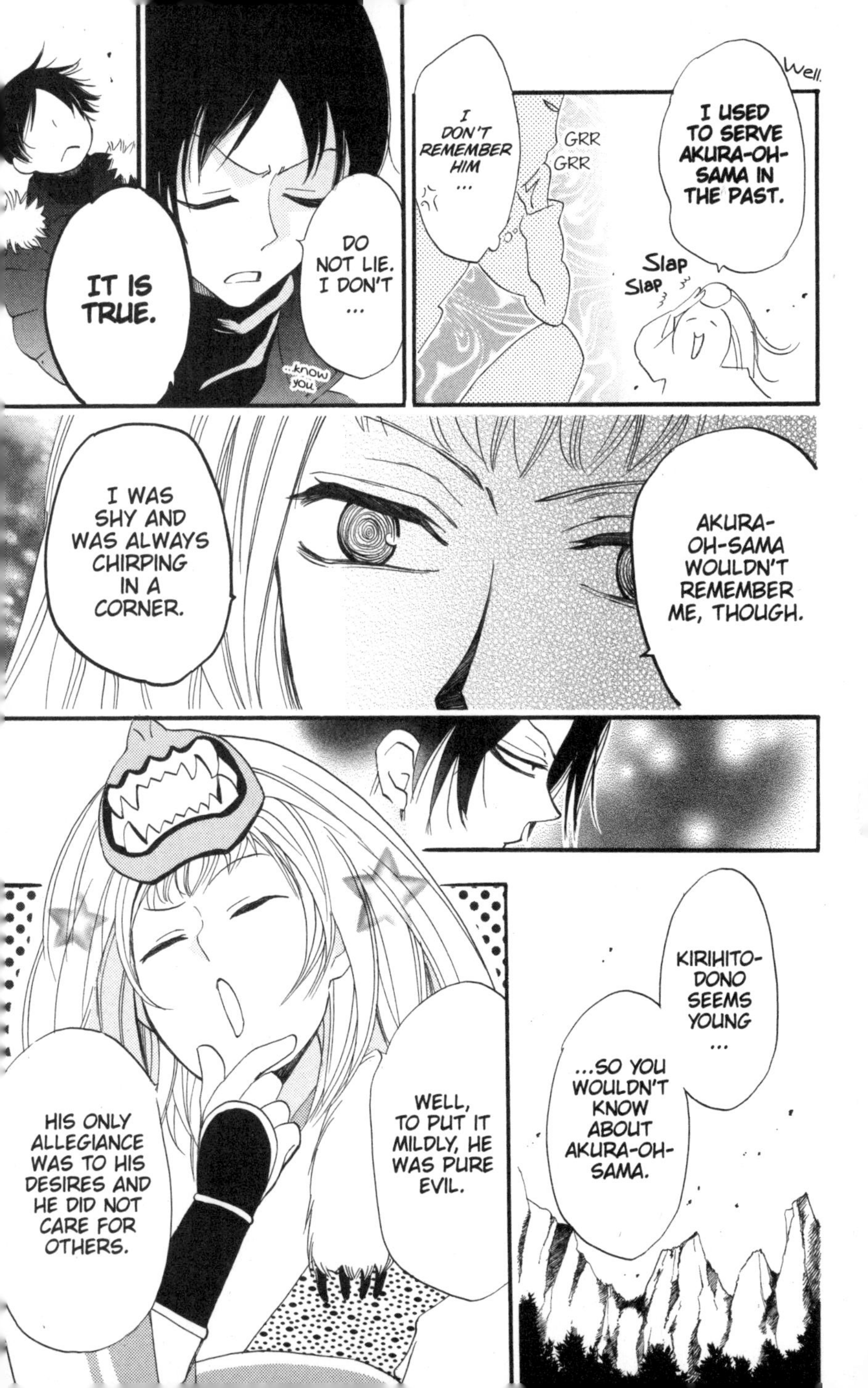
Well.
I USED TO SERVE AKURA-OH-SAMA IN THE PAST.
Slap
Slap
GRR
GRR
I DON'T REMEMBER HIM ...
DO NOT LIE. I DON'T ...
...know you.
IT IS TRUE.
AKURA-OH-SAMA WOULDN'T REMEMBER ME, THOUGH.
I WAS SHY AND WAS ALWAYS CHIRPING IN A CORNER.
KIRIHITO-DONO SEEMS YOUNG ...
...SO YOU WOULDN'T KNOW ABOUT AKURA-OH-SAMA.
WELL, TO PUT IT MILDLY, HE WAS PURE EVIL.
HIS ONLY ALLEGIANCE WAS TO HIS DESIRES AND HE DID NOT CARE FOR OTHERS.

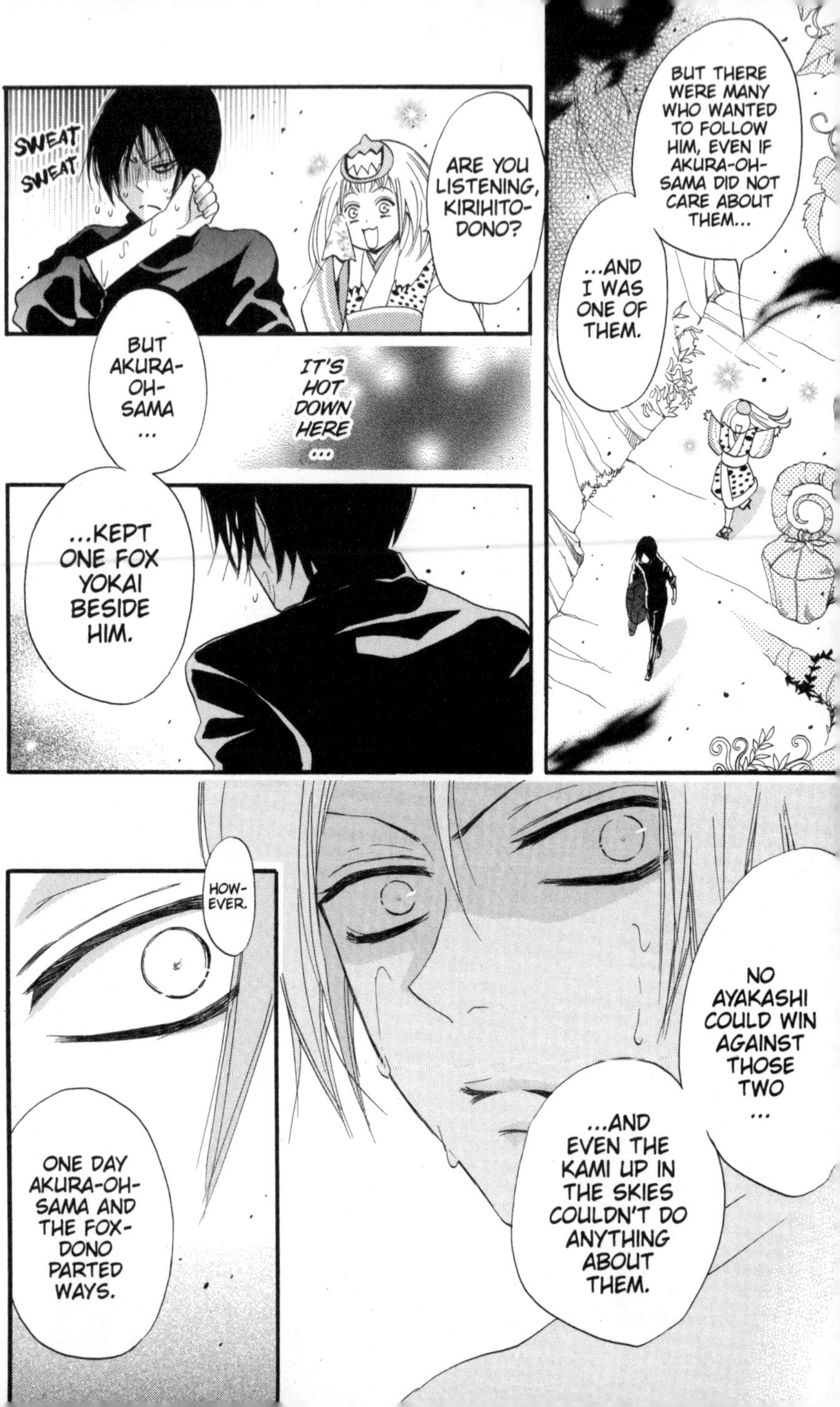
BUT THERE WERE MANY WHO WANTED TO FOLLOW HIM, EVEN IF AKURA-OH-SAMA DID NOT CARE ABOUT THEM...
...AND I WAS ONE OF THEM.
SWEAT SWEAT
ARE YOU LISTENING, KIRIHITO-DONO?
IT'S HOT DOWN HERE...
BUT AKURA-OH-SAMA...
...KEPT ONE FOX YOKAI BESIDE HIM.
NO AYAKASHI COULD WIN AGAINST THOSE TWO...
...AND EVEN THE KAMI UP IN THE SKIES COULDN'T DO ANYTHING ABOUT THEM.
HOW-EVER.
ONE DAY AKURA-OH-SAMA AND THE FOX-DONO PARTED WAYS.

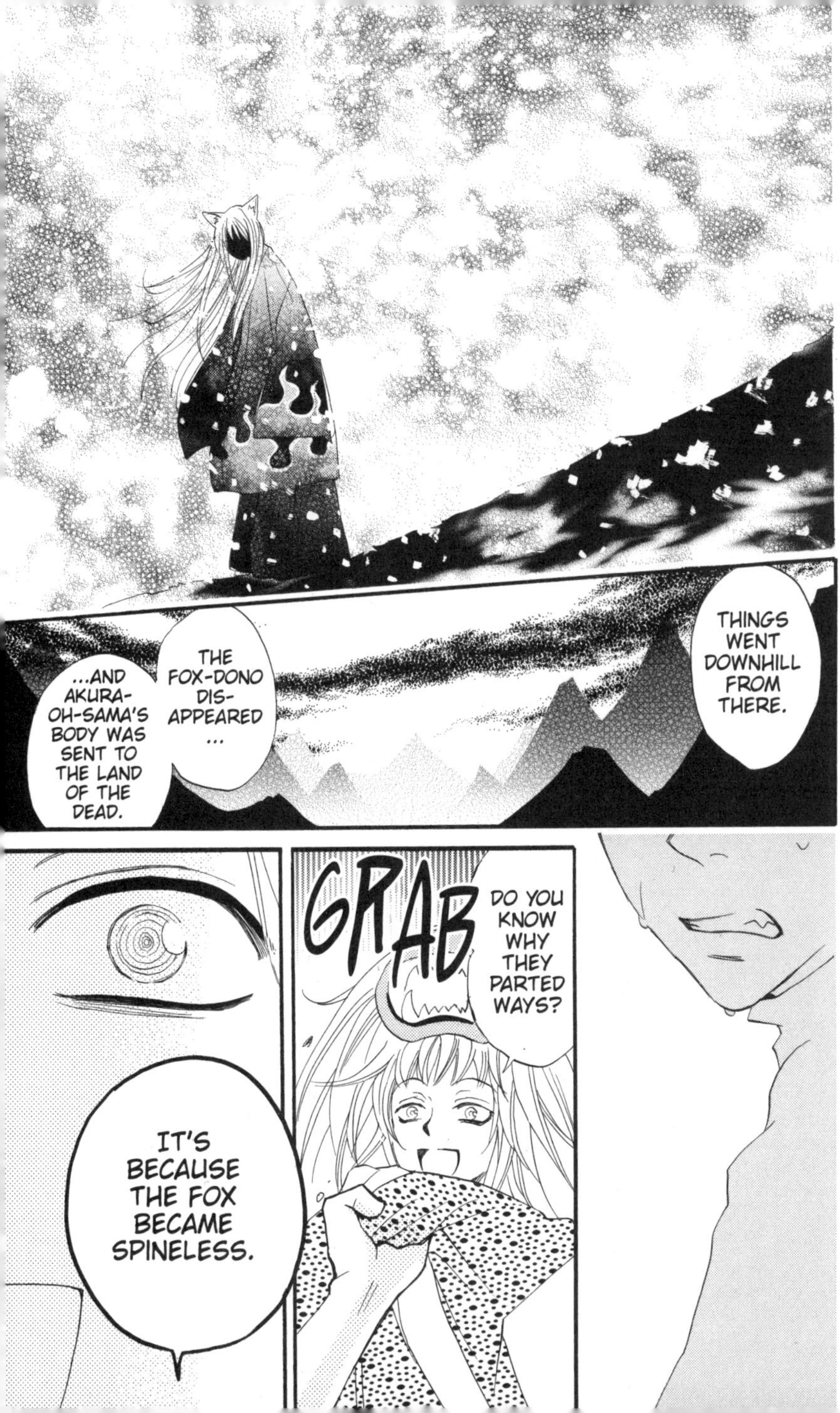
THINGS WENT DOWNHILL FROM THERE.
THE FOX-DONO DIS-APPEARED ...
...AND AKURA-OH-SAMA'S BODY WAS SENT TO THE LAND OF THE DEAD.
DO YOU KNOW WHY THEY PARTED WAYS?
GRAB
IT'S BECAUSE THE FOX BECAME SPINELESS.

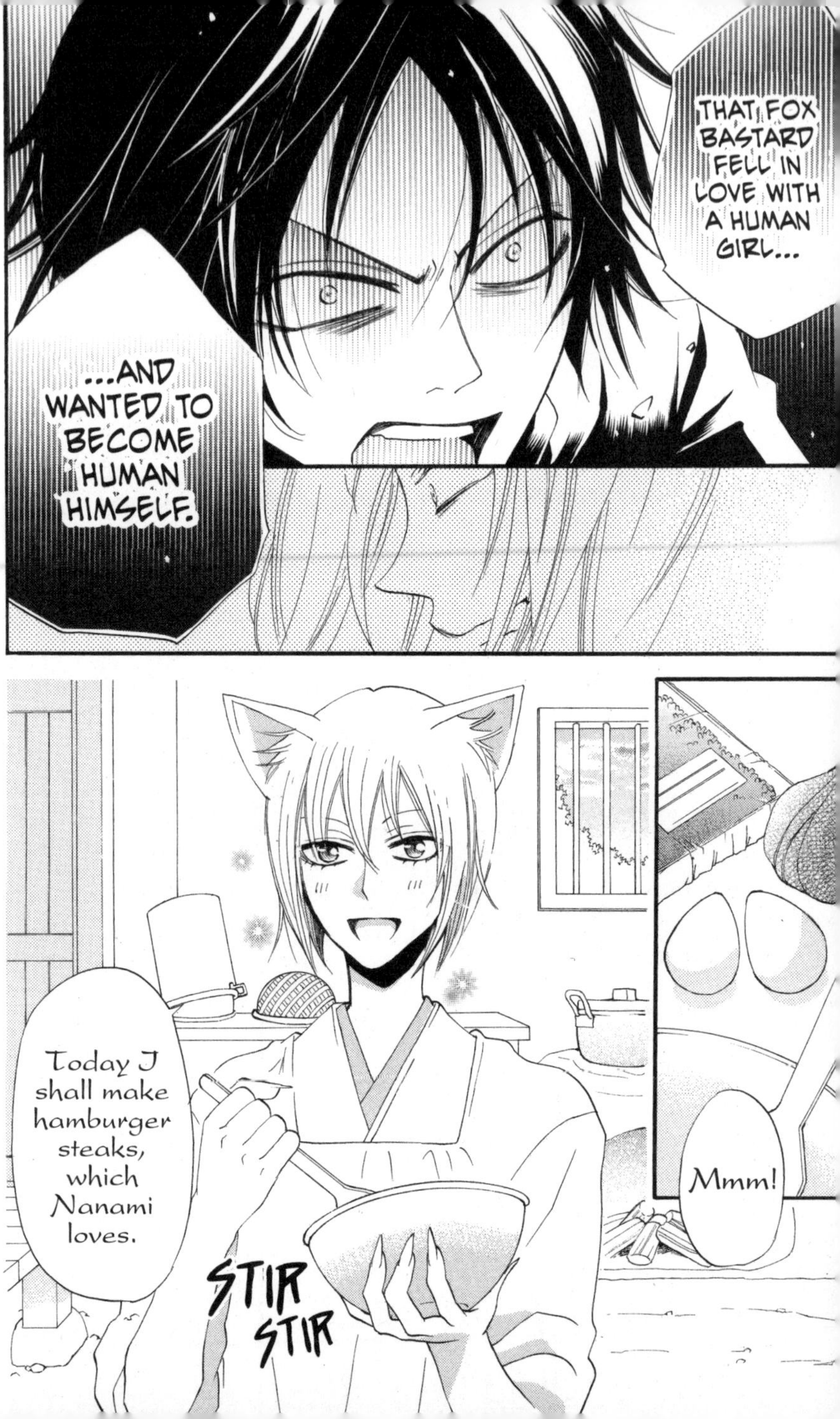
THAT FOX BASTARD FELL IN LOVE WITH A HUMAN GIRL...
...AND WANTED TO BECOME HUMAN HIMSELF.
Mmm!
Today I shall make hamburger steaks, which Nanami loves.
STIR STIR

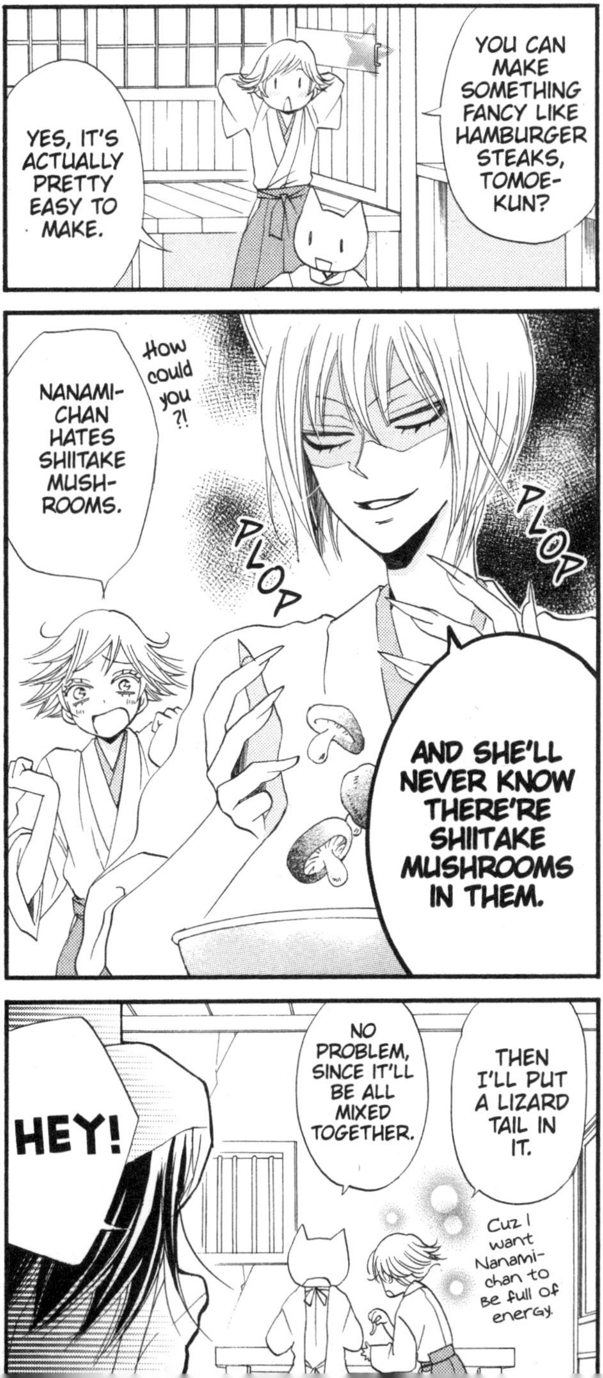
YOU CAN MAKE SOMETHING FANCY LIKE HAMBURGER STEAKS, TOMOE-KUN?
YES, IT'S ACTUALLY PRETTY EASY TO MAKE.
PLOP
How could you?!
NANAMI-CHAN HATES SHIITAKE MUSH-ROOMS.
PLOP
AND SHE'LL NEVER KNOW THERE'RE SHIITAKE MUSHROOMS IN THEM.
THEN I'LL PUT A LIZARD TAIL IN IT.
NO PROBLEM, SINCE IT'LL BE ALL MIXED TOGETHER.
Cuz I want Nanami-chan to be full of energy.
HEY!

(Assistant)

Okazaki's Kamisama Working Hell Recipe ①

In volume 11, I am introducing recipes of dishes that Juli Sensei liked. I made them while everyone was working.

◉ Pork wrapped with plums and shiso leaves

① Salt and pepper the pork loin.

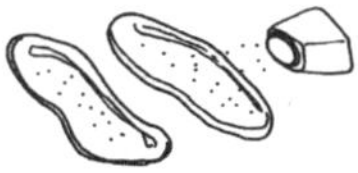

② Remove the pits from the pickled plums, and smash them using the side of the cooking knife.

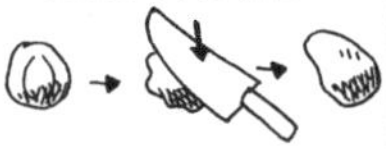

③ Remove the stem of the shiso leaves, and chop them up.

④ Layer a shiso leaf and some plum on the pork, and roll it up.

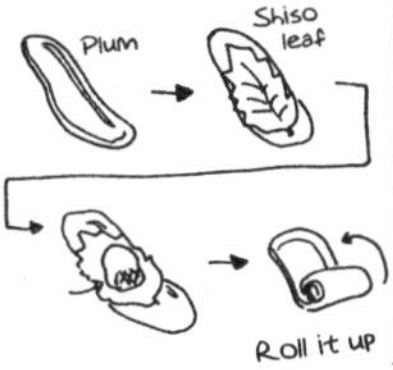
Plum
Shiso leaf
Roll it up

To be continued.

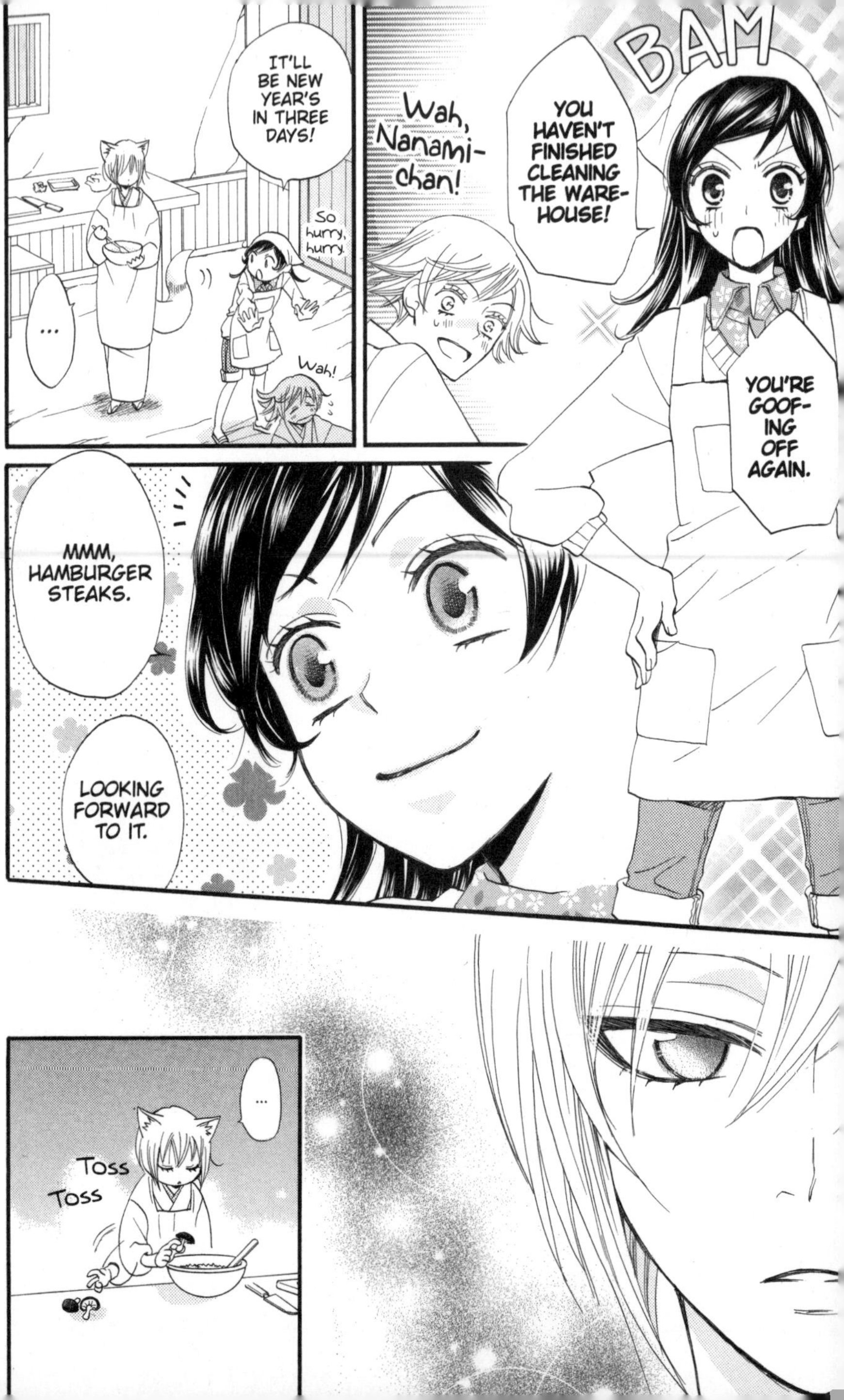
BAM
YOU HAVEN'T FINISHED CLEANING THE WAREHOUSE!
Wah, Nanami-chan!
YOU'RE GOOFING OFF AGAIN.
IT'LL BE NEW YEAR'S IN THREE DAYS!
So hurry, hurry.
Wah!
...
MMM, HAMBURGER STEAKS.
LOOKING FORWARD TO IT.
...
Toss
Toss

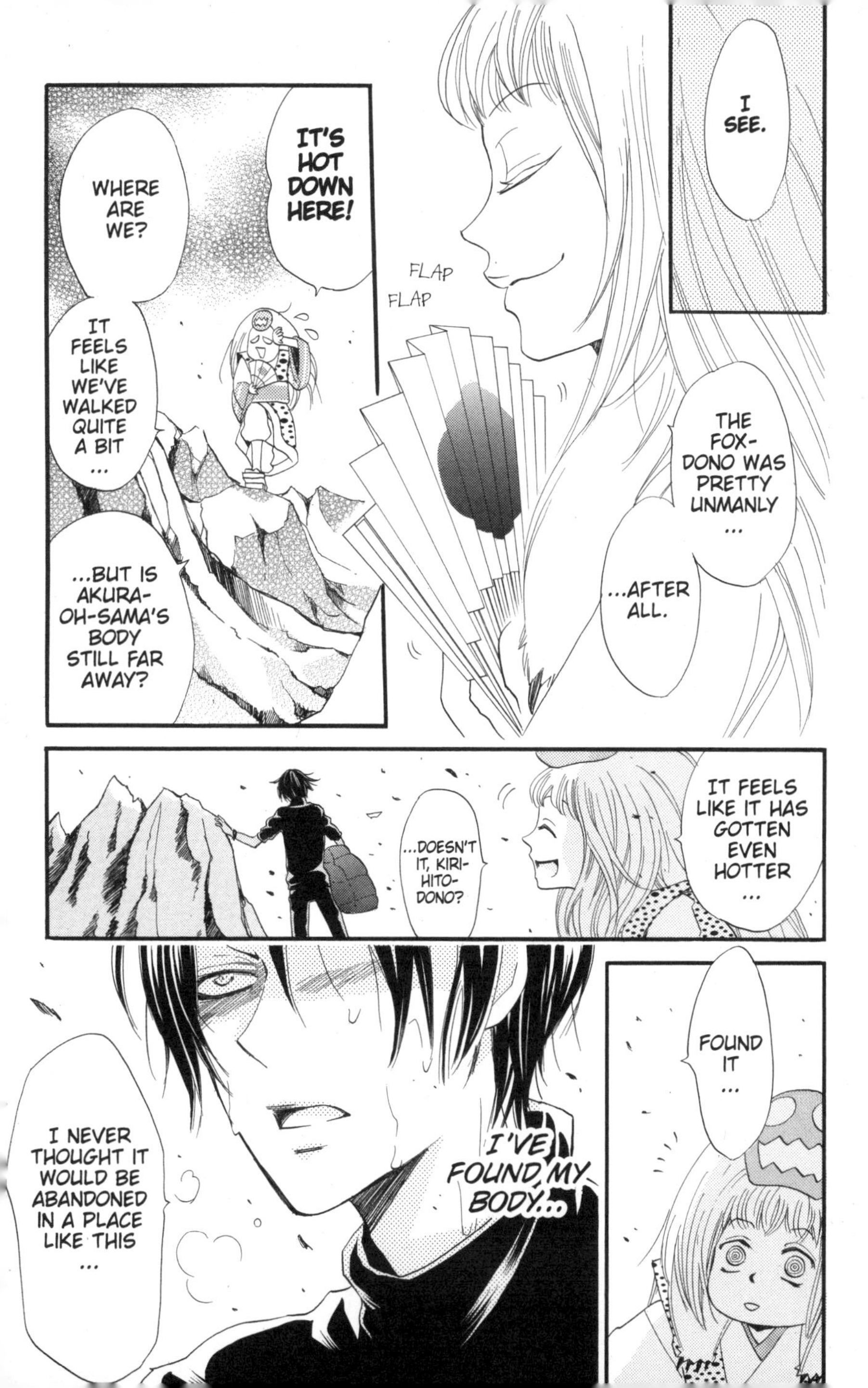
I SEE.
FLAP
FLAP
THE FOX-DONO WAS PRETTY UNMANLY...
...AFTER ALL.
IT'S HOT DOWN HERE!
WHERE ARE WE?
IT FEELS LIKE WE'VE WALKED QUITE A BIT...
...BUT IS AKURA-OH-SAMA'S BODY STILL FAR AWAY?
IT FEELS LIKE IT HAS GOTTEN EVEN HOTTER...
...DOESN'T IT, KIRIHITO-DONO?
FOUND IT...
I'VE FOUND MY BODY...
I NEVER THOUGHT IT WOULD BE ABANDONED IN A PLACE LIKE THIS...

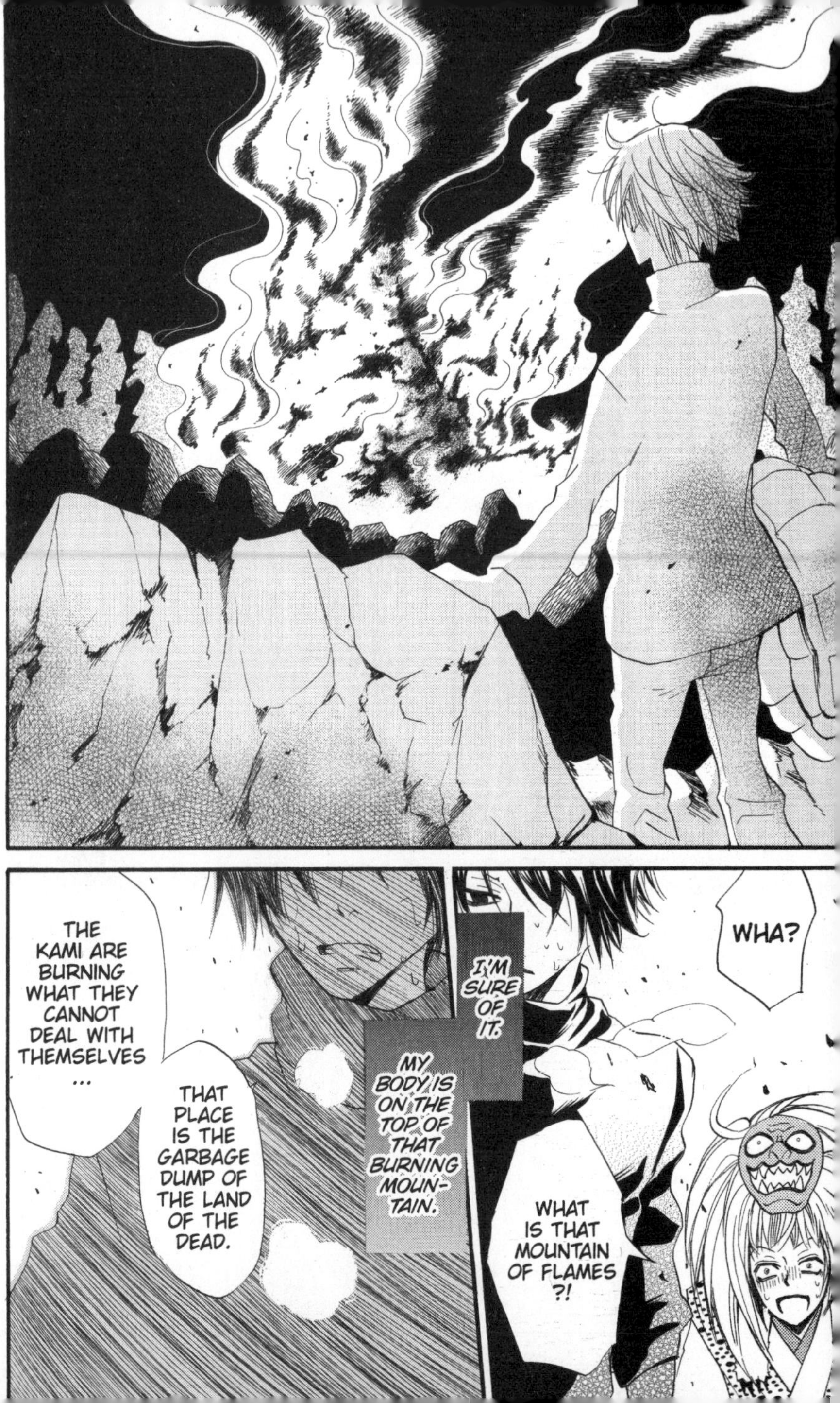
WHA?
WHAT IS THAT MOUNTAIN OF FLAMES?!
I'M SURE OF IT.
MY BODY IS ON THE TOP OF THAT BURNING MOUN-TAIN.
THE KAMI ARE BURNING WHAT THEY CANNOT DEAL WITH THEMSELVES...
THAT PLACE IS THE GARBAGE DUMP OF THE LAND OF THE DEAD.

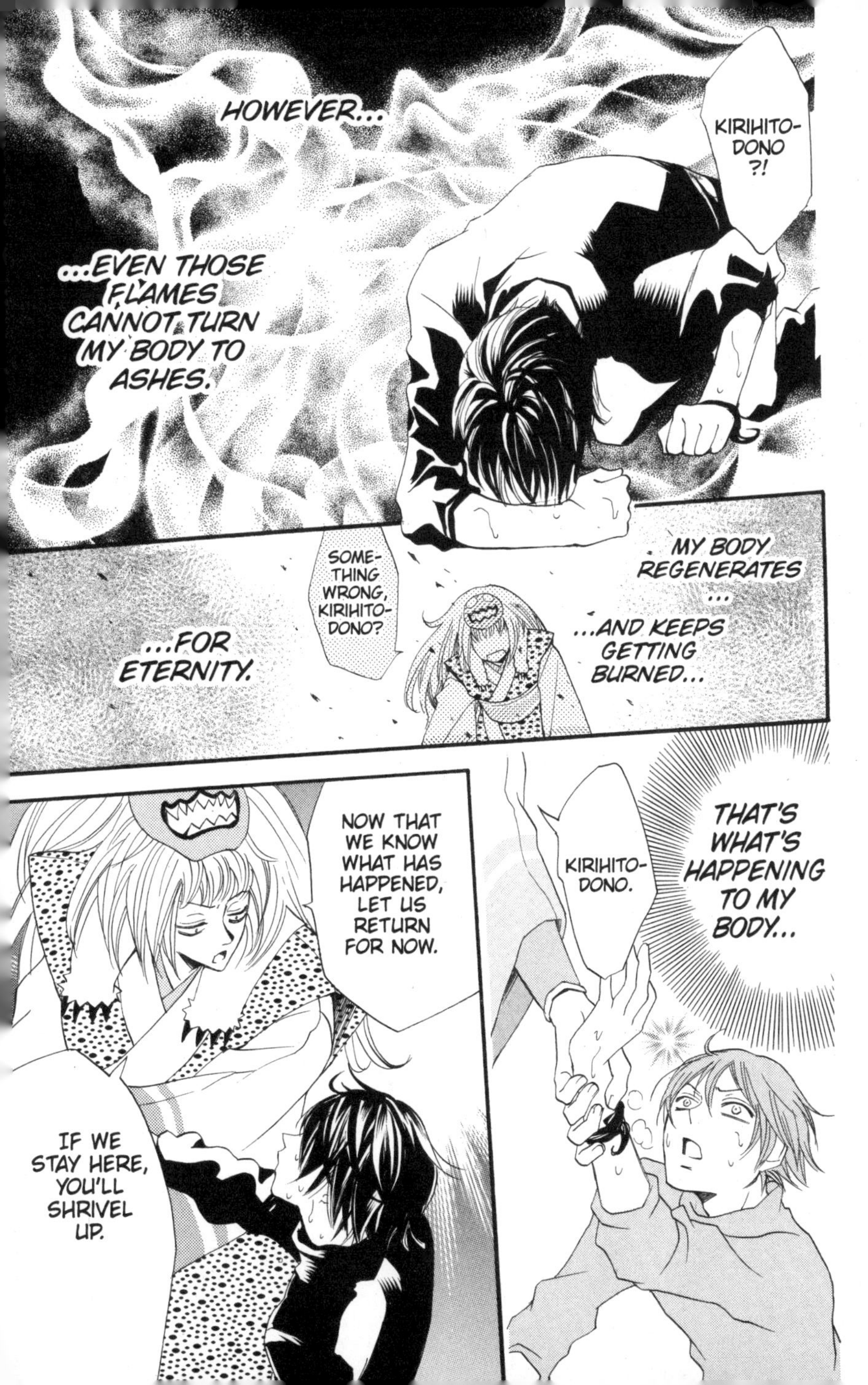
KIRIHITO-DONO?!
HOWEVER...
...EVEN THOSE FLAMES CANNOT TURN MY BODY TO ASHES.
MY BODY REGENERATES...
...AND KEEPS GETTING BURNED...
SOME-THING WRONG, KIRIHITO-DONO?
...FOR ETERNITY.
THAT'S WHAT'S HAPPENING TO MY BODY...
KIRIHITO-DONO.
NOW THAT WE KNOW WHAT HAS HAPPENED, LET US RETURN FOR NOW.
IF WE STAY HERE, YOU'LL SHRIVEL UP.

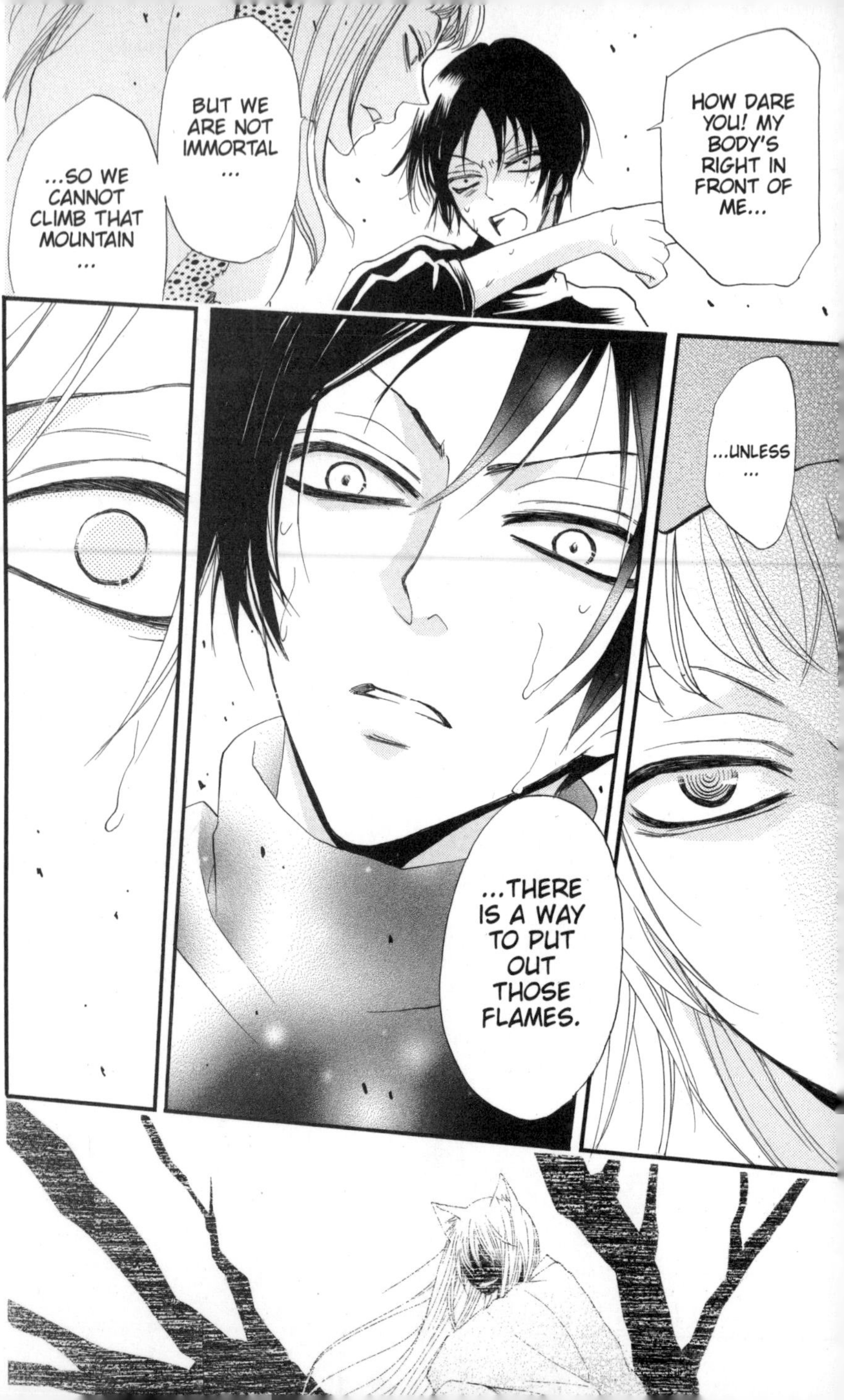
HOW DARE YOU! MY BODY'S RIGHT IN FRONT OF ME...
BUT WE ARE NOT IMMORTAL...
...SO WE CANNOT CLIMB THAT MOUNTAIN...
...UNLESS...
...THERE IS A WAY TO PUT OUT THOSE FLAMES.

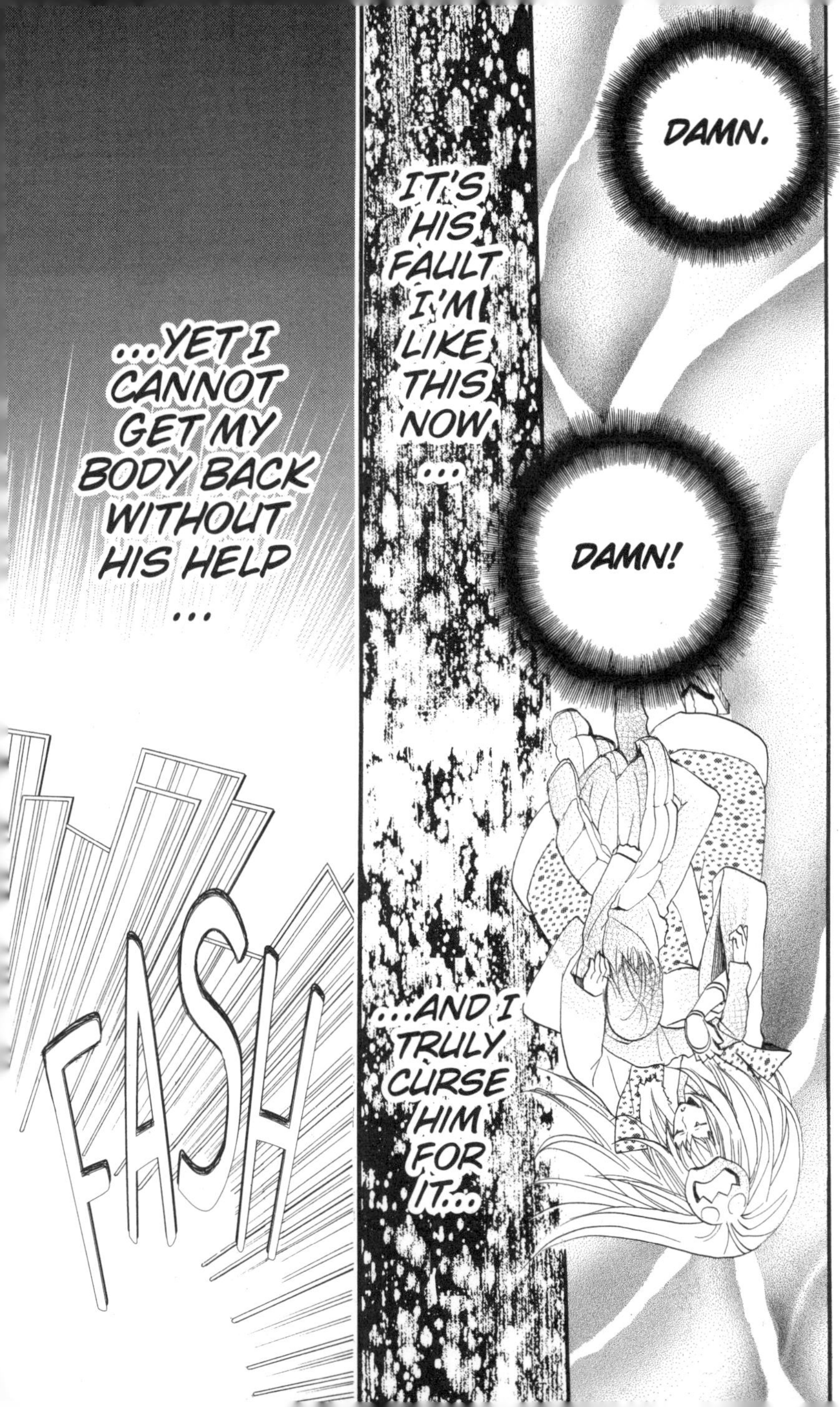
DAMN.
IT'S HIS FAULT I'M LIKE THIS NOW...
DAMN!
...AND I TRULY CURSE HIM FOR IT...
...YET I CANNOT GET MY BODY BACK WITHOUT HIS HELP...
FASH

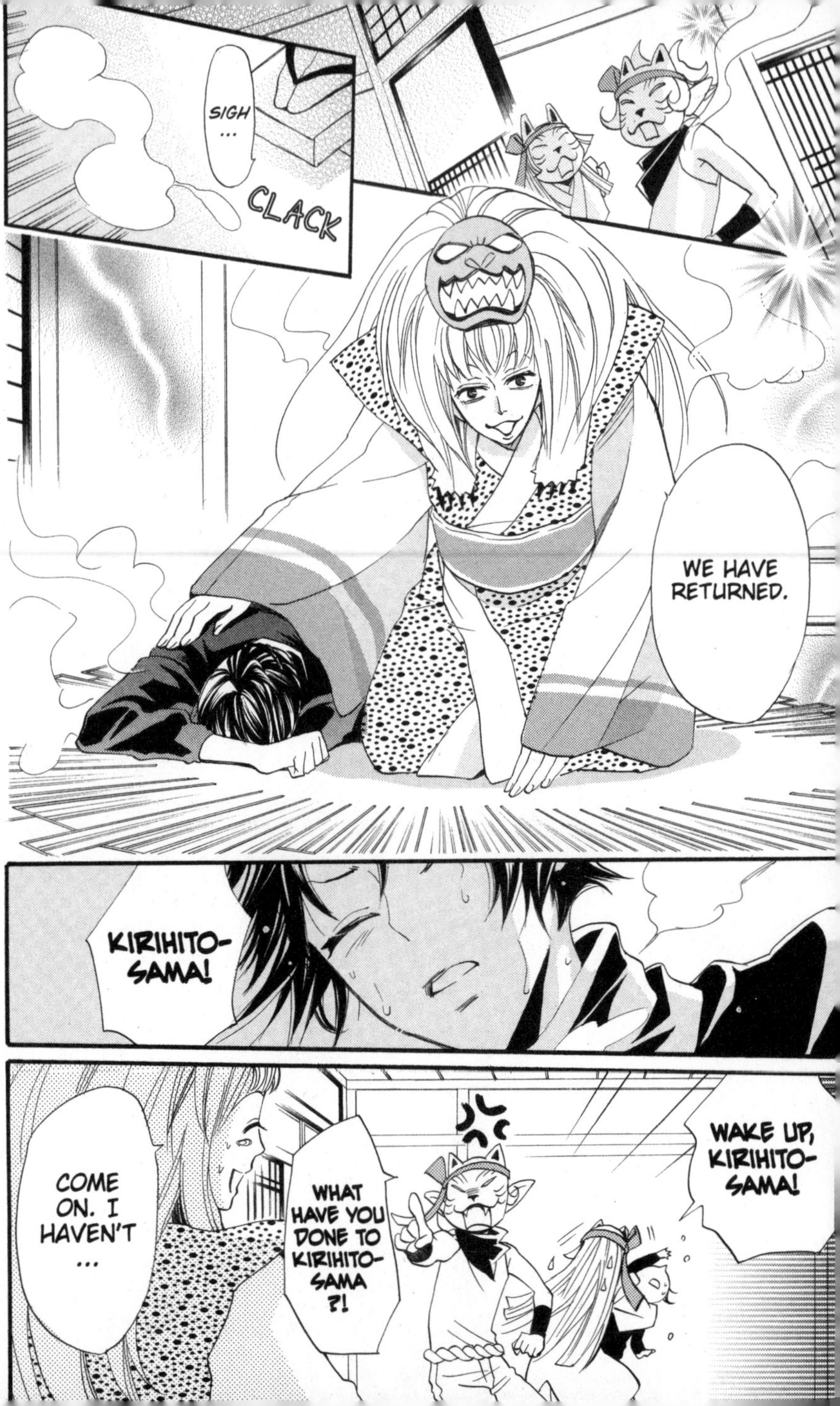
SIGH ...
CLACK
WE HAVE RETURNED.
KIRIHITO-SAMA!
WAKE UP, KIRIHITO-SAMA!
WHAT HAVE YOU DONE TO KIRIHITO-SAMA ?!
COME ON. I HAVEN'T ...

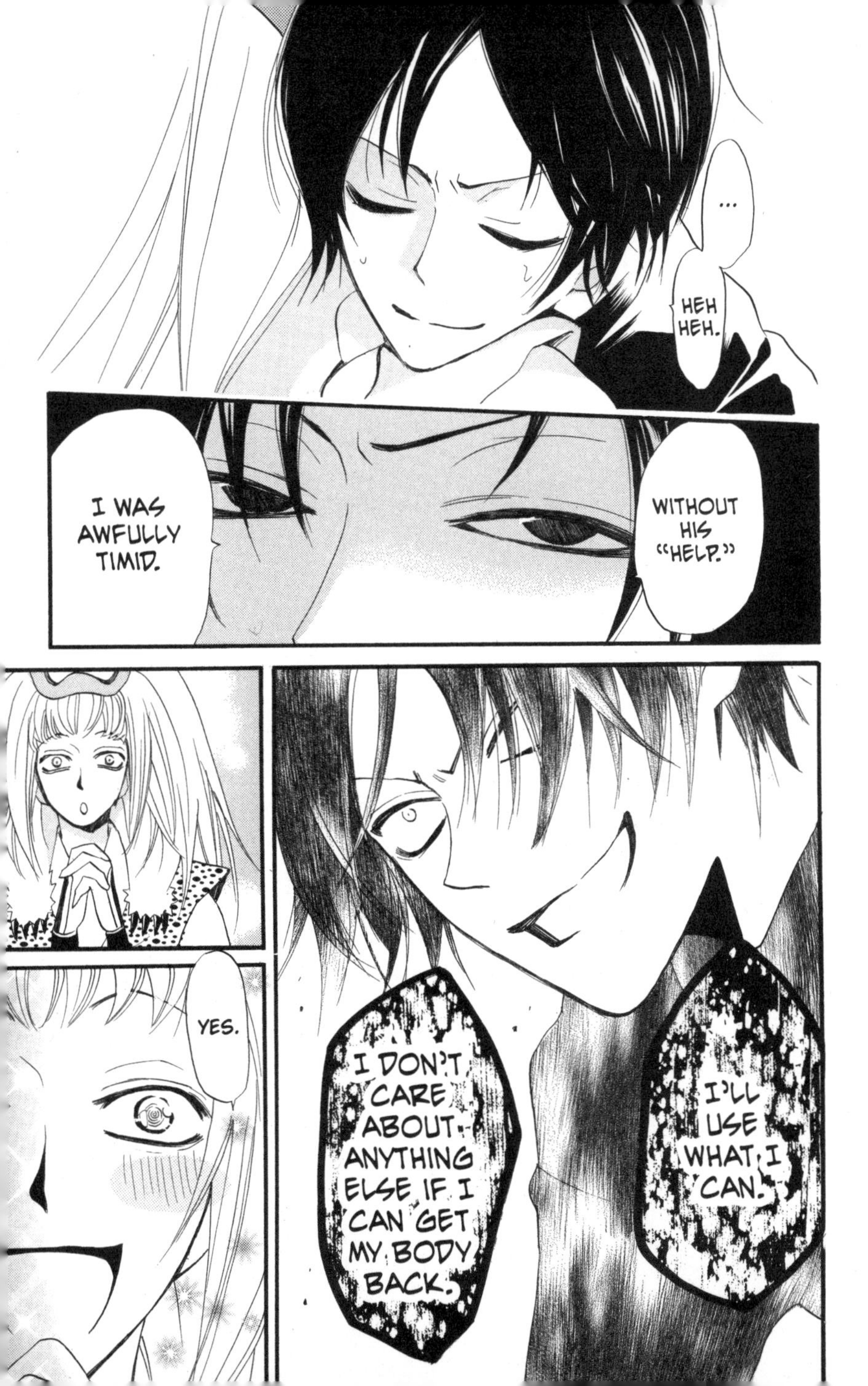
...
HEH HEH.
WITHOUT HIS "HELP."
I WAS AWFULLY TIMID.
I'LL USE WHAT I CAN.
I DON'T CARE ABOUT ANYTHING ELSE IF I CAN GET MY BODY BACK.
YES.

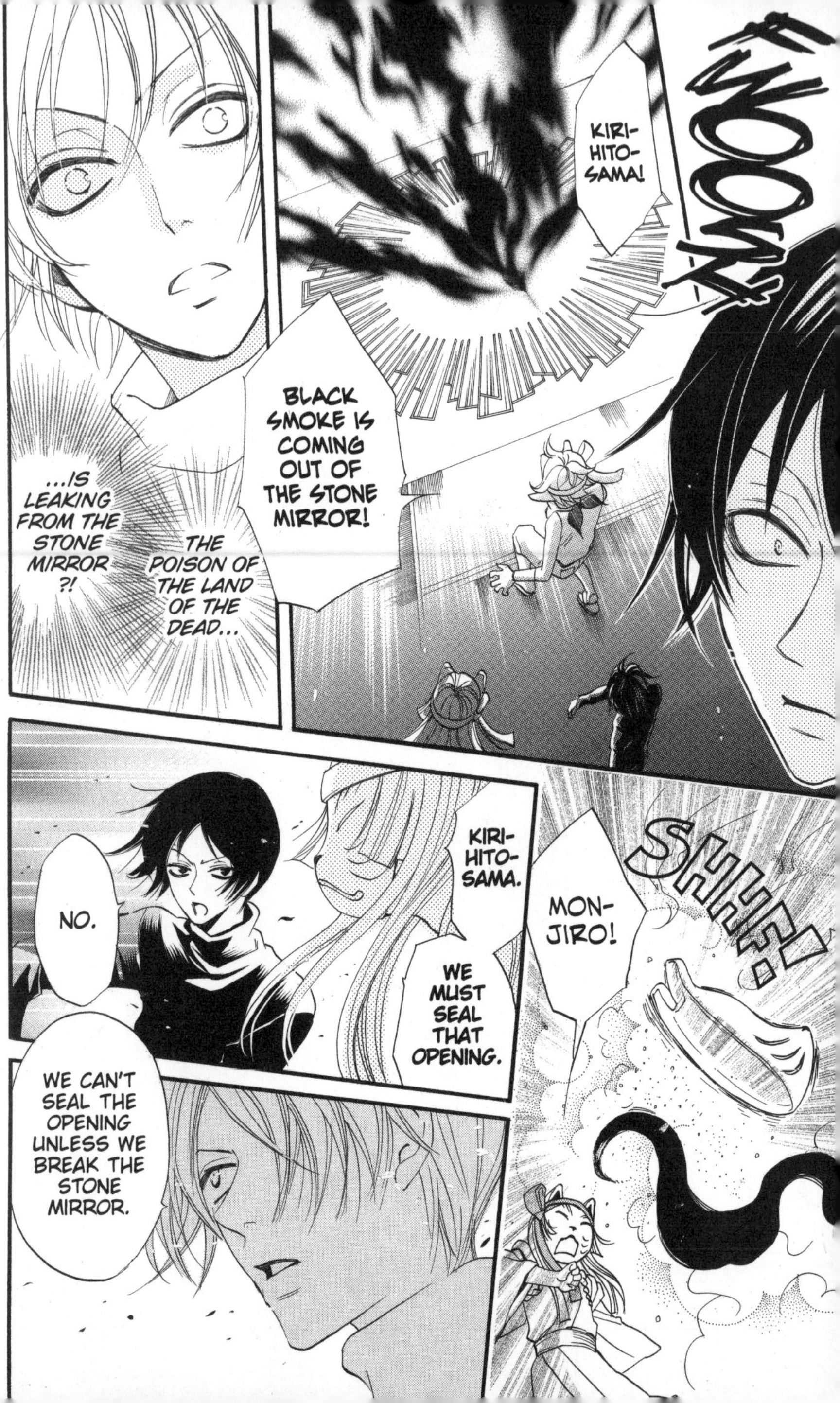
FWOOM
KIRI-HITO-SAMA!
BLACK SMOKE IS COMING OUT OF THE STONE MIRROR!
THE POISON OF THE LAND OF THE DEAD...
...IS LEAKING FROM THE STONE MIRROR ?!
SHHF!
MON-JIRO!
KIRI-HITO-SAMA.
WE MUST SEAL THAT OPENING.
NO.
WE CAN'T SEAL THE OPENING UNLESS WE BREAK THE STONE MIRROR.

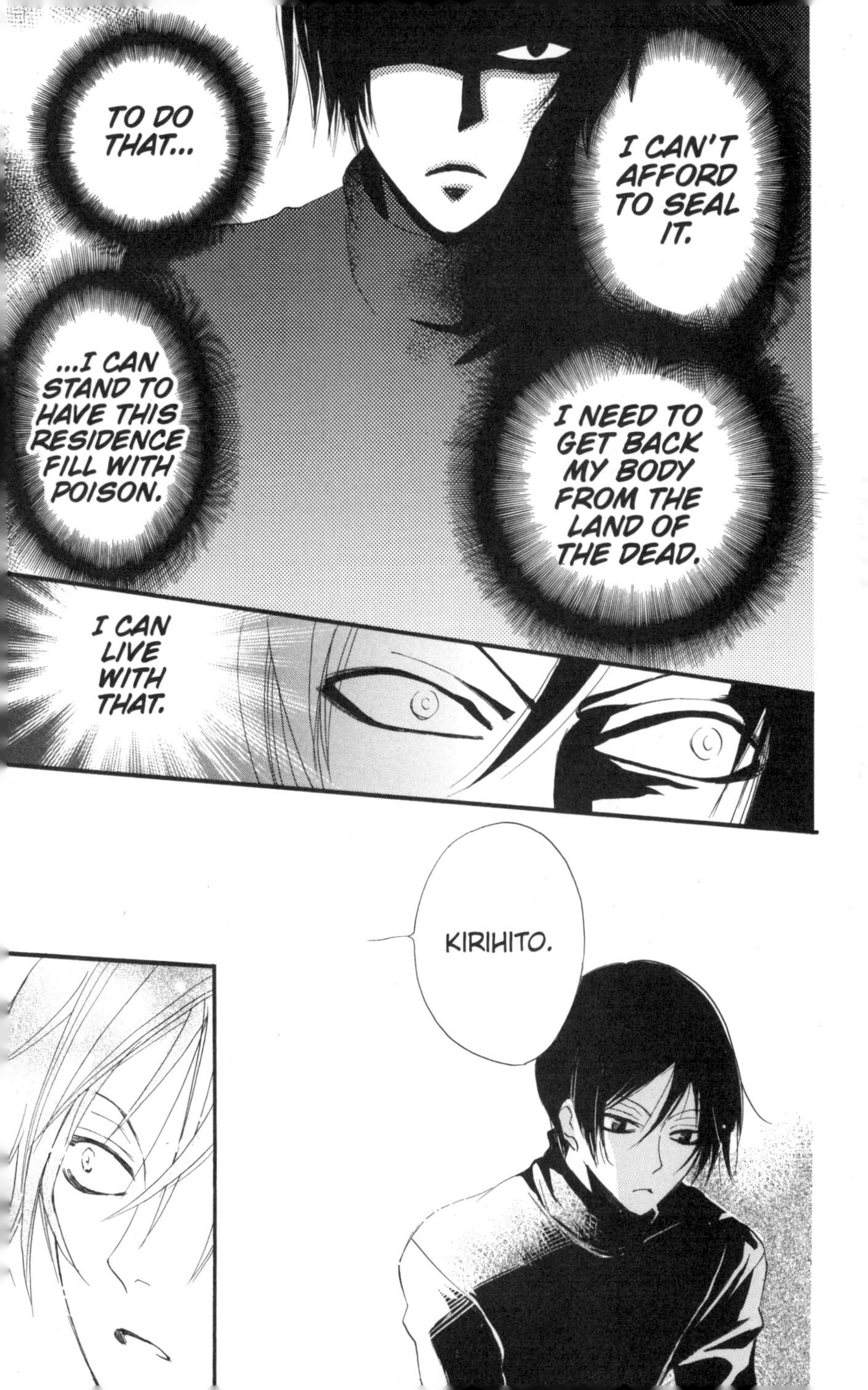
I CAN'T AFFORD TO SEAL IT.
I NEED TO GET BACK MY BODY FROM THE LAND OF THE DEAD.
TO DO THAT...
...I CAN STAND TO HAVE THIS RESIDENCE FILL WITH POISON.
I CAN LIVE WITH THAT.
KIRIHITO.

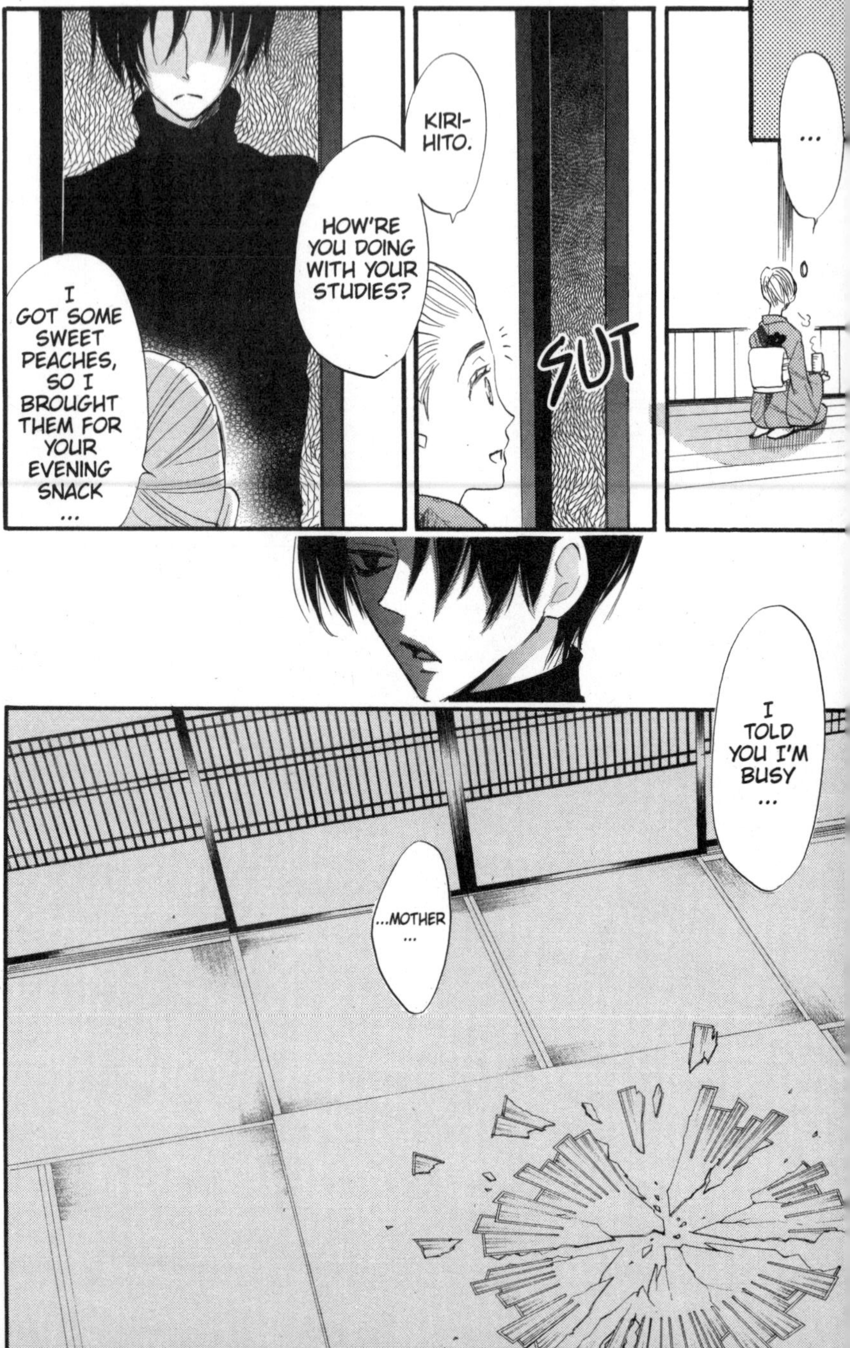
...
KIRI-HITO.
HOW'RE YOU DOING WITH YOUR STUDIES?
SUT
I GOT SOME SWEET PEACHES, SO I BROUGHT THEM FOR YOUR EVENING SNACK ...
I TOLD YOU I'M BUSY ...
...MOTHER ...

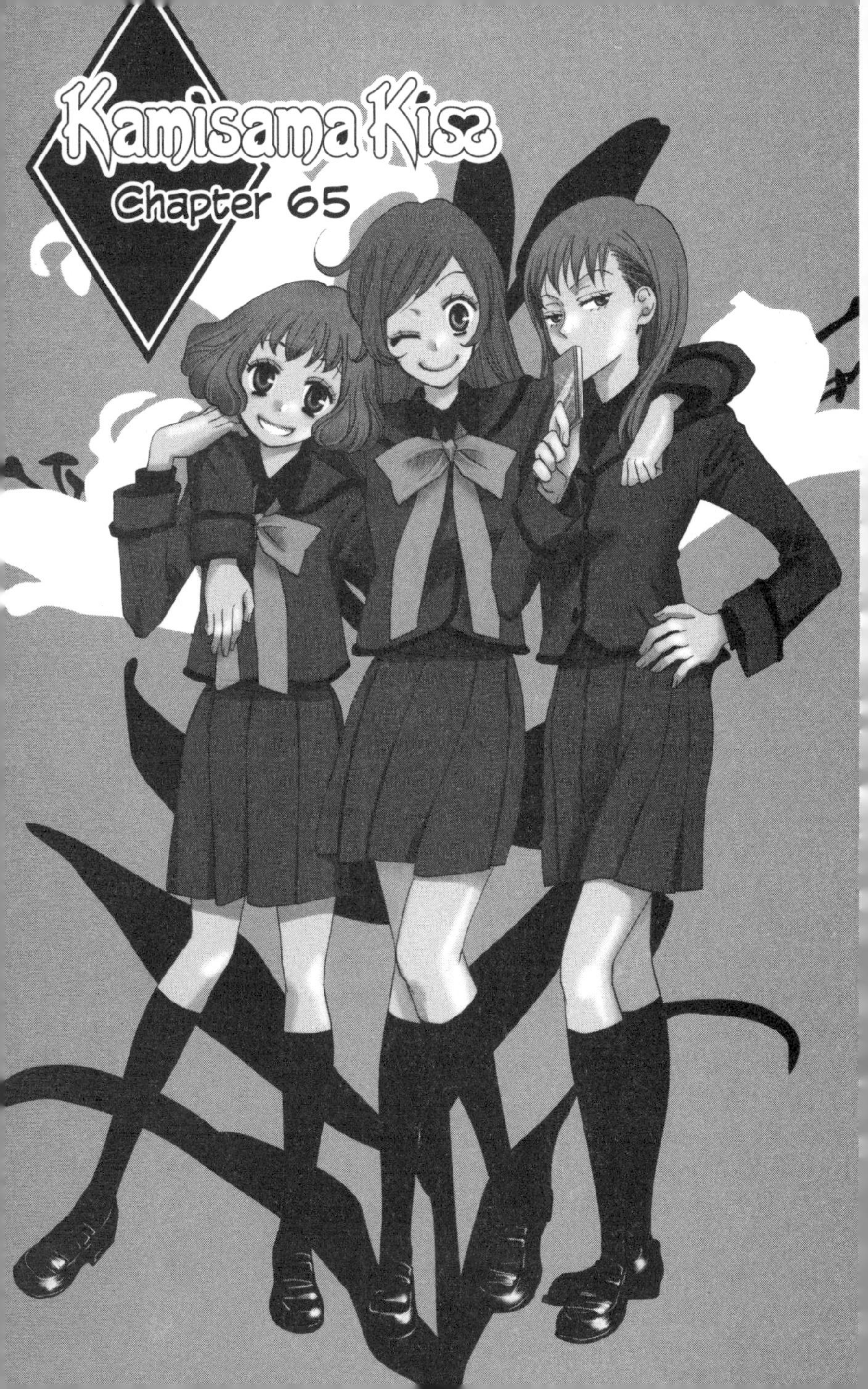
Kamisama Kiss
Chapter 65

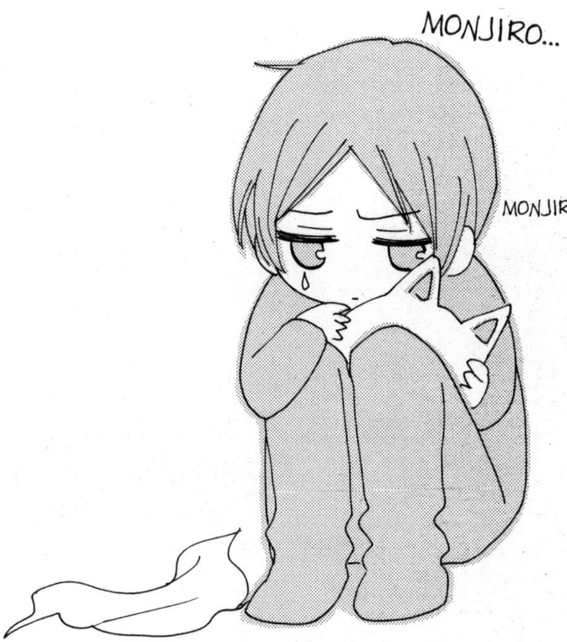

MONJIRO...
MONJIRO...

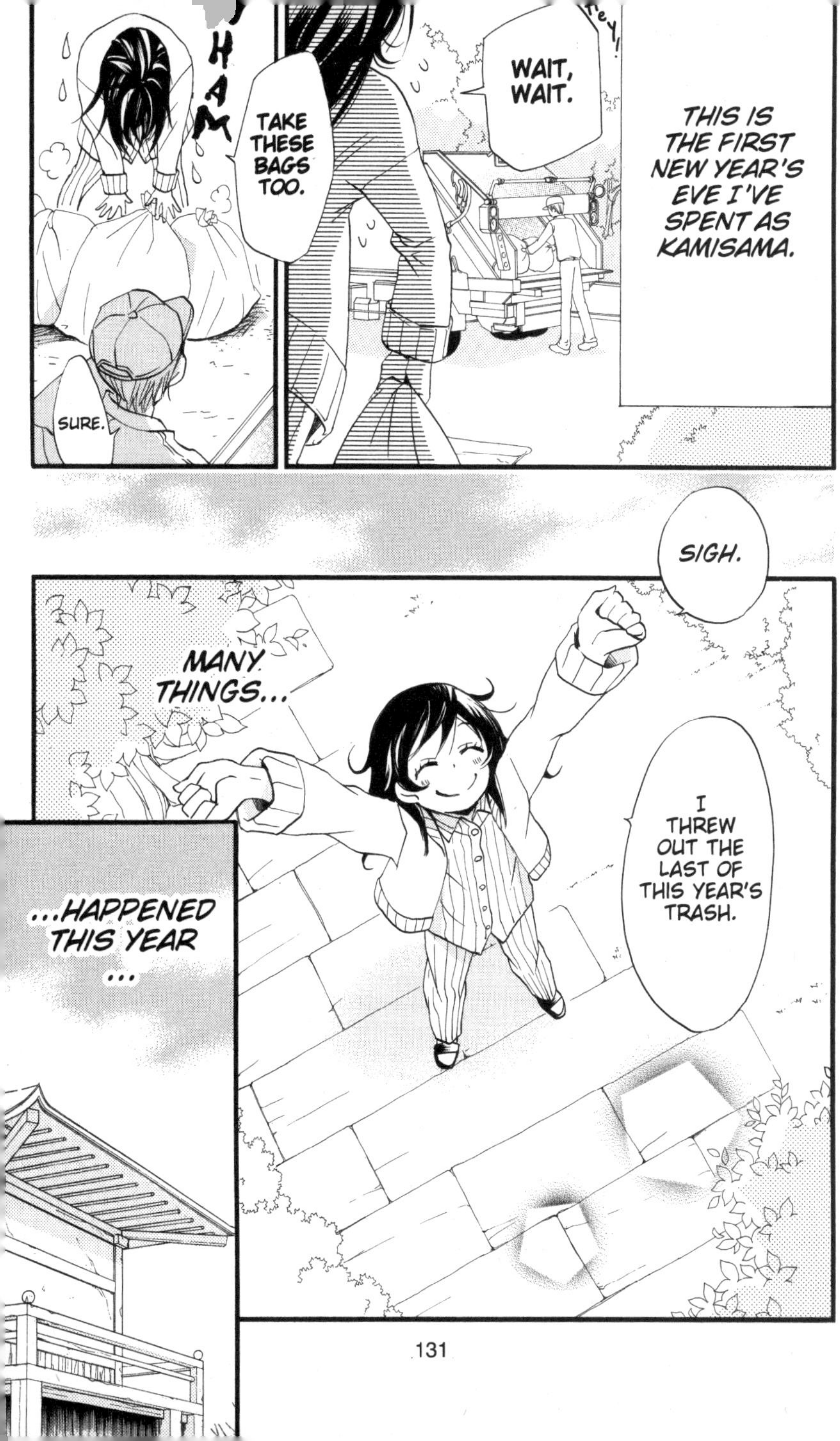
THIS IS THE FIRST NEW YEAR'S EVE I'VE SPENT AS KAMISAMA.
WAIT, WAIT.
TAKE THESE BAGS TOO.
HAM
SURE.
SIGH.
I THREW OUT THE LAST OF THIS YEAR'S TRASH.
MANY THINGS...
...HAPPENED THIS YEAR ...

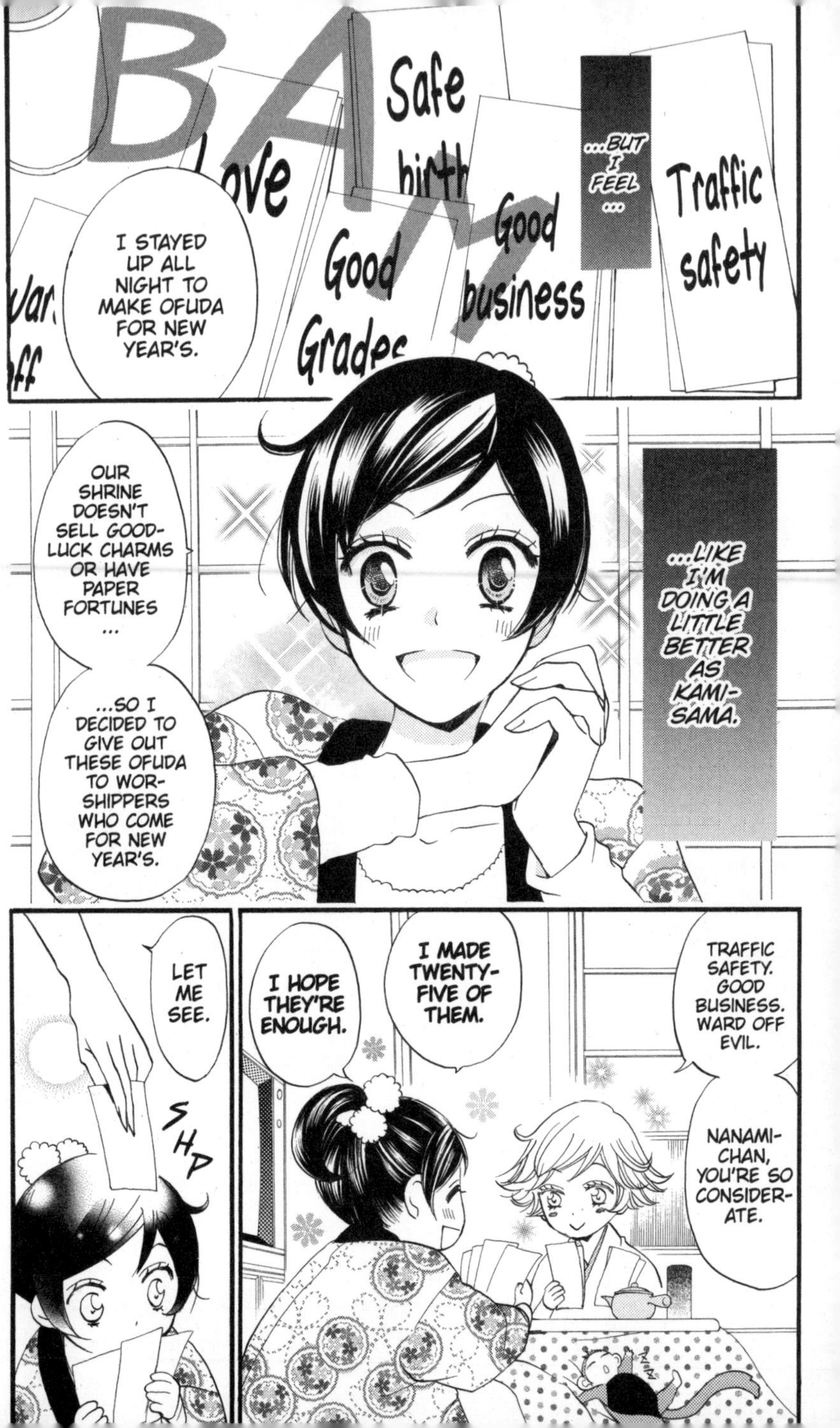
Traffic safety
...BUT I FEEL ...
Safe birth
Good business
Love
Good Grades
I STAYED UP ALL NIGHT TO MAKE OFUDA FOR NEW YEAR'S.
...LIKE I'M DOING A LITTLE BETTER AS KAMI-SAMA.
OUR SHRINE DOESN'T SELL GOOD-LUCK CHARMS OR HAVE PAPER FORTUNES ...
...SO I DECIDED TO GIVE OUT THESE OFUDA TO WOR-SHIPPERS WHO COME FOR NEW YEAR'S.
TRAFFIC SAFETY. GOOD BUSINESS. WARD OFF EVIL.
NANAMI-CHAN, YOU'RE SO CONSIDER-ATE.
I MADE TWENTY-FIVE OF THEM.
I HOPE THEY'RE ENOUGH.
LET ME SEE.
SHP

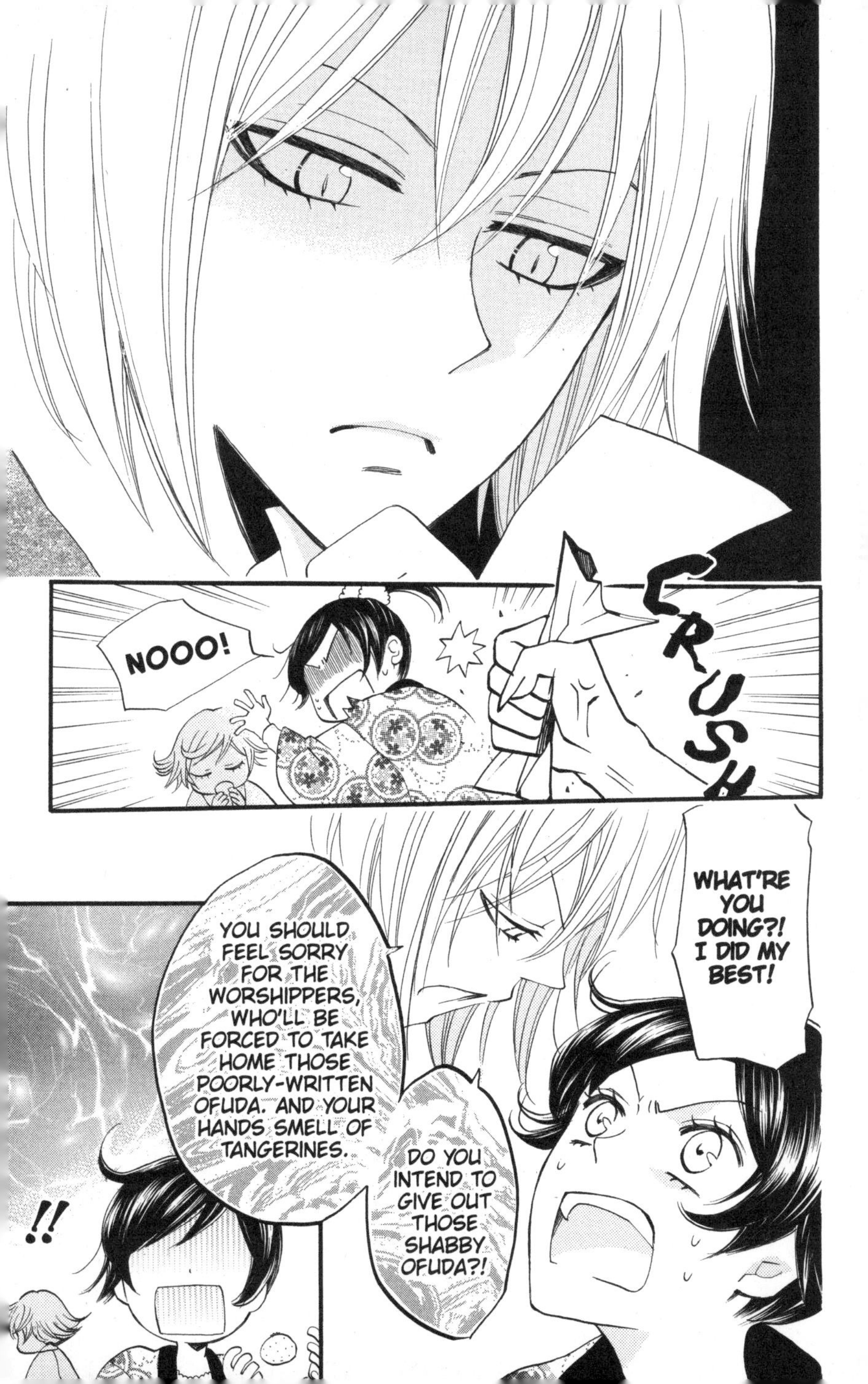
CRUSH
NOOO!
WHAT'RE YOU DOING?! I DID MY BEST!
YOU SHOULD FEEL SORRY FOR THE WORSHIPPERS, WHO'LL BE FORCED TO TAKE HOME THOSE POORLY-WRITTEN OFUDA. AND YOUR HANDS SMELL OF TANGERINES.
DO YOU INTEND TO GIVE OUT THOSE SHABBY OFUDA?!
!!

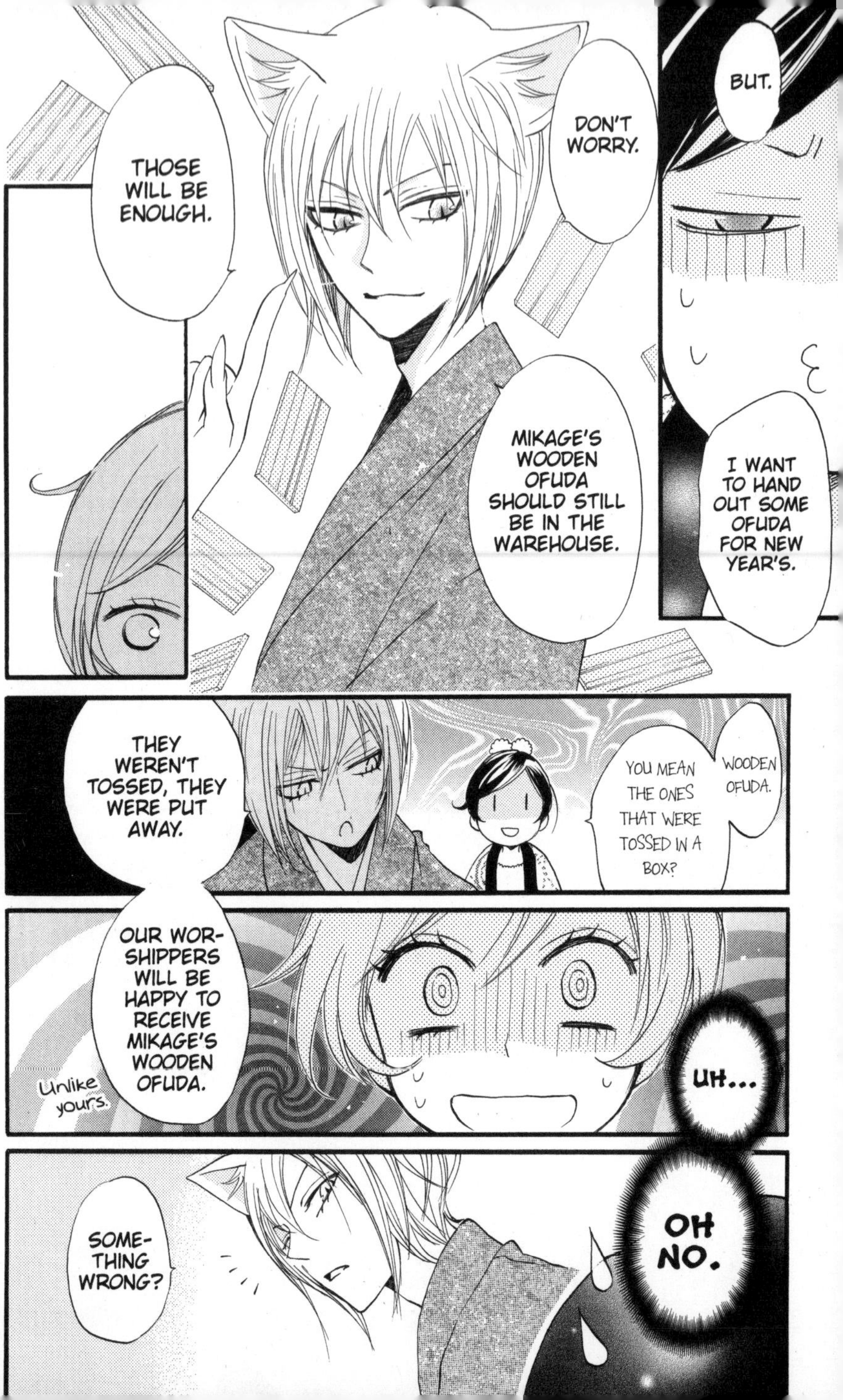
BUT.
I WANT TO HAND OUT SOME OFUDA FOR NEW YEAR'S.
DON'T WORRY.
MIKAGE'S WOODEN OFUDA SHOULD STILL BE IN THE WAREHOUSE.
THOSE WILL BE ENOUGH.
WOODEN OFUDA.
YOU MEAN THE ONES THAT WERE TOSSED IN A BOX?
THEY WEREN'T TOSSED, THEY WERE PUT AWAY.
OUR WOR-SHIPPERS WILL BE HAPPY TO RECEIVE MIKAGE'S WOODEN OFUDA.
Unlike yours.
UH...
OH NO.
SOME-THING WRONG?

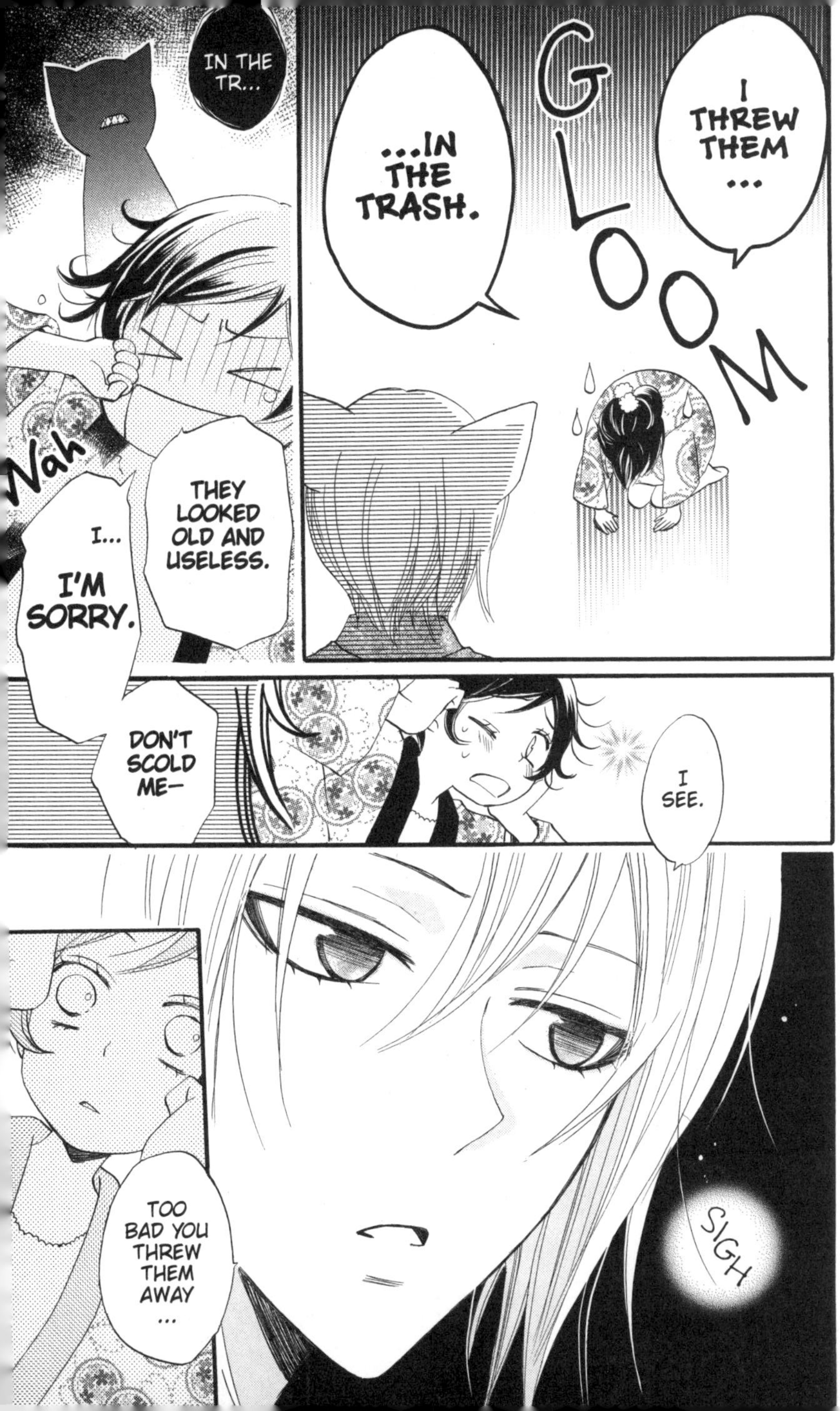
I THREW THEM...
GLOOM
...IN THE TRASH.
IN THE TR...
Wah
THEY LOOKED OLD AND USELESS.
I... I'M SORRY.
I SEE.
DON'T SCOLD ME—
SIGH
TOO BAD YOU THREW THEM AWAY...

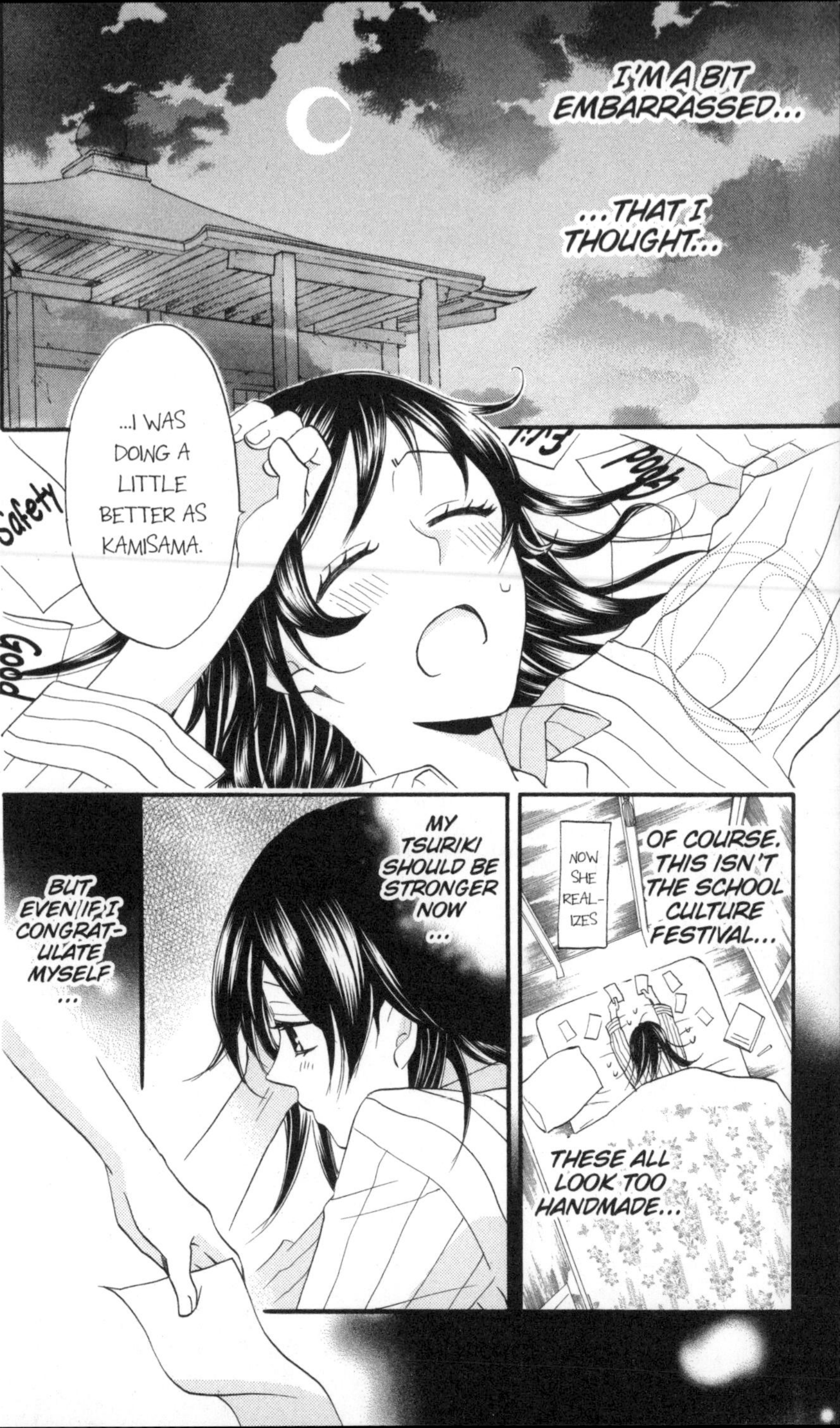
I'M A BIT EMBARRASSED...
...THAT I THOUGHT...
...I WAS DOING A LITTLE BETTER AS KAMISAMA.
Good
Safety
Good
OF COURSE. THIS ISN'T THE SCHOOL CULTURE FESTIVAL...
NOW SHE REAL-IZES
THESE ALL LOOK TOO HANDMADE...
MY TSURIKI SHOULD BE STRONGER NOW ...
BUT EVEN IF I CONGRAT-ULATE MYSELF ...

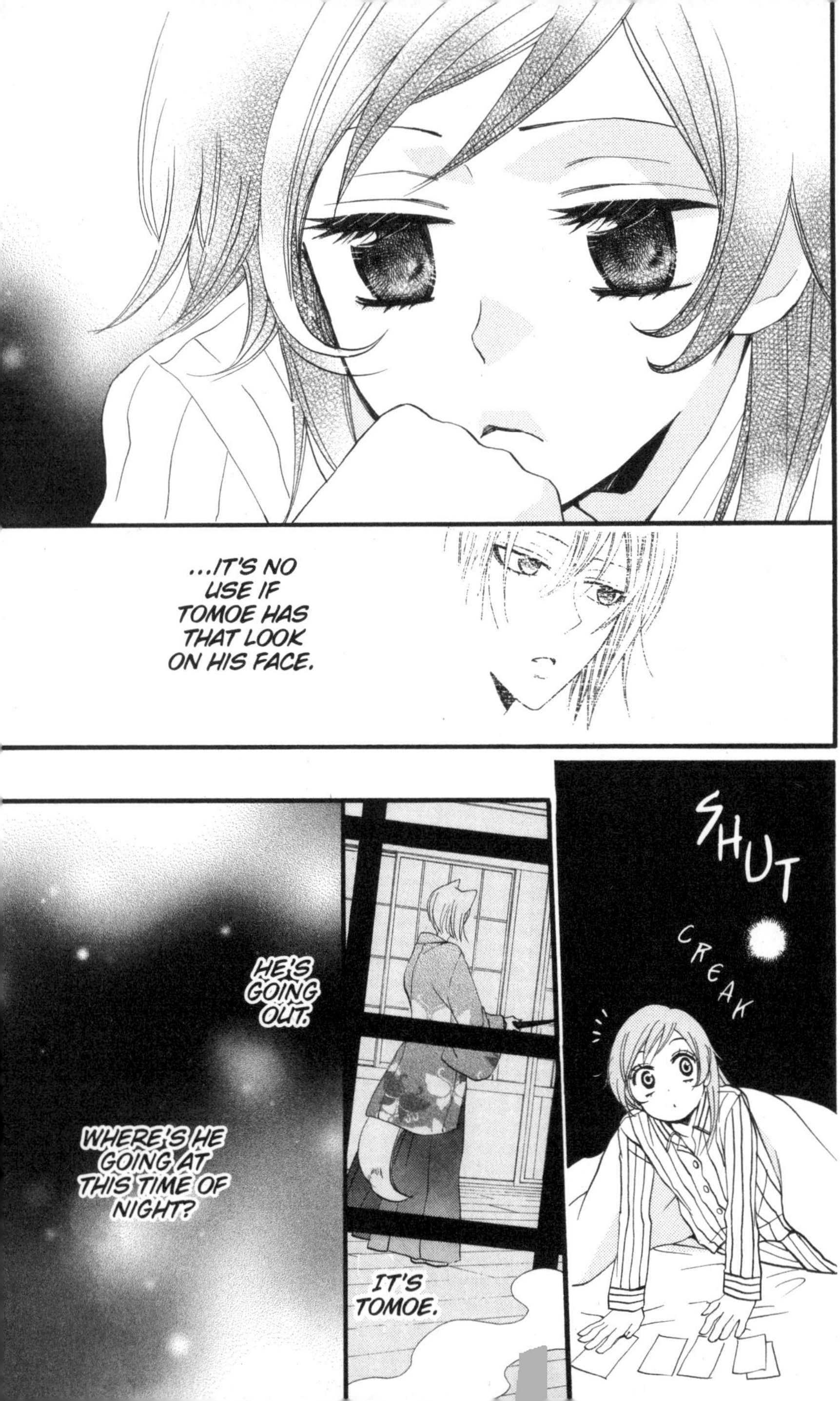
...IT'S NO USE IF TOMOE HAS THAT LOOK ON HIS FACE.
SHUT
CREAK
IT'S TOMOE.
HE'S GOING OUT.
WHERE'S HE GOING AT THIS TIME OF NIGHT?

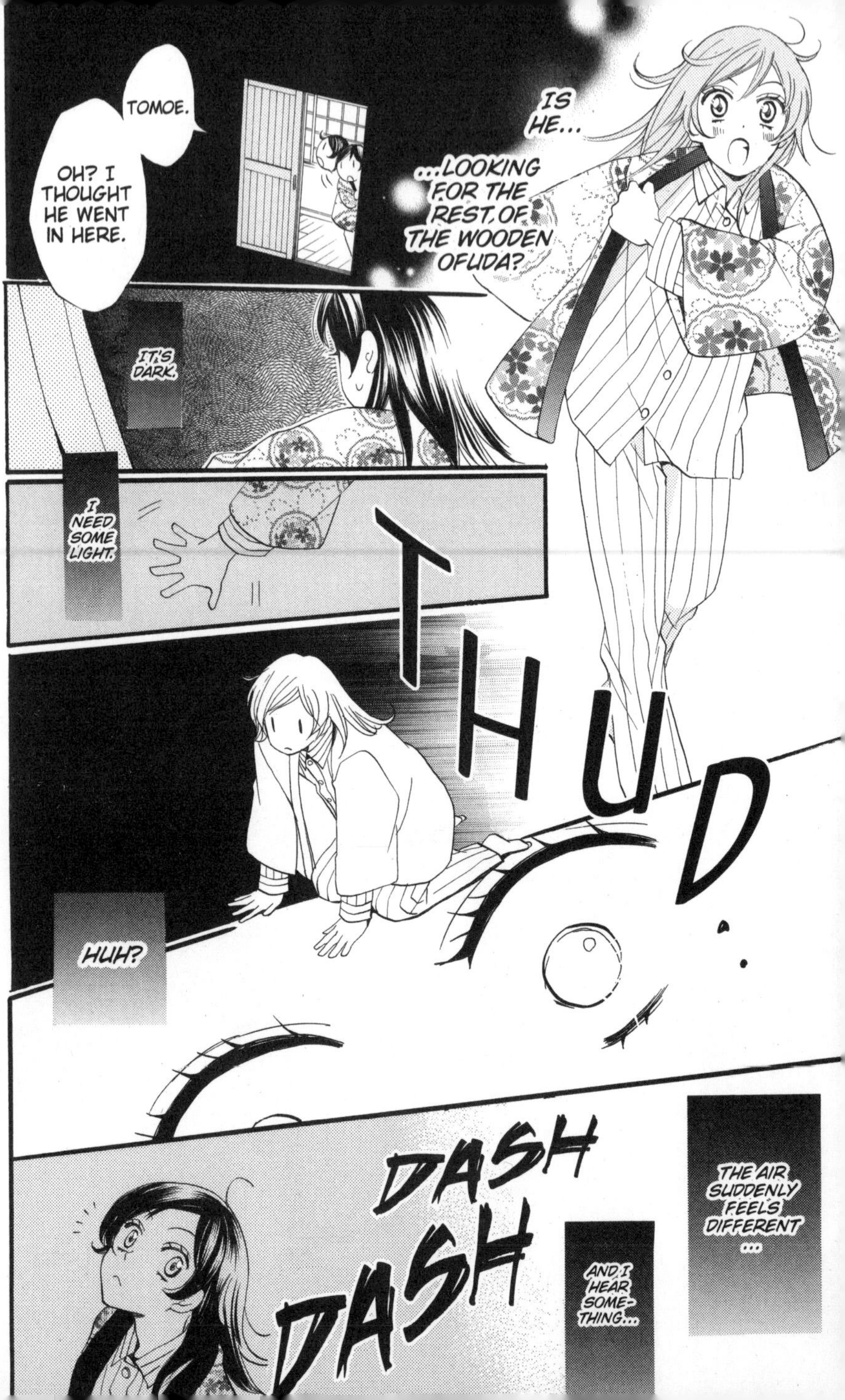
IS HE...
...LOOKING FOR THE REST OF THE WOODEN OFUDA?
TOMOE.
OH? I THOUGHT HE WENT IN HERE.
IT'S DARK.
I NEED SOME LIGHT.
THUD
HUH?
THE AIR SUDDENLY FEELS DIFFERENT...
AND I HEAR SOMETHING...
DASH
DASH

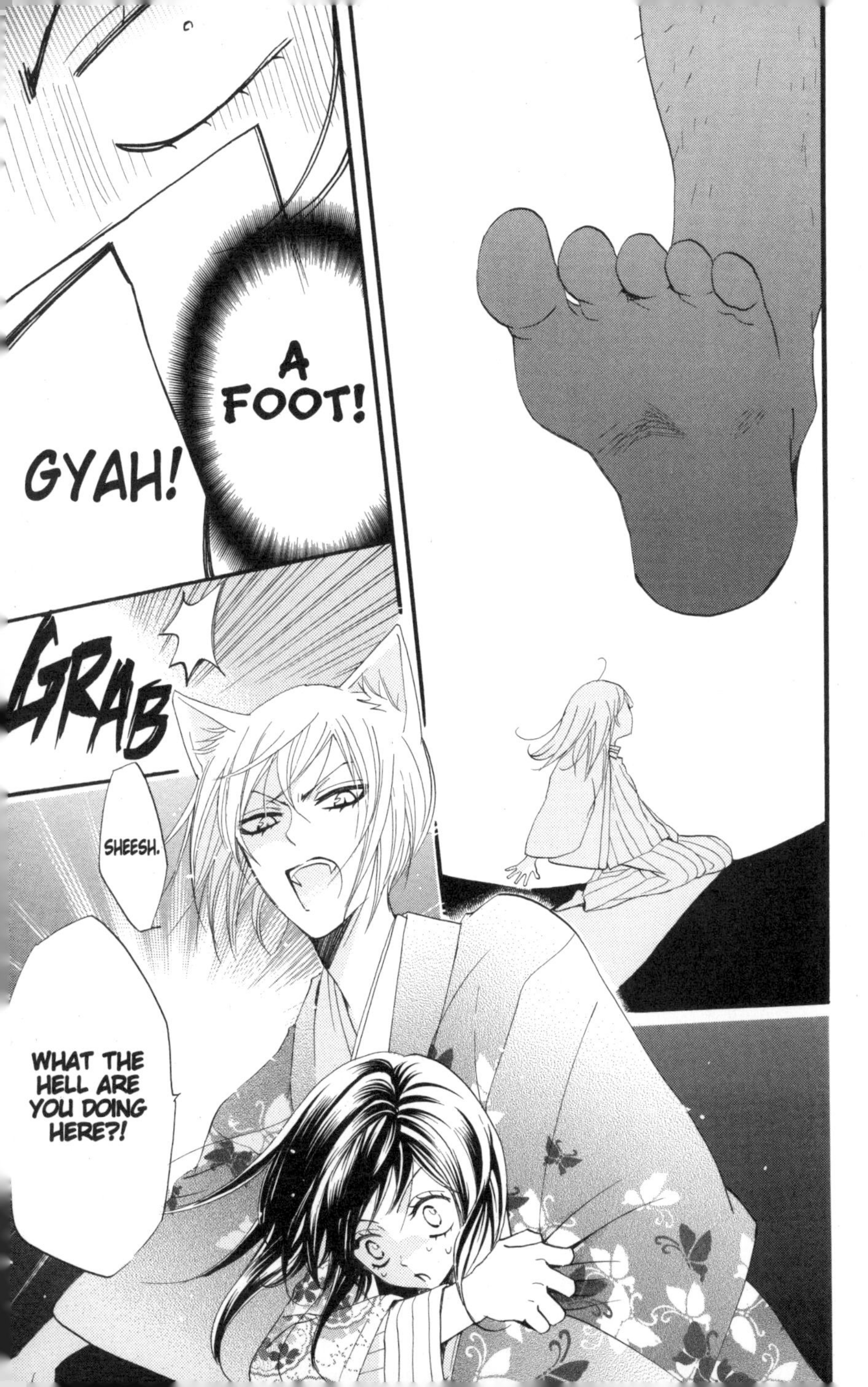
A FOOT!
GYAH!
GRAB
SHEESH.
WHAT THE HELL ARE YOU DOING HERE?!

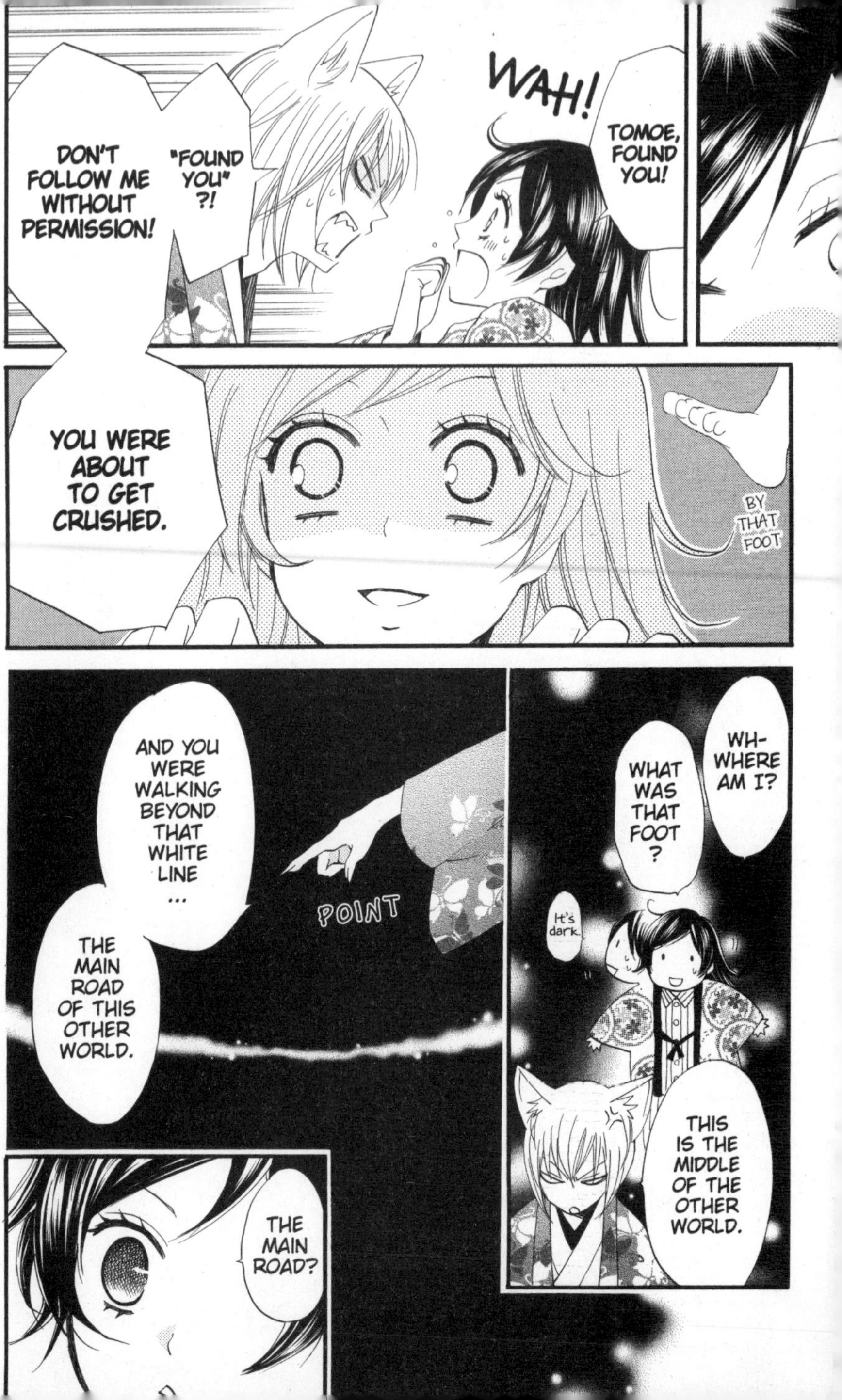
WAH!
TOMOE, FOUND YOU!
"FOUND YOU"?!
DON'T FOLLOW ME WITHOUT PERMISSION!
YOU WERE ABOUT TO GET CRUSHED.
BY THAT FOOT
WH-WHERE AM I?
WHAT WAS THAT FOOT?
It's dark.
THIS IS THE MIDDLE OF THE OTHER WORLD.
AND YOU WERE WALKING BEYOND THAT WHITE LINE...
POINT
THE MAIN ROAD OF THIS OTHER WORLD.
THE MAIN ROAD?

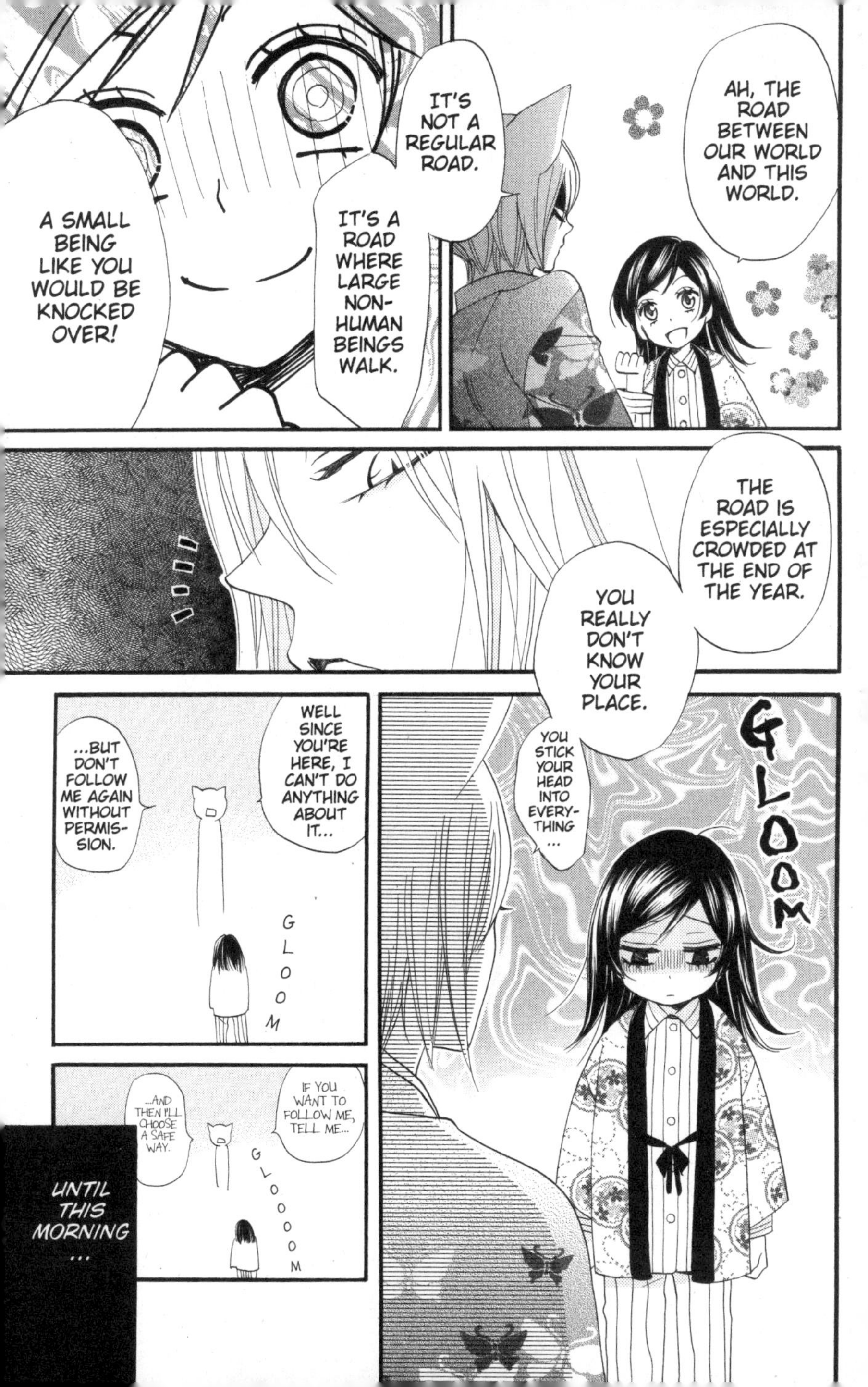
AH, THE ROAD BETWEEN OUR WORLD AND THIS WORLD.
IT'S NOT A REGULAR ROAD.
IT'S A ROAD WHERE LARGE NON-HUMAN BEINGS WALK.
A SMALL BEING LIKE YOU WOULD BE KNOCKED OVER!
THE ROAD IS ESPECIALLY CROWDED AT THE END OF THE YEAR.
YOU REALLY DON'T KNOW YOUR PLACE.
YOU STICK YOUR HEAD INTO EVERYTHING...
GLOOM
WELL SINCE YOU'RE HERE, I CAN'T DO ANYTHING ABOUT IT...
...BUT DON'T FOLLOW ME AGAIN WITHOUT PERMISSION.
GLOOM
IF YOU WANT TO FOLLOW ME, TELL ME...
...AND THEN I'LL CHOOSE A SAFE WAY.
GLOOOOOM
UNTIL THIS MORNING...

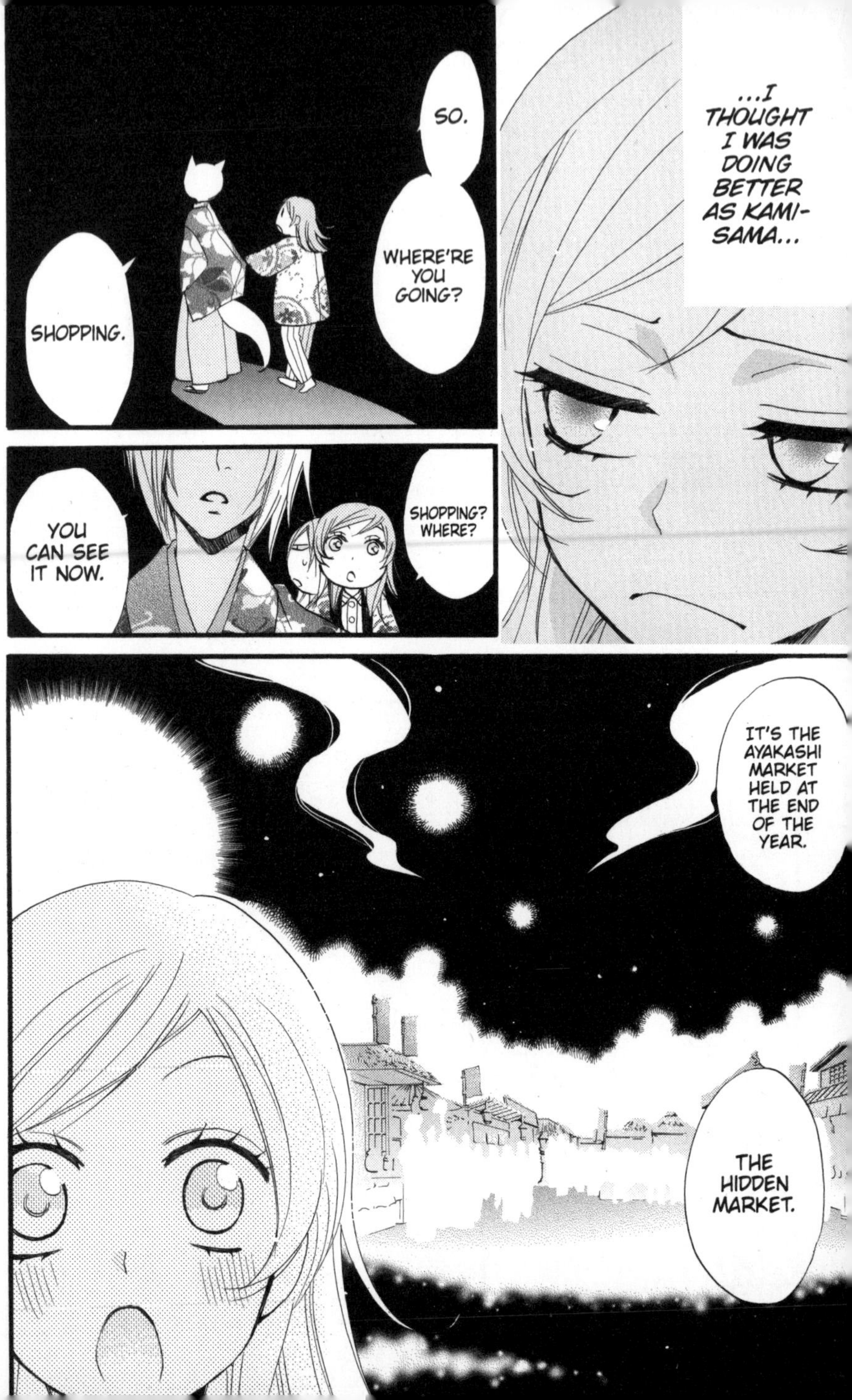
...I THOUGHT I WAS DOING BETTER AS KAMI-SAMA...
SO.
WHERE'RE YOU GOING?
SHOPPING.
SHOPPING? WHERE?
YOU CAN SEE IT NOW.
IT'S THE AYAKASHI MARKET HELD AT THE END OF THE YEAR.
THE HIDDEN MARKET.

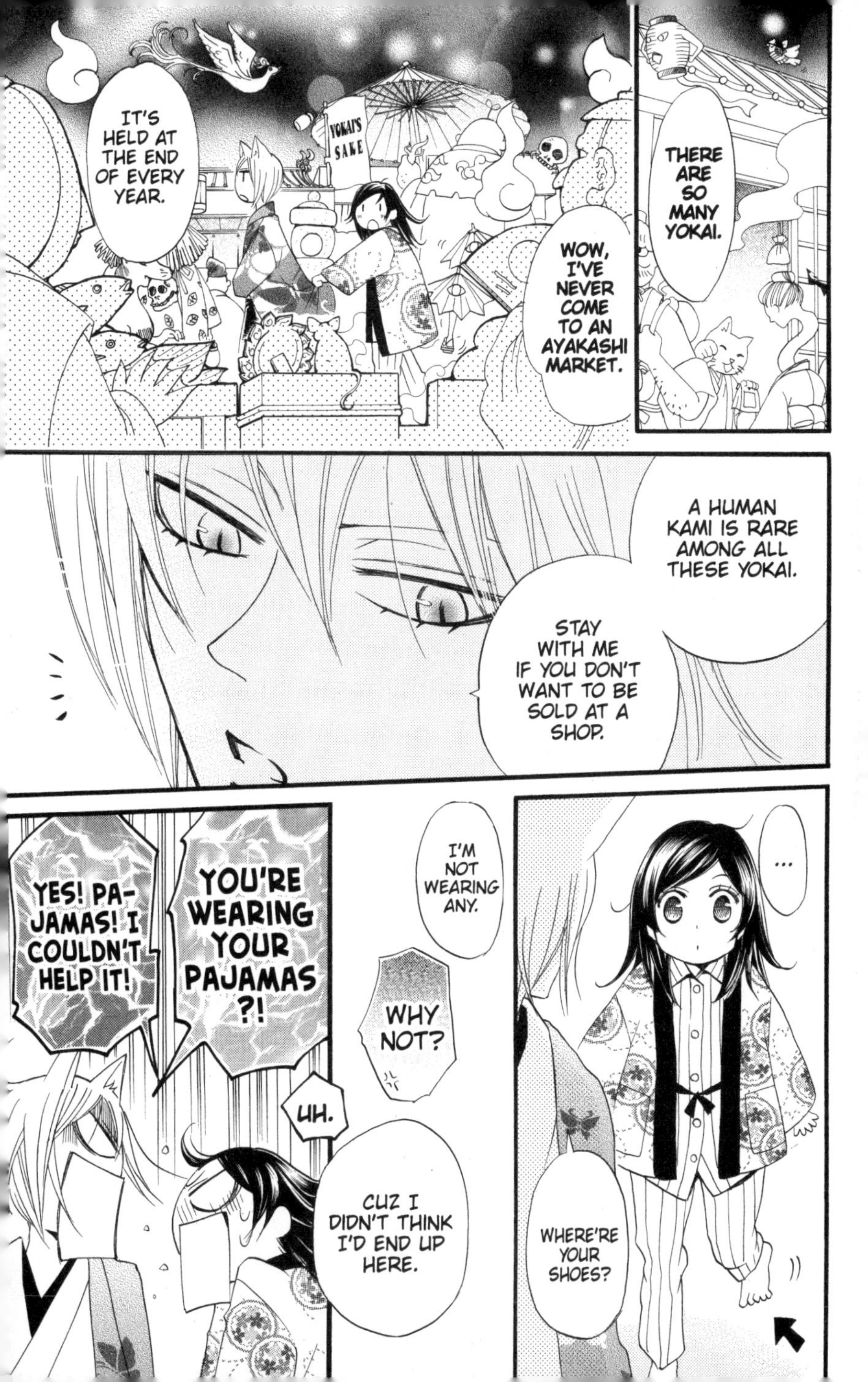
THERE ARE SO MANY YOKAI.
WOW, I'VE NEVER COME TO AN AYAKASHI MARKET.
YOKAI'S SAKE
IT'S HELD AT THE END OF EVERY YEAR.
A HUMAN KAMI IS RARE AMONG ALL THESE YOKAI.
STAY WITH ME IF YOU DON'T WANT TO BE SOLD AT A SHOP.
...
WHERE'RE YOUR SHOES?
I'M NOT WEARING ANY.
WHY NOT?
CUZ I DIDN'T THINK I'D END UP HERE.
UH.
YOU'RE WEARING YOUR PAJAMAS?!
YES! PA-JAMAS! I COULDN'T HELP IT!

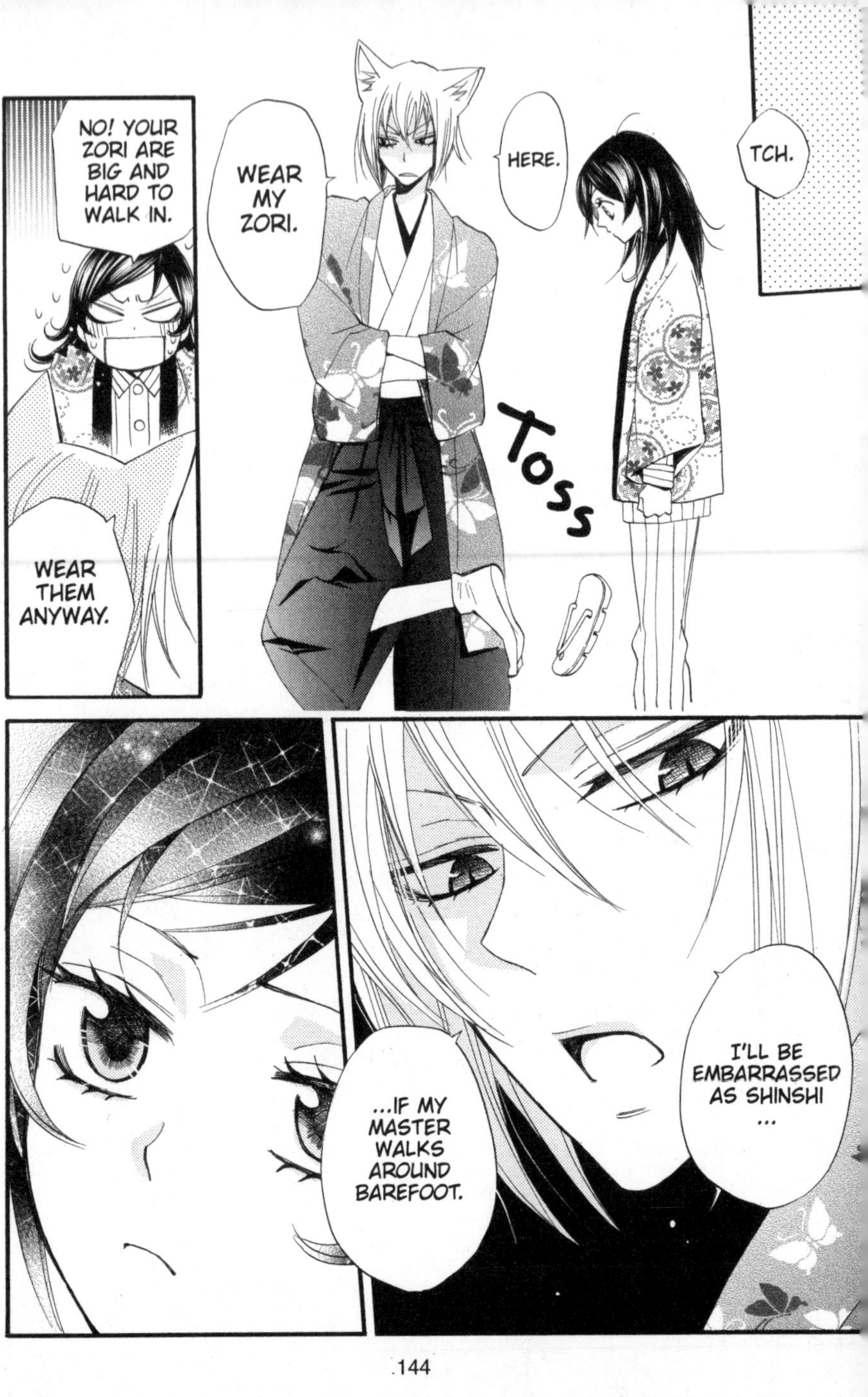
TCH.
HERE.
WEAR MY ZORI.
TOSS
NO! YOUR ZORI ARE BIG AND HARD TO WALK IN.
WEAR THEM ANYWAY.
I'LL BE EMBARRASSED AS SHINSHI ...
...IF MY MASTER WALKS AROUND BAREFOOT.

(Assistant) Okazaki's

Kamisama Working Hell

Recipe ②

⑥ Coat the pork with flour.

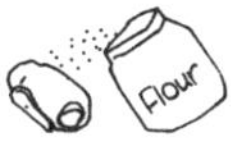

Flour

⑦ Heat up a frying pan, put a little oil in it, and cook the pork.

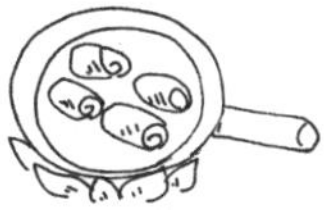

⑧ Pour a little soy sauce for flavor, and it's done.

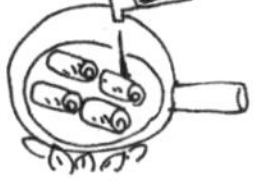

Stir-fry some veggies as garnishing and it's done!

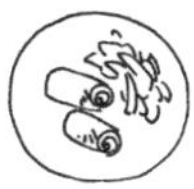

You can use kidney beans stir-fried in butter instead of the pickled plums and beefsteak leaves.

Try it!

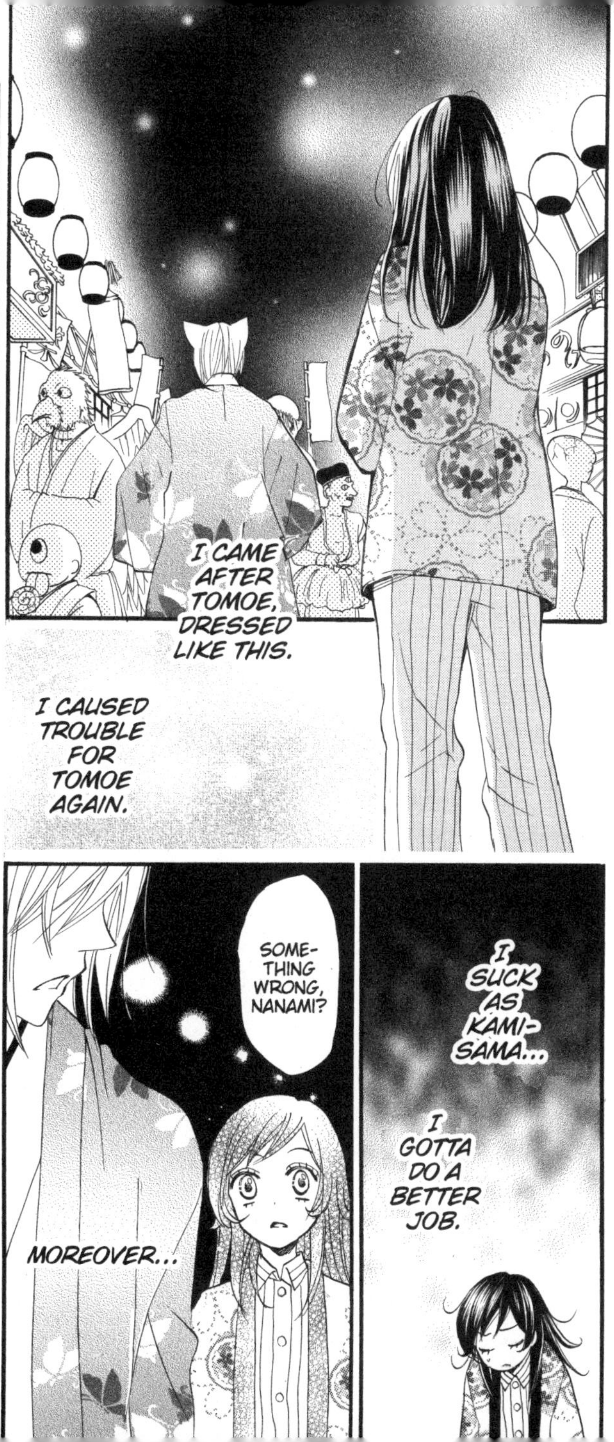

I CAME AFTER TOMOE, DRESSED LIKE THIS.
I CAUSED TROUBLE FOR TOMOE AGAIN.
SOME-THING WRONG, NANAMI?
MOREOVER...
I SUCK AS KAMI-SAMA...
I GOTTA DO A BETTER JOB.

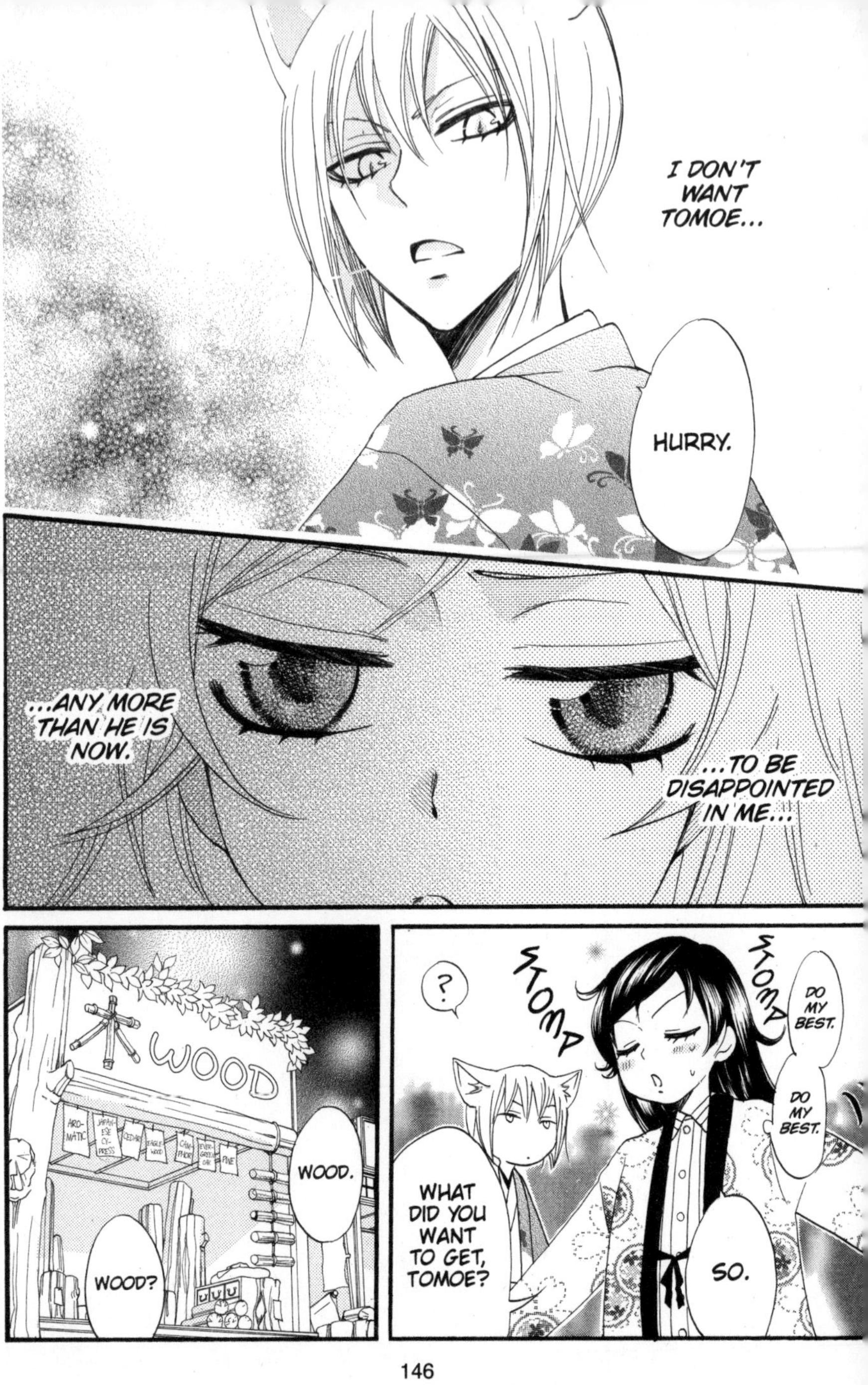
I DON'T WANT TOMOE...
HURRY.
...TO BE DISAPPOINTED IN ME...
...ANY MORE THAN HE IS NOW.
STOMP
STOMP
DO MY BEST.
DO MY BEST.
?
SO.
WHAT DID YOU WANT TO GET, TOMOE?
WOOD
ARO-MATIC
JAPAN-ESE CY-PRESS
CEDAR
EAGLE WOOD
CAM-PHOR
EVER-GREEN OAK
PINE
WOOD.
WOOD?

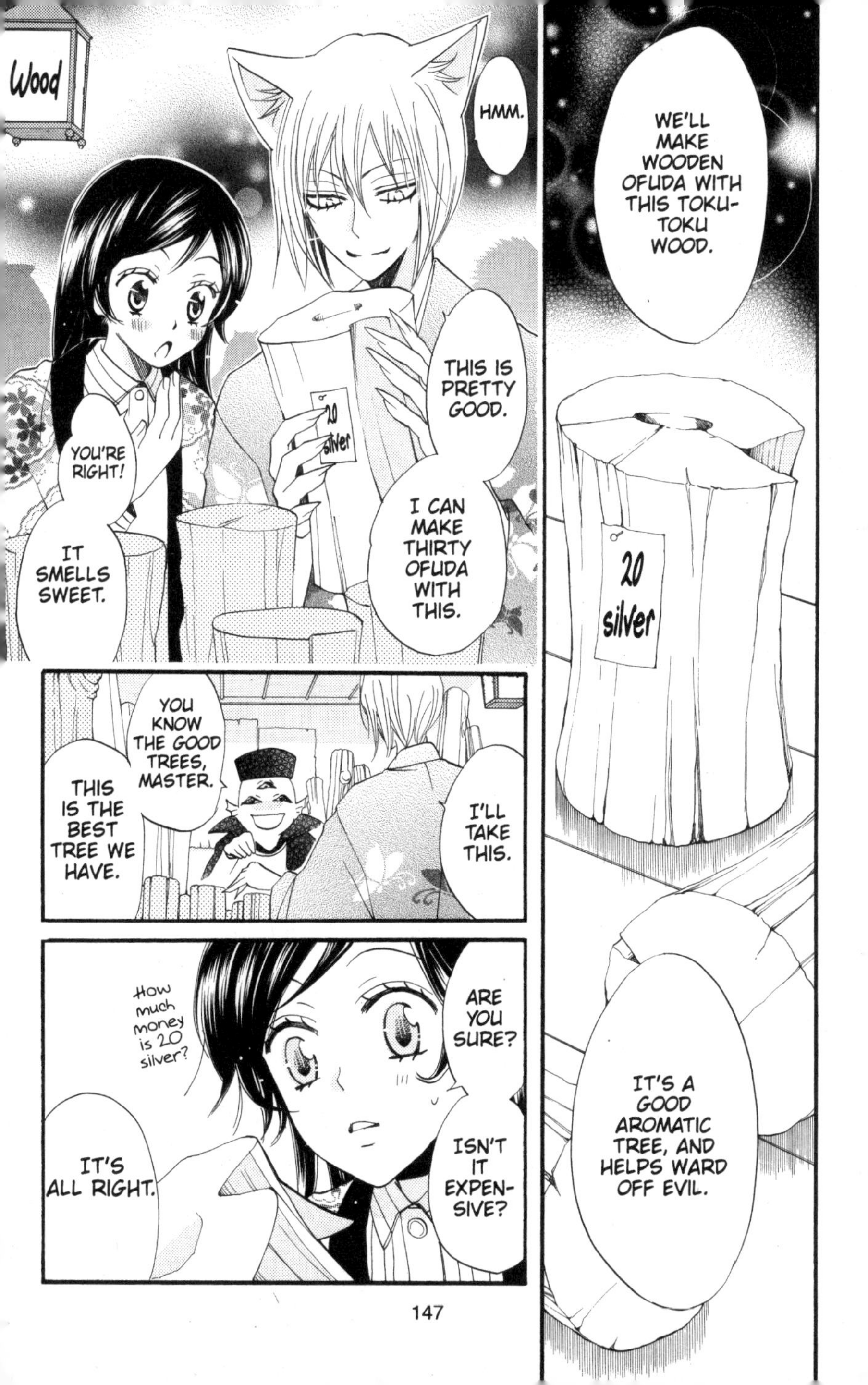
WE'LL MAKE WOODEN OFUDA WITH THIS TOKU-TOKU WOOD.
20 silver
IT'S A GOOD AROMATIC TREE, AND HELPS WARD OFF EVIL.
Wood
HMM.
THIS IS PRETTY GOOD.
I CAN MAKE THIRTY OFUDA WITH THIS.
20 silver
YOU'RE RIGHT!
IT SMELLS SWEET.
I'LL TAKE THIS.
YOU KNOW THE GOOD TREES, MASTER.
THIS IS THE BEST TREE WE HAVE.
ARE YOU SURE?
ISN'T IT EXPENSIVE?
How much money is 20 silver?
IT'S ALL RIGHT.

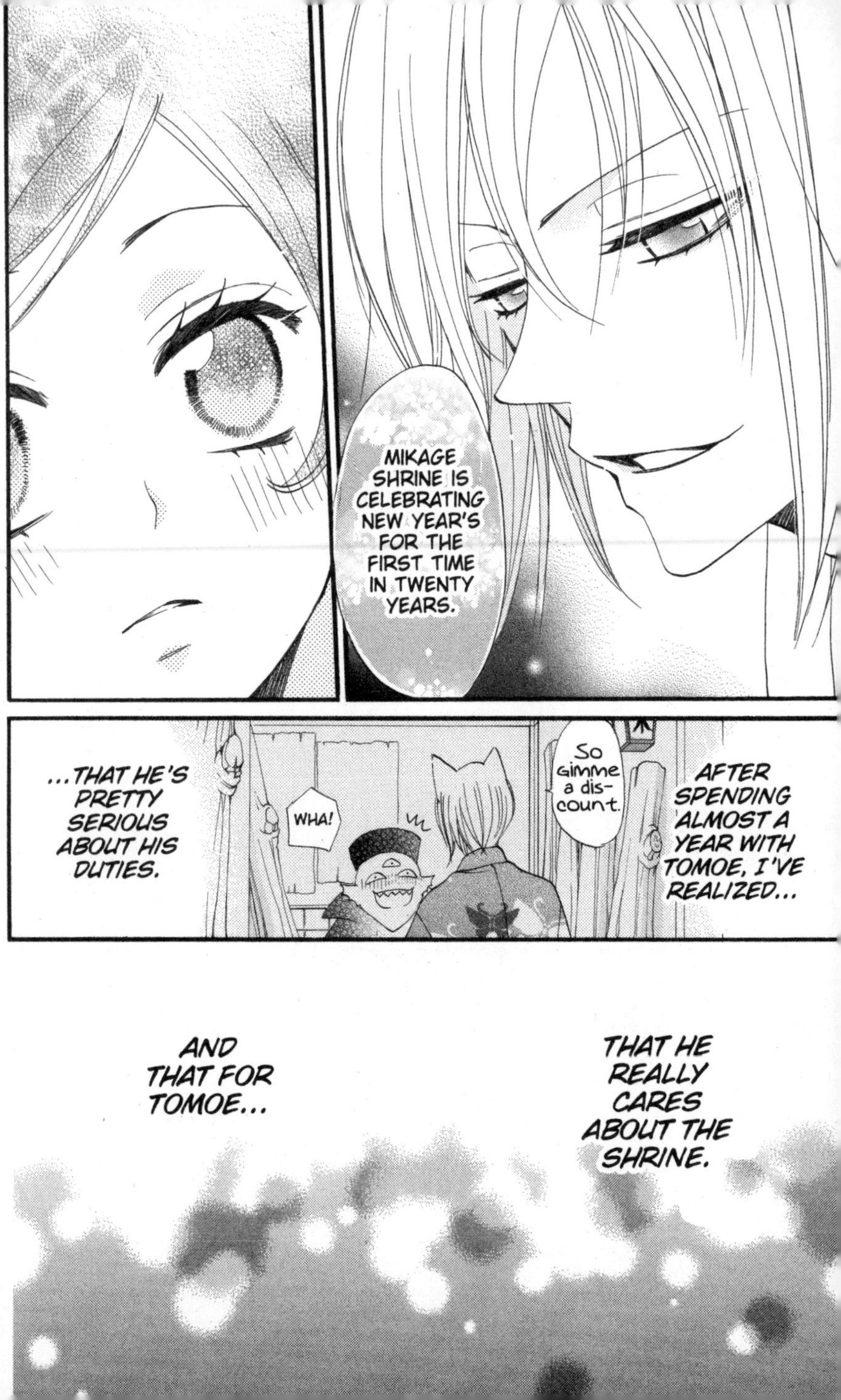
MIKAGE SHRINE IS CELEBRATING NEW YEAR'S FOR THE FIRST TIME IN TWENTY YEARS.
AFTER SPENDING ALMOST A YEAR WITH TOMOE, I'VE REALIZED...
So gimme a dis-count.
WHA!
...THAT HE'S PRETTY SERIOUS ABOUT HIS DUTIES.
THAT HE REALLY CARES ABOUT THE SHRINE.
AND THAT FOR TOMOE...

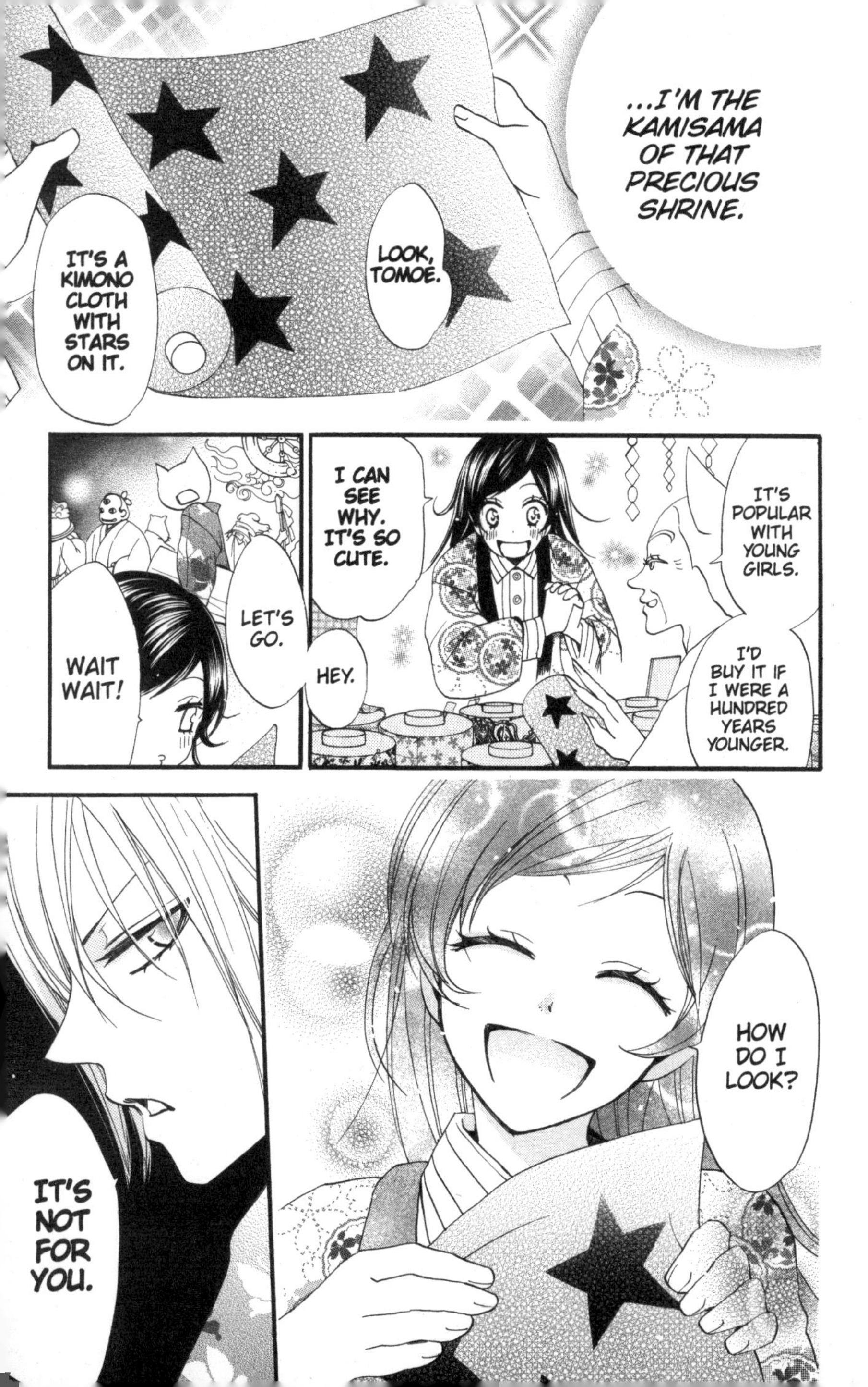
...I'M THE KAMISAMA OF THAT PRECIOUS SHRINE.
LOOK, TOMOE.
IT'S A KIMONO CLOTH WITH STARS ON IT.
IT'S POPULAR WITH YOUNG GIRLS.
I CAN SEE WHY. IT'S SO CUTE.
I'D BUY IT IF I WERE A HUNDRED YEARS YOUNGER.
HEY.
LET'S GO.
WAIT WAIT!
HOW DO I LOOK?
IT'S NOT FOR YOU.

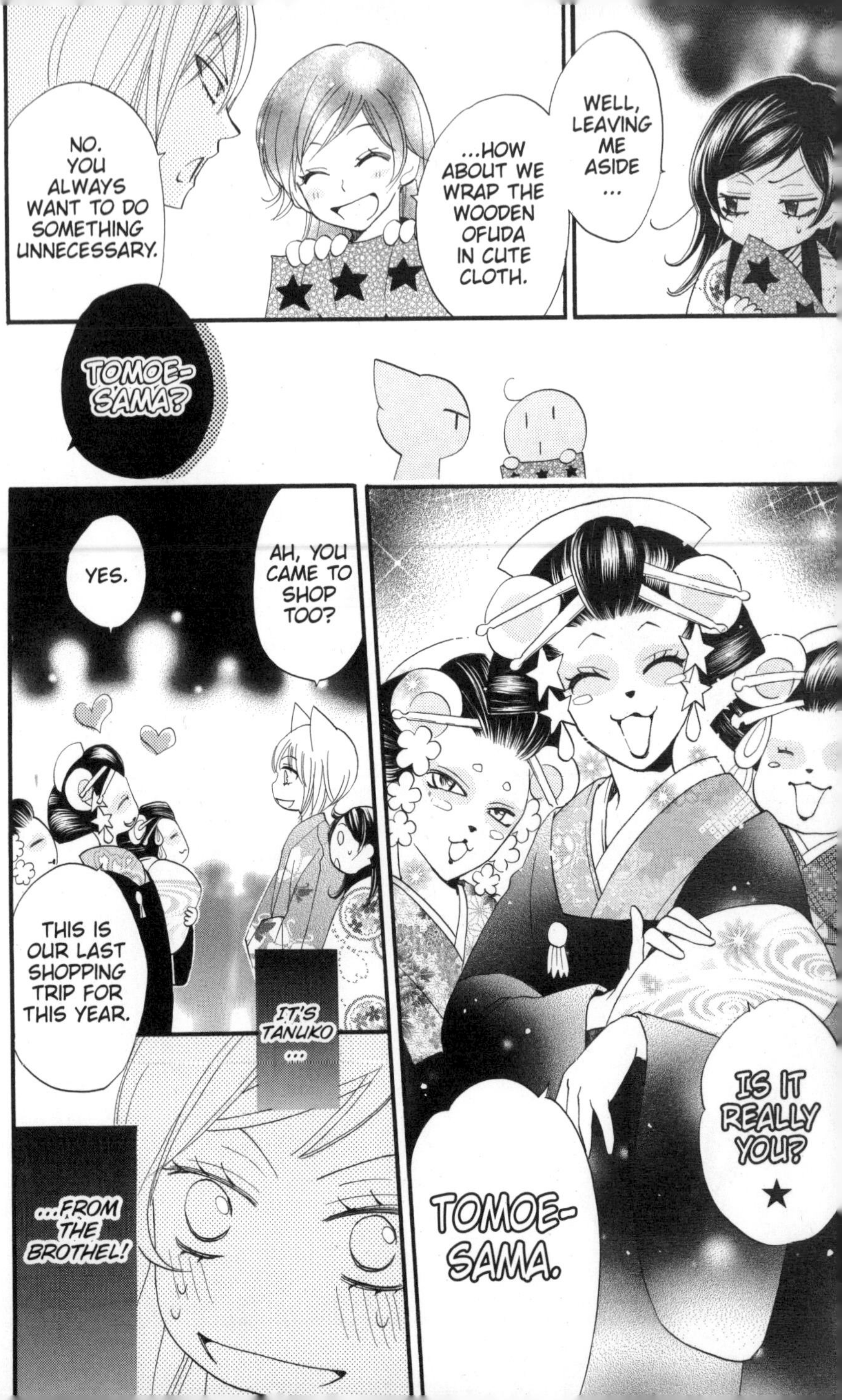
WELL, LEAVING ME ASIDE...
...HOW ABOUT WE WRAP THE WOODEN OFUDA IN CUTE CLOTH.
NO. YOU ALWAYS WANT TO DO SOMETHING UNNECESSARY.
TOMOE-SAMA?
IS IT REALLY YOU? ★
TOMOE-SAMA.
AH, YOU CAME TO SHOP TOO?
YES.
THIS IS OUR LAST SHOPPING TRIP FOR THIS YEAR.
IT'S TANUKO...
...FROM THE BROTHEL!

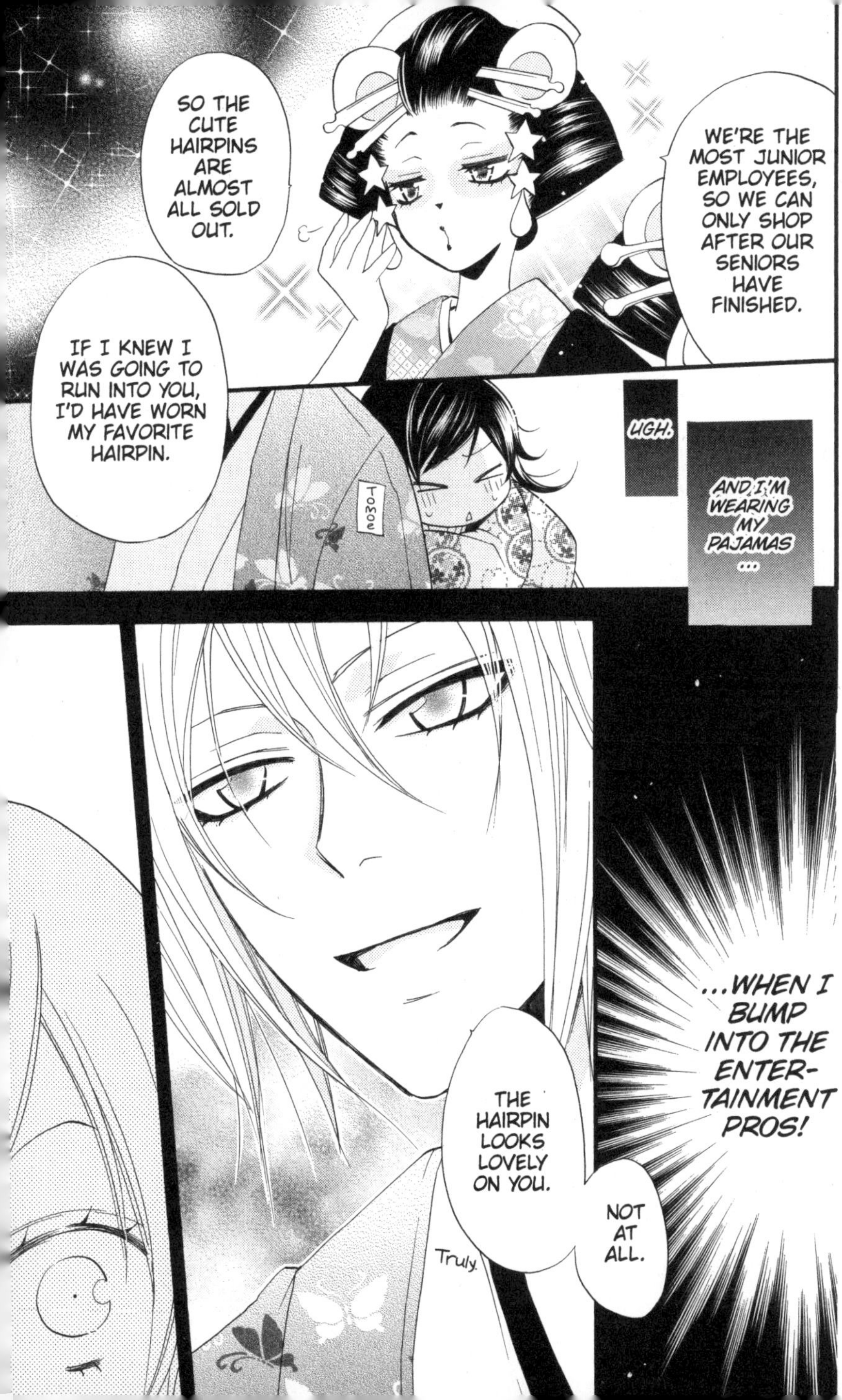
WE'RE THE MOST JUNIOR EMPLOYEES, SO WE CAN ONLY SHOP AFTER OUR SENIORS HAVE FINISHED.
SO THE CUTE HAIRPINS ARE ALMOST ALL SOLD OUT.
IF I KNEW I WAS GOING TO RUN INTO YOU, I'D HAVE WORN MY FAVORITE HAIRPIN.
UGH.
AND I'M WEARING MY PAJAMAS...
Tomoe
...WHEN I BUMP INTO THE ENTER-TAINMENT PROS!
THE HAIRPIN LOOKS LOVELY ON YOU.
NOT AT ALL.
Truly.

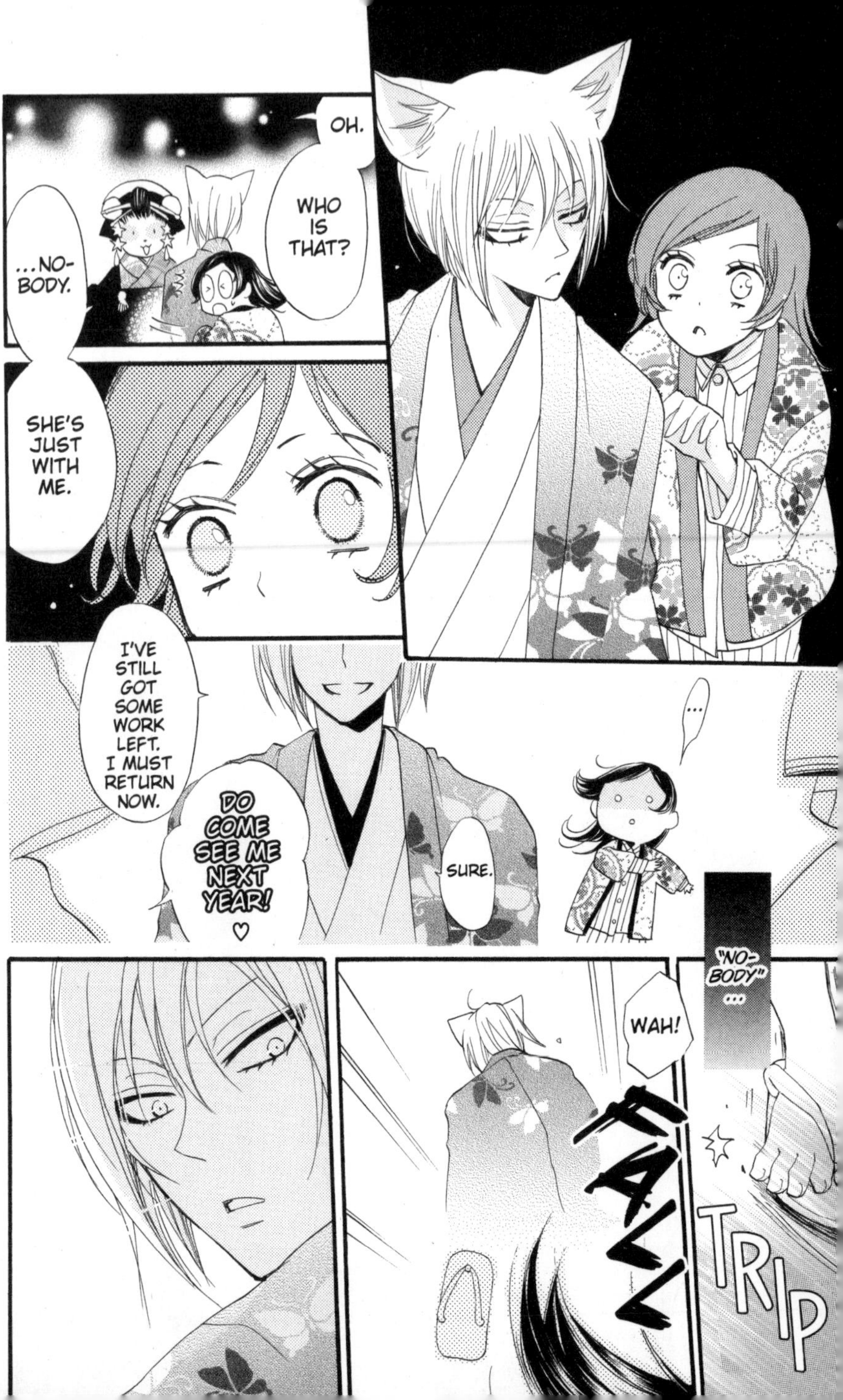
OH.
WHO IS THAT?
...NO-BODY.
SHE'S JUST WITH ME.
...
I'VE STILL GOT SOME WORK LEFT. I MUST RETURN NOW.
DO COME SEE ME NEXT YEAR! ♡
SURE.
"NO-BODY"...
WAH!
FALL
TRIP

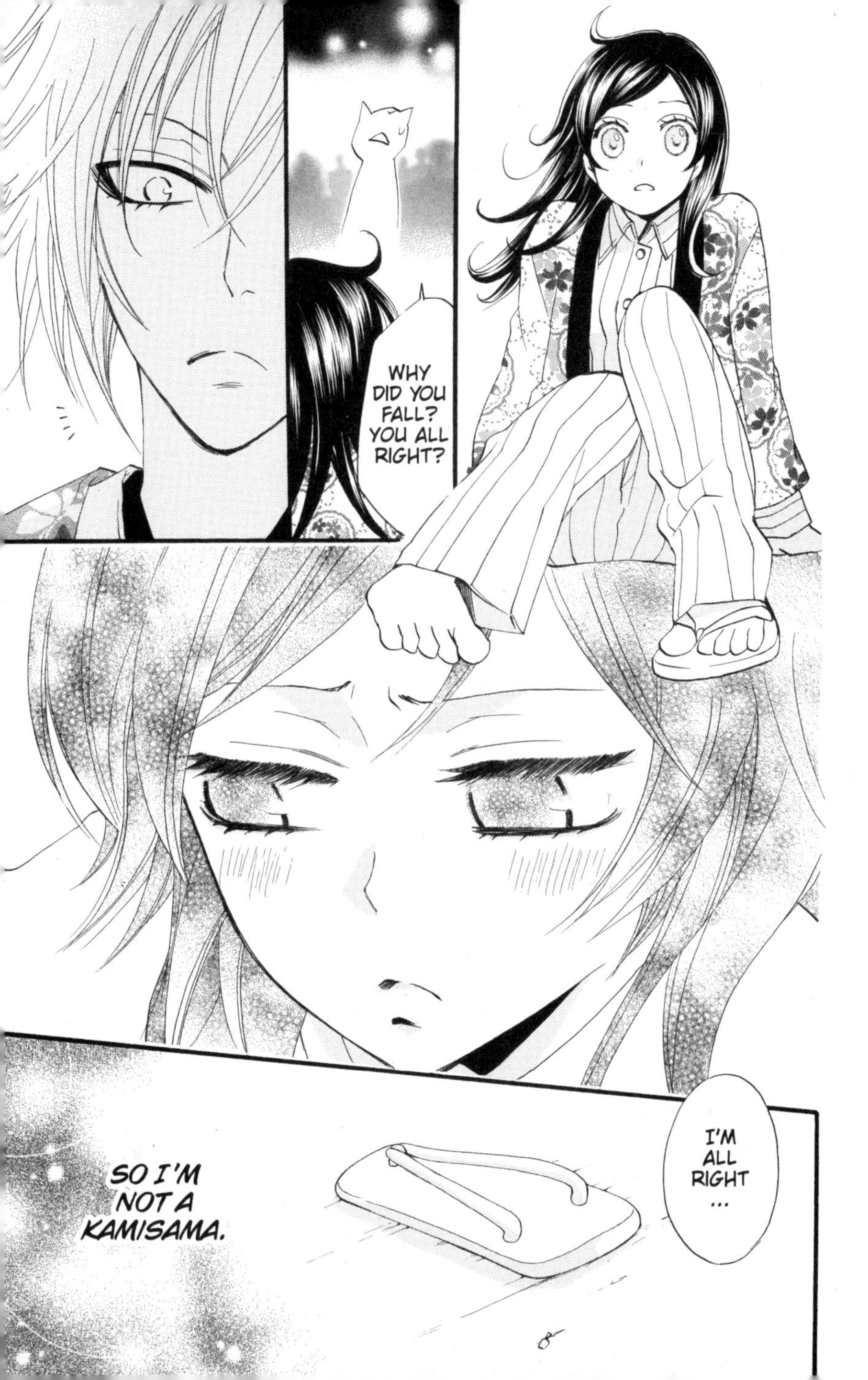
WHY DID YOU FALL? YOU ALL RIGHT?
I'M ALL RIGHT ...
SO I'M NOT A KAMISAMA.

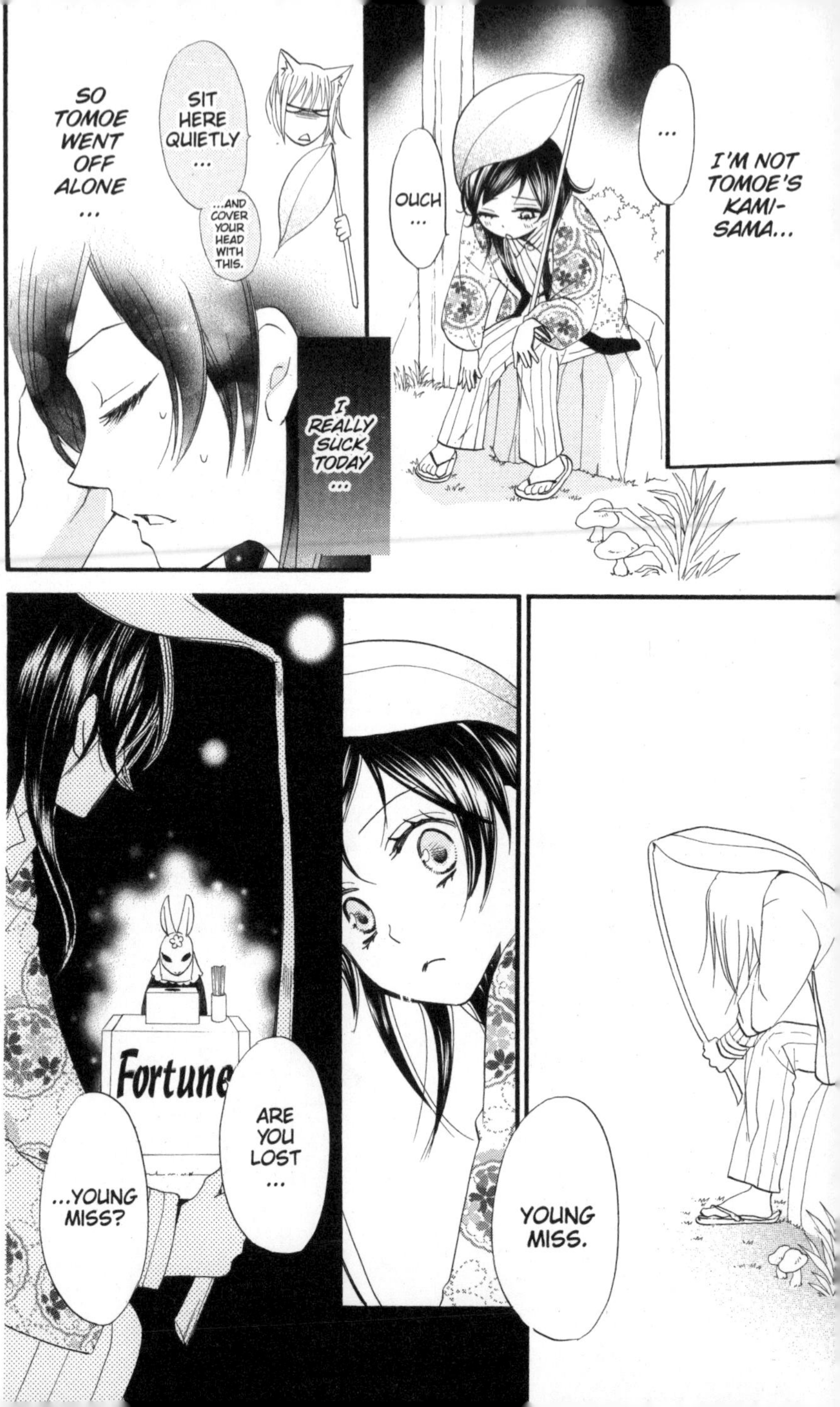

...
I'M NOT TOMOE'S KAMI-SAMA...
OUCH...
SIT HERE QUIETLY...
...AND COVER YOUR HEAD WITH THIS.
SO TOMOE WENT OFF ALONE...
I REALLY SUCK TODAY...
YOUNG MISS.
Fortune
ARE YOU LOST...
...YOUNG MISS?

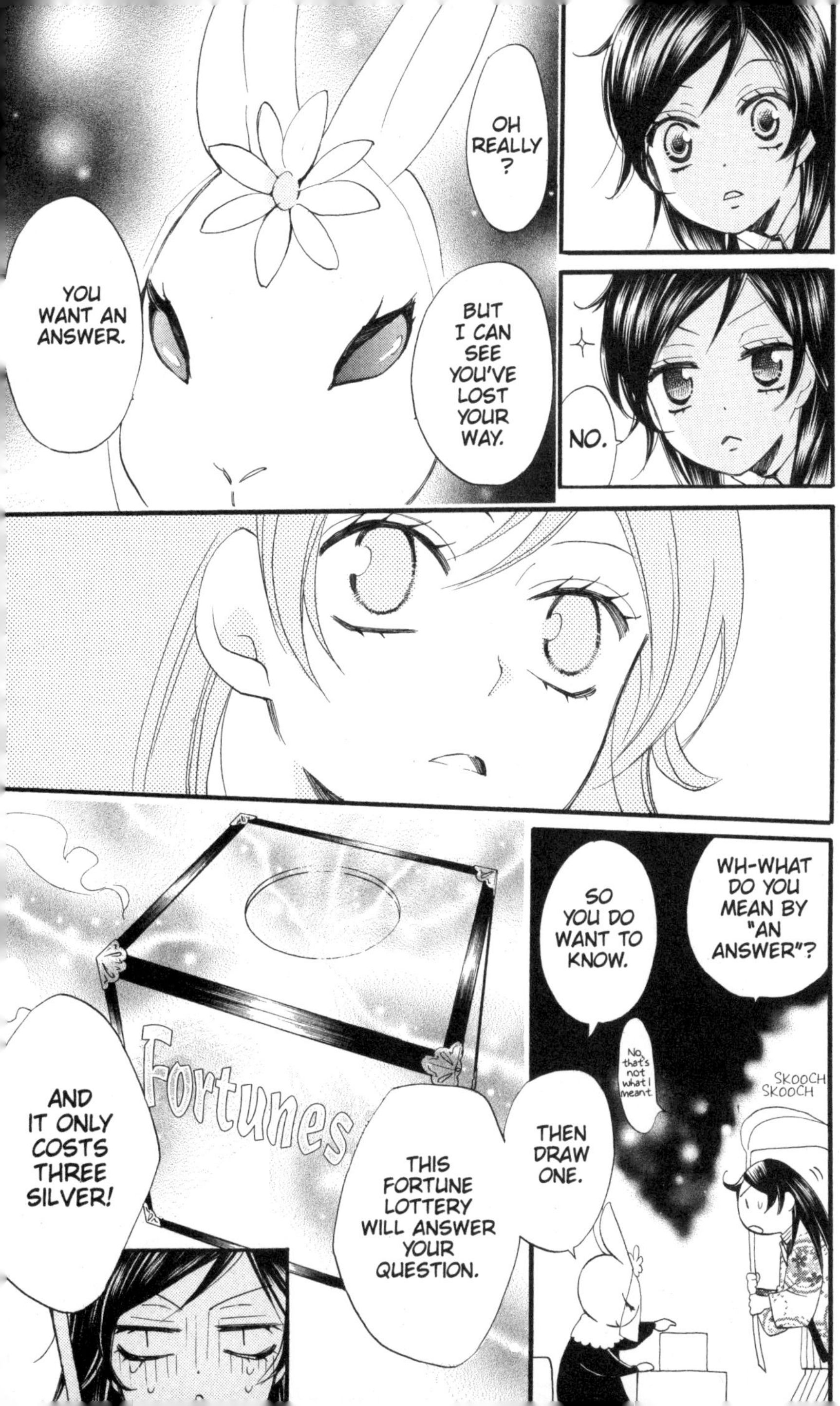
NO.
OH REALLY ?
BUT I CAN SEE YOU'VE LOST YOUR WAY.
YOU WANT AN ANSWER.
WH-WHAT DO YOU MEAN BY "AN ANSWER"?
SO YOU DO WANT TO KNOW.
No, that's not what I meant.
SKOOCH SKOOCH
THEN DRAW ONE.
THIS FORTUNE LOTTERY WILL ANSWER YOUR QUESTION.
Fortunes
AND IT ONLY COSTS THREE SILVER!

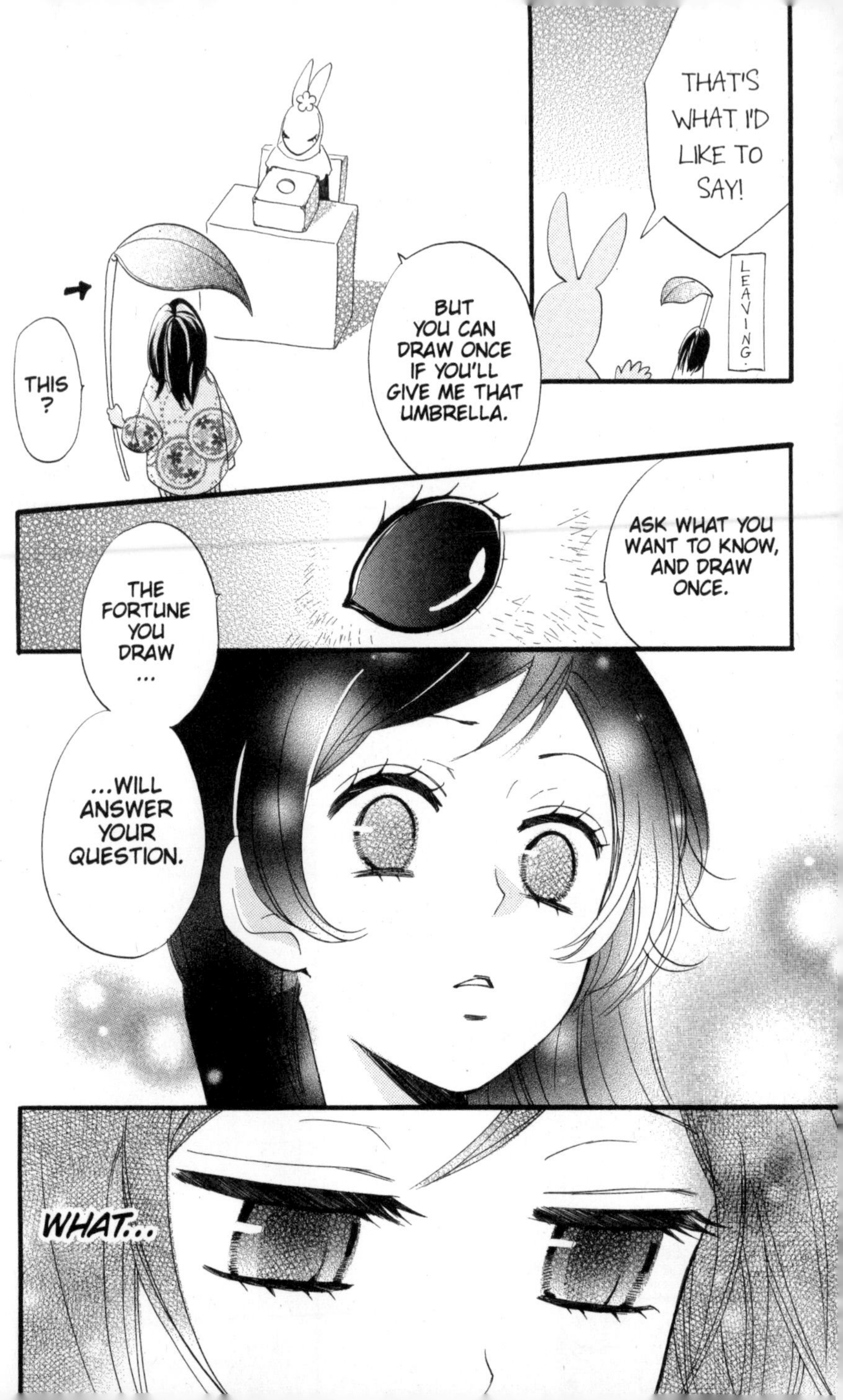
THAT'S WHAT I'D LIKE TO SAY!
LEAVING.
BUT YOU CAN DRAW ONCE IF YOU'LL GIVE ME THAT UMBRELLA.
THIS?
ASK WHAT YOU WANT TO KNOW, AND DRAW ONCE.
THE FORTUNE YOU DRAW...
...WILL ANSWER YOUR QUESTION.
WHAT...

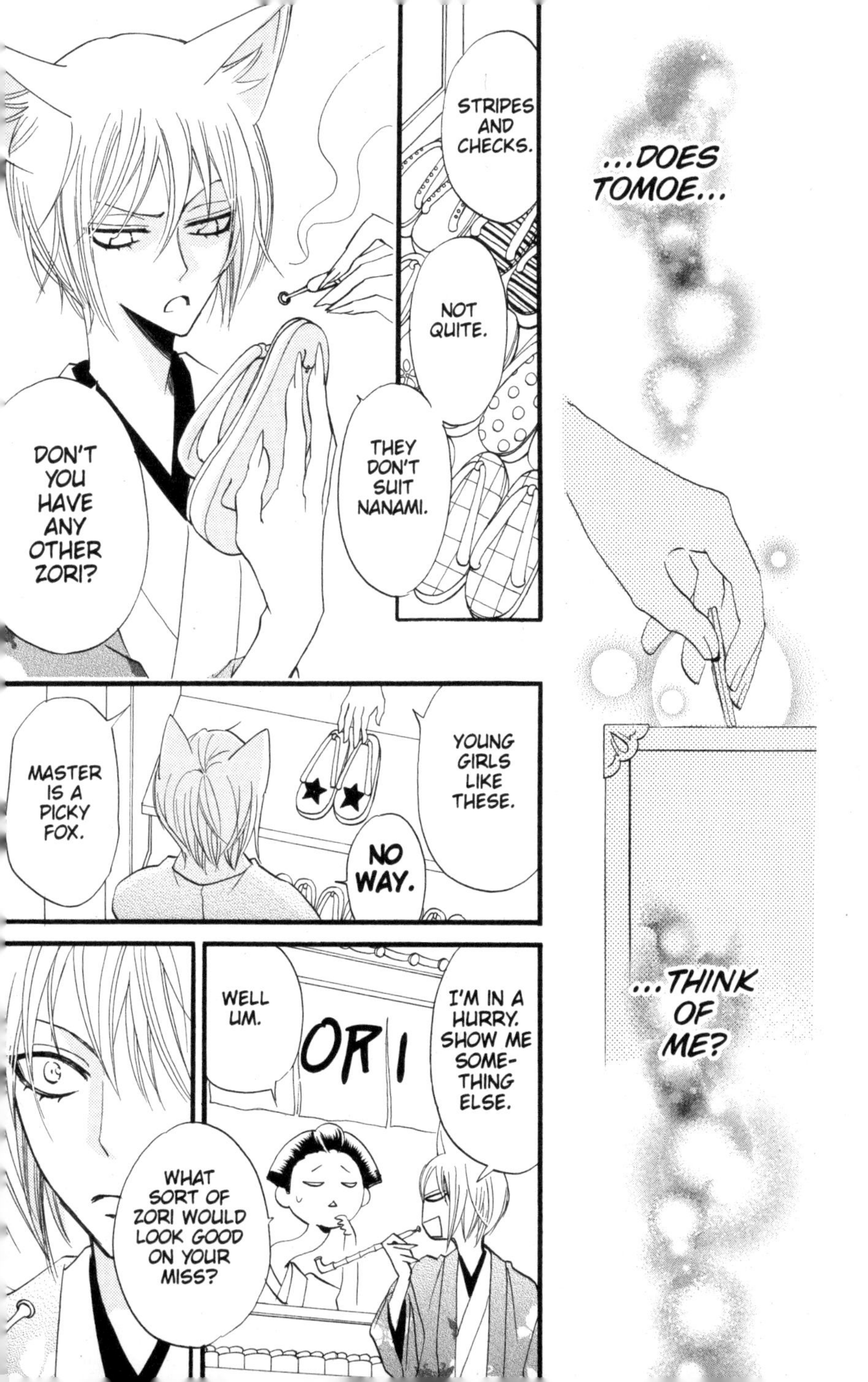
...DOES TOMOE...
...THINK OF ME?
STRIPES AND CHECKS.
NOT QUITE.
THEY DON'T SUIT NANAMI.
DON'T YOU HAVE ANY OTHER ZORI?
YOUNG GIRLS LIKE THESE.
NO WAY.
MASTER IS A PICKY FOX.
I'M IN A HURRY. SHOW ME SOMETHING ELSE.
WELL UM.
ORI
WHAT SORT OF ZORI WOULD LOOK GOOD ON YOUR MISS?

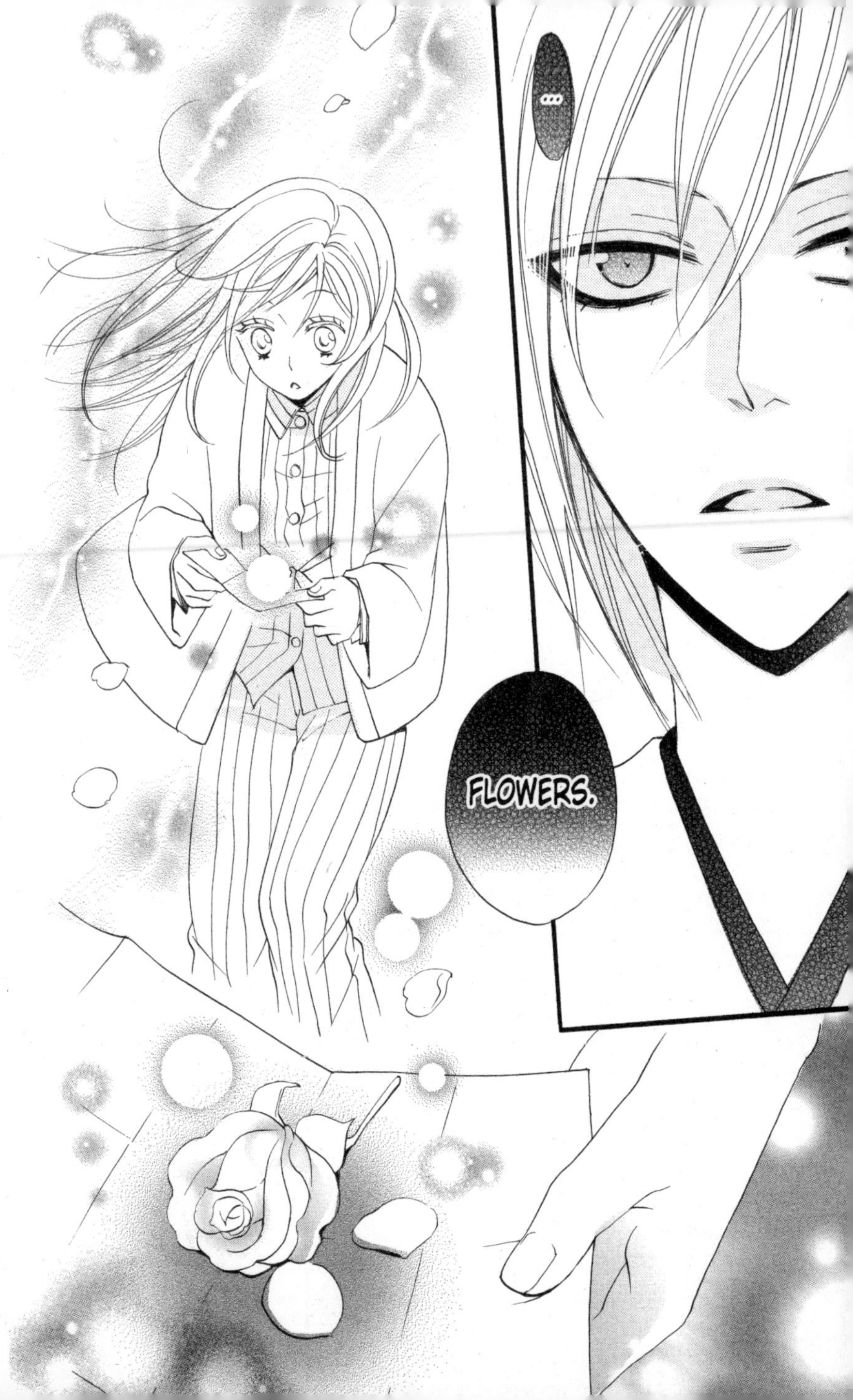
...
FLOWERS.

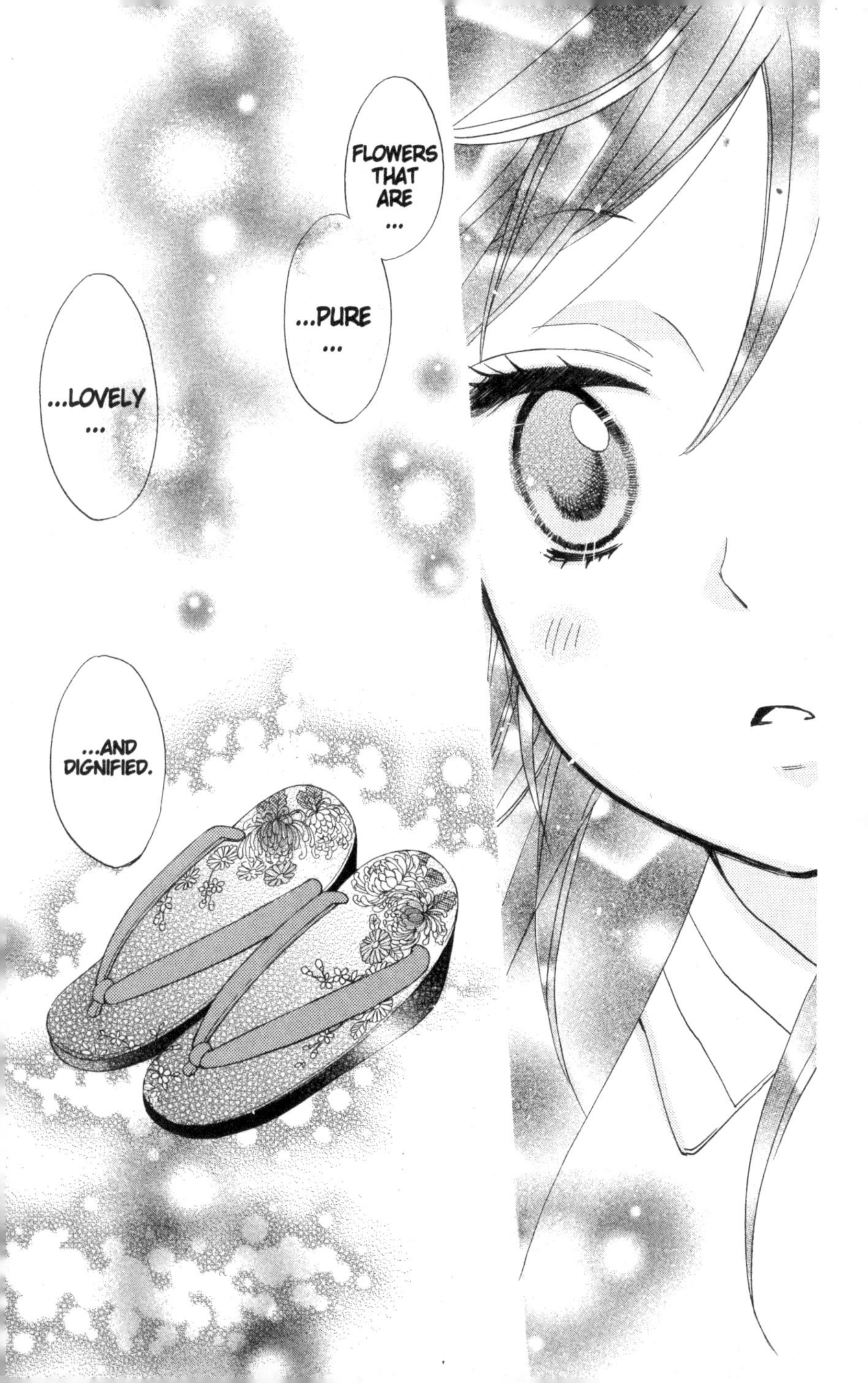
FLOWERS THAT ARE ...
...PURE ...
...LOVELY ...
...AND DIGNIFIED.

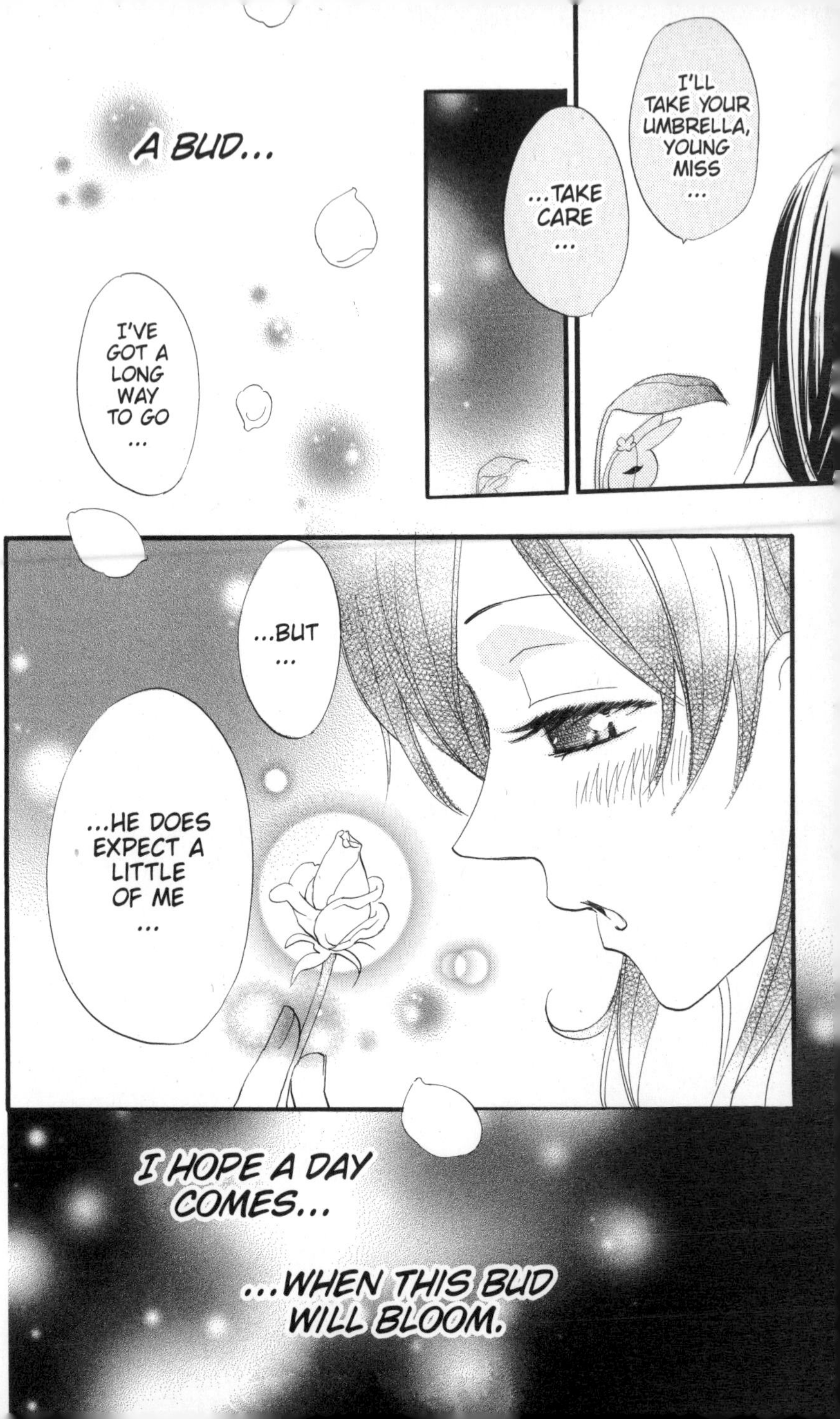
I'LL TAKE YOUR UMBRELLA, YOUNG MISS ...
...TAKE CARE ...
A BUD...
I'VE GOT A LONG WAY TO GO ...
...BUT ...
...HE DOES EXPECT A LITTLE OF ME ...
I HOPE A DAY COMES...
...WHEN THIS BUD WILL BLOOM.

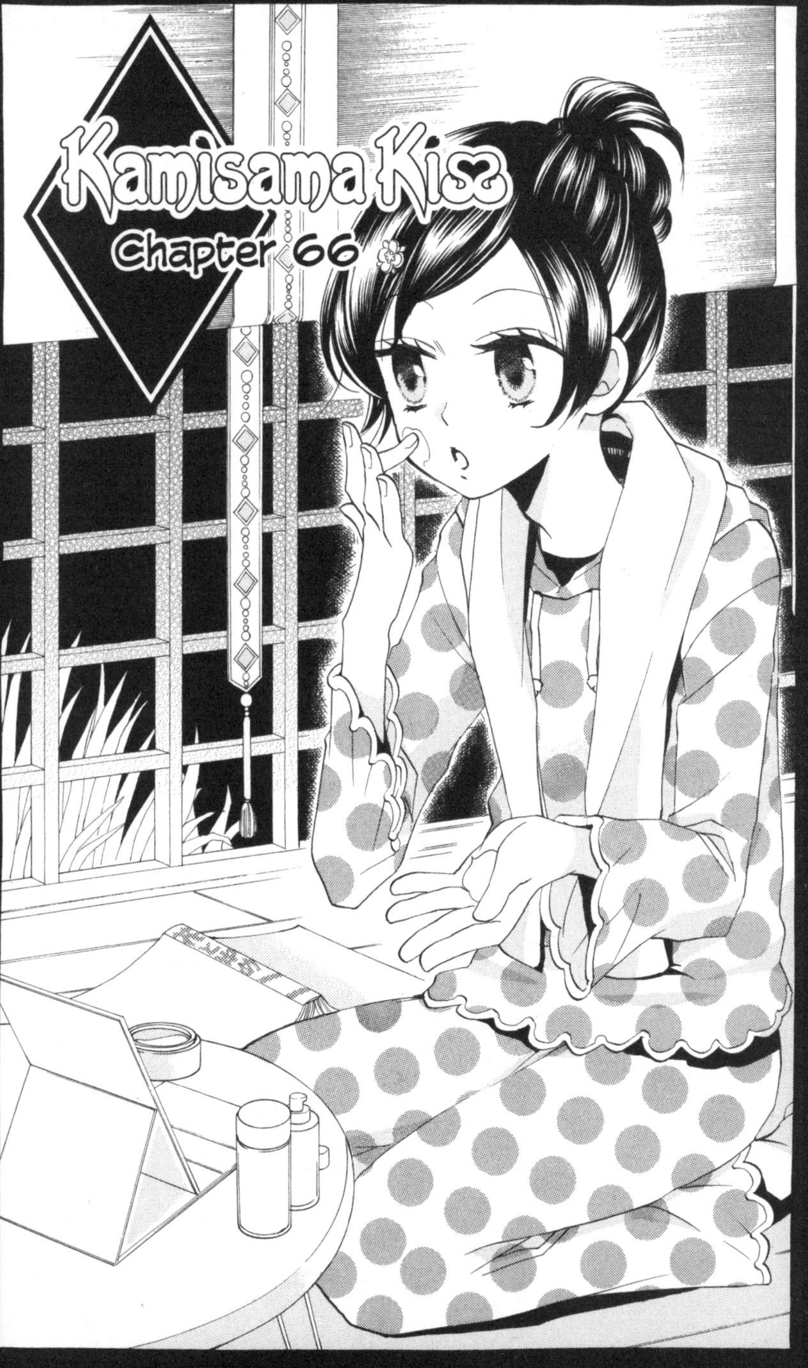
Kamisama Kiss
Chapter 66

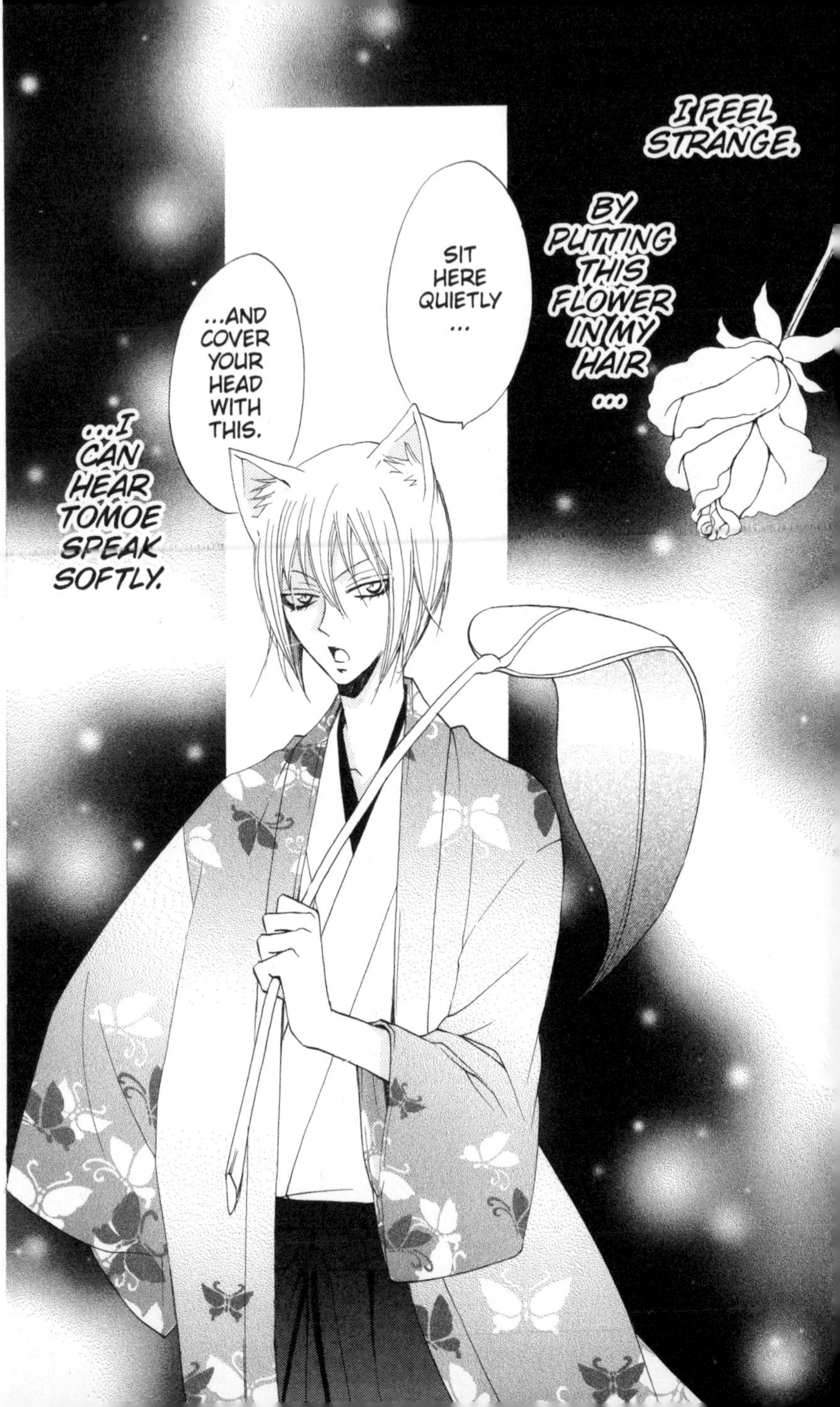
I FEEL STRANGE.
BY PUTTING THIS FLOWER IN MY HAIR...
SIT HERE QUIETLY...
...AND COVER YOUR HEAD WITH THIS.
...I CAN HEAR TOMOE SPEAK SOFTLY.

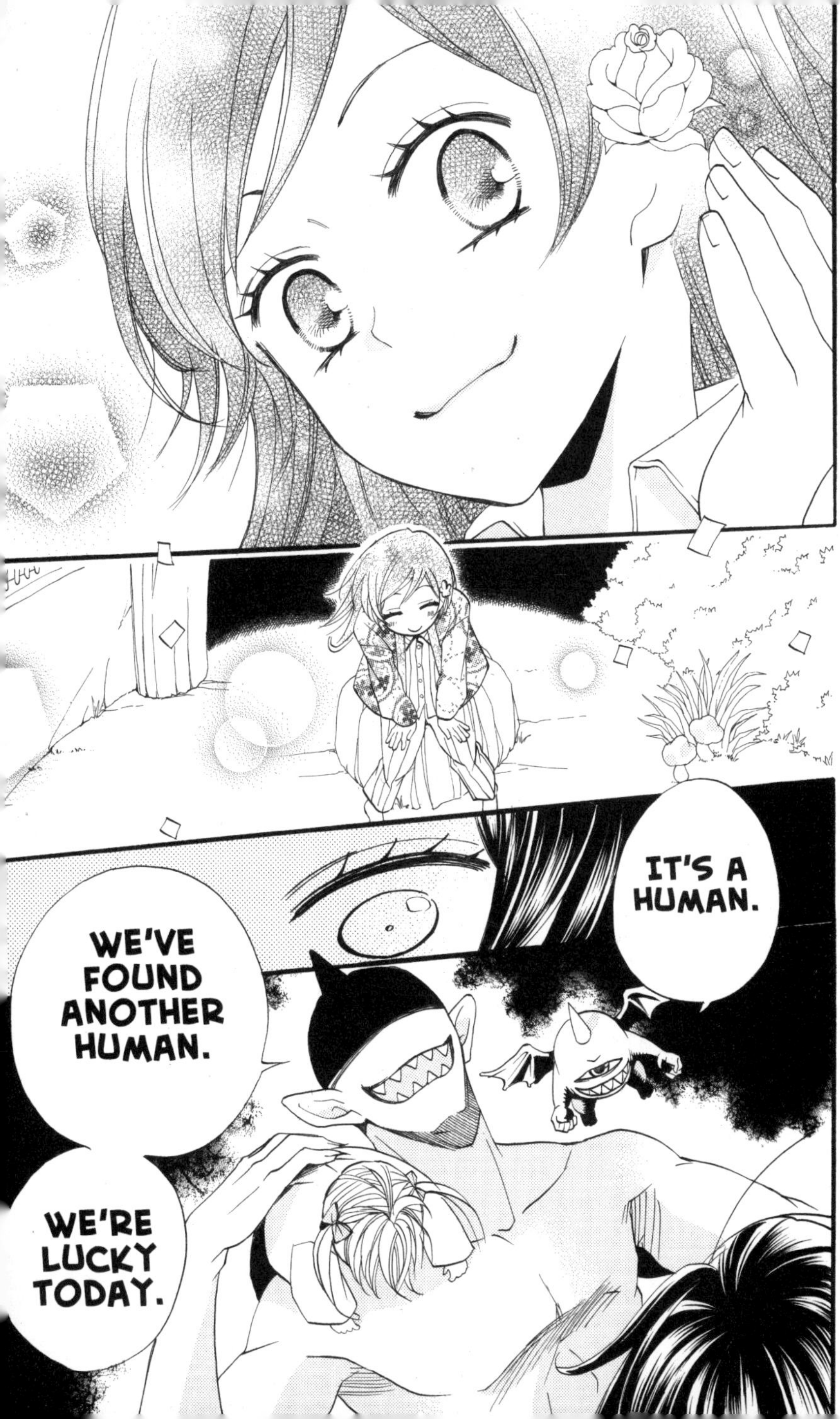
IT'S A HUMAN.
WE'VE FOUND ANOTHER HUMAN.
WE'RE LUCKY TODAY.

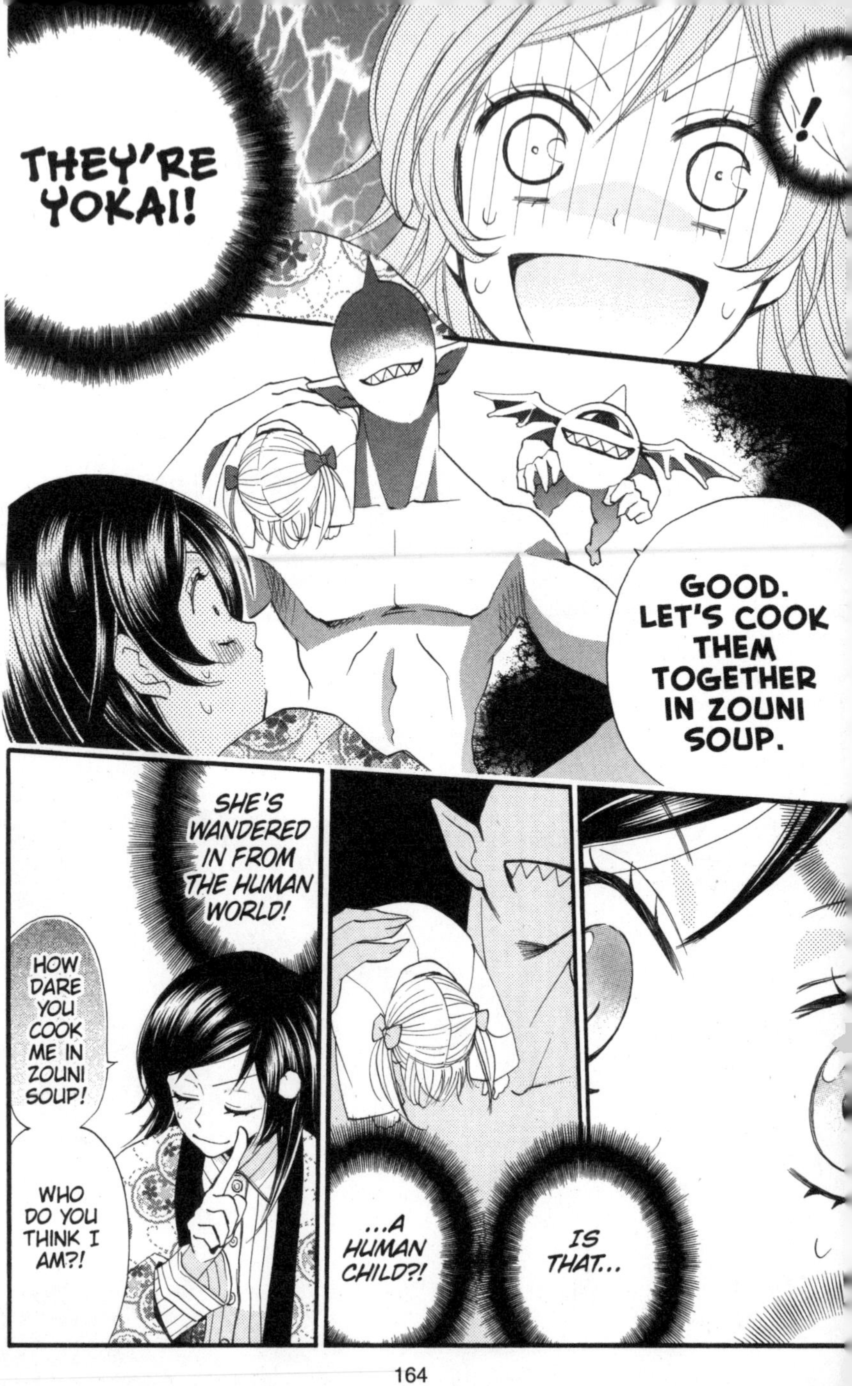
!
THEY'RE YOKAI!
GOOD. LET'S COOK THEM TOGETHER IN ZOUNI SOUP.
IS THAT...
...A HUMAN CHILD?!
SHE'S WANDERED IN FROM THE HUMAN WORLD!
HOW DARE YOU COOK ME IN ZOUNI SOUP!
WHO DO YOU THINK I AM?!

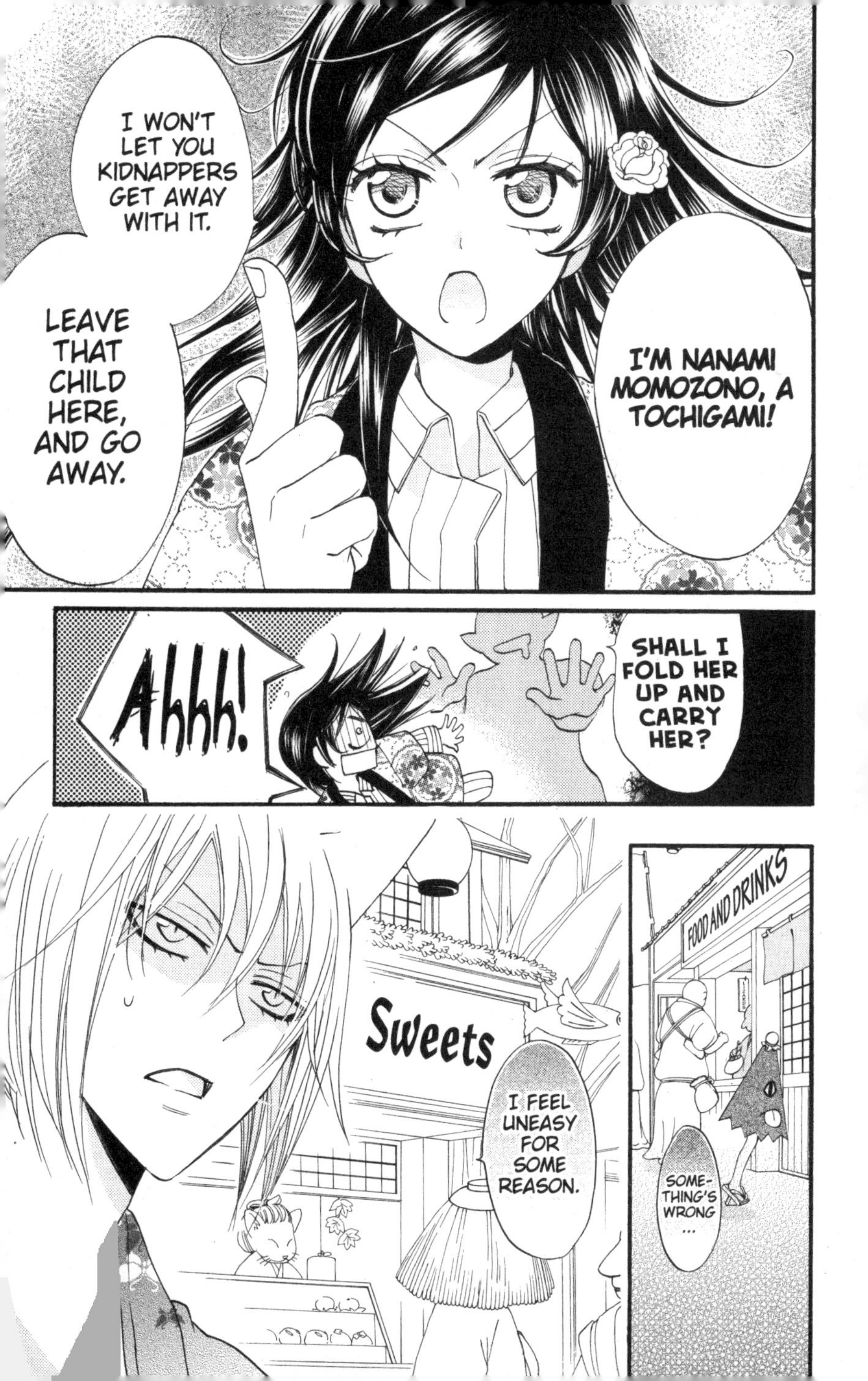
I'M NANAMI MOMOZONO, A TOCHIGAMI!
I WON'T LET YOU KIDNAPPERS GET AWAY WITH IT.
LEAVE THAT CHILD HERE, AND GO AWAY.
SHALL I FOLD HER UP AND CARRY HER?
Ahhh!
FOOD AND DRINKS
SOME-THING'S WRONG ...
Sweets
I FEEL UNEASY FOR SOME REASON.

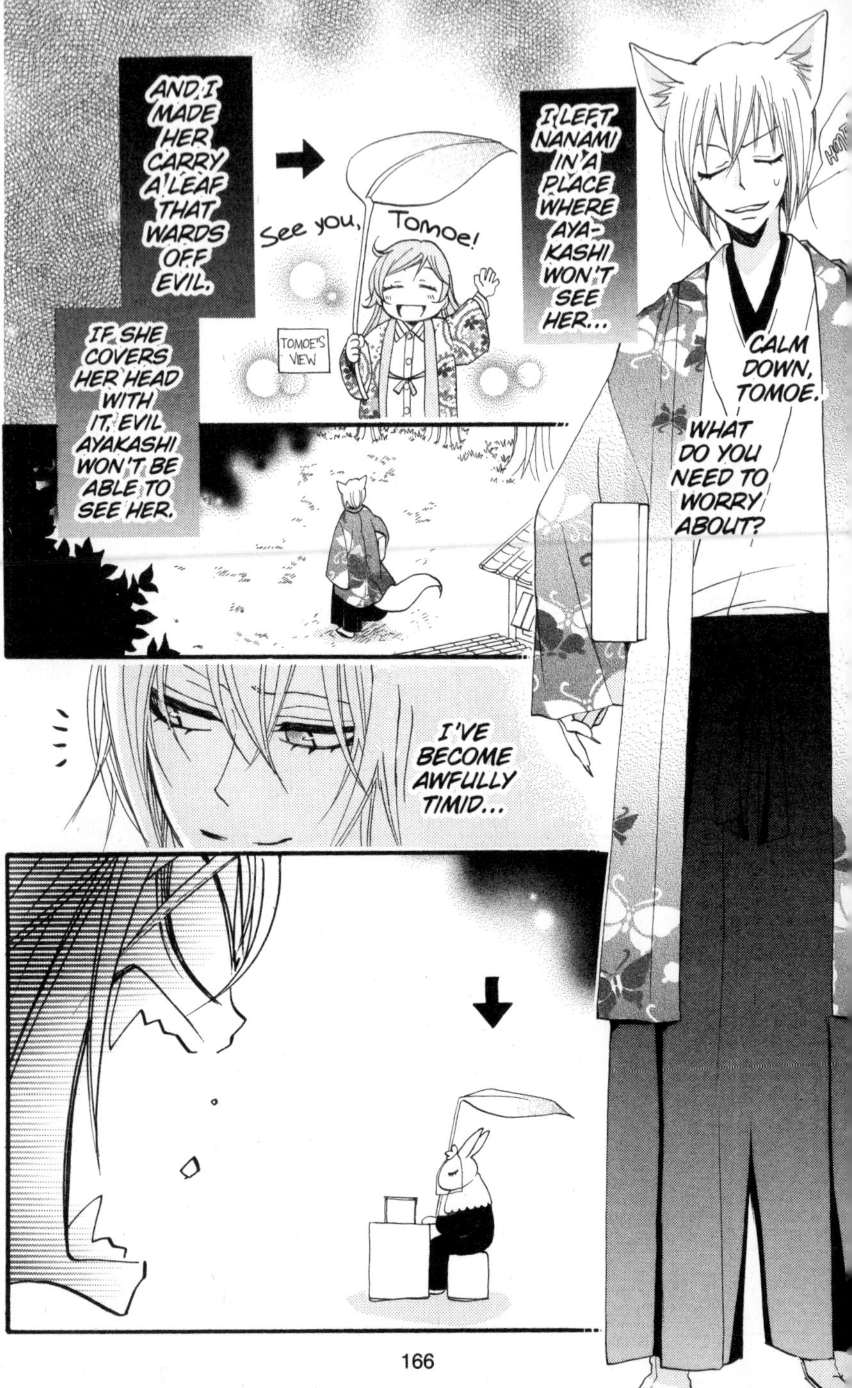
CALM DOWN, TOMOE.
WHAT DO YOU NEED TO WORRY ABOUT?
I LEFT NANAMI IN A PLACE WHERE AYAKASHI WON'T SEE HER...
AND I MADE HER CARRY A LEAF THAT WARDS OFF EVIL.
See you, Tomoe!
TOMOE'S VIEW
IF SHE COVERS HER HEAD WITH IT, EVIL AYAKASHI WON'T BE ABLE TO SEE HER.
I'VE BECOME AWFULLY TIMID...

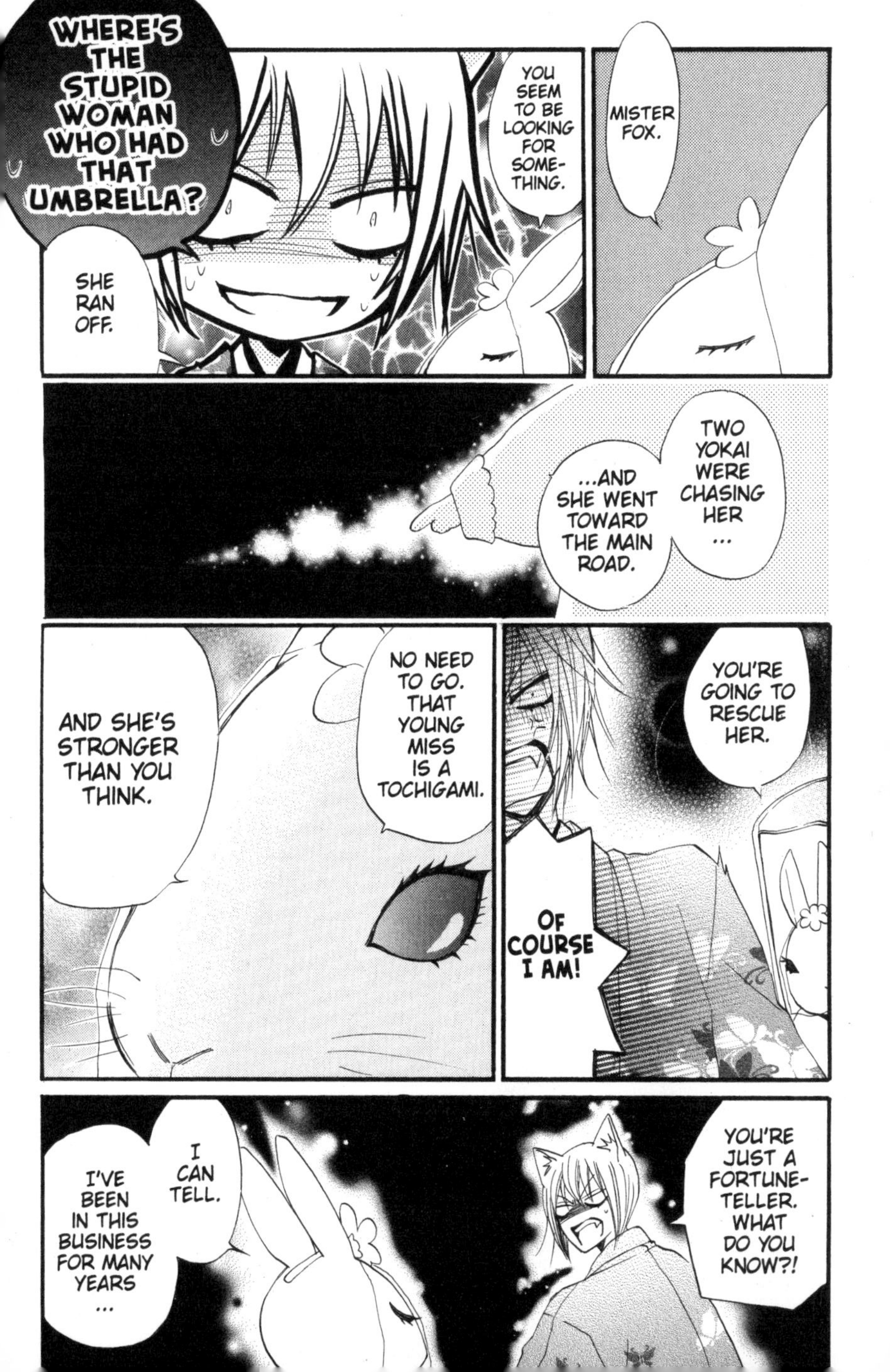
MISTER FOX.
YOU SEEM TO BE LOOKING FOR SOME-THING.
WHERE'S THE STUPID WOMAN WHO HAD THAT UMBRELLA?
SHE RAN OFF.
TWO YOKAI WERE CHASING HER ...
...AND SHE WENT TOWARD THE MAIN ROAD.
YOU'RE GOING TO RESCUE HER.
OF COURSE I AM!
NO NEED TO GO. THAT YOUNG MISS IS A TOCHIGAMI.
AND SHE'S STRONGER THAN YOU THINK.
YOU'RE JUST A FORTUNE-TELLER. WHAT DO YOU KNOW?!
I CAN TELL.
I'VE BEEN IN THIS BUSINESS FOR MANY YEARS ...

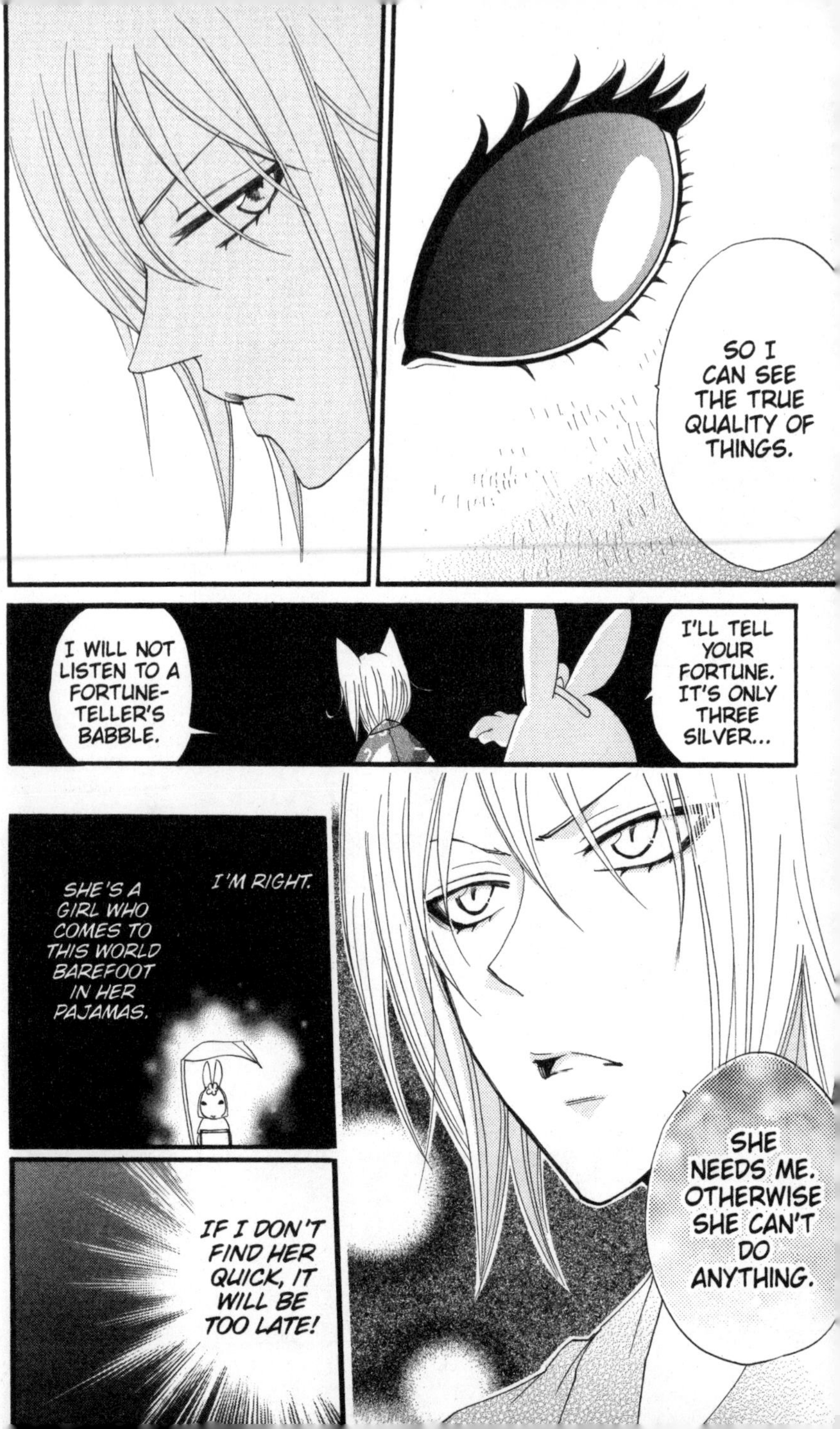
SO I CAN SEE THE TRUE QUALITY OF THINGS.
I'LL TELL YOUR FORTUNE. IT'S ONLY THREE SILVER...
I WILL NOT LISTEN TO A FORTUNE-TELLER'S BABBLE.
SHE NEEDS ME. OTHERWISE SHE CAN'T DO ANYTHING.
I'M RIGHT.
SHE'S A GIRL WHO COMES TO THIS WORLD BAREFOOT IN HER PAJAMAS.
IF I DON'T FIND HER QUICK, IT WILL BE TOO LATE!

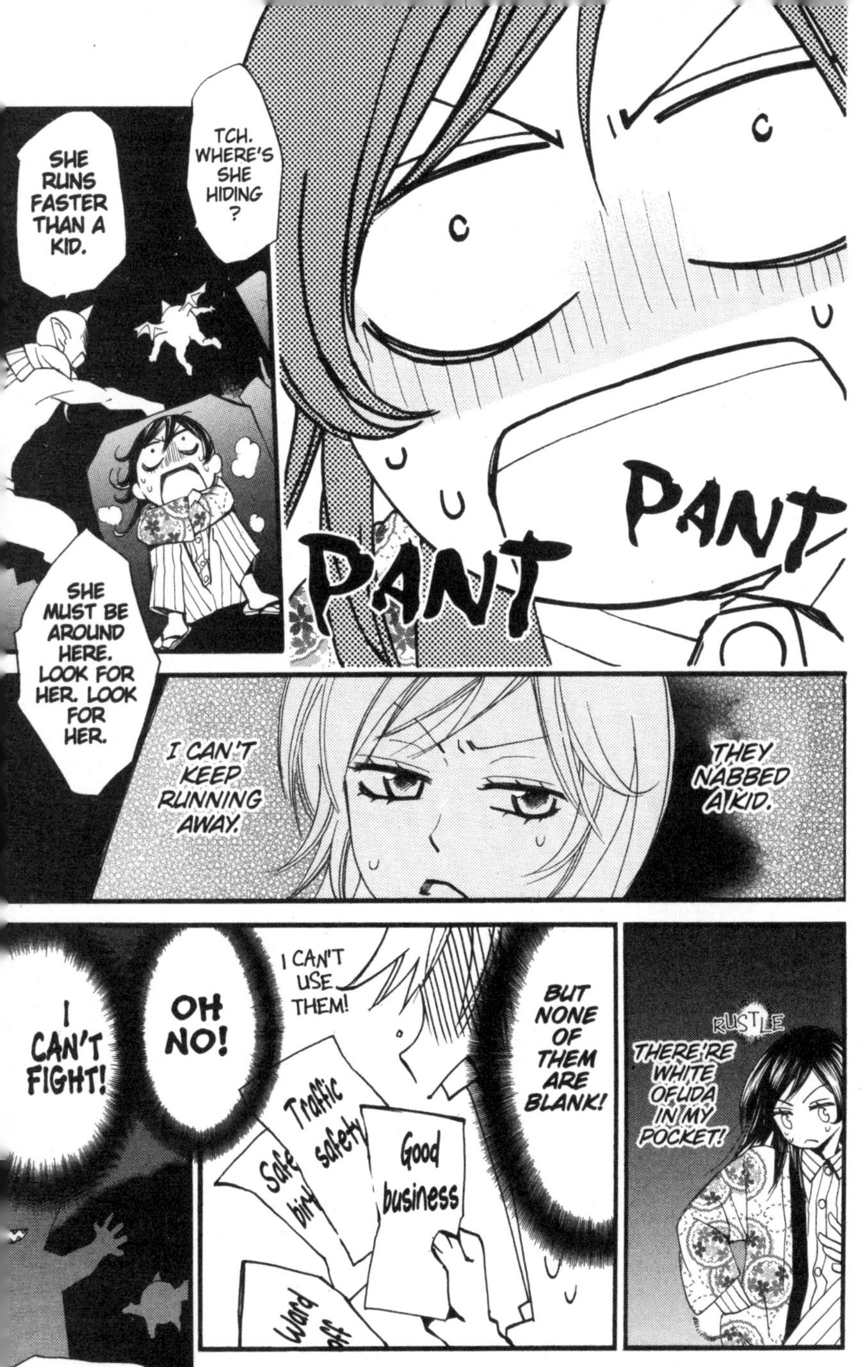
PANT
PANT
TCH. WHERE'S SHE HIDING?
SHE RUNS FASTER THAN A KID.
SHE MUST BE AROUND HERE. LOOK FOR HER. LOOK FOR HER.
THEY NABBED A KID.
I CAN'T KEEP RUNNING AWAY.
RUSTLE
THERE'RE WHITE OFUDA IN MY POCKET!
BUT NONE OF THEM ARE BLANK!
I CAN'T USE THEM!
Good business
Traffic safety
OH NO!
I CAN'T FIGHT!

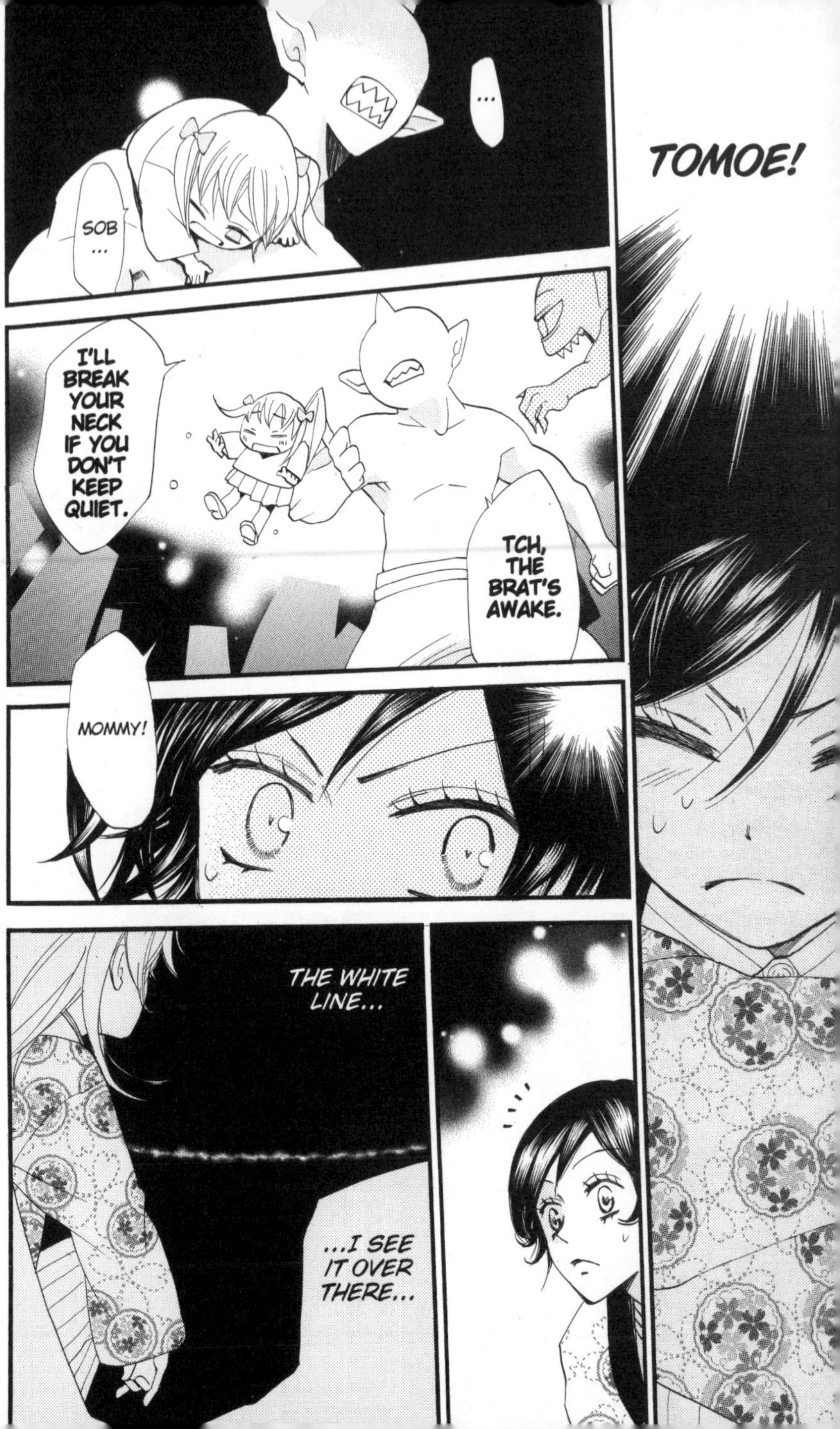
TOMOE!
...
SOB ...
TCH, THE BRAT'S AWAKE.
I'LL BREAK YOUR NECK IF YOU DON'T KEEP QUIET.
MOMMY!
THE WHITE LINE...
...I SEE IT OVER THERE...

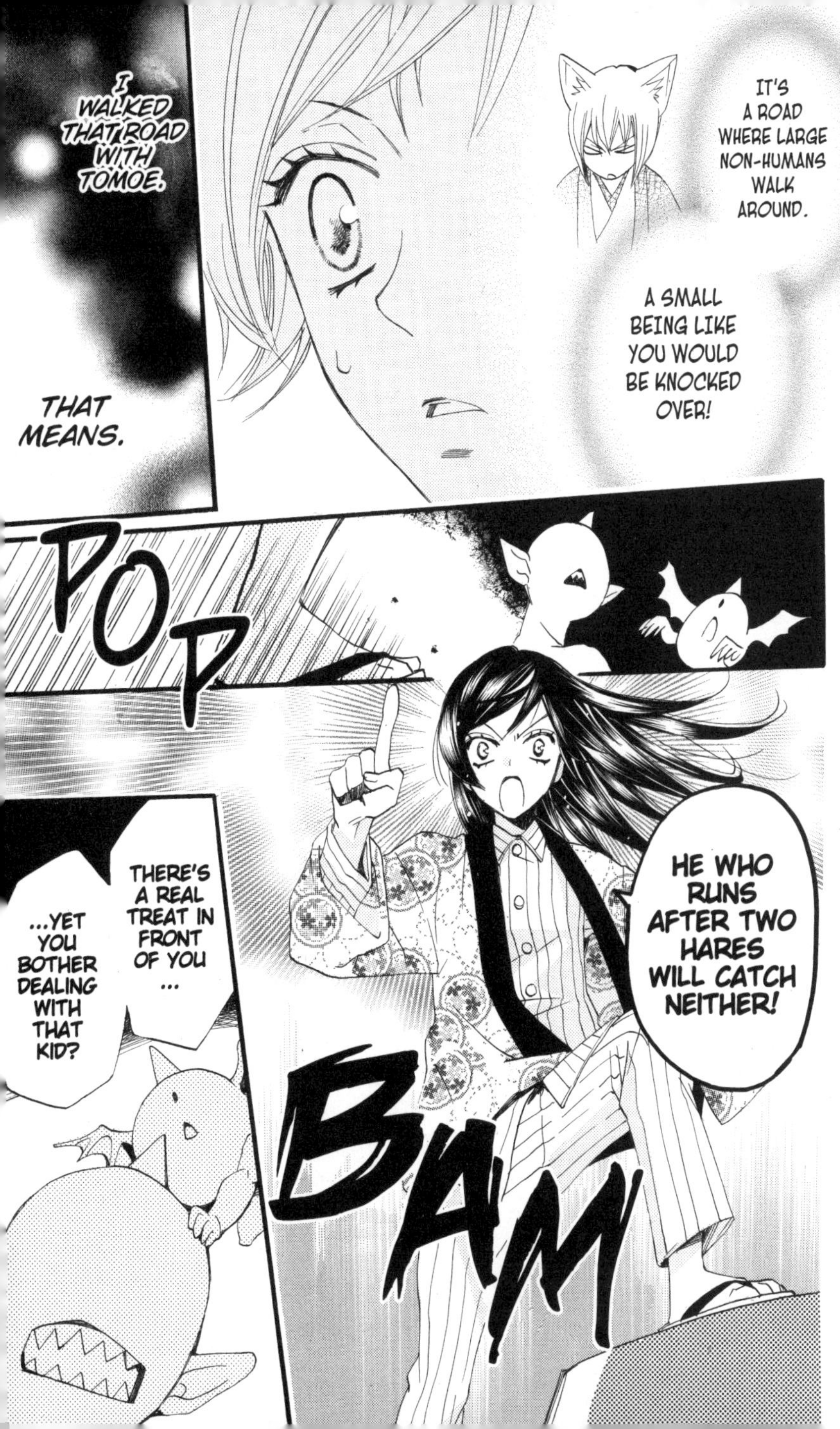
IT'S A ROAD WHERE LARGE NON-HUMANS WALK AROUND.
A SMALL BEING LIKE YOU WOULD BE KNOCKED OVER!
I WALKED THAT ROAD WITH TOMOE.
THAT MEANS.
POP
HE WHO RUNS AFTER TWO HARES WILL CATCH NEITHER!
BAM
THERE'S A REAL TREAT IN FRONT OF YOU ...
...YET YOU BOTHER DEALING WITH THAT KID?

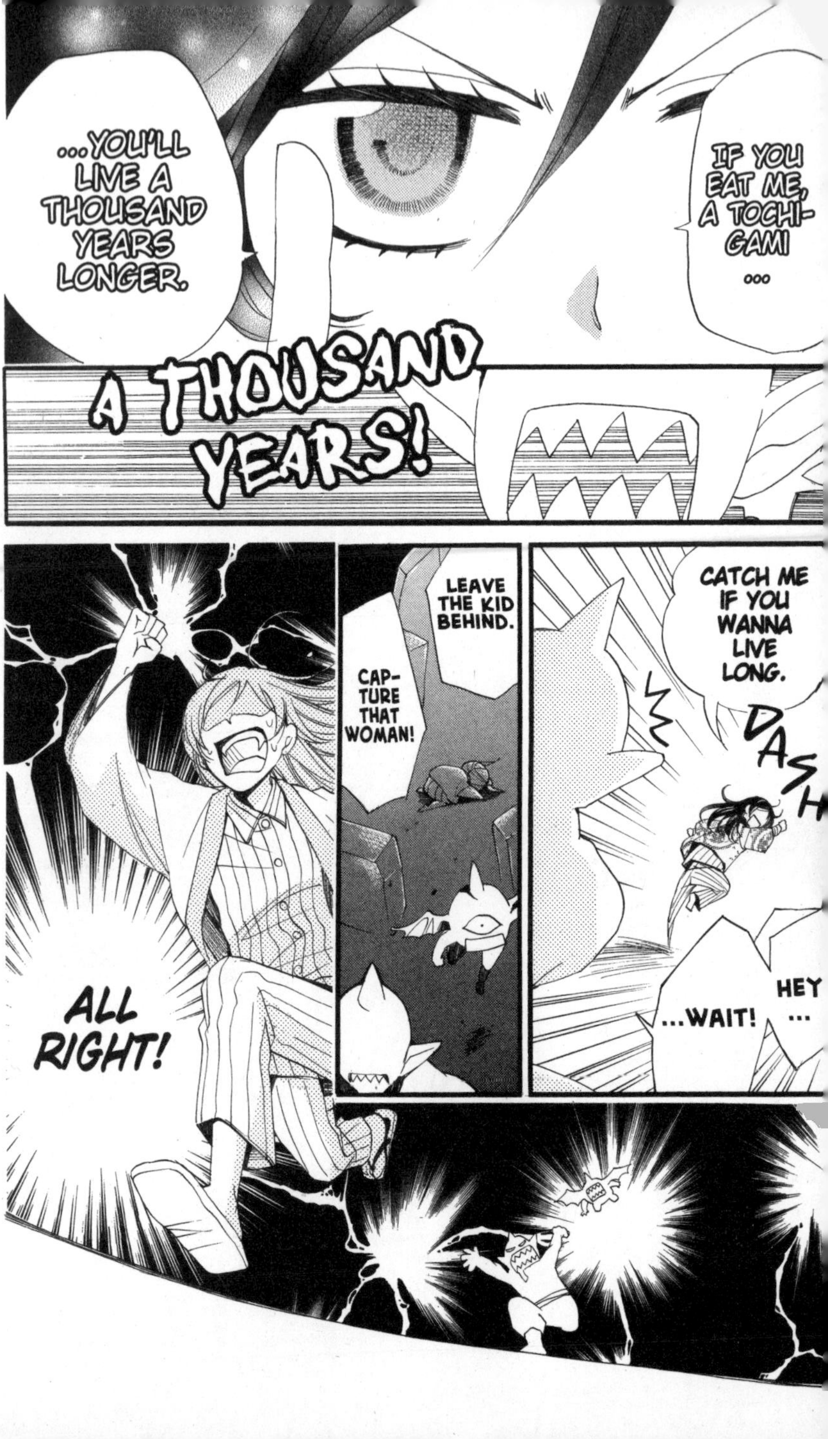
IF YOU EAT ME, A TOCHI-GAMI ...
...YOU'LL LIVE A THOUSAND YEARS LONGER.
A THOUSAND YEARS!
CATCH ME IF YOU WANNA LIVE LONG.
DASH
HEY ...
...WAIT!
LEAVE THE KID BEHIND.
CAP-TURE THAT WOMAN!
ALL RIGHT!

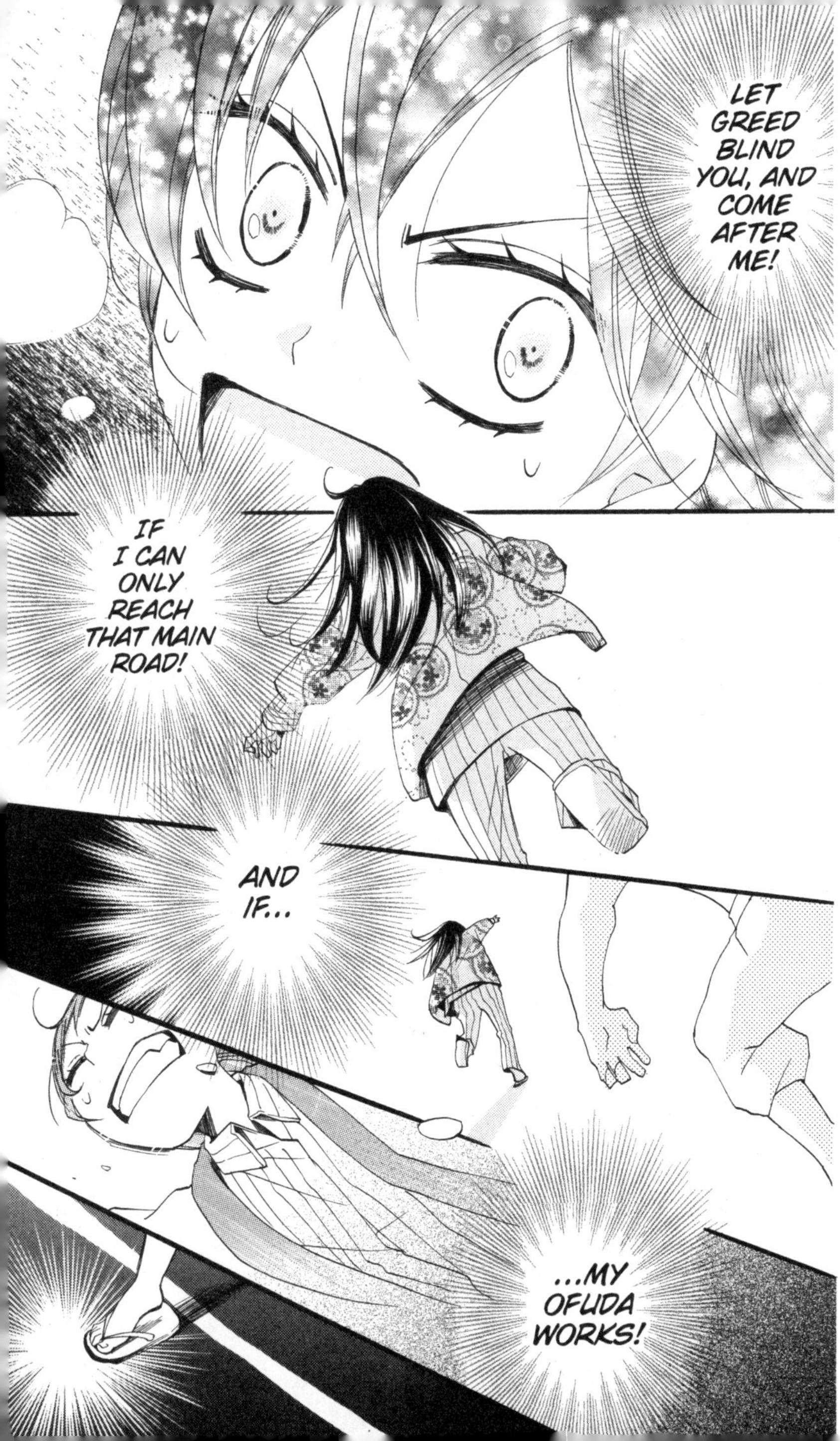
LET GREED BLIND YOU, AND COME AFTER ME!
IF I CAN ONLY REACH THAT MAIN ROAD!
AND IF...
...MY OFUDA WORKS!

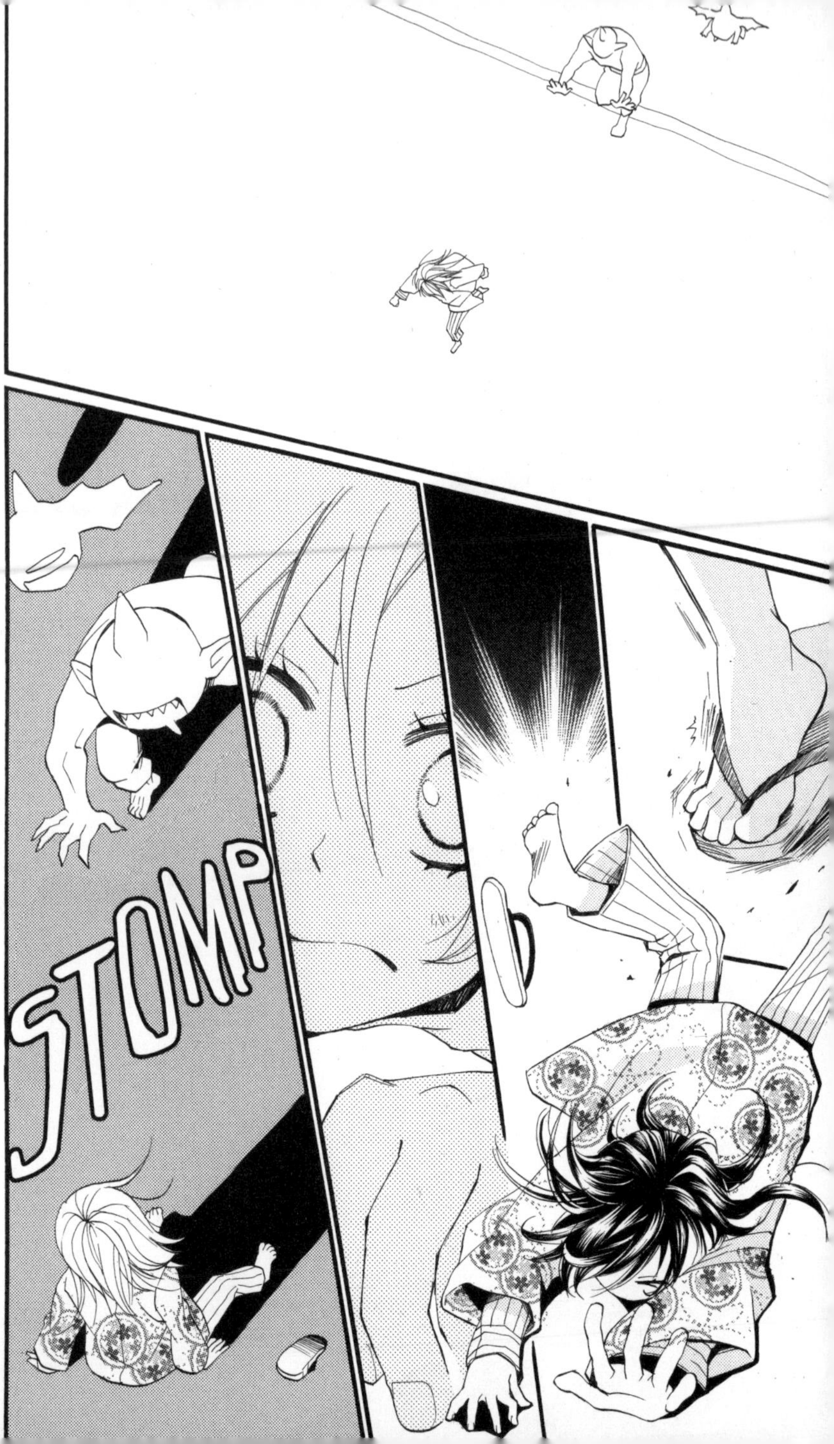
STOMP

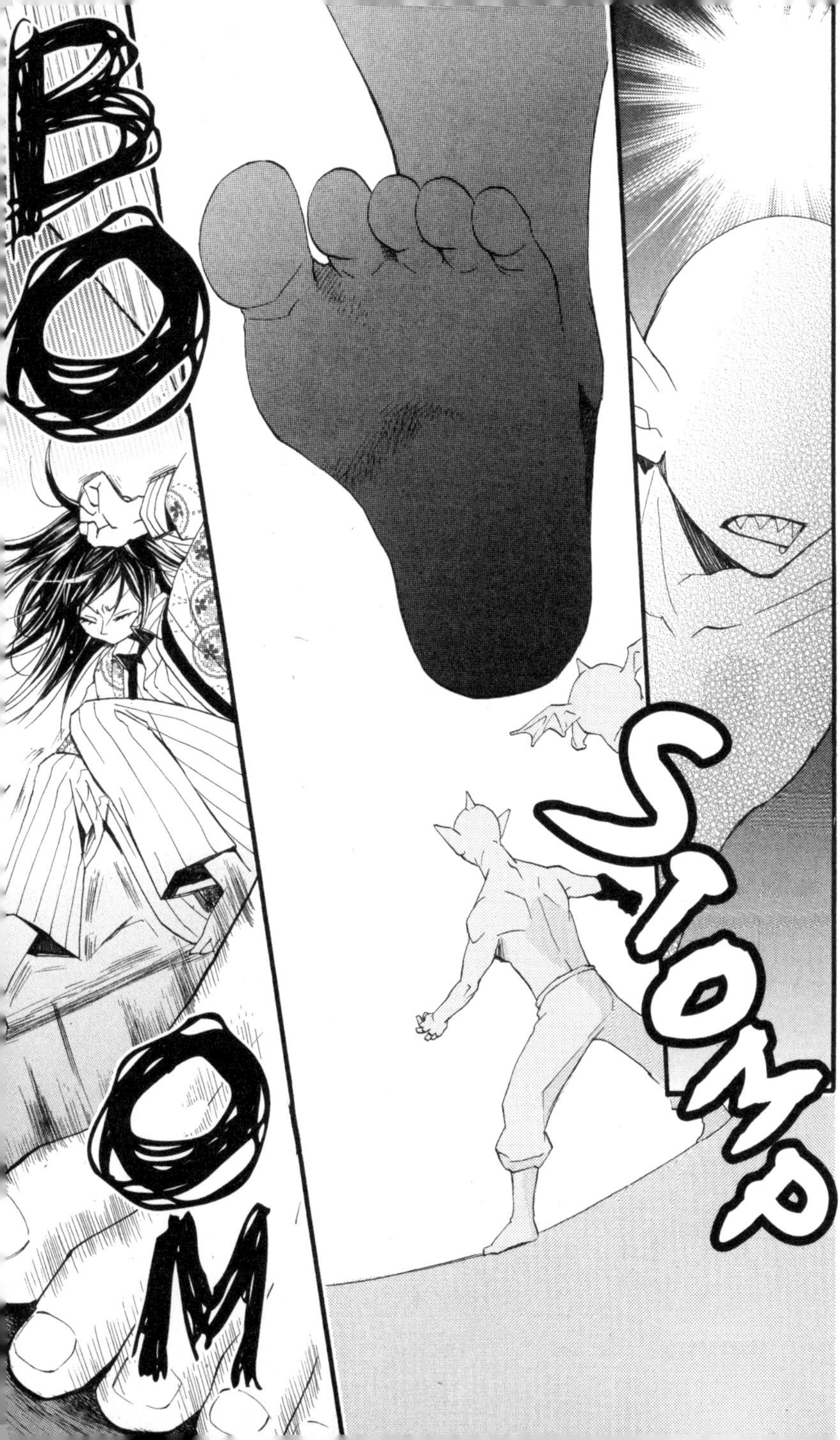
STOMP
BOOM

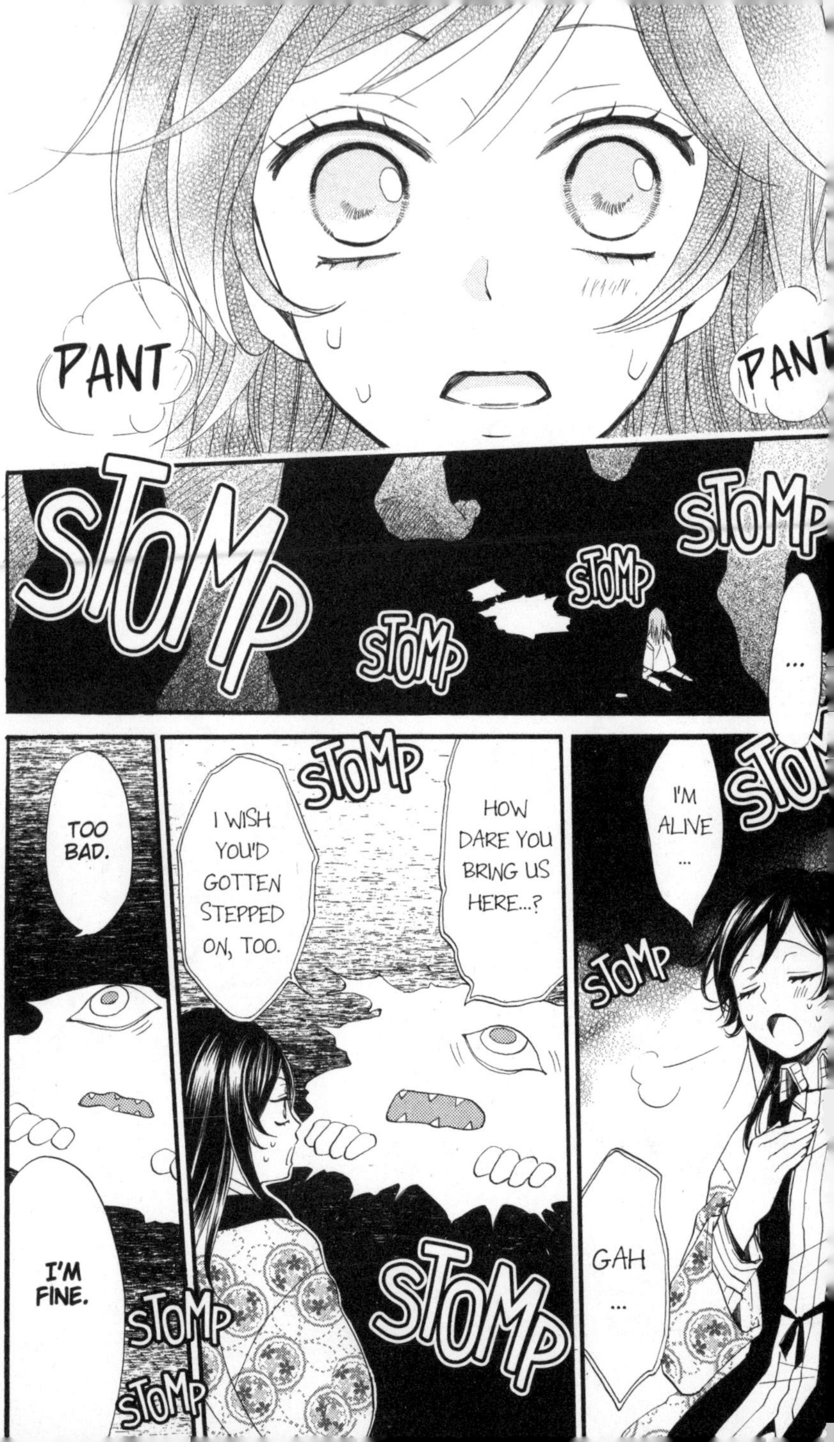
PANT
PANT
STOMP
...
STOMP
STOMP
STOMP
STOMP
I'M ALIVE ...
STOMP
GAH ...
HOW DARE YOU BRING US HERE...?
STOMP
I WISH YOU'D GOTTEN STEPPED ON, TOO.
STOMP
TOO BAD.
I'M FINE.
STOMP
STOMP

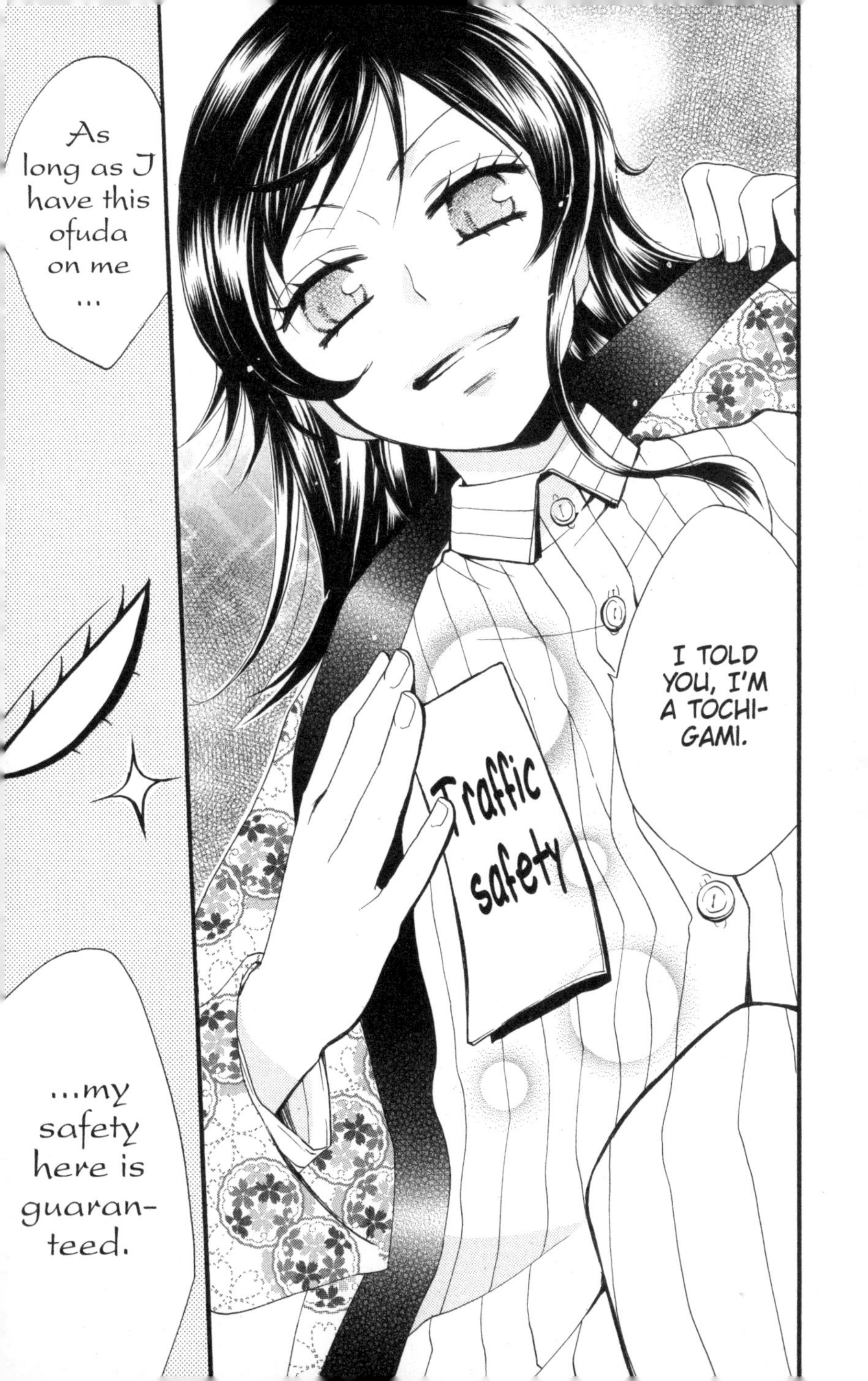
I TOLD YOU, I'M A TOCHI-GAMI.
Traffic safety
As long as I have this ofuda on me ...
...my safety here is guaran-teed.

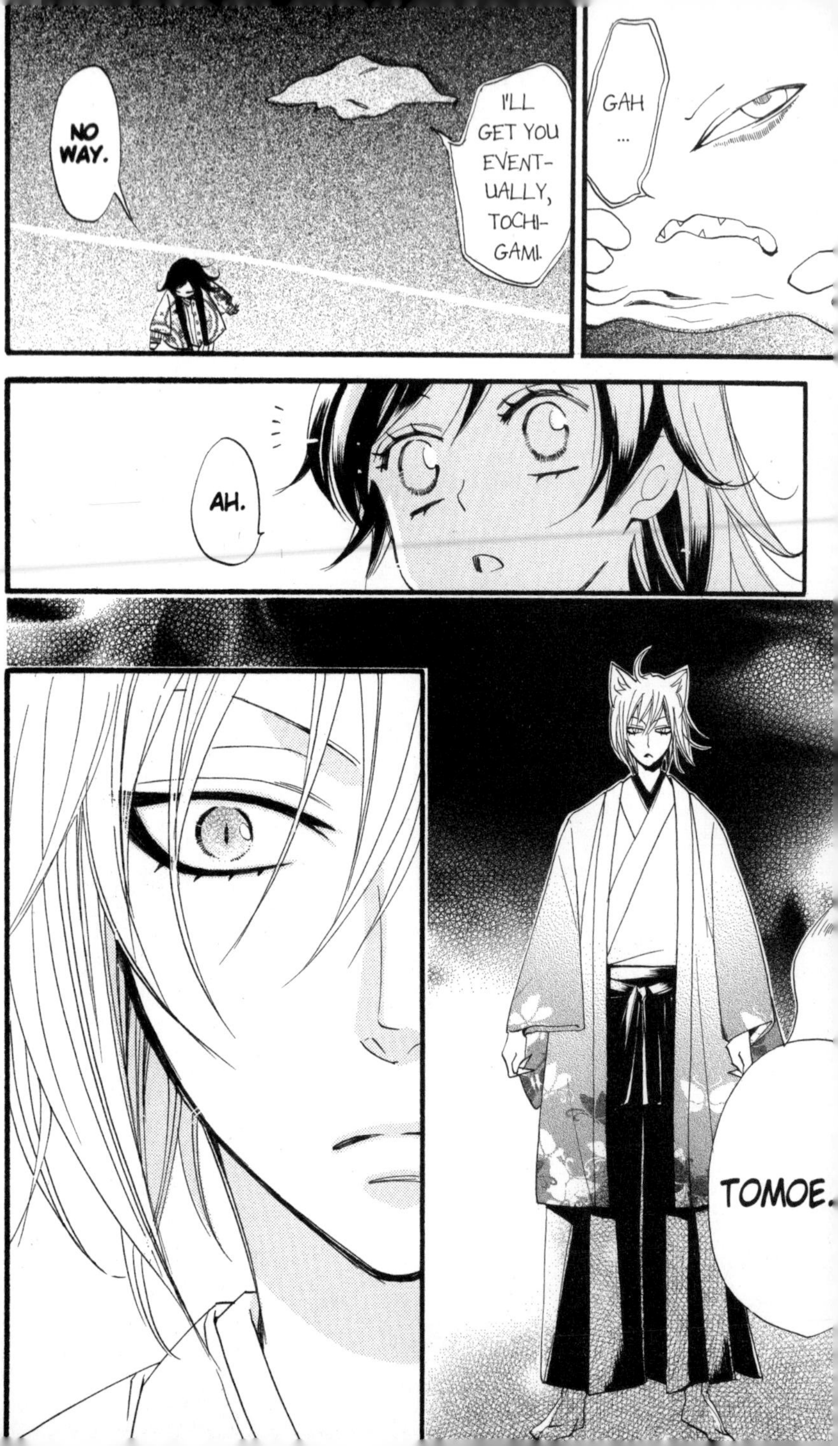
GAH ...
I'LL GET YOU EVENT-UALLY, TOCHI-GAMI.
NO WAY.
AH.
TOMOE.

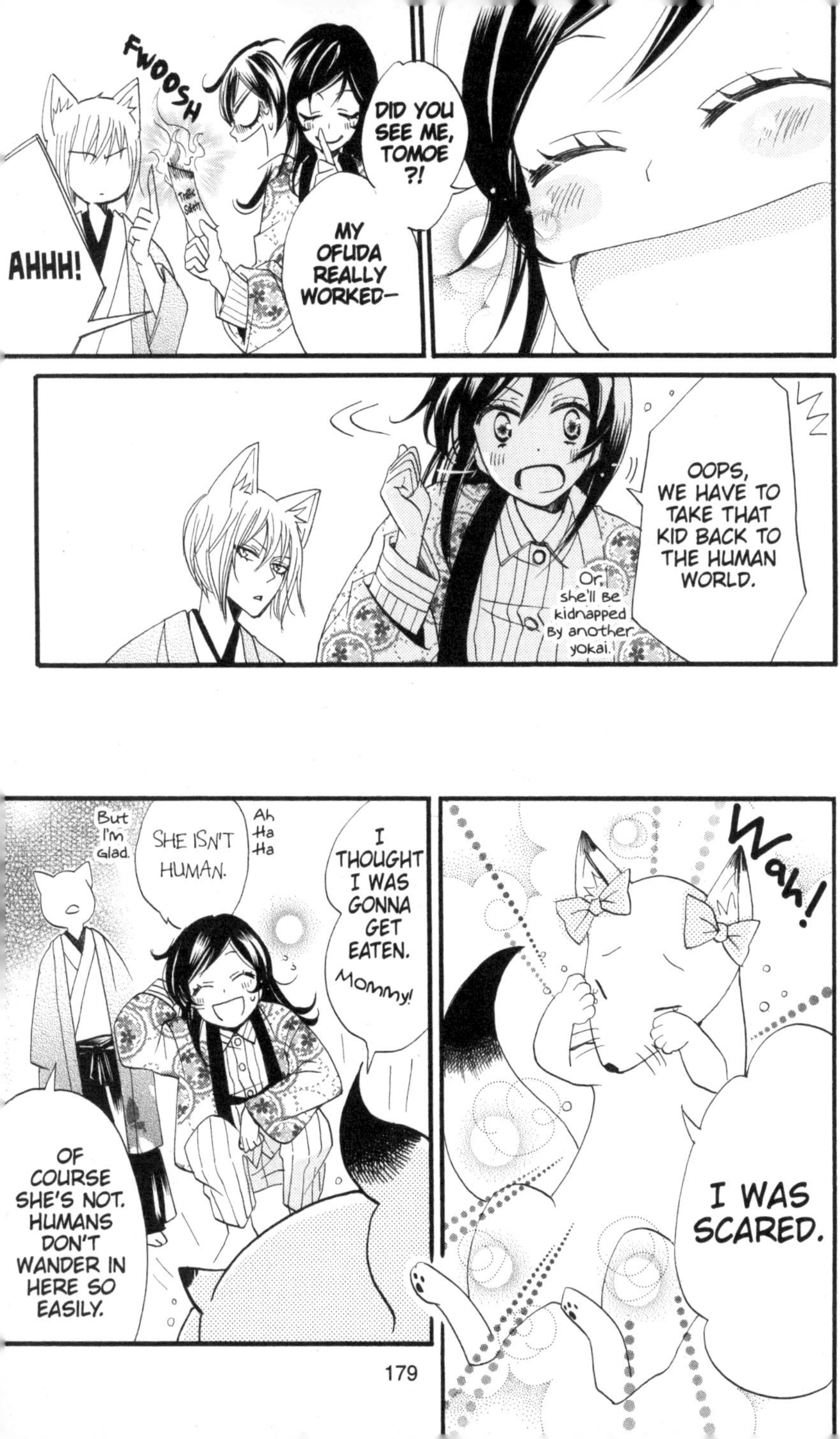
DID YOU SEE ME, TOMOE ?!
MY OFUDA REALLY WORKED—
FWOOSH
Traffic Safety
AHHH!
OOPS, WE HAVE TO TAKE THAT KID BACK TO THE HUMAN WORLD.
Or, she'll be kidnapped by another yokai.
Wah!
I WAS SCARED.
I THOUGHT I WAS GONNA GET EATEN.
Mommy!
Ah Ha Ha
SHE ISN'T HUMAN.
But I'm Glad.
OF COURSE SHE'S NOT. HUMANS DON'T WANDER IN HERE SO EASILY.

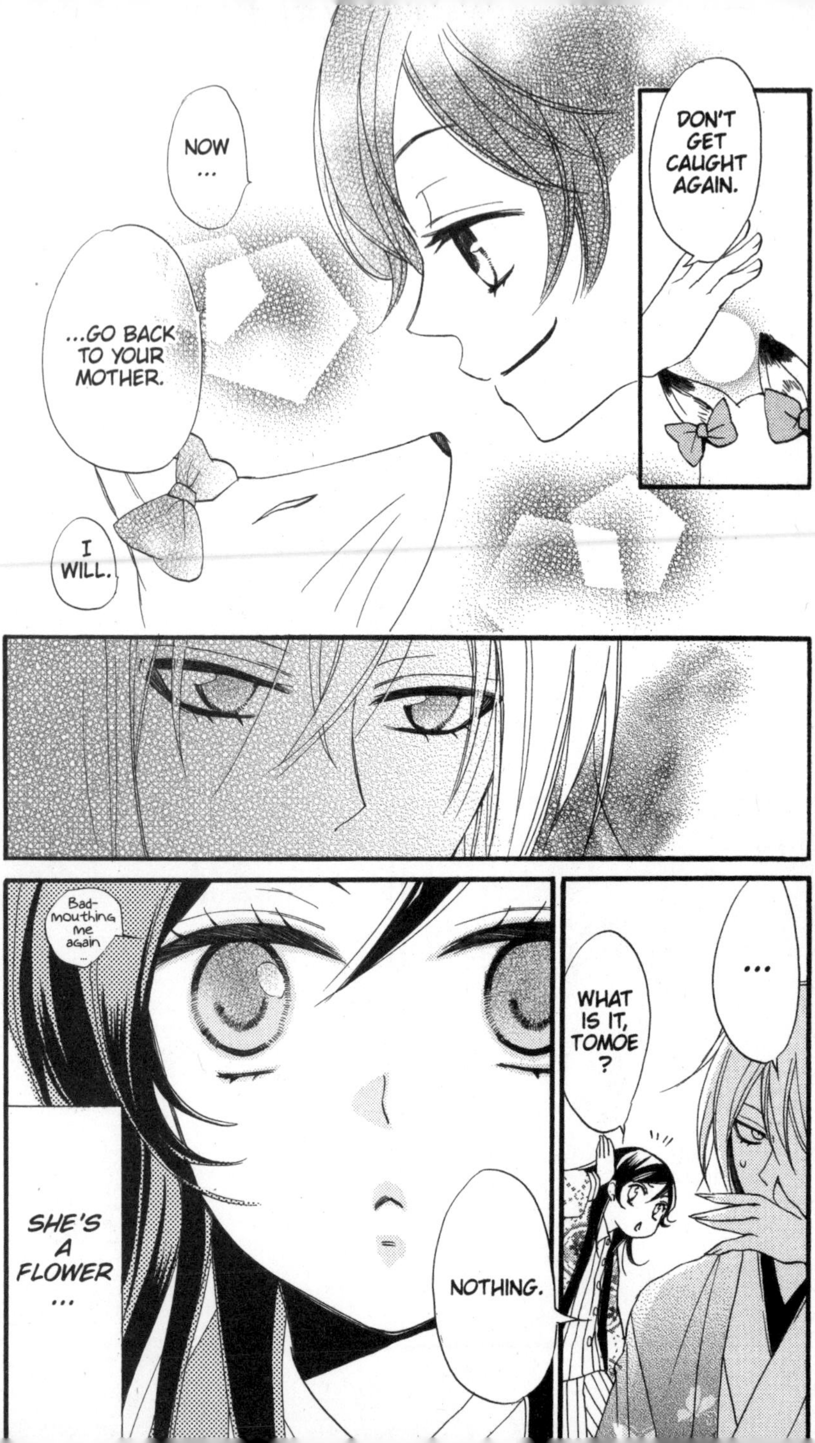
DON'T GET CAUGHT AGAIN.
NOW ...
...GO BACK TO YOUR MOTHER.
I WILL.
...
WHAT IS IT, TOMOE?
NOTHING.
Bad-mouthing me again ...
SHE'S A FLOWER ...

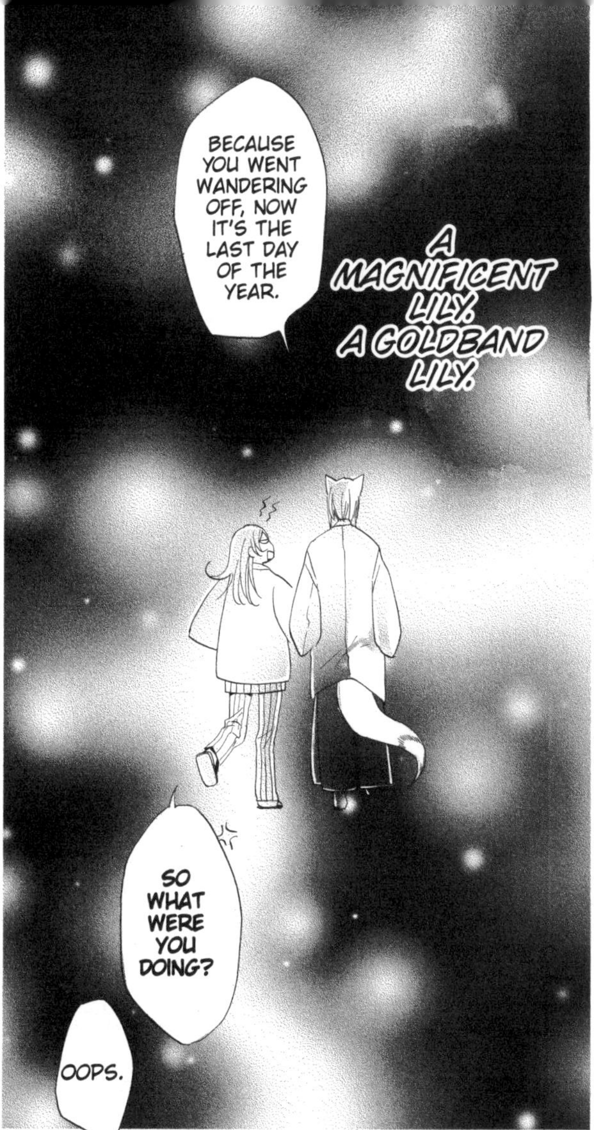
A MAGNIFICENT LILY. A GOLDBAND LILY.
BECAUSE YOU WENT WANDERING OFF, NOW IT'S THE LAST DAY OF THE YEAR.
SO WHAT WERE YOU DOING?
OOPS.

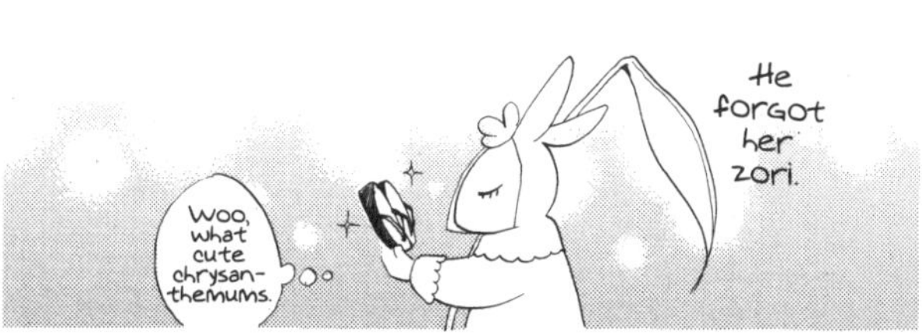
He forgot her zori.
Woo, what cute chrysan-themums.

Thank you for reading this far!

This time, I had Okazaki-san, who's done a great job assisting me since Odette, draw a guest manuscript and some sidebars. Thank you!

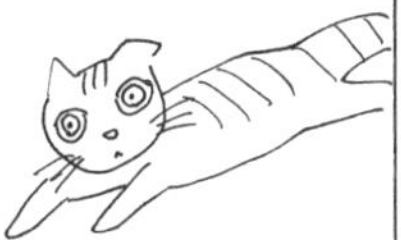

I write a BLOG, and I twitter as well.

My BLOG

http://suzuju.jugem.jp/

I write about my work and my daily life, so please come take a look.

If you have any comments, please let me hear you.

Julietta Suzuki
c/o Shojo Beat
VIZ Media, LLC
P.O. Box 77010
San Francisco
CA 94107

Thank you.

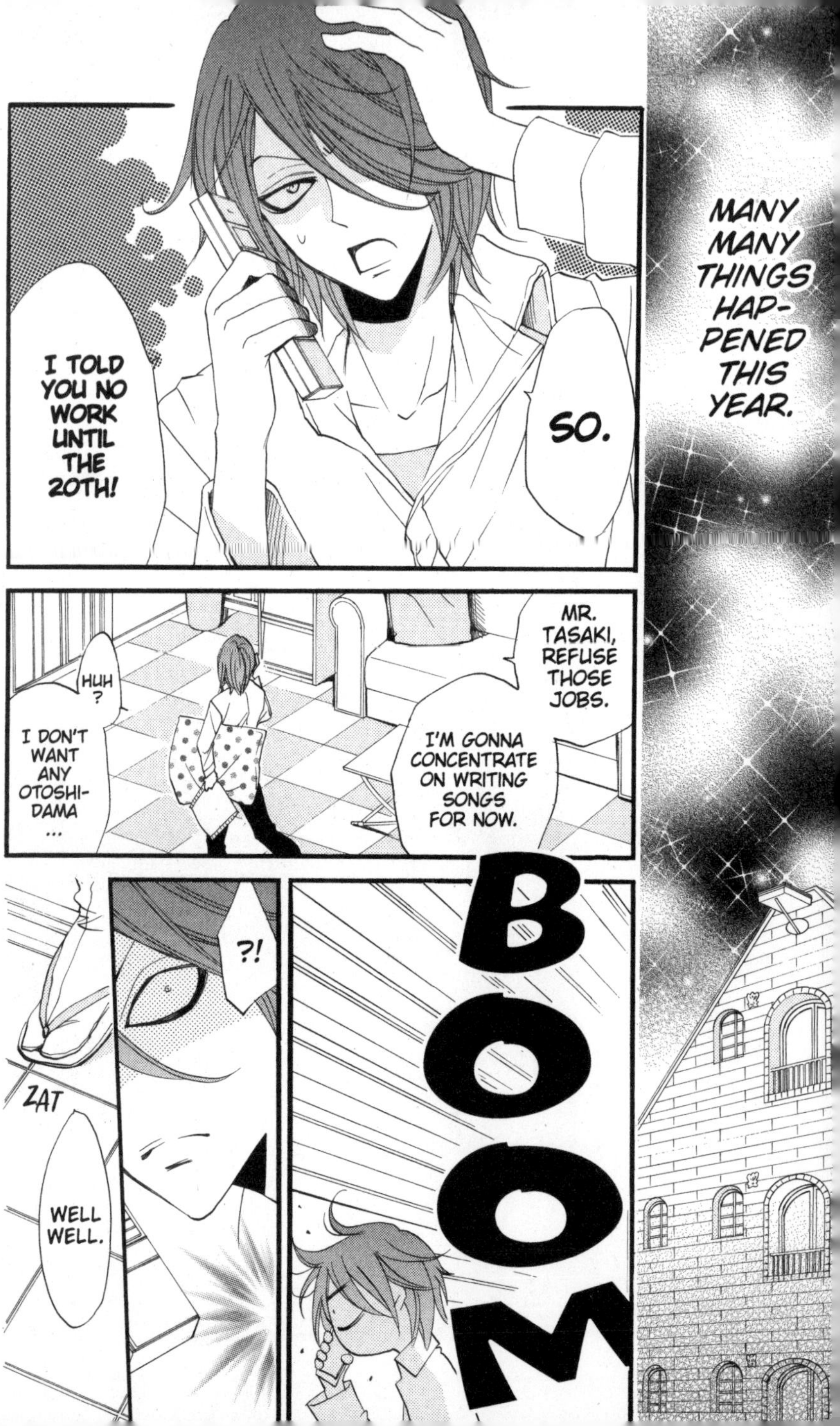
MANY MANY THINGS HAP-PENED THIS YEAR.
SO.
I TOLD YOU NO WORK UNTIL THE 20TH!
MR. TASAKI, REFUSE THOSE JOBS.
I'M GONNA CONCENTRATE ON WRITING SONGS FOR NOW.
HUH?
I DON'T WANT ANY OTOSHI-DAMA...
BOOM
?!
ZAT
WELL WELL.

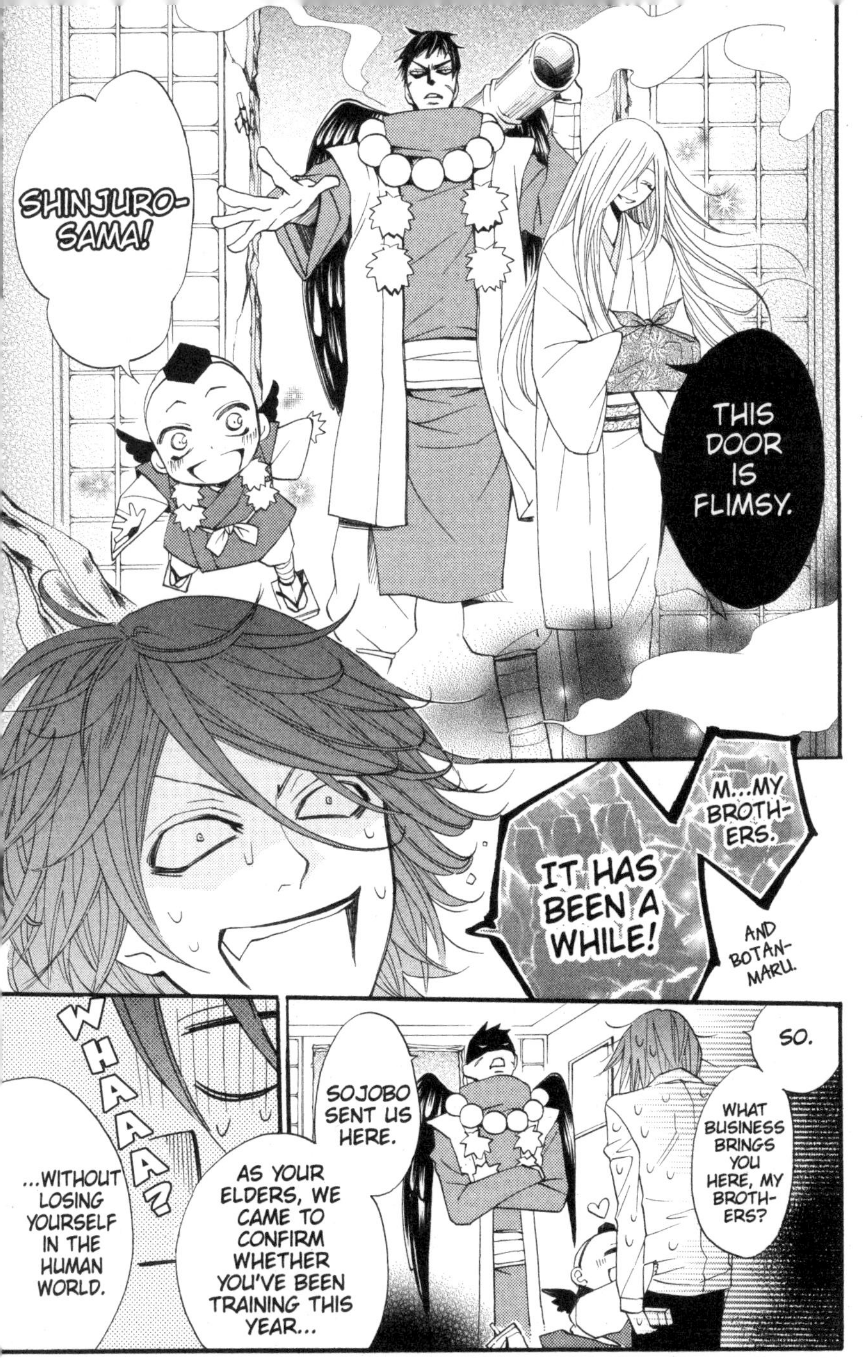
THIS DOOR IS FLIMSY.
SHINJURO-SAMA!
M...MY BROTHERS.
IT HAS BEEN A WHILE!
AND BOTAN-MARU.
SO.
WHAT BUSINESS BRINGS YOU HERE, MY BROTHERS?
SOJOBO SENT US HERE.
AS YOUR ELDERS, WE CAME TO CONFIRM WHETHER YOU'VE BEEN TRAINING THIS YEAR...
...WITHOUT LOSING YOURSELF IN THE HUMAN WORLD.
WHAAAA?

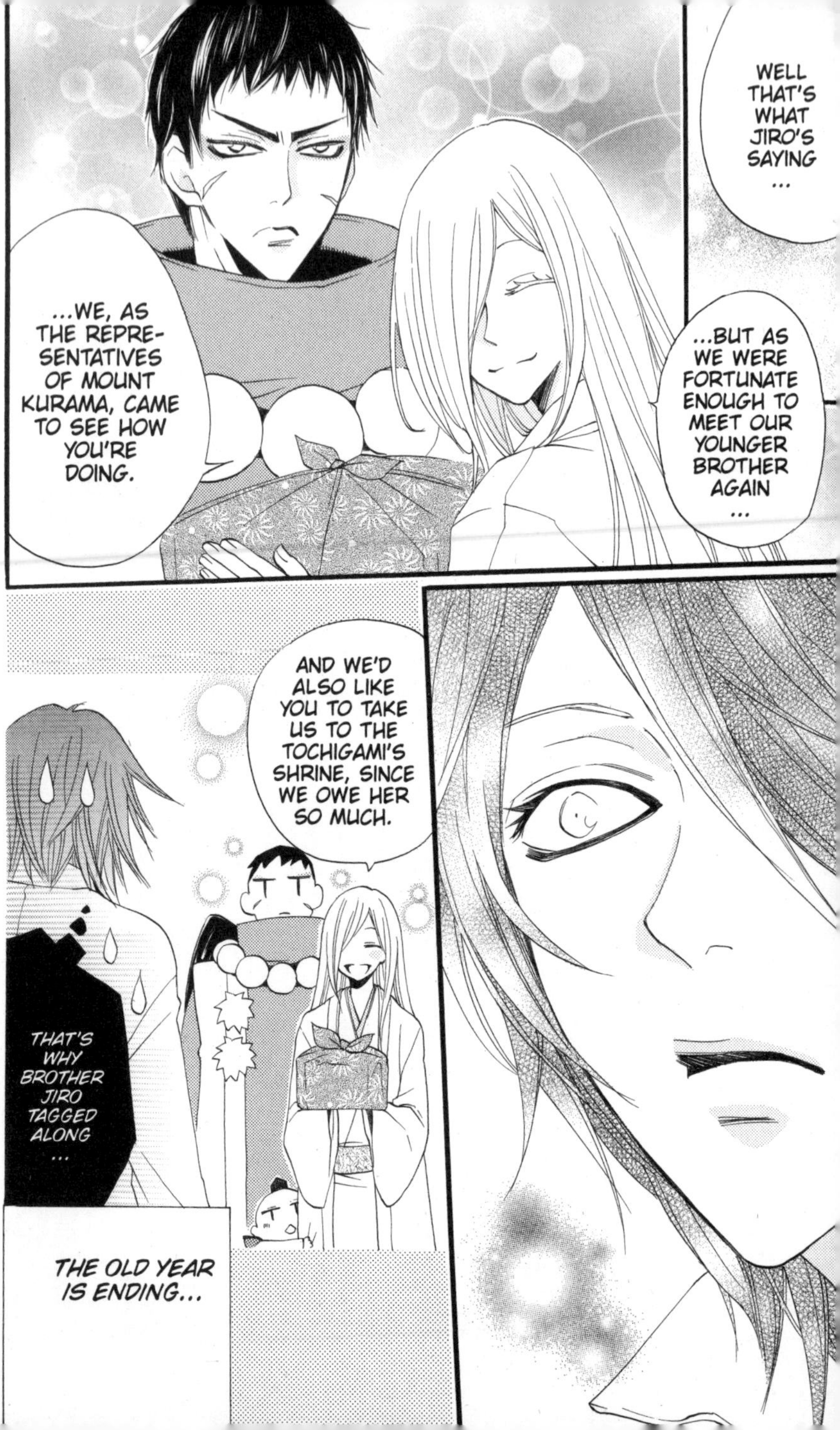
WELL THAT'S WHAT JIRO'S SAYING ...
...WE, AS THE REPRESENTATIVES OF MOUNT KURAMA, CAME TO SEE HOW YOU'RE DOING.
...BUT AS WE WERE FORTUNATE ENOUGH TO MEET OUR YOUNGER BROTHER AGAIN ...
AND WE'D ALSO LIKE YOU TO TAKE US TO THE TOCHIGAMI'S SHRINE, SINCE WE OWE HER SO MUCH.
THAT'S WHY BROTHER JIRO TAGGED ALONG ...
THE OLD YEAR IS ENDING...

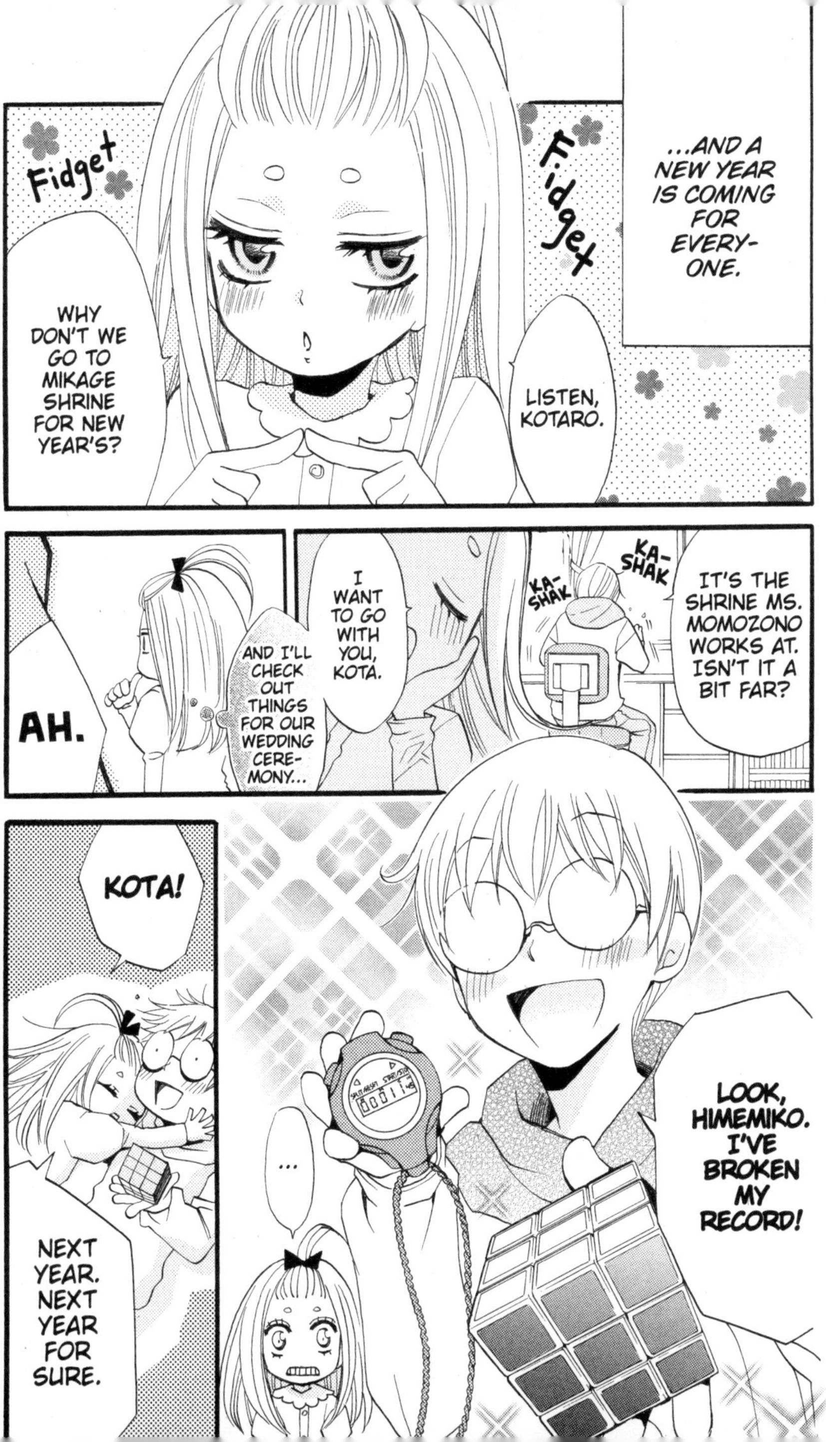
...AND A NEW YEAR IS COMING FOR EVERY-ONE.
Fidget
LISTEN, KOTARO.
Fidget
WHY DON'T WE GO TO MIKAGE SHRINE FOR NEW YEAR'S?
KA-SHAK
KA-SHAK
IT'S THE SHRINE MS. MOMOZONO WORKS AT. ISN'T IT A BIT FAR?
I WANT TO GO WITH YOU, KOTA.
AND I'LL CHECK OUT THINGS FOR OUR WEDDING CEREMONY...
AH.
LOOK, HIMEMIKO. I'VE BROKEN MY RECORD!
...
KOTA!
NEXT YEAR. NEXT YEAR FOR SURE.

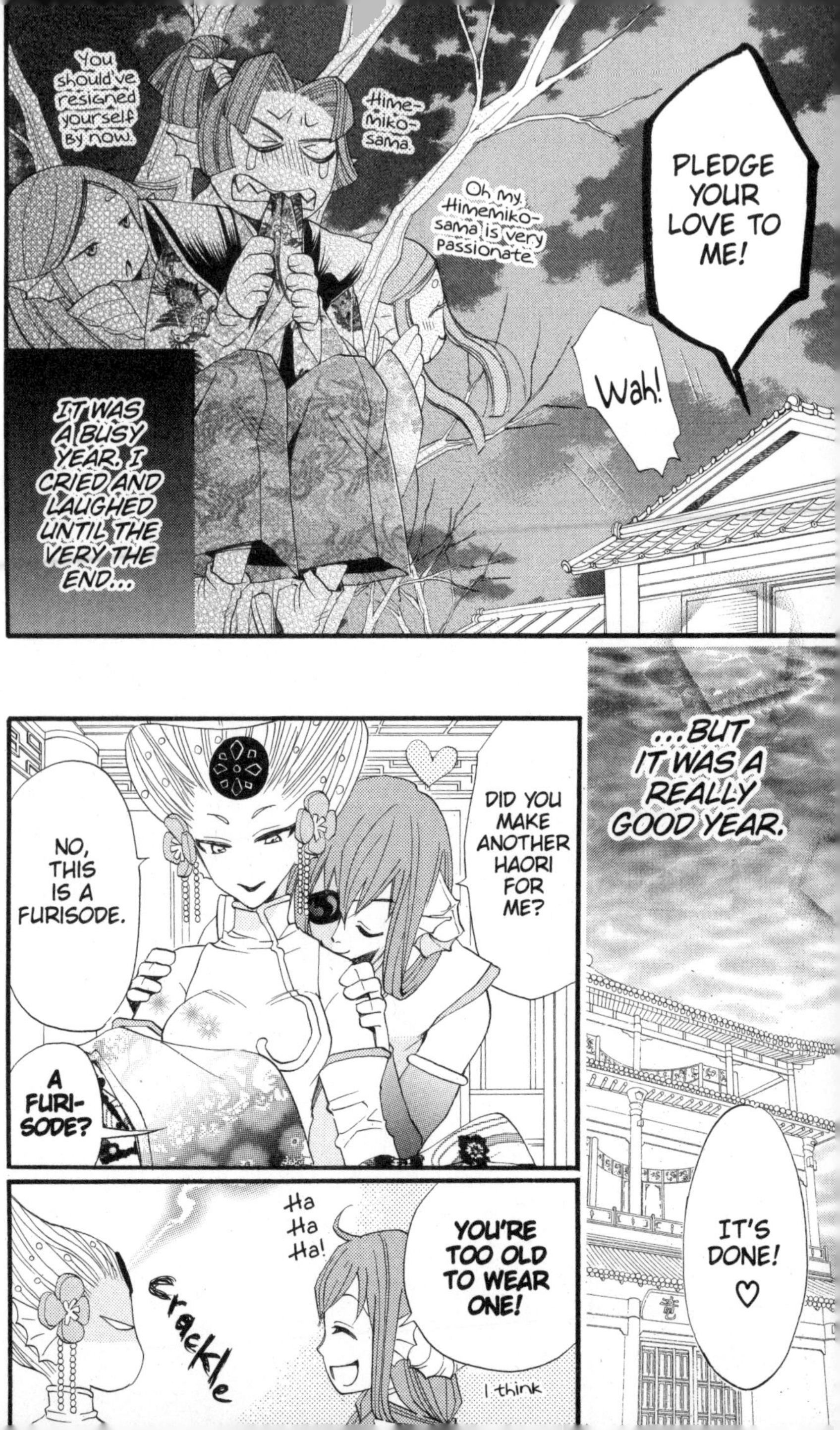
PLEDGE YOUR LOVE TO ME!
Wah!
Oh my. Himemiko-sama is very passionate.
Hime-miko-sama.
You should've resigned yourself by now.
IT WAS A BUSY YEAR. I CRIED AND LAUGHED UNTIL THE VERY THE END...
...BUT IT WAS A REALLY GOOD YEAR.
IT'S DONE! ♡
DID YOU MAKE ANOTHER HAORI FOR ME?
NO, THIS IS A FURISODE.
A FURI-SODE?
YOU'RE TOO OLD TO WEAR ONE!
Ha Ha Ha!
I think
Crackle

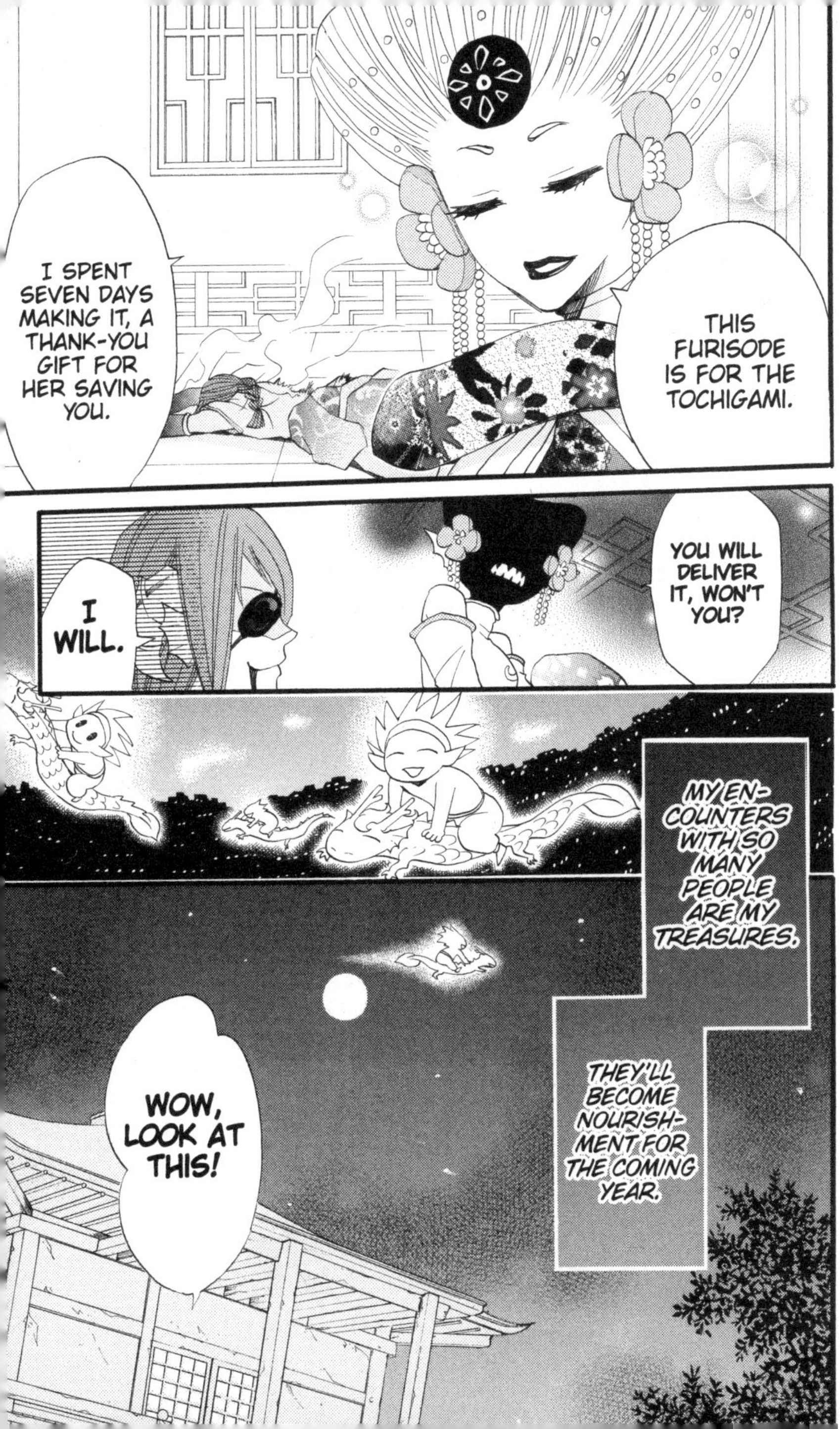
THIS FURISODE IS FOR THE TOCHIGAMI.
I SPENT SEVEN DAYS MAKING IT, A THANK-YOU GIFT FOR HER SAVING YOU.
YOU WILL DELIVER IT, WON'T YOU?
I WILL.
MY ENCOUNTERS WITH SO MANY PEOPLE ARE MY TREASURES.
THEY'LL BECOME NOURISHMENT FOR THE COMING YEAR.
WOW, LOOK AT THIS!

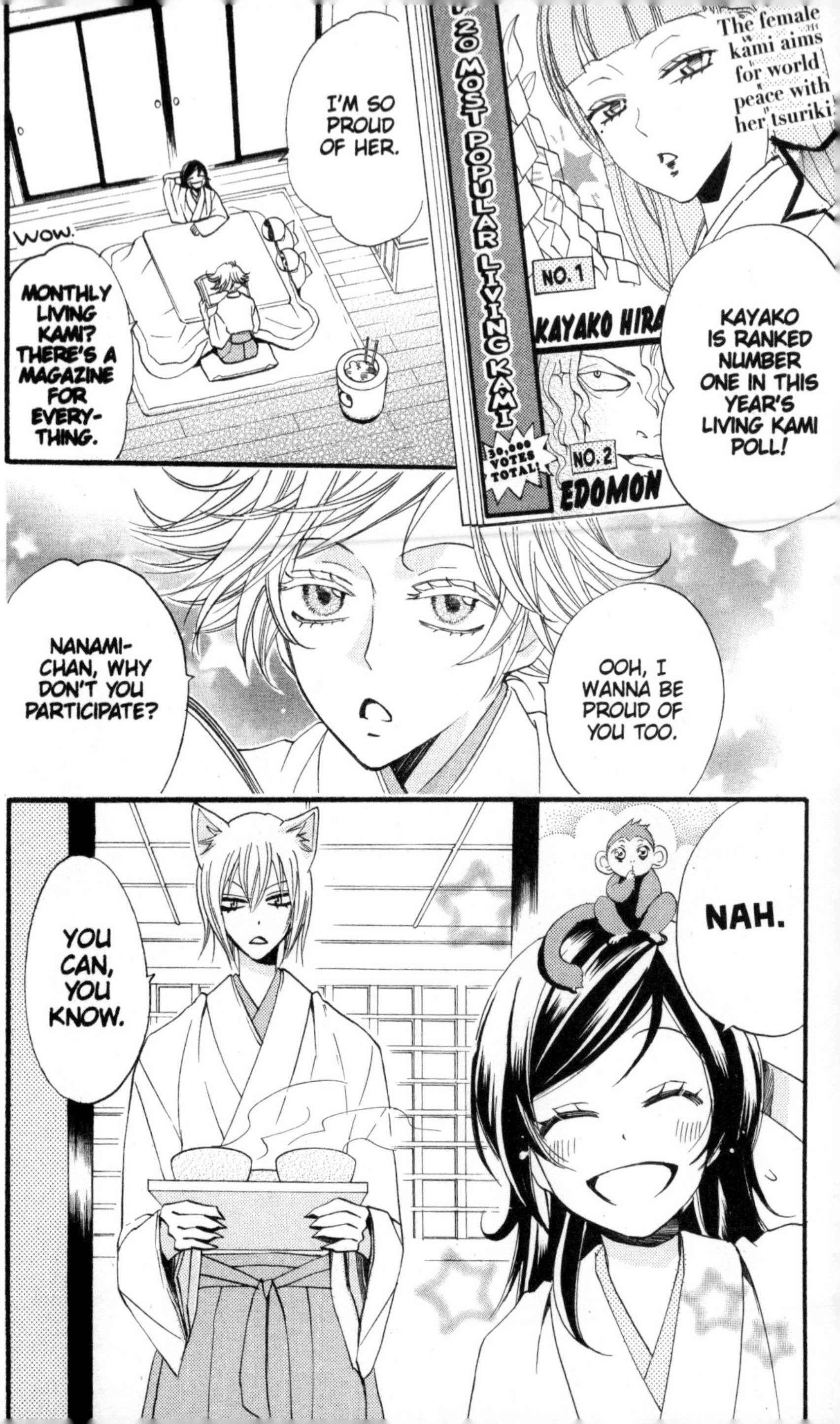

The female kami aims for world peace with her tsuriki
20 MOST POPULAR LIVING KAMI
NO. 1
KAYAKO HIRA
30,000 VOTES TOTAL!
NO. 2
EDOMON
KAYAKO IS RANKED NUMBER ONE IN THIS YEAR'S LIVING KAMI POLL!
I'M SO PROUD OF HER.
WOW.
MONTHLY LIVING KAMI? THERE'S A MAGAZINE FOR EVERYTHING.
OOH, I WANNA BE PROUD OF YOU TOO.
NANAMI-CHAN, WHY DON'T YOU PARTICIPATE?
NAH.
YOU CAN, YOU KNOW.

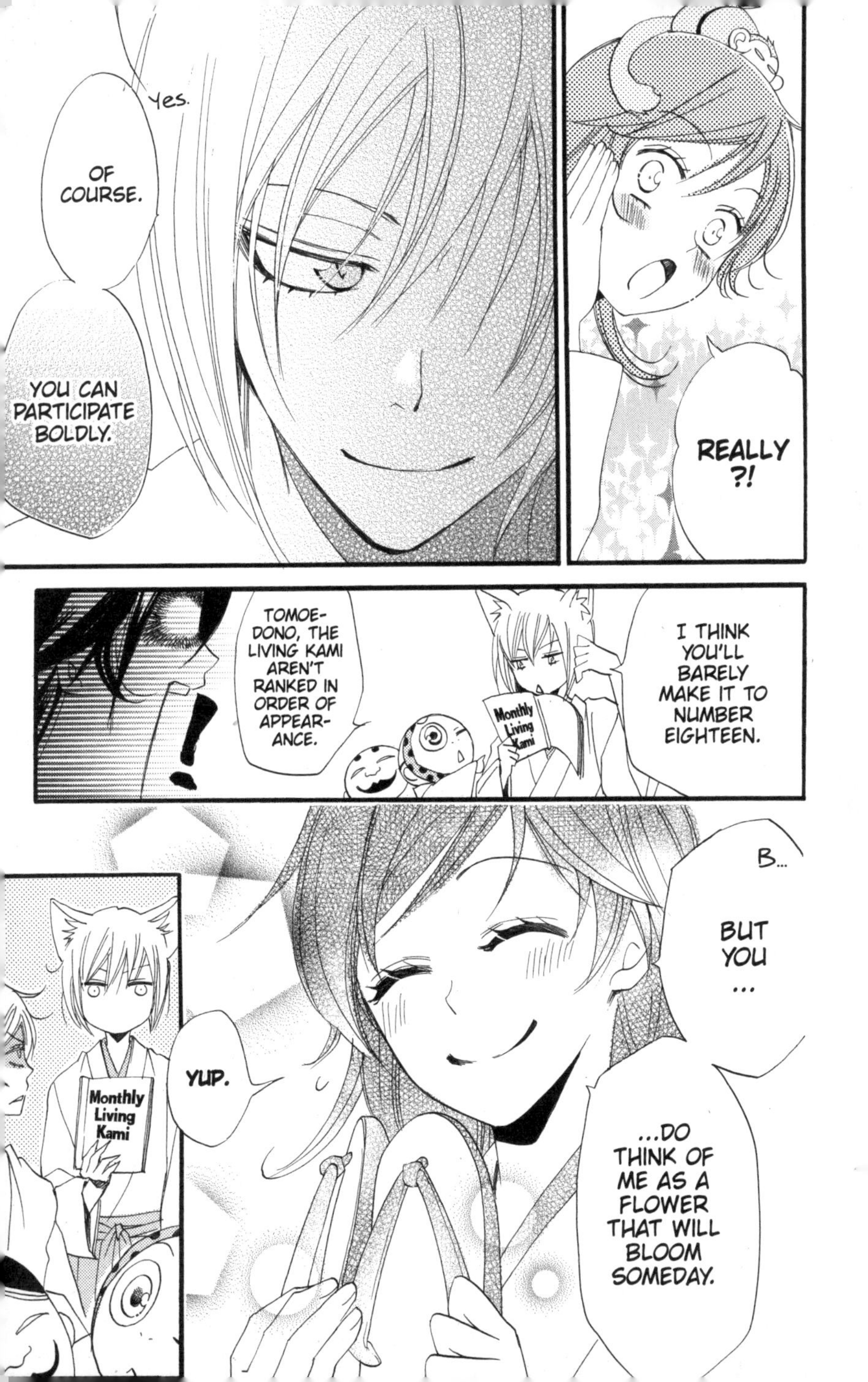
REALLY ?!
Yes.
OF COURSE.
YOU CAN PARTICIPATE BOLDLY.
I THINK YOU'LL BARELY MAKE IT TO NUMBER EIGHTEEN.
Monthly Living Kami
TOMOE-DONO, THE LIVING KAMI AREN'T RANKED IN ORDER OF APPEARANCE.
!
B...
BUT YOU ...
...DO THINK OF ME AS A FLOWER THAT WILL BLOOM SOMEDAY.
YUP.
Monthly Living Kami

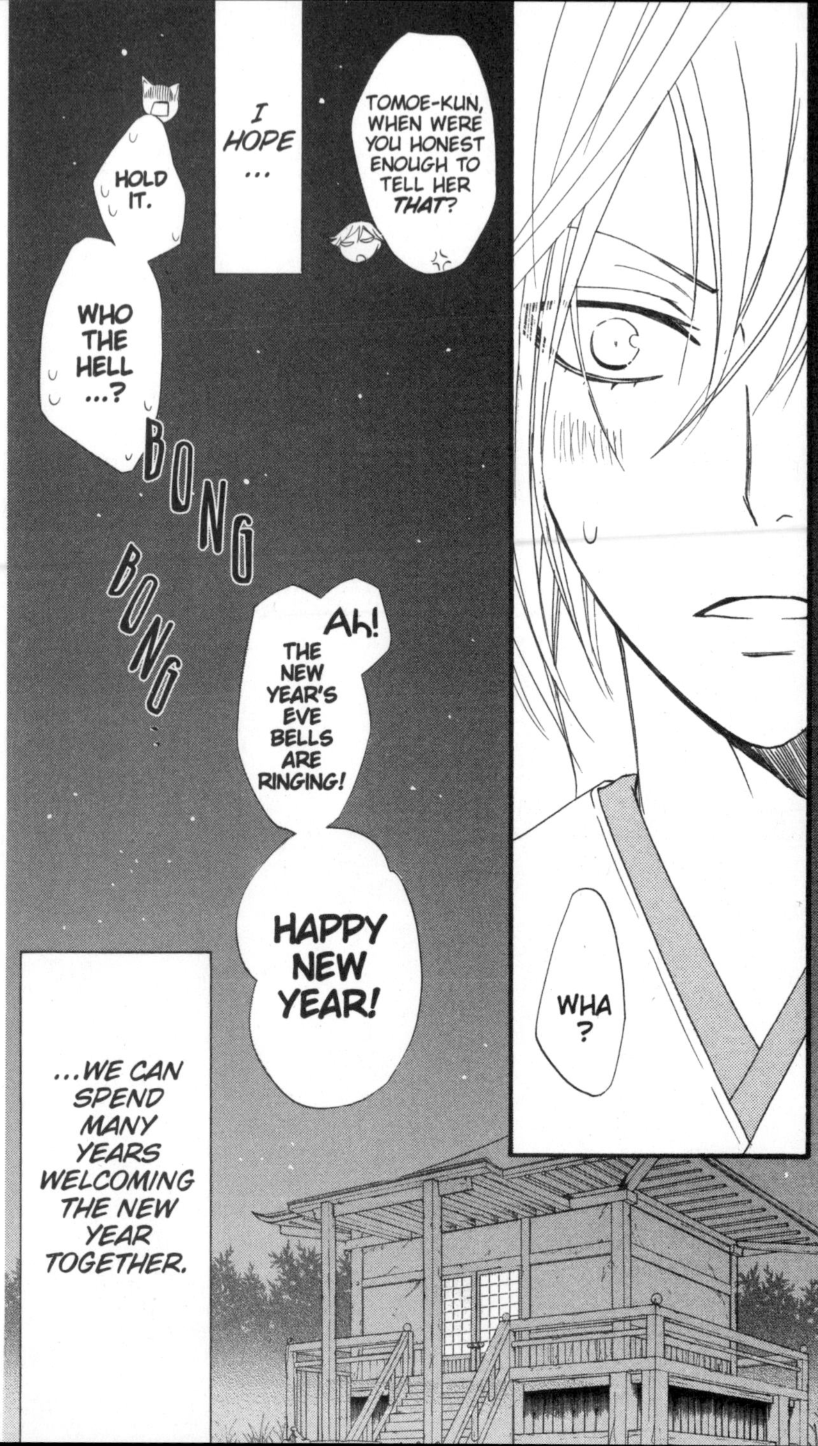
WHA ?
TOMOE-KUN, WHEN WERE YOU HONEST ENOUGH TO TELL HER THAT?
I HOPE ...
HOLD IT.
WHO THE HELL ...?
BONG
BONG
Ah! THE NEW YEAR'S EVE BELLS ARE RINGING!
HAPPY NEW YEAR!
...WE CAN SPEND MANY YEARS WELCOMING THE NEW YEAR TOGETHER.

The Otherworld

Ayakashi is an archaic term for yokai.

Kami are Shinto deities or spirits. The word can be used for a range of creatures, from nature spirits to strong and dangerous gods.

Onibi-warashi are like will-o'-the-wisps.

Shikigami are spirits that are summoned and employed by *onmyoji* (Yin-Yang sorcerers).

Shinshi are birds, beasts, insects or fish that have a special relationship with a kami.

Tengu are a type of yokai. They are sometimes associated with excess pride.

Tochigami (or *jinushigami*) are deities of a specific area of land.

Honorifics

-chan is a diminutive most often used with babies, children or teenage girls.

-dono roughly means "my lord," although not in the aristocratic sense.

-san is a standard honorific similar to Mr., Mrs., Miss, or Ms.

-sama is used with people of much higher rank.

Notes

Page 14, panel 4: Kagamimochi
Rice cakes piled one on top of another in order of size.
Kagamimochi literally means "mirror rice cake" and are used as a New Year's offering for the toshigami, then cut and eaten on January 11.

Page 17, panel 3: Torii
Torii is a Shinto archway or gate.

Page 26, panel 2: Bread crusts
Japanese bakeries often sell bags of crusts cut from bread loaves for a small price.

Page 26, panel 5: Pachinko
Pachinko is a gambling game often described as a cross between pinball and slot machines. Players earn winnings in the form of pachinko balls, which can be traded in for prizes. Winnings can also be surreptitiously exchanged for cash.

Page 39, panel 2: Sasamochi
Mochi (sticky rice cakes) wrapped in *sasa* (bamboo leaves).

Page 77, panel 3: Seahorse
Seahorses are called *tatsunoko* in Japanese, which literally means "dragon child."

Page 78, panel 3: Beast of the Zodiac
The Japanese zodiac is very similar to the Chinese one, except the pig is a boar.

Page 87, panel 3: Ryu-bo
Ryu literally means "dragon," and *–bo* is an honorific for boys.

Page 144, panel 2: Zori
Japanese sandals, worn with kimonos.

Page 164, panel 2: Zouni soup
A soup with rice cakes, veggies, and other ingredients eaten at New Year's.

Page 182, panel 3: Otoshidama
Otoshidama are gifts of money given to children by adults on New Year's Day in little envelopes of Japanese paper.

Page 186, panel 3: Haori, furisode
A *haori* is a lightweight silk jacket that is worn over a kimono. It is traditionally a part of a man's formal outfit. A *furisode* is a kind of kimono for young, unmarried women characterized by long sleeves.

Page 190, panel 2: New Year's Eve bells
One hundred eight bells rung by Buddhist temples at New Year's. The number is commonly described as the number of earthly desires humans possess.

Julietta Suzuki's debut manga *Hoshi ni Naru Hi* (The Day One Becomes a Star) appeared in the 2004 *Hana to Yume Plus*. Her other books include *Akuma to Dolce* (The Devil and Sweets) and *Karakuri Odette*. Born in December in Fukuoka Prefecture, she enjoys having movies play in the background while she works on her manga.

KAMISAMA KISS

VOL. 11
Shojo Beat Edition

STORY AND ART BY
Julietta Suzuki

English Translation & Adaptation/Tomo Kimura
Touch-up Art & Lettering/Joanna Estep
Design/Yukiko Whitley
Editor/Pancha Diaz

KAMISAMA HAJIMEMASHITA by Julietta Suzuki
© Julietta Suzuki 2012
All rights reserved.
First published in Japan in 2012 by HAKUSENSHA, Inc., Tokyo.
English language translation rights arranged with
HAKUSENSHA, Inc., Tokyo.

Printed in Italy

Published by VIZ Media, LLC
P.O. Box 77010
San Francisco, CA 94107

10 9 8
First printing, November 2012
Eighth printing, September 2023

viz.com

shojobeat.com

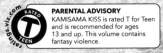

Behind the Scenes!!

STORY AND ART BY **BISCO HATORI**

Ranmaru Kurisu comes from a family of hardy, rough-and-tumble fisherfolk and he sticks out at home like a delicate, artistic sore thumb. It's given him a raging inferiority complex and a permanently pessimistic outlook. Now that he's in college, he's hoping to find a sense of belonging. But after a whole life of being left out, does he even know how to fit in?!

RATED **T** FOR TEEN
ratings.viz.com

VIZ MEDIA
www.viz.com

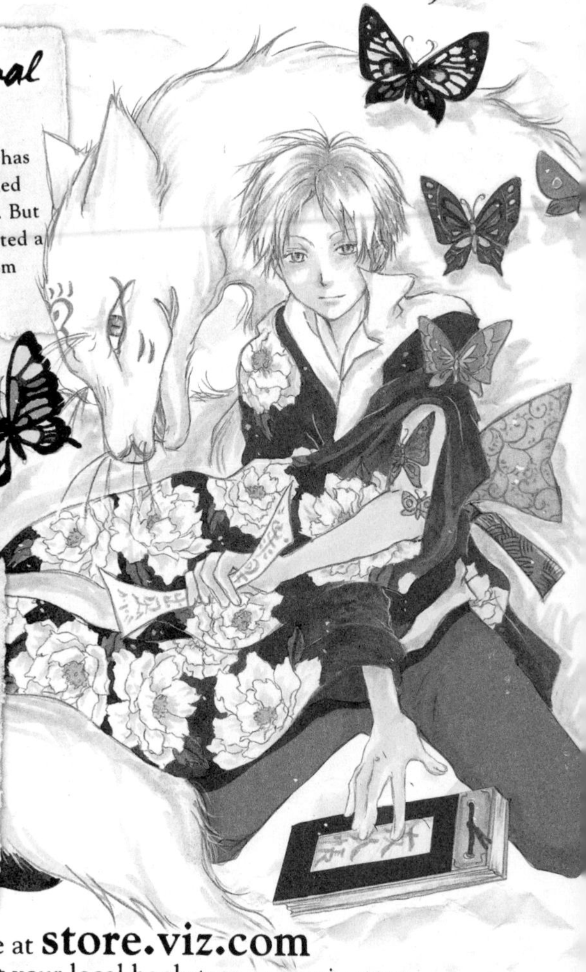

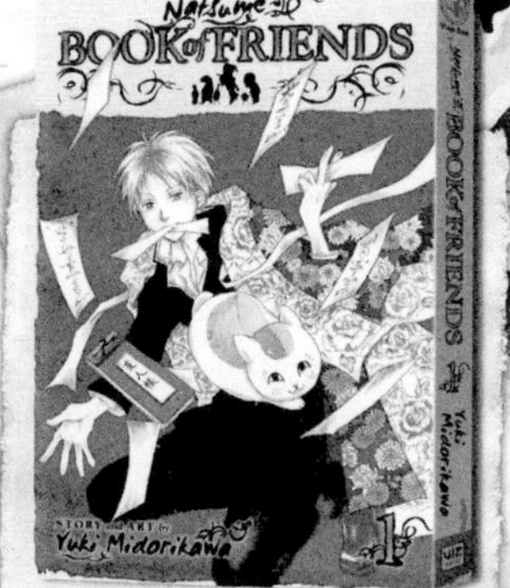

Natsume's
BOOK of FRIENDS
STORY and ART by
Yuki Midorikawa
1

ISBN: 978-1-4215-3243-1

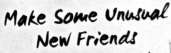

This is the last page.

In keeping with the original Japanese comic format, this book reads from right to left—so action, sound effects, and word balloons are completely reversed. This preserves the orientation of the original artwork—plus, it's fun! Check out the diagram shown here to get the hang of things, and then turn to the other side of the book to get started!

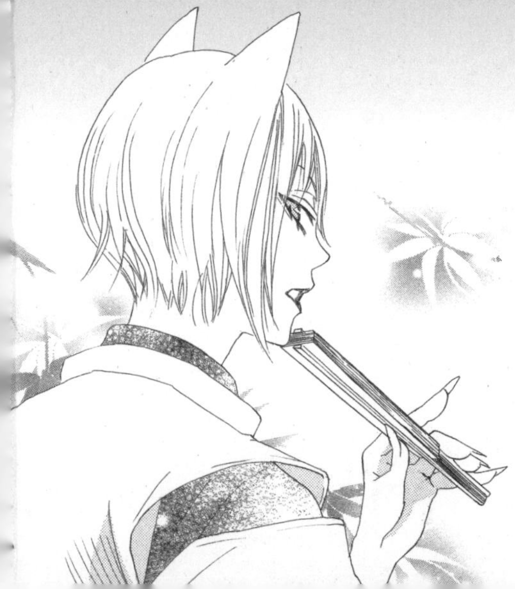

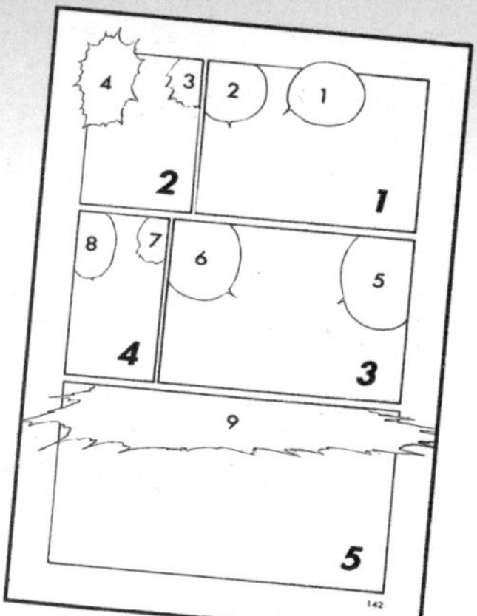
1
2
1
3
4
2
5
6
3
7
8
4
9
5
142